Praise for *The Roots of Goodness and Resistance to Evil*

"In this excellent book, Ervin Staub writes from a lifetime of knowledge and experience, both personal and professional. He has never been a bystander. You will cherish his insight, and perhaps even more the goodness of his heart."

—Richard Rhodes, historian and author of the Pulitzer
Prize–winning *The Making of the Atomic Bomb*

"Ervin Staub has devoted his life—from his childhood Holocaust escape to his distinguished career—to resisting evil and pursuing goodness. This important volume recaps his career as the world's leading expert on evil and goodness, harm and helping, radicalization and reconciliation. His life and scholarship point the way to wider circles of "moral inclusion," to responding with moral courage, to raising children who become helpful and even heroic adults, and to empathy nurtured by suffering."

—David G. Myers, Professor of Psychology, Hope College,
and author of *Social Psychology, 11th Edition*

"This book is a compilation of the insights of a devoted scholar who has studied good and evil for approximately 45 years. Staub deals with some of the most important issues of our time: violence against out-group members; altruism, moral courage, and reconciliation; and how and why a person is a perpetrator versus a helper. This book is an important resource for anyone interested in fostering compassion, helping behavior, and caring societies."

—Nancy Eisenberg, Regents' Professor of Psychology,
Arizona State University

"In *The Roots of Goodness and Resistance to Evil*, Ervin Staub helps us understand how each of us can tap into our own compassion and moral courage. Drawing on many years of comprehensive research and work in real-world settings, and inspired by his own experience as a childhood survivor of the Holocaust, Staub has written a book with the unique power to illuminate the best of humanity in individuals and societies."

—Arianna Huffington, chair, president, and editor-in-chief of
the *Huffington Post* and author of *Thrive: The Third Metric to
Redefining Success and Creating a Life of Well-Being,
Wisdom, and Wonder*

The Roots of Goodness and Resistance to Evil

Other Books by Ervin Staub

Positive Social Behavior and Morality, Vol. 1.
Personal and Social Influences. 1978

Positive Social Behavior and Morality, Vol. 2.
Socialization and Development. 1979

Personality: Basic Aspects and Current Research. Edited, 1980

The Development and Maintenance of Prosocial Behavior:
International Perspectives on Positive Morality.
Co-edited, with Daniel Bar-Tal, Jerzy Karylowski, Janusz Reykowski, 1984

The Roots of Evil: The Origins of Genocide and Other Group Violence. 1989

Social and Moral Values: Individual and Societal Perspectives.
Co-edited, with Nancy Eisenberg and Janusz Reykowski, 1989

Patriotism in the Lives of Individuals and Nations.
Co-edited, with Daniel Bar-Tal, 1997

The Psychology of Good and Evil: Why Children, Adults and Groups Help and
Harm Others. 2003

Overcoming Evil: Genocide, Violent Conflict and Terrorism. 2011

The Roots of Goodness and Resistance to Evil

Inclusive Caring, Moral Courage,
Altruism Born of Suffering,
Active Bystandership, and Heroism

Ervin Staub

OXFORD
UNIVERSITY PRESS

OXFORD

UNIVERSITY PRESS

Oxford University Press is a department of the University of
Oxford. It furthers the University's objective of excellence in research,
scholarship, and education by publishing worldwide.

Oxford   New York

Auckland   Cape Town   Dar es Salaam   Hong Kong   Karachi
Kuala Lumpur   Madrid   Melbourne   Mexico City   Nairobi
New Delhi   Shanghai   Taipei   Toronto

With offices in

Argentina   Austria   Brazil   Chile   Czech Republic   France   Greece
Guatemala   Hungary   Italy   Japan   Poland   Portugal   Singapore
South Korea   Switzerland   Thailand   Turkey   Ukraine   Vietnam

Oxford is a registered trademark of Oxford University Press
in the UK and certain other countries.

Published in the United States of America by
Oxford University Press
198 Madison Avenue, New York, NY 10016

© Oxford University Press 2015

Library of Congress Cataloging-in-Publication Data
Staub, Ervin.
The roots of goodness and resistance to evil : inclusive caring, moral courage, altruism born of
suffering, active bystandership, and heroism / Ervin Staub.
pages cm
Includes bibliographical references and index.
ISBN 978–0–19–538203–7
1. Good and evil—Psychological aspects.   2. Altruism—Psychological aspects.
3. Courage—Psychological
aspects.   I. Title.
BF789.E94S833 2015
177'.7—dc23
2014025877

3 5 7 9 8 6 4 2
Printed in the United States of America
on acid-free paper

To Vera, Dora, Georgia, Noah, Oona, Rory, and Willie. May you be surrounded by goodness and be creators of goodness.

To the memory of Maria Gogan and Raoul Wallenberg, two heroes, and my courageous parents and aunt Julia.

Contents

Acknowledgments

The author of a book stands on the shoulder of many others. I will mention here a few of them. With regard to my work on helping and altruism, especially important were my associations with Marian Radke-Yarrow, Carolyn Zahn-Waxler, Martin Hoffman, Nancy Eisenberg, and Janusz Reykowski of Poland, and the influence of the research of Bibb Latane and John Darley. I am also grateful to Facing History and Ourselves, and to schools, teachers and students who enabled me to work in a practical way on how to create caring classrooms and raise caring children. Helen Fein's writing was an inspiration for my study of the roots of genocide, and Daniel Bar-Tal was important for my work on patriotism.

Two of the chapters I included in the book are coauthored, and two are authored by others. I am immensely grateful for the kindness of these authors for allowing me to publish them.

I am grateful to Maria Gogan and Raoul Wallenberg, heroic helpers, and to my mother and aunt, two courageous women, who by their actions when was I a young child in Hungary inspired me as an adult about the possibilities of goodness in the world (see Preface and Chapters 25, 26).

I was also inspired by Perry London, a visiting professor at Stanford when I was a graduate student there and later a friend, who was the first to study "rescuers," and by the guidance of my advisor and friend Walter Mischel. An important colleague at Harvard was Stanley Milgram, whose office was next door to mine when I started there. My colleagues at the University of Massachusetts at Amherst, the Psychology Department and the University made my work possible in faraway places like Rwanda. They and generous anonymous donors made it possible for me to start a doctoral program on the Psychology of Peace and Violence.

There have been a number of associates, former students who are now professors, and other Westerners, crucial to our work on reconciliation in Rwanda. They are mentioned in Chapter 19. There were a large number of important Rwandan associates, whom I mention in my book *Overcoming Evil*. There were other important collaborators in Burundi and the Congo (DRC) when our projects expanded to these countries. Here I will only refer to

Charles Murigande, who inspired us to go to Rwanda and has been a consistent supporter of our work there, and George Weiss, of Amsterdam, a producer with whom we developed our prototype radio programs in Rwanda and whose organization, LaBenevolencija, has produced our radio programs in all three countries.

My primary associate on our work in Rwanda has been my wife, Laurie Anne Pearlman, a clinical psychologist and trauma specialist. She and I worked together on all aspects of our projects in Africa. Her expertise was extraordinarily important for the deeply traumatized people there. Her amazing support for all I do has been extraordinarily important to me.

Preface

Why I Have Been Studying Goodness (and Evil and Its Prevention)

I have engaged for many years in research and writing about the roots of caring and helping and ways to promote them, and the roots and prevention of violence, especially violence between groups, but also by individuals and children. I have also worked in real-world settings on reconciliation after violence between group, thereby to prevent new violence and improve the lives of both survivors, and members of the group or in case of mutual violence both groups that perpetrated the violence. I have also worked with teachers and children to promoting caring and helping.

This book is a summary of what I know and believe is important to know about how children can become people who will help others in need and who as adults will do what they can to enhance other people's well-being, protect people, and be active bystanders to prevent violence and build harmonious, peaceful societies. The book is also about our responsibilities and possibilities to act when people in other parts of the world are in danger. It aims to offer relevant knowledge and hopefully also inspiration to help each other, prevent harm, and build peaceful and harmonious societies that fulfill human needs, not only material but also psychological needs—societies that help people lead fulfilled lives.

My early experiences had a profound influence in leading to this work. As a young child I survived the Holocaust in Hungary. I then lived under communism, a system with both positive ideals and very bad ideas and practices, such as dictatorship of the proletariat, greatly restricting citizens' freedom and choices, repression and violence against them. I escaped from Hungary when I was 18, three weeks after Soviet troops defeated the revolution there. I lived in Vienna for three years until I received a US visa. I finished my undergraduate education at the University of Minnesota, received a PhD at Stanford, and in my first job at Harvard began my lifelong engagement with goodness and evil.

There were many specific early experiences that motivated me to begin on this road, beyond being the member of a persecuted group designated for murder during the Holocaust and living under communism. I and my immediate family survived because of the actions of Raoul Wallenberg, a member of a poor branch of a wealthy Swedish banking family and in 1944 partner in an export–import firm that did business in Hungary. After about 450,000 Hungarian Jews were deported to Auschwitz in the summer of 1944, most of them killed immediately, he was asked to go to Hungary to try to save lives. He was appointed a diplomat, went to Hungary, and, acting with intelligence, determination, and heroic courage, saved many lives.

Especially important in shaping me, and in inspiring my later professional work, was a Christian woman who worked for my family, Maria. She took my sister and me into hiding. She later moved with us and endangered herself to get food for us and others in one of the "protected houses" Wallenberg set up. Many people survived in these houses, but there were constant raids and many were taken away. She prepared dough, took it in a baby carriage to a bakery, and brought back the bread after it was baked. She continued to do such things after Hungarian Nazis stopped her and threatened her. They made her stand at a wall for hours with her hands up in the air and told her they will kill her for what she was doing.

She lived with us after the war, and her past actions and loving presence taught me more about the possibility of goodness than anything else. I had no direct contact with Wallenberg, but Maria was very much part of my life until age 18 when I escaped from Hungary and later when I visited my family, and then continued to visit her, the last surviving member of my family. She was my second mother. Between 1975, when my mother, the last member of my immediate family died, and 1991, when Maria died, I went to Hungary at least every second year to visit her (See Chapter 25).

I was also shaped by the persistent, courageous actions of my mother and aunt during the Holocaust to save us, the children, which included my three cousins, as well as themselves. Many people had no possibility to save themselves in those inhumane times. Our opportunities were narrow, but my family acted again and again when possible. To survive required the courage not to obey those who were ready to kill us. On the part of my father it required the courage to escape when the people in his forced labor camp were taken to Germany. The example of their actions, and even my own action at age six, which at the time of a raid on the protected house contributed to my father's survival—who after his escape was staying there in hiding—shaped who I became. All these experiences have also shaped the focus of my work, especially what makes people passive in the face of others' (and their own) needs and what leads them to act.

As I engaged with questions like these, my motivation deepened, my concerns expanded. I learned and changed by my choices and actions—a core principle in the development of both intense violence and helping, and in other aspects of life as well. After studying caring, helping, and active bystandership, I began to study the roots of great violence, such as mass killing and genocide, their prevention, and reconciliation between groups as a way of preventing new violence—or even great violence in the first place. But in recent times and in this book I have returned to my original concerns. This is partly because it is very difficult to change the world to eliminate great violence, but it is very much possible to raise children, and for adults to come to care about and help others and resist the influences that lead to violence. This book is primarily about the roots of caring and helping, but it is also about active bystandership, moral courage, and heroism in the service of rescuing endangered people, preventing violence, and creating harmonious human relations.

About half of this book consists of mostly recent already published articles and book chapters. I selected writings that I hope are accessible. I wrote a couple of the recently published chapters, for example, the long Chapter 22 that is just being published in a Handbook, already with the consideration of how they would contribute to this book.

The other half of the book is new writing. A few short chapters that aim to make the topics and issues of the book especially accessible I wrote for the book, but also published along the way as a *Psychology Today* blog. The previously published material, according to academic custom, has many references to sources of research and ideas. The chapters I wrote for this book refer to sources, but fewer, to make it easier on the reader. While each chapter should be understandable and I hope useful on its own, I selected and wrote chapters so that they build on each other as they present how goodness originates and evolves, how resistance to evil comes about, and the possibility of creating caring societies.

The Roots of Goodness and Resistance to Evil

1

Introduction
Examples of Goodness and Passivity
and Overview of the Book

The woman I am interviewing is Tutsi, a member of the group that was the victim of the genocide in Rwanda—a survivor. She is part of a workshop I and my associates are conducting in Kigali, the capital of Rwanda. She tells me that men came to the door of their house and took away her husband. One of them worked for her family; he sent another man to protect her. This man arrived with a Bible under his arm and moved into one of the rooms of the house. He left her alone, but when other men come, repeatedly, to take her away, he would meet them at the door and stop them. When the genocide is ended by a primarily Tutsi military group, this Hutu man, afraid of retaliation for the genocide, together with about a million and a half Hutus, escaped to neighboring Zaire, now the Congo. We do not know why this particular man did what he did.

But there is much that we have learned about the roots of helping, and even of heroic actions. This book is about what leads people to act in caring and helpful ways, in relation to people immediately around them, people in their society, or those in the outside world in danger of being harmed or who have been harmed and suffer its aftermath. It is about how socialization and life experience develop personal characteristics, which join with people's immediate surroundings and their broader circumstances—what is happening in their group, culture, society, and world—in giving rise to or inhibiting "active bystandership." This includes helping other people, preventing and resisting violence, and working to improve society and the world. *A guiding vision of this book is that it is possible to create a world in which people care about other human beings, caring that is expressed in helpful actions and in fostering values and creating institutions that promote well-being.*

One central focus of the book is the socialization of children and the experiences of children and adults that lead them to become caring and helpful—or not. Another focus is the socialization and experiences required for moral courage, for people to express their caring and moral values by acting in others' behalf, or in behalf of the social good, even if they have to do so in the face of opposition and at risk of potential or actual negative consequences to themselves. The book is also about how people become heroic helpers, those who endanger themselves to help or save others. There is some focus on "heroic rescuers," who saved the lives of designated victims of group violence or genocide, because they are the heroes who have been most studied in research. Some chapters are about how to move people to become active bystanders who take action against harmful actions they witness, or resist the influences that lead groups to turn violently against others such as a minority in their own society, and do what they can to build harmonious relations between individuals and groups.

I begin this introductory chapter with examples of material relevant to these topics, especially passive and active bystandership, mostly from my own research and experiences in real-world settings. Some examples are from my early experimental research, some have to do with bullying in schools, some with training police and students in schools in active bystandership, some with helping groups of people reconcile after genocide or mass killing, in particular in Rwanda, and some with how people who have suffered can become caring and helpful—what I have called "altruism born of suffering." The examples follow each other, without breaks between them.

In what may be regarded as a second introductory chapter, chapter 3 substantively engages with several dimensions of generating goodness. It extensively discusses the socialization of children by parents and peers. A number of topics in it are treated in greater detail in subsequent chapters. Near the end of the book Chapter 22 again reviews topics, and adds to them, especially in what approaches people can take to resist and present violence between groups.

Examples of Passivity and Helping/Active Bystandership

We would expect children to become more helpful with age—with more time to learn to care about others and with more competence to help. However, helping in response to hearing a crash and sounds of a child's distress from an adjoining room increased from kindergarten to first grade and from first to second grade, remained at the same level in fourth grade, and then sharply declined in sixth grade to about the level of kindergarten children (Staub, 1970). Helping in this case meant that children who were working on a drawing either went into the room from which the distress sounds came or reported it to the adult when she returned to the room. When, in order to learn what inhibited helping, we individually asked sixth graders why they acted as they did, they told us that they thought the person in charge would get mad if they interrupted working on their task or went into the other room (in this strange environment). This suggested that the reason for the decline in helping was that children learned rules of appropriate everyday behavior, which inhibited helping.

To explore this further, we conducted another study in which seventh graders, instructed to work on a drawing, were either told nothing else, as in the previous study, or told *not* to go into the other room because someone else was working there, or told that they can go into the other room if they needed more drawing pencils. Being told nothing seemed to function as a prohibition, since both in this condition and when they were prohibited from going into the other room, the same small percentage of children helped (about 25%). When children were permitted to go into the other room for an irrelevant reason, almost 90% did so when they heard the distress sounds. One girl, listening to the sounds, broke the edge of both of her drawing pencils and then ran into the other room (Staub, 1971b). She apparently needed to exactly fulfill the condition under which she was permitted to go in there. It seems important to teach children that, under certain circumstances, morally relevant rules/values override conventional rules.

Around the same age I found the decline in emergency helping, other researchers have also found a decline in prosocial behavior—in varied forms of sharing and helping (Eisenberg, Spinrad, & Eggum, in press). One reason for this may be because children are learning and focusing on appropriate social behaviors, which diminishes the influence of values and beliefs that promote helping. Other reasons may include increased self-focus and increased desire for approval by peers. Concern about appropriate behavior and approval by peers would be especially likely to inhibit helping that requires stepping forward and calling attention to oneself, which may lead to disapproval of one's actions.

Concern about appropriate behavior may not only reduce helping, both in children and adults, but may make it more likely that people go along with authorities that direct them to engage in harmful behavior. This may have been one reason for many participants going along in Stanley Milgram's "obedience experiments," where as part of a study, ostensibly of the effectiveness of punishment in learning, participants were told and pressured to administer increasingly powerful electric shocks to another person. (This person did not actually receive the shocks). Having agreed to participate, it was appropriate behavior to live up to one's "contract" and to fulfill one's role well (Staub, 2014).

In the study on changes in helping with age, we also explored whether pairs of children help more than individual children. At younger ages, they did. This was at odds with the usually found "bystander effect," a decrease in the likelihood of any one person helping with an increase in the number of people who witness an "emergency." One of the explanations proposed for this effect is "pluralistic ignorance," the idea that people in public put on a poker face and hide their reactions to events (Latane & Darley, 1970). As people look at others and see no reaction, they assume that there is nothing to be concerned about or that the appropriate action is to do nothing. However, when young children heard sounds of distress, they talked to each other. They said things like "what is that?" or "someone is hurt." By calling attention to it and expressing concern, they influenced each other and acted together. These responses to the distress sounds, and the joining in helping, unfortunately disappear by second grade, and the bystander effect appears.

Witnesses, bystanders, and other people can have a powerful influence on each other, and on harmdoers, by their passivity, by what they say, and by what they do. One example of this in the Milgram study was the behavior of the "teacher" who was administering shocks of increasing intensity to the "learner" when he made mistakes on a task. The person in charge insisted that the teacher administer a shock, a level higher than the previous shock, after each mistake. But when others who were working with the person in charge opposed doing this, teachers stopped administering shocks (Milgram, 1974; Staub, 2014). I provide many examples of the power of bystanders in the book, both from research and life events. I later describe one of my studies in which what one person says, encouraging or discouraging helping, powerfully affects what another person does in response to distress sounds from another room.

Empathy and feelings of or beliefs in one's responsibility to help others are very important influences on helping. Darley and Latane (1970) suggested diffusion of responsibility when a number of people are present as another explanation of the bystander effect. Feelings of responsibility or the belief that one is responsible can be the result of circumstances focusing responsibility on a person. Or one's values and beliefs can lead a person to feel responsible—which is a central element in "prosocial value orientation," a personal characteristic my students and I have studied extensively. While empathy, sympathy, and compassion for others are important, and at least partly the building blocks of a prosocial orientation, the feeling of responsibility for others' welfare may well be the most powerful influence leading people to help (see Chapters 3, 22). One central question for us is what socialization by adults and peers and what experiences, including education and training (Chapters 3, 17), give rise to empathy, responsibility, prosocial orientation—and competence in helping others.

In one study, when a child heard a crash and sounds of distress from the other room, if the adult in charge before leaving the room interacted with the child in a warm, affectionate manner, the child was more likely to try to help than if the adult acted in a matter-of-fact, distant manner (Staub, 1971a). In another study, kindergarten-age children role-played situations in which one of them helped the other, and then they exchanged roles. This led the children to be more helpful at a later time than children who did not have this experience (Staub, 1971c).

Getting children engaged in real helping is also important. Both helping and violence evolve progressively. *People change as a result of their actions; they learn by doing.* When we engaged children in helping others, for example, making toys for poor, hospitalized children or older children teaching younger ones, they later helped more than children who engaged in an activity that did not involve helping (Staub, 1979, 2003). Many rescuers of people targeted by genocide also became more committed helpers over time (Staub, 1989, 1997, 2011; Chapters 5 and 7).

A young man, a Harvard student, collapses on a quiet street in Cambridge, Massachusetts, when there are passers-by approaching on the other side of the street. Some passers-by immediately rush over. Some look, hesitate, and sometimes others approach the person who collapsed. But some passers-by look away after a single glance and never look back, and some of them even turn off the street at the next corner (Staub & Baer, 1974). Presumably, they try to avoid taking in information about what is happening so that they don't feel responsible to engage with it. This study, other research, and the observation of similar avoidance of information about events in various countries by government officials, media, and citizens (Staub, 2011) led me to define bystanders as "witnesses who are in a *position to know* what is happening and in a *position to take action*" (Staub, 2005; Chapter 3). Even though they are in a position to know, sometimes bystanders close their eyes and minds and make themselves not know.

In one experiment, a male student in William James Hall at Harvard University is working on a task when he hears distress sounds (groaning) from another room. Sometimes the student responds by going into the other room. If he does not, the person there comes in and says that he has strong stomach pains. In either case the student has further opportunities to help. He can go to a pharmacy in Harvard Square, a 10-minute walk, to fill a prescription, or make a phone call to the roommate of the person in distress so that he can come and help, or do something even more limited such as escorting this person to another floor where there is a couch to lie down on. Or he can do nothing. A few students are so eager to get the medication that they immediately start running down the stairs from the 14th story of the building, with the person in charge having difficulty catching up and explaining that this was part of a research study. Weeks before, in a different, seemingly unrelated setting, the participants filled out a long questionnaire. Those who demonstrate a greater degree of what I call *prosocial value orientation* (a combination of a positive view of human beings, caring about others' welfare, and, perhaps most important, a feeling of personal responsibility to help people) help more. Students who were "impulsive" on another test, reacting fast (but often less accurately), also respond fast to the distress sounds by getting up, listening, and walking around, but they helped more only if they also had a strong prosocial value orientation (Staub, 1974). A similar personal disposition was identified by Oliner and Oliner (1988) as characterizing many rescuers of Jews during the Holocaust.

As some students are harassed, intimidated, victimized—bullied—by peers in school, most student bystanders remain passive. But some attempt to help. The targets of harmful actions feel better about their lives at school if they have had the experience of a peer intervening. The active bystanders also feel better about their lives at school than those who remained passive (Staub & Spielman, 2003; Staub, Fellner, Berry, & Morange, 2003; Chapters 15 and 16).

As Jews are deported from Germany (mostly to extermination camps in the East), a group of German wives of Jewish men gather day after day in front of government buildings in Berlin to protest the deportation of their husbands. The deportations stop and some of the men already deported are brought back from Auschwitz and other camps. These were the only public protests against the persecution of Jews in Germany (Staub, 2011).

As hostility and violence progressively increase in a society toward a minority group, the bystanders, witnesses who are neither perpetrators nor victims, tend to remain passive. But once the evolution of violence reaches an extreme (e.g. genocide), a very small number of people endanger themselves to help intended victims. Their parents tended to tended to raise them with reasoning and good values, with one parent often a caring person and therefore a positive model. The parents of many of them were inclusive, engaged with people outside their own group, including Jews (Oliner & Oliner, 1988; Staub, 1997—Chapters 7 and 22 in this book).

In a meeting I had with a group of about 25 Germans in 1987 in Trier who were teenagers or slightly older during the 1930s (one was a nurse who worked in a facility involved in the so-called euthanasia program, in which physically or mentally handicapped and some homosexual Germans were killed)—a meeting that lasted four hours—they could hardly stop talking about the satisfaction of their lives during that time. They talked about sitting around campfires and singing songs, their experience of an embracing community. They were so engaged with their own satisfying lives that they hardly noticed the very public persecution of Jews (Staub, 1989). It took one man a long time to remember that someone came from the local Nazi headquarters to tell his father, who was renting out rooms, not to rent to Jews. All this was not denial, I think. They seemed comfortable with me, my status as professor balanced by my halting German, which was good enough that I did not have to ask the German graduate student who accompanied me to translate. Thus preoccupation with their own lives (which can be based on the difficulties of life but also because life is engaging and satisfying) is one reason that people remain passive.

US and other foreign corporations were busy doing business in Germany during the 1930s, in spite of the brutal practices of its government. However, people in many countries began to protest apartheid in South Africa, and in response to their demands many international corporations stopped doing business there. This was rare behavior for "external bystanders," and it contributed to the change in government and the end of apartheid in South Africa. In response to the boycott, internal groups, like the South African business community, also exerted pressure on the government to change policies (Staub, 2011).

> I sit on a chair in a field in Rwanda, with a lovely view of hills all around, at the edge of a large group of people from the local community. There is canvas stretched over our heads, which protects most but not all of us from the sun. There are not enough benches and chairs, so some people are standing. Children play near us. I am here to attend the weekly community meeting, called the *gacaca*, at which local people elected to serve as judges lead the community through a process of establishing who was killed and what other crimes were committed during the genocide and then try people from the community who are accused of perpetrating these acts. . . . My translator sitting next to me, a young journalist in her regular job, is a survivor of the genocide. (Staub, 2011, p. 3)

A couple of chapters in this book are about the work my associates and I have been doing in Rwanda to promote healing and reconciliation in the aftermath of the 1994 genocide, in order to prevent new violence and help improve people's lives. This work soon expanded to Burundi, where there has also been great violence, and to the Democratic Republic of the Congo where many groups have been involved in violence, which is still ongoing. One primary aim of this work has been to provide knowledge and understanding and enable people to notice and resist influences that tend to lead to violence. Another aim is to help with healing and generate motivation that leads people to become active bystanders who build positive relations between long-hostile groups (Chapters 18, 19).

I stress in this book how circumstances and personality combine in determining our actions (Chapter 22). But it is even more complex; different aspects of the environment and facets of our personality enter into shaping our feelings, motivations, and actions. I interviewed in Rwanda a rescuer, together with the woman his family rescued. She was a neighbor, and they hid her in a hole in a field. Late in the evening, when it was dark, someone from the family went to take away her refuse and bring her food and water. While the whole family participated, it was the father, the head of the family, who decided to do this. At the time of this interview he was in prison, accused of involvement in the killing of some children. He deviated from his group and endangered his family for the sake of a young neighbor, but if the accusation was correct, he was also acting as a member of his group, perpetrating violence.

Some Past Engagements in "Real-World" Settings

As a researcher/scholar, I want to gain knowledge both from formal research and from experience in real-world settings; and I also want to contribute in whatever way I can to building a less violent, more caring world. I believe that this can be a world in which people care about and help others, in which societies are harmonious and peaceful, with different groups within societies as well as nations having constructive relations. But for this to happen requires much work, and the immediate task is to identify and promote the processes that can create it. It requires that both leaders and people in general acquire relevant knowledge and develop motivation to engage in persistent, committed, determined action. Such a world has to be created through socialization that develops inclusive caring and moral courage, by people who as active bystanders promote positive values, create just institutions, and engage in societal practices that create conditions for people to at least minimally fulfill basic material and psychological needs.

I have conducted research on what leads children and adults to help others, or not to help when help is needed (see Staub, 1978, 1979, 2005) and how caring and helping can be promoted in children. I then worked with parents, and with teachers through organizations such as Facing History and Ourselves, and directly with schools, to create classrooms in which children learn to care about other people and help others (see Staub, 2003). This work is referred to in a number of chapters.

In several projects I worked to generate active bystandership. I developed a program for police training in California after the Rodney King incident, which aimed to make unnecessary violence by police less likely. Rodney King, not stopping his car when a police officer tried to stop him, was chased down by the police. Lying on the ground he was beaten with batons by a couple of policemen, while others stood around watching. This scene was captured on video and became an international sensation.

A central element in the training was police officers becoming positive, active bystanders to each other. Normally police officers work in pairs. The culture that develops in police groups requires a police officer to support his or her colleague no matter what the colleague does. This can be very bad bystandership, allowing harm to civilians. It can also lead at times to serious problems for an officer whose violence to civilians is exposed. Positive bystandership and good teamwork means engaging early when a fellow officer gets increasingly and inappropriately heated during interaction with someone, to help neutralize and redirect the interaction (Staub, 2003; Chapter 14 in this book). As I write this, I and a group of committed people in New Orleans, including lawyers and former police officers from there and around the country, are creating an expanded program for the city, where for many years the police have used unnecessary force, and are already working to extend its use around the United States. I also worked with a local organization in New Orleans after Hurricane Katrina, developing a training to help improve community relations, and was an expert witness at one of the Abu Ghraib trials.

After the genocide in Rwanda in 1994, starting in early 1999, clinical psychologist and trauma specialist Laurie Anne Pearlman and I have conducted trainings and workshops there with members of local organizations that worked with groups in the community, with the media, with community leaders, and with national leaders to promote healing and reconciliation between Tutsis and Hutus. One component was about how intense violence between groups develops and the influences that lead to it, based primarily on the research and theory in my book *The Roots of Evil: The Origins of Genocide and Other Group Violence* (Staub, 1989). Another focus was on the impact of violence on people, the traumatic effects of violence (Pearlman, 2001), or the psychological wounds they create (Staub, 1998) and the consequences of this on people's behavior. The trainings were also about how to prevent violence between groups and how to promote reconciliation that prevents renewed violence (Staub, 2006, 2011; Staub & Pearlman, 2006).

Encouraged to expand the reach of our program by many parties in Rwanda, including national leaders, we developed educational radio programs, both radio dramas and informational programs, first in Rwanda and then in Burundi and the Congo, using and further developing the approach in our trainings. We did this in collaboration with Radio LaBenevolencija, a Dutch nongovernmental organization that is producing the programs. The first of these programs, a radio drama, *Musekeweya* (New Dawn), is a story of two villages in conflict. There are attacks and counterattacks, a leader who incites violence, followers, positive bystanders, a Romeo and Juliet love story between the sister of the leader who is inciting violence and a young man from the other village, with the two of them working with other youth to prevent violence, trauma and healing, and trials of perpetrators, with the story slowing moving to reconciliation.

This radio drama began to broadcast in 2004 and is still ongoing in 2015. Separate evaluations of how people were affected by the trainings (Staub, Pearlman, Gubin, & Hagengimana, 2005) and the radio drama (Paluck, 2009; Staub & Pearlman, 2009) showed a variety of positive and important effects. It was my sense that knowledge and understanding, especially what I call "experiential understanding," deep knowledge that comes from people applying information to their own experience, can have powerful positive effects. These "interventions," among other effects, appear to give rise to active bystandership. (For a detailed description of the trainings, the educational radio programs, and the evaluation studies see Staub, 2011; see also Chapters 18 and 19). What I learned from my research, work with the police, and our work in Africa entered into the creation of a curriculum to train students as active bystanders in schools when they witness bullying of a fellow student (Chapter 16).

Another of my engagements was in the Netherlands, at the invitation of the Amsterdam city government, after Theo van Gogh, a journalist, was killed by a Muslim man. The burning of mosques, Muslim schools, and churches followed, unusual for that historically peaceful society, creating much concern. I was asked to make recommendations for improving

Dutch–Muslim relations and preventing future violence, which I did after studying the situation there (Staub, 2007; also Staub, 2011; see Chapter 20, 21). These recommendation are relevant to other settings as well.

Overview of the Main Topics of the Book

Before addressing the substantive issues, I start in Chapter 2 by discussing the reasons we should help others. A primary reason is that our actions can, both through direct and generalized reciprocity, come back to us and our children and grandchildren. By what we do we can create more caring and helping or hostility and violence in the world. Caring, altruistic behavior not only benefits others but shows enlightened self-interest. Another reason is that being empathic, compassionate, and helpful contributes to our well-being and happiness (Seppala, 2013; Svoboda, 2013). I also discuss why aggression does not benefit us, how it is handed down to our children, and how it shapes the world around us—and toward us. I also briefly discuss the nature of genetic and temperamental influences on empathy, compassion, and altruism.

Raising Helpful, Inclusively Caring Children

How does a child become a person who cares about others' well-being and takes action on others' behalf when they are in distress, when they suffer, or when they just need help to accomplish their goals? How can parents, teachers, even neighbors and peers guide a child so that she or he cares about the well-being of people, and not only those in the family or a close group but also people outside the group, ideally all human beings. A number of the chapters in this book address the question of how to raise children so that they become caring, helpful people (Eisenberg, Fabes, & Spinrad, 2006; Eisenberg et al., in press; Staub, 1979), and an issue of longstanding concern for me (Staub, 2003, 2005), how caring can become inclusive and expand beyond one's own group.

McFarland, Webb, and Brown (2012) studied identification with all humanity. People who on their measure identified more with all humanity valued people outside their group more, were more concerned for their needs, and were more willing to contribute to international humanitarian efforts. Clearly, this concept greatly overlaps with inclusive caring. But only a small percentage of people score very high on this measure. One of the issues I address in this book is how to promote inclusive caring.

Changing Ourselves Into Active Bystanders and Training in Active Bystandership

As our wok in Africa indicates, I believe in the power of information. It can help us transform ourselves. Our sensitive and effective use of information, as well as our actions, can help us create change in society. One chapter describes the inspiring example of single individuals who as active bystanders brought impressive change (Chapter 12). In another chapter I discuss how we can turn ourselves into active bystanders, understanding and overcoming inhibitors, generating in ourselves motivation for action, turning to other people as allies

(Chapter 13). I also describe a training to provide students in schools with the knowledge and skills to be active` bystanders when they witness harassment, intimidation, and harmful actions by peers, that is, bullying (Chapter 16). The practices in this training can also be applied to other domains. Part of this training is assessing and reducing the risk involved in active bystandership.

Moral Courage

Children and adults who hold moral values and feel empathy for other people, even believe in their responsibility for others' welfare, will not necessarily act in others behalf when they face certain adverse circumstances. How do people become morally courageous, acting on their moral values and beliefs and empathic, caring feelings, even in the face of potential or actual opposition and the possibility of harm to themselves? A number of chapters engage with this question.

Moral courage is important any time a person tries to bring about change. Individuals and groups embrace tradition and current practice and tend to consider what is customary as morally right. People justify existing systems (Jost, Kay, & Thorisdottir, 2009). Moral courage is needed in everyday situations, when one person harms another in words or actions. It is needed when people want to improve an institution or change its values, structure, or modes of operation. Changing a school, for example, from authoritarian methods of teaching and disciplining to more participatory and democratic practices is a substantial challenge.

Moral courage is very much needed in resisting the evolution of violence toward another group. Great harm done to members of a group, usually a minority in society, does not just erupt. It is almost always, if not always, the outcome of progressive change in individuals and society. Saying derogatory things about members of some group, excluding them from certain kinds of jobs or restricting their admission to universities, or treating them badly in other ways are way stations to violence. Engaging in violence further changes individuals, group norms, and institutions and tends to gives rise to greater violence.

Speaking out and acting against this evolution requires moral courage and sometimes, depending on circumstances, physical courage. Inherent in morally courageous action is the possibility of physical danger to the actor. There is less physical danger earlier when other people, leaders, or society in general are as yet less committed to harmful actions. The danger initially may be disapproval and ostracism. As commitment to doing harm increases, opposition becomes physically more dangerous. But if people are able to attract allies who join them in their morally courageous behavior, the danger is reduced and the likelihood of success greater.

Helping others and morally courageous behavior are the outcome of personality, as they join with circumstances surrounding us. Sometimes circumstances are so powerful that they lead most people to help; at other times they inhibit helping, and only people with strong empathy or personal responsibility are likely to help. A feeling of competence adds to this likelihood. In addition to personal characteristics and the influence of immediate circumstances, this book considers the influence of the larger social situation—the circumstances in a society—in leading to or inhibiting helping.

Heroism and Heroic Rescue

Personal characteristics are important in giving rise to the motivation for heroic helping. There is some question about what these characteristics are, which I address in Chapters 7, 22, and 23. However, moral courage is not always required. Rarely would anyone disapprove of or ostracize someone for jumping into the river to save the life of a drowning person. While the action is dangerous, the helper is likely to be celebrated.

But hiding the member of a group that is the target of genocide is another matter. All too often, many of the people in the society have developed such a negative view of these designated victims that they strongly disapprove of helping them. Or they may be afraid of retaliation by authorities against the whole community. The helper, or rescuer, may face betrayal, disapproval, exclusion by neighbors, and punishment by authorities, even death, and not only for herself or himself but also family members. While resisting the increasing hostility, persecution, and violence against a group may be regarded as a moral obligation, rescue that carries such danger seems a case of moral as well as physical heroism. Some of the chapters in this book address the question of what enables and leads some people to engage in these and other heroic actions.

Altruism Born of Suffering

Most research on the roots of caring, helping, and altruism has focused on positive socialization, such as nurturance and good guidance. Research has also focused on dysfunction, the perception of the world as hostile, and aggressiveness that frequently result from prior victimization. I have proposed the term "altruism born of suffering" to refer to people who have been victimized or suffered for other reasons but nonetheless act to prevent suffering or help those who have suffered (Staub, 2003, 2005). We know that there are people who have suffered greatly due to abuse by parents and other adults, who have been persecuted due to prejudice or as intended victims of mass violence, or have been affected by natural disasters who come to see their shared humanity with others and devote themselves to protecting and helping others.

The limited research on this suggests that even though severe prior victimization can have strong negative effects, it can also give rise to altruism in many people. Groups of people who have been victimized can also become altruistic, working to stop others' victimization. Some material in the book considers evidence for the existence of altruism born of suffering, as well as discusses experiences and influences that transform victimization and suffering into caring for and helping people (Staub & Vollhardt, 2008; Chapters 10, 11 in this book).

Resisting Evil; Working for Reconciliation and Positive Relations Between Groups; Building Harmonious, Peaceful, and Caring Societies

One chapter (18) gives an overview of our work in Rwanda using workshops/trainings to promote healing after the genocide in 1994 and reconciliation between groups as a way of preventing new violence. It also describes research evaluating and showing the positive effects of the training. Another chapter (19) describes our educational radio programs, including research evaluating it and showing its positive effects. It also describes their expansion through "grassroots projects," directly working with members of communities so that they can be agents in resolving conflict and preventing violence. Based on my prior work, my on-the-ground engagement with people in Amsterdam, and research about the conditions there, in Chapter 20 (see also 21) I discuss ways to prevent violence and build harmonious relations between ethnic Dutch and Muslims living in the Netherlands. This has relevance to all countries with substantial Muslim minorities.

Chapter 22 is in part an overview of the topics in the book. In addition, I discuss the personal characteristics and circumstances that lead to helpful and heroic actions. An important focus of this chapter is exploration of what is required to create active bystandership to resist the evolution of violence between groups—to overcome devaluation, promote positive relations across group lines, and create peaceful, harmonious societies. Practices that prevent violence and promote reconciliation go a long way to create such societies (see Staub, 2011, 2013).

In Chapter 23 I explore in greater depth than before moral courage and heroism. I discuss some research on courage, studied among military, that shows that preparation and practice in dangerous activities contribute to it. I describe some research related to moral courage and again consider how children can become morally courageous. I then discuss nonviolence as a strategy to accomplish some of the important goals of this book (Chapter 24). Chapter 25 is highly personal, about the heroic woman who helped me and my family during the Holocaust.

In the last section of the book, I include a long table that summarizes the central influences that lead people to become active bystanders (Chapter 27). In a concluding chapter (28) I write about creating caring societies. I discuss good societies and bad societies as they contrast with good societies, mostly as described by others. I describe the values and institutions that constitute a caring society and some of the practices that can help create them. Segments of the population (bottom up), leaders (top down), and groups in the middle (the media, churches, writers) can exert influence. An example I consider in some detail that involved all these levels was the civil rights movement in the United States. I discuss why its success, the great changes that it brought about, did not evolve further into genuinely equal race relations.

Basic Needs and Personal Goals

I have developed two theories over the years to help with understanding the origins of caring and helping and hostility and aggression, as well as their expression in action. One of these, basic needs theory, identifies universal psychological needs, the consequences of their satisfaction or frustration, and constructive and destructive modes of their fulfillment (part of Chapter 3 and Chapter 4). The other, personal goal theory, which I discuss at various places in the book as relevant to material there (especially Chapter 22), considers how personal values and related goals that people have developed influence their actions.

However, moral and caring values and goals can be subverted by circumstances. An awareness of this can create resistance to this "subversion."

Passive and Active (Positive and Harmful/Complicit) Bystanders and Upstanders

A central theme in this book is the bystander, the witness who is in a position to know that action is needed and in a position to take action. A bystander can remain passive, not act, even turn away, avoid information, close his or her eyes, and therefore make himself or herself "not know." In addition to individuals, collections of individuals—groups, whole societies, leaders who could initiate actions by groups—can be passive. Or bystanders can be active, take action to address an immediate need, or attempt to improve the well-being of people in their society, or respond to harmful conditions and violence against people within their countries or in other societies.

The concept of active bystander, which I have been using for a very long time (see Staub, 1978, and especially 1989), has become widely used. On Google on August 21, 2014, it had 1.7 million hits. Universities offer trainings in active bystandership, so that students will stop or prevent harm done to fellow students. Some high schools and middle schools do this as well (for a training I developed with coworkers to stop bullying, that is also applicable to other settings, see Chapter 16).

In 2014 there has been a great deal of attention to sexual harassment on campuses, and President Barack Obama has called for action, with a focus on active bystandership by students. The University of Massachusetts at Amherst has a campus-wide project called UMatter. The goal is to create a campus environment in which everyone feels that he or she matters. Active bystandership is at the heart of this, with a focus not only on sexual harassment but also suicide prevention and preventing harm in general.

A more recent, related but less widely used concept is the upstander (with 77,100 hits on Google). We can think of active bystandership as a continuum, ranging from small acts to heroic actions such as rescuers hiding a Tutsi in Rwanda or a Jew in Germany, to heroism that immediately risks the actor's life as he or she tries to save another person in great danger at that moment. If the idea of an upstander is used, it seems more appropriate for actions toward the high end of this continuum. Asking someone to please not tell a racist joke is active bystandership; the term *upstander* seems too strong to describe this. *Active bystander* also implicitly provides a contrast to *passive bystander*.

When I write about active bystanders in this book I mean positive bystanders who take action to help people in need, improve society, and create benefit. Often it is obvious when a person or group is a positive bystander. But individuals and groups can hold beliefs and values that lead them to support actions that, from their perspective, are positive but from a disinterested or moral perspective perpetrate harm. The same is true of the upstander. In the United States, some people believe that individuals—at least those who are not seriously ill—should be responsible for their own circumstances in life regardless of their social situation, history, or other conditions that make them understandably dependent on some form of societal support.

Before all the recent attention to bullying in schools, my students and I interviewed teachers as part of a study of students verbally or physically harming other students (as well as behaving in positive ways) in a whole school system. Some teachers believed that it is best to let students take care of their own conflicts (Staub, 2003). This makes sense up to a point, but when some students greatly suffer due to what fellow students do to them, adults need to get involved. These teachers did not believe in intervening themselves and presumably did not regard well other teachers who intervened.

Even perpetrators of genocide or other mass violence normally believe that they are acting for a higher good. The Khmer Rouge, the communists in Cambodia who perpetrated genocide, wanted to create a society of total social equality. They believed that people who, in their view, would not contribute to or accept the existence of such a state had to be eliminated (Staub, 1989).

Judging bystander actions as beneficial or harmful is not a simple matter; perspectives can vary, and there are not always definitive answers. Even people usually called terrorist are sometimes, by some groups (and occasionally justifiably) regarded as fighting for freedom or liberation. It can be helpful to consider the actions' aims and their actual or potential consequences. Does it provide benefit or contribute to harm? How do the actions or institutions that active bystanders support look in relation to universal moral principles, such as justice, the sanctity of life, and utilitarianism, the greatest good for the greatest number? Are the actions consistent with or contrary to international law?

It is difficult to draw a line between harmful bystanders and complicit bystanders, whose intention is not to support harmdoing but by their actions make perpetrators believe that at the very least they accept what they do. Kids who stand around and laugh while a peer is bullied are complicit. Presumably the intention of most US and other corporations busily doing business in Germany during the 1930s, while the Nazis violently eliminated opposition, assumed dictatorial powers, and increasingly persecuted Jews, was not to support these practices, which would have made them into harmful bystanders, but to make money, which made them complicit. However, intentions are hard to establish, and complicity and harmful bystandership are hard to separate. I therefore use only the term *complicit bystanders*.

What about supporting a person, one's country, or another country, that engages in self-defense? Everyone has the right to self-defense. But supporting a person or country that claims to engage in self-defense but uses overwhelming force not commensurate with threat, provocation, or attack is also harmful or complicit bystandership. An example is supporting the legal right to shoot a person when someone *believes* that this person *intends* to harm him or her, an issue that has received wide attention in the United States as a result of a few such actions.

What, How, and Who

We should identify the what, how, and who in creating change. *What* goals do we need to accomplish to contribute to "goodness"? Positive attitudes by members of groups toward others, or inclusive caring, and constructive ideologies, a vision of social relations, and societal arrangements that embrace all groups are examples of goals. *How* can we bring these about, by what practices? For example, positive attitudes can be promoted by deep connections, as people from different groups work on joint projects for shared goals, and by the media writing in positive ways about the lives of people in each group, making them known and understood. *Who* are the actors to accomplish different goals? They include school personnel, creating classrooms in which children belonging to different groups experience positive connections to each other, experts training leaders and members of the media in understanding the influences that lead to violence and ways they can exert positive influence, leaders and members of the media exerting such influence, churches and civic organizations that move their members to active bystandership, and writers, intellectuals, government officials—any individuals—propagating positive visions, or engaging in positive actions.

Each parent and each teacher can contribute to children becoming caring people. But to do so, many parents and teachers have to change themselves. Change, therefore, is interconnected; changes in institutions and society help change individuals, while changes in individuals and actions by them can change institutions and society. For schools to change, parents and societal authorities need to exert influence. Change in the values and mode of operation of a school means that teachers and administrators changed, which affects children and in turn can also affect parents. This is not an easy process, since parents who are most preoccupied with the pressures and stresses of life and least engaged with the raising of their children are least likely to engage with schools and be affected by changes in their child's school environment. Schools have to be proactive to engage parents.

As parents and teachers can raise caring children, so leaders—in government, churches, corporations, and other institutions—can contribute to a caring society. But here again, they often have to change first in order to become agents of positive change. The starting point for change can come from individuals, collections of individuals, leaders, or institutions. As I discuss in the concluding chapter on creating caring societies, they have to promote values that connect (rather than divide) people and build just institutions that express these values in policies and practices.

References

Eisenberg, N., Fabes, R. A., & Spinrad, T. L. (2006). Prosocial development. In W. Damon (Ed.), *Handbook of child psychology: Vol. 3. Social, emotional, and personality development* (5th ed., pp. 646–718). New York: Wiley.

Eisenberg, N., Spinrad, T. L., & Eggum, N. D. (in press). The development of prosocial behavior. In D. A. Schroeder & W. Graziano (Eds.), *Oxford handbook of prosocial behavior*. New York: Oxford University Press.

Jost, J. T., Kay, A. C., & Thorisdottir, H. (Eds.). (2009). *Social and psychological bases of ideology and system justification*. New York: Oxford University Press.

Latane, B., & Darley, J. (1970). *The unresponsive bystander: Why doesn't he help?* New York: Appleton-Crofts.

McFarland, S., Webb, M., & Brown, D. (2012). All humanity is my ingroup: A measure and studies of identification with all humanity. *Journal of Personality and Social Psychology, 103*, 850–853.

Milgram, S. (1974). *Obedience to authority: An experimental view*. New York: Harper and Row.

Oliner, S. B., & Oliner, P. (1988). *The altruistic personality: Rescuers of Jews in Nazi Europe*. New York: Free Press.

Paluck, E. L. (2009). Reducing intergroup prejudice and conflict using the media: A field experiment in Rwanda. *Journal of Personality and Social Psychology, 96,* 574–587.

Pearlman, L. A. (2001). The treatment of persons with complex PTSD and other trauma-related disruptions of the self. In J. P. Wilson, M. J. Friedman, & J. D. Lindy (Eds.), *Treating psychological trauma & PTSD* (pp. 205–236). New York: Guilford Press.

Seppala, E. (2013). The compassionate mind. *Observer, 26*(5). 20–24.

Staub, E. (1970). A child in distress: The influence of age and number of witnesses on children's attempts to help. *Journal of Personality and Social Psychology, 14,* 130–140.

Staub, E. (1971a). A child in distress: The influence of modeling and nurturance on children's attempts to help. *Developmental Psychology, 5,* 124–133.

Staub, E. (1971b). Helping a person in distress: The influence of implicit and explicit "rules" of conduct on children and adults. *Journal of Personality and Social Psychology, 17,* 137–145.

Staub, E. (1971c). The use of role playing and induction in children's learning of helping and sharing behavior. *Child Development, 42,* 805–817.

Staub, E. (1974). Helping a distressed person: Social, personality and stimulus determinants. In L. Berkowitz (Ed.), *Advances in experimental social psychology* (Vol. 7., pp. 203–342). New York: Academic Press.

Staub, E. (1978). *Positive social behavior and morality: Vol. 1. Personal and social influences.* New York: Academic Press.

Staub, E. (1979). *Positive social behavior and morality: Vol. 2. Socialization and development.* New York: Academic Press.

Staub, E. (1989). *The roots of evil: The origins of genocide and other group violence.* New York: Cambridge University Press.

Staub, E. (1997). The psychology of rescue: Perpetrators, bystanders and heroic helpers. In J. Michalczyk (Ed.), *Resisters, rescuers and refugees: Historical and ethical issues* (pp. 137–47). Kansas City, MO: Sheed and Ward.

Staub, E. (1998). Breaking the cycle of genocidal violence: Healing and reconciliation. In J. Harvey (Ed.), *Perspectives on loss* (pp. 231–241). Washington, DC: Taylor & Francis.

Staub, E. (2003). *The psychology of good and evil: Why children, adults and groups help and harm others.* New York: Cambridge University Press.

Staub, E. (2005). The roots of goodness: The fulfillment of basic human needs and the development of caring, helping and nonaggression, inclusive caring, moral courage, active bystandership, and altruism born of suffering. In G. Carlo & C. Edwards (Eds.), *Moral motivation through the life span: Theory, research, applications* (pp. 33–73). Nebraska Symposium on Motivation. Lincoln: Nebraska University Press.

Staub, E. (2006). Reconciliation after genocide, mass killing or intractable conflict: Understanding the roots of violence, psychological recovery and steps toward a general theory. *Political Psychology, 27*(6), 865–895.

Staub, E. (2007). Preventing violence and terrorism and promoting positive relations between Dutch and Muslim communities in Amsterdam. *Peace and Conflict: Journal of Peace Psychology, 13*(3), 333–361.

Staub, E. (2011). *Overcoming evil: genocide, violent conflict and terrorism.* New York: Oxford University Press.

Staub, E. (2013). Building a peaceful society: Origins, prevention, and reconciliation after genocide and other group violence. *American Psychologist, 68*(7), 576–589.

Staub, E. (2014). Obedience, joining, following and resistance in the Milgram situation and in genocide and other group violence: Situation, personality, bystanders. *Journal of Social Issues, 70*(3), 501–514.

Staub, E., & Baer, R. S. Jr. (1974). Stimulus characteristics of a sufferer and difficulty of escape as determinants of helping. *Journal of Personality and Social Psychology, 30,* 279–285.

Staub, E., Fellner, D. Jr., Berry, J., & Morange, K. (2003). Passive and active bystandership across grades in response to students bullying others students. In E. Staub (Ed.), *The psychology of good and evil: Why children, adults and groups help and harm others* (pp. 240–244). New York: Cambridge University Press.

Staub, E., & Pearlman, L. A. (2006). Advancing healing and reconciliation. In L. Barbanel & R. Sternberg (Eds.), *Psychological interventions in times of crisis* (pp. 213–245). New York: Springer-Verlag.

Staub, E., & Pearlman, L. A. (2009). Reducing intergroup prejudice and conflict: A commentary. *Journal of Personality and Social Psychology, 96,* 588–594.

Staub, E., Pearlman, L. A., Gubin, A., & Hagengimana, A. (2005). Healing, reconciliation, forgiving and the prevention of violence after genocide or mass killing: An intervention and its experimental evaluation in Rwanda. *Journal of Social and Clinical Psychology, 24*(3), 297–334.

Staub, E., & Spielman, D. A. (2003). Students' experience of bullying and other aspects of their lives in middle school in Belchertown: Report summary. In E. Staub (Ed.), *The psychology of good and evil: Why children, adults and groups help and harm others* (pp. 227–240). New York: Cambridge University Press.

Staub, E., & Vollhardt, J. (2008). Altruism born of suffering: The roots of caring and helping after experiences of personal and political victimization. *American Journal of Orthopsychiatry, 78,* 267–280.

Svoboda, E. (2013). *What makes a hero? The surprising science of selflessness.* New York: Current.

2

Why We Should Help and Not Harm Others

Why should a person be caring and helpful? Why not simply look out for our own interests and pursue them, even employing as much aggression as necessary to fulfill them? Why should parents raise children who feel empathy, care about others' welfare and help others? And to what extent do our human genetic makeup and individual heredity contribute to our empathy for and caring about others?

The Consequences of Aggression to Us, Our Children, Our Group

When children are aggressive, they often grow into aggressive adults and then raise aggressive children. Boys whose peers rate them as aggressive at age eight are more aggressive as adults against their spouse, use more physical punishment with their children, and have more of a criminal record at age 30 than other boys. The more aggressive these boys are at age eight, the more fantasy aggression their own children engage in when they are about age eight (Huesmann, Eron, Lefkowitz, & Walder, 1984).

Aggression—behavior that harms other people and that brings loss, pain, and injury to others—often brings harm to the aggressor as well. The aggressive behavior of children, adults, ethnic groups, and whole nations usually ends in harm to everyone. Aggressive children are usually disliked by their peers, which affects their continued development (Coie & Dodge, 1997). There are many examples of how violence by groups ultimately brings harm to the perpetrators. In recent times these include Nazi Germany, the Khmer Rouge in Cambodia, the genocide by Hutus of the Tutsis in Rwanda, and the mass killings by Serbs in Bosnia. Perpetrators of terrorism, like many of the leaders of Al Qaeda, also bring harm to themselves.

Becoming caring and helpful does not mean that we cannot act on our own behalf and work on fulfilling our own goals, or cannot use force when necessary to defend ourselves.

People can be caring and helpful and still know how to balance pursuing their own goals and acting in behalf of others. Part of caring is to know when others' needs have become so great that they should supersede our own. Rushing to get to a movie when we are with a friend when he learns that his child was killed in a car accident would be an absurd disregard for his need—and also show disrespect for ourselves. But giving a friend a ride to a movie while I am seriously ill would show lack of respect for my own needs.

Enlightened Self-Interest, Reciprocity, Community, and Caring

Much of the time helping others ultimately benefits us, if not immediately then in the long run. There is a norm of reciprocity that is apparently universal, held in every society (Mauss, 1954). A norm is a social expectation that people will behave in a certain way. People believe that they should help, and not harm, people who have helped them. While this does not mean that people will always follow this norm, many research studies show that people usually help others who were helpful or generous to them, especially when they interpret the others' behavior as benevolent, rather than selfish, wanting to gain something in return. They also withhold kindness from or retaliate against people who have harmed them (Staub, 1978).

In one of our studies, two fourth graders were in the same room (Staub & Noerenberg, 1981). We asked each of them to make a drawing but gave a drawing pencil to only one of the children. Later we gave candy to the second child. The more the first child shared the drawing pencil, the more candy the second child shared. Or, to put it another way, the less the first child shared, the less the second child shared in return. But human relationships are not simple. Friends behaved in a different way. When a child was selfish with a friend, the friend shared *more* in return. How we respond to someone's actions depends on its meaning for us. A friend's selfishness may make us wonder about their feelings for us, may endanger the relationship, and at least initially we may make extra efforts to repair the relationship.

We also found strong reciprocity in our observations of the classroom and playground interactions of second to fourth grade children (Staub & Feinberg, 1980). Children who helped and shared with others were the recipients of help and generosity. Those who were aggressive and unhelpful were the objects of others' aggression and received little help. This was not the case with children who acted aggressively only to defend themselves.

Reciprocity does not depend only on actions but also on their meaning. It strongly depends on how we perceive a helper's or aggressor's intentions. Helping or sharing can be perceived as selfish, its purpose to gain something by inducing reciprocity. It is more likely that others will reciprocate our helpful acts if we act unselfishly, not to gain benefits, and/or if others believe that this is the case. This is also true in the case of harmful actions. Children retaliated much less when they believed that an older child who messed up a game they played did this because he was very tired and in a bad mood and not because he wanted to harm them personally (Mallick & McCandless, 1966). Adults retaliate less if they believe that a person who was verbally rude and abusive was under extreme pressure.

Aggression and selfishness do not beget love, friendship, and respect. In our observations of interactions among elementary school children (Staub & Feinberg, 1980) aggressive children were the recipients of more aggressive and less kind behavior. In contrast, girls with a sophisticated, advanced form of empathy (which the second to fourth grade boys we studied did not yet possess) were the recipients of more helpful, generous, and cooperative acts than other children.

Empathy is sometimes defined as role taking, understanding others' situation and feelings (cognitive empathy). More often empathy is seen as an emotional experience, as feeling at least to some degree what others feel, that is, feeling an emotion not because of what is happening to us but because of what is happening to another person and/or because that person has that emotion. These girls did not necessary feel the same thing another person felt, like sadness upon seeing a sad child. Instead, they reacted with feelings of their own. On seeing the picture of a dispirited, Black child standing in front of an empty, grungy refrigerator, some felt angry about the injustice of this child's situation. We called this *reactive empathy*. Possibly what they felt had elements of sympathy, which Eisenberg, Fabes and Spinrad (2006, p. 647) defined as "feeling sorrow or concern for the distressed or needy other," or compassion, which Emma Seppala (2013) defined as "the emotional response when perceiving suffering and involves an authentic desire to help." Perhaps they already felt responsibility for others' welfare, which I see as the strongest influence on helping (see later chapters).

Perhaps because they cared about and were sensitive to other children, their peers helped them with tasks; sought them out to work with; and shared candy, pencils, or other possessions with them (Staub & Feinberg, 1980). We help those who have helped us partly because of the norm of reciprocity in society, which we learn and adopt. But when someone shows empathy and helps us, especially repeatedly, and we believe that this is based on good intentions, we also help them and not harm them because we come to like and value that person.

What comes around goes around. When in a group, whether it is a small community or a whole society, helping contributes to "generalized reciprocity." People will help a stranger because they were helped. If we help others we are contributing to creating a society in which we can rely on others' help when we need it, whether after an accident, or when we are sick, or have lost someone we love, or have become old, fragile, and helpless, or lost our job. Norms or expectations of mutual help develop. Through their experiences people come to trust, value, and like other people. They come to have a positive view of human beings and human nature, and see people as worth helping. There is the potential for this happening in a classroom, a school, a workplace, a society, or in the relations between nations. This view is consistent with research findings of a contagion in helping, with generous and helpful acts giving rise to generosity and helping by other people (Fowler & Christiakis, 2010).

In contrast, if we have been frequently harmed we will mistrust, dislike, and devalue people. We will help others less and engage in violence more, both because that has become the norm, the usual and even expected behavior, and because we have come to fear and mistrust each other. Like aggressive boys (Dodge & Frame, 1982), individuals and even social groups (Staub, 2011) develop an inclination to interpret others' actions as hostile and use force to defend themselves.

Helping others also contributes to success in our lives. We have the myth in the United States that it is selfish and aggressive people who are successful, especially in the business world. But to become successful, people have to be able to cooperate with their coworkers. Without that they will not receive from them the help and support necessary for success. In business, leaders who care about their coworkers and demonstrate caring are the most successful. Cooperation between children fosters cooperative tendencies (Lippitt & White, 1943) and often does so among adults as well. However, people can cooperate for purely instrumental reasons, to accomplish a task or gain benefits, or to manipulate others, thus making it less likely that cooperation leads to learning by doing and contributes to a lasting disposition.

Implicit in this discussion is that we humans live in communities and that we need each other. The concept of enlightened self-interest, while its starting point is self-interest, recognizes this. It is to the benefit of the community, as well as ourselves in need of connection and community, to care about and value each other. Most communities therefore develop and transmit to their members' caring values and foster caring emotions, at least toward their own members. In doing so they build on the human potential or even disposition for empathy, sympathy, and compassion.

But people tend to draw lines between "us" and "them," and even more so if they have as individuals, or as members of their group, experienced victimization. While they may cooperate even with members of the group that has hurt them or their families as part of essential coexistence, since the groups continue to live together in the same society, even in the same villages, as Hutus and Tutsis have done in Rwanda for a long time, they do not allow themselves to develop a positive emotional connection. As I will suggest in later chapters, a combination of healing, deep engagement, as well as other experiences can develop positive attitudes toward the other, foster reconciliation, and overcome this (see especially Chapter 22 and also 18, 19, 20).

The Costs of Passivity in the Face of Others' Need

Remaining passive when people suffer or need help for other reasons, and harming others, diminishes our openness to them, our capacity for empathy with them, and in turn our ability to grow as persons. An important way for us to develop and grow is through "taking in" other people. By understanding others we come to look at events that affect them from their perspective and develop varied perspectives on life. Understanding who they are, what they feel and think, we can absorb some of their knowledge, wisdom, and experience of the world. We can feel what they feel and respond to their situation.

As I studied mass violence, my observation of what happens to people who are passive bystanders to discrimination, persecution, or violence against other people in their society has convinced me that passively standing by when others suffer changes people in profound ways (Staub, 1989, 2011). This is also true when people are passive in the face of everyday suffering, like homelessness or the abuse of children. Our passivity often leads us to distance ourselves from those who suffer, and even to justify their suffering. This reduces our guilt and empathic pain. When people are passive, they tend to explain others' suffering as a result of something these others have done, or some failure or omission, or as due to basic faults in them. The more suffering surrounds us, and the more we do this, the smaller we make our world. We progressively lose part of our humanity.

This has happened in many instances of group violence: in Argentina as neighbors were abducted to be tortured and killed, in Rwanda, and elsewhere (Staub, 1989). It happened to Germans in the Nazi Germany of the 1930s. When the Nazis called upon the German people to boycott Jewish stores, to stop friendship and love relationship with Jews, they complied. They passively stood by as Jews were increasingly persecuted and harmed. By the time Jews were deported from Germany to concentration and extermination camps, only a very small number of people cared enough to attempt to rescue someone.

The Benefits of Helping Others: Well-Being, Happiness, and Health

Our needs or interests go way beyond material well-being. We deeply need and want security. We want close, loving relationships with family and friends, connection to a community, and a harmonious relationship to the world around us. These are required for our well-being. Deep connections to people, and to a community, are very satisfying. Even if aggression brings material gains, our aggressive behavior, as well as our passivity, affects our connections to people. Taking positive action and seeing or knowing how others' suffering diminishes and their well-being increases tends to enhance our own well-being. There is increasing amount of research that shows this.

Both acting in others' behalf and seeing others do so are uplifting. People who spend money on others feel happy, at times even happier than if they spend money on themselves (Dunn, Aknin, & Norton, 2008). Somewhat surprisingly Dunn and associates found that around the world, in poor and rich countries, among poor and rich people, giving and spending money on others made people happier than spending money on themselves (also discussed in Seppala, 2013). Earlier interview studies also found that people who help others report more well-being and even happiness, although this is more likely when they do so more extensively rather than on a single occasion (Svoboda, 2013).

While with such an association we do not know whether it is helping that causes happiness or happier people help more, a number of studies have shown that giving money to a charity activates the "pleasure center" of the brain. In one study, when people gave to charities, both voluntarily but to a lesser extent even when they were "taxed" (part of the money they received in the study was simply taken for a charity), the same part of the brain became active as when they rewarded themselves (Harbaugh, Mayr, & Burghart, 2007). Helping others (Seppala, 2013), and even seeing others helping appears to be good for our health. Students who saw Mother Theresa tending to suffering Indian children had an increase in the number of immune cells in their blood (McClelland, 1989).

A further example comes from my work. The magazine *Psychology Today* asked me in 1989 to create a questionnaire about values, caring, and helping. It included questions about how often people engaged in different forms of helping, such as giving up a seat on the bus for someone, helping in emergencies when someone had an accident or an attack of illness, helping a friend move, contributing money for charity, helping in a soup kitchen, trying to help a friend who is distressed. There were also questions about the last times people helped, as an attempt to validate to some degree self-reports of helping. We asked readers to fill out and return the questionnaire, and more than 7,000 people did so. People reported feeling good after they helped. Those who helped more experienced more satisfaction and happiness in helping. (*Psychology Today* stopped publication for a couple of years just as an article about this was about to be published; an article, and the questionnaire in an appendix, are in Staub, 2003.)

What is rarely studied is whether all people, or only or primarily people who care more about others' welfare, feel good after helping. The *Psychology Today* study showed that the stronger a prosocial value orientation, also measured by the questionnaire, the more people reported that they felt good after helping. This personal characteristic includes a positive view of human beings, concern about their welfare, and a feeling of responsibility for others' welfare. Colby and Damon (1992) described the history and actions of altruists who were deeply committed to helping. For these people, helping others became a source of deep satisfaction. The roots of this happening may lie in people's childhood experience. It may also lie in the important principle of learning by doing—that we change as a result of our own actions, and having started to help others we tend to become increasingly caring (see Chapter 5). As people engage in helping, they may develop more empathy and more of a feeling of responsibility for others' welfare. An increased capacity for these can even be an outcome of a person's past suffering, which leads some people to want to prevent others' suffering or to help those who have suffered (see Chapters 10 and 11). All these sources of helping were evident in these histories of the altruists Colby and Damon wrote about; all these I will discuss in subsequent chapters.

Even if socialization and experience develop the characteristics that motivate us to help and make helping satisfying, that does not mean that we will help on a particular occasion. Obviously, we often do not. The pursuit of our own goals, the sacrifices required, and other inhibitors I will discuss in later chapters can stop us from helping. We are least likely to help people we see as different from us and not worthy of our help. If we see human beings, or particular individuals or groups, in a negative light, we tend to feel less empathy and concern for them and would expect little satisfaction from helping them.

Research findings indicate that people who are more powerful, which may just be power in a particular situation, pay less attention to those who are less powerful. They give less indication of interest and interrupt more, even in a short, getting-acquainted situation. They are also less compassionate when they hear less powerful people describe their difficulties in life. Rich, powerful people may feel protected by their privilege or wealth, and reciprocity may matter to them only with regard to people similar to themselves.

In a brief, lucid discussion of this, Goleman (2013) suggests that "high status people attend to those of equal rank . . . those with most power in society seem to pay particularly little attention to those with least power" (p. 12). He also suggests that these attitudes, together with the absence of role taking and empathy by the powerful, make it difficult to address economic inequality. However, great economic inequality in a society is harmful to everyone (see Chapter 28).

In contrast to the advantaged in society, both past and recent research indicate that less advantaged people are more tuned in to other people. They need each other more and rely on each other's help in small and at times big ways, such as borrowing a food item or caring for a child. Presumably, therefore, they gain satisfaction from helping. Of course, people vary in empathy and prosocial orientation. While the charitable contributions of many wealthy people (and people in general) are to their church or for the arts, some are to help people in need. These must provide some satisfaction. It is possible that if people disinclined to help certain kinds of people in need were moved to help, especially in direct ways, the experience of improving others welfare would be satisfying for them. For reciprocity and enlightened self-interest, and satisfaction gained from helping to contribute to more equal, harmonious, and therefore well-functioning and peaceful societies, people have to develop not only empathy and feelings of responsibility for other close to them, but also inclusive caring.

Does Goodness (or Evil) Arise out of Our Genetic Makeup or Socialization and Experience?

There are a number of questions about the role of our human genetic characteristics in contributing to caring, empathy, compassion, helping, and altruism. One of them is simply how humans could have developed genetic characteristics that make the inclinations for such emotions and behaviors possible. We humans must have the genetic potential for caring emotions and behavior, since we can relatively naturally develop the tendency for them with socialization and experience. We can develop caring and engage in helping others even when this requires great effort or involves great danger to us. Another question is whether such dispositions and behaviors are the direct outcome of our genetic makeup or whether our genetic makeup provides the basis out of which they can develop with appropriate experience. The third one is whether individual genetic makeup, or differences in heredity, contributes to differences in these tendencies.

Scholars concerned with evolution and genetics have struggled with the question of how altruism can become part of our genetic makeup. This includes Darwin. The challenge is that in order to reproduce their genes, presumably an evolutionary imperative as the notion of the selfish gene suggests, it is assumed that humans have to focus on their own advantage, rather than endure costs and dangers in helping others. Scholars have proposed various ideas to account for how people who are more altruistic, in spite of the risks they take, would be more likely to pass on their genes, so that altruism can become part of the human gene pool. These include kin selection (by helping others related to us we help propagate our genes), reciprocal altruism (by saving the child of a neighbor from drowning in the creek, the neighbor will reciprocate and help members of our family in need), and group selection (helping members of our group improves our chances of survival, since we need other group members for survival and thus "reproductive success").

With regard to the second question, there are thinkers and scholars who see empathy, compassion, and altruism, once a child is old enough for these tendencies to demonstrate themselves, as simply present in us due to our genetic makeup (Seppala, 2013). One study did find that newborn infants cry more when they hear the sounds of another infant's crying than when they hear sounds of similar intensity (Sagi & Hoffman, 1976). This suggests that we are born with a rudimentary form of empathy. However, the most reasonable perspective supported by both research and observation of behavior is that we have the genetic potential for empathy, compassion, the tendency to help others, and altruism (unselfish helping motivated by the desire to benefit others), as well as for hostility and aggression, potentials that develop to different extent with experience. The rudimentary form of empathy is an expression of this potential.

Children show at an early age both helpful and aggressive behavior. They may more naturally come to aggressive behavior, since it often demonstrates itself as a very young child wants a toy another is playing with and uses force to take it. No hostility may be intended; the behavior is simply instrumental, focused on getting the toy. Grabbing the toy is an expression of wanting and may not require special learning. It is not grabbing it that may require the learning to inhibit this seemingly natural tendency for wanting.

Early helpful behaviors that have been observed, such as a child taking to a distressed boy his favorite blanket, may require more learning from experience. But children learn to orient themselves to a caretaker in the first hour of their lives. They observe many acts of caretaking, of themselves, and of others, from birth on. These are all opportunities for learning through imitation. Moreover, adults engage in active socialization from birth on. Three-year-olds whose parents more often point out to them the consequences of their behavior on other people are more empathic (Zahn-Wexler & Radke-Yarrow, 1990).

With regard to the third question, apart from a shared human genetic makeup, there are individual variations in heredity. There is now research that shows that heredity does play some role in "prosocial behavior," behavior that benefits others. There have been attempts to identify particular genes that may have a role (for a discussion see Eisenberg, Spinrad, & Eggum, in press). One aspect of the contribution of heredity is through differences in temperamental characteristics, such as outgoingness and activity level. Such temperamental characteristics may attract socializing practices and relationships that lead to caring and helping. High activity levels may also contribute to the development of what I have called "action orientation" (Staub, 1978). This makes helping that requires fast action more likely.

As in many other realms as well, heredity and environment interact, or join together, in exerting influence. It has, for example, been demonstrated that children with one type of gene reacted differently to low and high quality socialization by parents. Children with more temperamental reactivity were also differently affected by socialization practices (Eisenberg et al., in press). It is unlikely that in the foreseeable future we will test for particular genes and effectively adjust socialization practices accordingly. But parental sensitivity and adjustment to the child's temperament, and to other characteristics, whether based on genetic makeup or not, is important.

As I noted brain research, which now enjoys great popularity and flowering, has demonstrated that when people share or do helpful things, the same areas of the brain may become active as when they gain benefits for themselves. Such research shows that helping is satisfying, not that it is the result of our genetic makeup. It may be satisfying because of values a person has learned, because of the connection it creates between people, or because of the empathic experience of someone's increased well-being. Helping may then get connected to and stimulate areas of the brain associated with reward.

Temperament, Attachment, Harmdoing, and Fending Off Harmdoing

Some research on children's early experience and behavior has implications for the role of heredity versus the dominant role of socialization. Variations in children's temperamental characteristics are present already at birth. Initial temperamental characteristics, such as activity level, are regarded as to a large extent due to heredity. In early research on temperament, children were characterized as easy, slow to warm up, and difficult—having irregular waking and sleeping patterns, difficult to soothe, and not responding well to new situations.

Children's attachment to caretakers has also been extensively studied. Infants' attachment has been categorized as secure, anxious, and avoidant (the latter two sometimes together referred to as insecure), and also as occasionally disorganized, with consequences for their behavior and relationships to peers and later in life to partners as well. The question has been posed to what extent the kind of attachment children form to caretakers is due to heredity versus the way caretakers engage with them.

Adults' caretaking appears to be a strong influence on the quality of attachment. At the very least, heredity and experience with caretakers jointly shape attachment, with the latter influence dominant. An adult's sensitivity, or responsiveness to the child and his or her needs, is a primary contributor to secure attachment.

Mothers (who have been most studied, but the research findings generally apply to fathers and other important caretakers as well) establish secure attachment with the majority of infants who have some aspect of difficult temperament. Infants can be securely attached to one adult caretaker and insecurely attached to another, which would not be likely if temperament primarily determined attachment. For example, infants can be insecurely attached to the mother while securely attached to a caretaker in daycare, which can be a saving grace for them. Also, when a mother's life changes for the better (e.g., getting a job that improves her economic situation) or for the worse (a divorce, loss of job), the quality of attachment changes. Decrease or increase in stress change the adult's way of relating to the child (Bretherton, 1992; Cassady & Shaver, 2010).

Children with varying attachment show significant differences in behavior in interaction with peers. A striking study (Troy & Sroufe, 1987) found that preschool boys who as infants were avoidantly attached were aggressive when paired with an anxiously attached child at kindergarten age. When paired with another avoidantly attached child, they were either aggressors or themselves the object of the other child's aggression. Children who were anxiously attached as infants were frequently victims when paired with an avoidant child.

The victimization consisted of dominating, controlling toys, as well as verbal and physical aggression, with lack of empathy and even obvious enjoyment following the other child's distress. For example, playing doctor and using a play hypodermic needle, an avoidantly attached child promised it would not hurt, then slowly increased the pressure until the other child cried out in pain. Then the aggressor smiled and walked away. Anxiously attached children tended to continue to initiate engagement with the child who was aggressive with them, even though they were often rejected.

But children identified as securely attached were neither aggressive nor the victims of aggression. They were able to inhibit aggressive behavior toward themselves when paired with avoidant children (Troy & Sroufe, 1987). Other research has also found children who are avoidantly attached as infants to be hostile and aggressive with peers. In contrast, those who are securely attached engage in positive behavior and tend to have positive relations with peers. Such peer relations, in turn, are associated with prosocial, helpful behavior (see Eisenberg et al., in press). The mothers' or caretakers' sensitivity and responsiveness contribute both to secure attachment and prosocial, helpful behaviors.

Caring, Harmonious Societies and Active Bystandership by Groups and Nations

Our enlightened self-interest requires that we care about other people and help them, and help create societies of caring and benevolence. We cannot have security, love, connection, and continued personal (or material) growth without living in a benevolent and reasonably harmonious society. It is in such a society that our human potentials can fully develop.

I am not talking about a utopian world, a society without conflict and difficulty. We have needs that are sometimes in conflict with the needs of others; we have a proclivity to divide the world into "us" and "them" and to favor those whom we consider "us," whether we define "us" on the basis of familial, ethnic, religious, political, or national categories. We can even be violent against "them" because they are Yankee fans rather than Red Sox fans, or vice versa. But we can also work to create a society in which conflict can be resolved without aggression between individuals and subgroups of the society (see especially Chapters 22, 28).

When it comes to other countries, we can passively stand by when another group in their society, or their government, harms a minority. Or we can take action as individuals, as community groups—churches, chambers of commerce, members of schools or universities, civic groups concerned with human rights and human welfare—and nations and members of the international community. We can exert influence on our government to act. Moral values, caring emotions, and feelings of responsibility for our fellow human beings can guide us, as well as enlightened self-interest. Violence in a society often expands. The genocide in Rwanda led to great violence in the Congo, with 5 million to 6 million people dying due to violence and disease (Staub, 2011). The cost of addressing the consequences of violence, providing people food, and helping them rebuild their society are often huge; these are costs often partly borne by other countries.

Awareness of the principle of enlightened self-interest and satisfaction inherent in helping develop with age. Moreover, without caring about other people becoming deeply ingrained in us, at particular times our needs may overwhelm us, and their fulfillment becomes paramount, whatever the consequences to others and ourselves. Also, if our experiences lead us to mistrust, dislike, or hate other people, we will see our interest as defending ourselves, while containing and overcoming others. Socialization, and when it is lacking later experiences, are essential to develop perspectives on the world, views of other people, and emotional orientations and values that lead to people to care about and help each other.

A Summary of Why We Ought to Help and Not Harm Others

In summary, we have shared genetic dispositions to both help and harm others. Which one develops depends on experience and in turn has great consequences for our individual and group lives. Enlightened self-interest is a core philosophical and psychological reason to be caring and helpful. Caring and helping provide satisfaction and create connections through which we can fulfill essential psychological, as well as material needs. By helping others, by shaping values, by raising children to be caring we can contribute to a society in which everyone will be cared about.

Many parents may be concerned about their children becoming too caring. They think, therefore: Let them care a little, but not too much. People who care too much are suckers; at best it is only one's immediate family who really cares. We do not want our child to give away the roast that is cooking in the oven to the beggar who comes to the door. In fact, in these days we do not want the beggar to come to the door; he or she might be a dangerous, violent person. In 2014, a man shot a young woman who came to his door late at night after a car accident. If we choose to give, we want to do it without the pressure of a needy person, by making a contribution in an envelope.

Parents may be reluctant to emphasize caring and helping in an age where the world seems dangerous. We have become afraid of each other. Parents teach children not to talk to strangers. Teachers and adults in general worry about touching a child, fearing that it will be seen as a sexual rather than affectionate act. While in some places it is dangerous to be on the streets, television and the movies make the world appear more violent that it is.

We want our children to learn to take care of themselves and are afraid that if they become too caring and helpful they will become incapable of doing just that. But the experiences that lead children to be caring and helpful have a great deal in common with those that enable them to pursue their own goals effectively. Children and adults who care about others' welfare do not lose their capacity to make judgments. People who trust other people are not gullible. When there are signs that the other person is not trustworthy, they start behaving accordingly (Rotter, 1971). Trust and caring, combined with the ability to judge events and people and protect ourselves from danger, the ability to balance our own needs and others' interests but recognize when others' needs should supersede our own, will serve us much better than lack of caring, distancing ourselves from others' needs, or hostility toward people and the world (Staub, 2005, 2011).

References

Bretherton, I. (1992). The origins of attachment theory: Joyn Bowlby and Mary Ainsworth. *Developmental Psychology, 28,* 759–775.

Cassidy, J., & Shaver, P. R. (2010). *Handbook of attachment: theory, research, and clinical applications.* New York: Guilford.

Coie, J. D., & Dodge, K. A. (1997). Aggression and antisocial behavior. In W. Damon (Ed.), N. Eisenberg (Vol. Ed.), *Handbook of child psychology: Vol. 3. Social, emotional, and personality development* (5th ed.). New York: Wiley.

Colby, A., & Damon, W. (1992). *Some do care.* New York: Free Press.

Dodge, K. A., & Frame, C. L. (1982). Social cognitive biases and deficits in aggressive boys. *Child Development, 53,* 620–635.

Dunn, E. W., Aknin, L. B., & Norton, M. I. (2008). Spending money on others promotes happiness. *Science, 319,* 1687–1688.

Eisenberg, N., Fabes, R. A., & Spinrad, T. L. (2006). Prosocial development. In W. Damon (Ed.), *Handbook of child psychology: Vol. 3. Social, emotional, and personality development* (5th ed., pp. 646–718). New York: Wiley.

Eisenberg, N., Spinrad, T. L., & Eggum, N. D. (in press). The development of prosocial behavior. In D. A. Schroeder & W. Graziano (Eds.), *Oxford handbook of prosocial behavior.* New York: Oxford University Press.

Fowler, J. H., & Christiakis, N. A. (2010). Cooperative behavior cascades in human social networks. *Proceedings of the National Academy of Sciences of the United States of America, 107,* 5334–5338.

Goleman, D. (2013, October 6). Rich people just care less. *The New York Times Sunday Review,* p. 12.

Harbaugh, W. T., Mayr, U., & Burghart, D. R. (2007). Neural responses to taxation and voluntary giving reveal motives for charitable donations. *Science, 316*(5831), 1622–1625.

Huesmann, L. R., Eron, L. D., Lefkowitz, M. M., & Walder, L. O. (1984). Stability of aggression over time and generations. *Developmental Psychology, 20*(6), 1120–1134.

Lippitt, R., & White, R. K. (1943). The "social climate" of children's groups. In R. G. Barker, J. S. Kounin, & H. F. Wright (Eds.), *Child behavior and development* (pp. 485–508). New York: McGraw-Hill.

Mauss, M. (1954). *The gift: Forms and functions of exchange in archaic societies.* Glencoe, IL: Free Press.

McClelland, D. C. (1989). Motivational factors in health and disease *American Psychologist, 44*(4), 675–683. doi:10.1037/0003

Mallick, S. K., & McCandless, B. R. (1966). A study of catharsis of aggression. *Journal of Personality and Social Psychology, 4,* 591–596.

Rotter, J. B. (1971). Generalized expectancies for interpersonal trust. *American Psychologist, 26,* 443–452.

Sagi, A., & Hoffman, M. (1976). Empathic distress in the newborn. *Developmental Psychology, 12,* 175–176.

Seppala, E. (2013). The compassionate mind. *Observer, 26*(5), 20–24.

Staub, E. (1978). *Positive social behavior and morality: Vol. 1. Personal and social influences.* New York: Academic Press.

Staub, E. (1989). *The roots of evil: The origins of genocide and other group violence.* New York: Cambridge University Press.

Staub, E. (2003). *The psychology of good and evil: Why children, adults and groups help and harm others.* New York: Cambridge University Press.

Staub, E. (2005). The roots of goodness: The fulfillment of basic human needs and the development of caring, helping and nonaggression, inclusive caring, moral courage, active bystandership, and altruism born of suffering. In G. Carlo & C. Edwards (Eds.), *Moral motivation through the life span: Theory, research, applications* (pp. 33–73). Nebraska Symposium on Motivation. Lincoln: Nebraska University Press.

Staub, E. (2011). *Overcoming evil: Genocide, violent conflict and terrorism.* New York: Oxford University Press.

Staub, E., & Feinberg, H. (1980). Regularities in peer interaction, empathy, and sensitivity to others. Paper presented at the American Psychological Association Symposium: Development of Prosocial Behavior and Cognitions, Montreal.

Staub, E., & Noerenberg, H. (1981). Property rights, deservingness, reciprocity and friendship: The transactional character of children's sharing behavior. *Journal of Personality and Social Psychology, 40,* 271–289.

Svoboda, E. (2013). *What makes a hero? The surprising science of selflessness.* New York: Current/Penguin Group.

Troy, M., & Sroufe, L. A. (1987). Victimization among preschoolers: The role of attachment relationship history. *Journal of the American Academy of Child & Adolescent Psychiatry, 26*(2), 166–172.

Zahn-Wexler, C., & Radke-Yarrow, M. (1990). The origins of empathic concern. *Motivation and Emotion, 14,* 107–130.

3

Inclusive Caring, Moral Courage, Basic Human Needs, Altruism Born of Suffering

Socialization and Experience

Caring that develops can be limited to a particular group of people, to some "in-group." When the basic needs of whole groups of people are frustrated by difficult social conditions, such as economic problems, political upheaval, and great societal change, psychological and social processes can lead these groups to turn against and victimize others (Staub, 1989a). If enough people in a group have developed inclusive caring (caring for the welfare of people who are not members of their group, ideally for all human beings) and moral courage (the courage to speak out and act according to one's values and beliefs in the face of potential or actual opposition, i.e., even if these beliefs and values are contrary to prevailing views in one's immediate environment or larger group), their active bystandership, their speaking out in behalf of their values and in behalf of the people who are harmed, can inhibit the evolution of increasing harmdoing and violence. I will note the importance of inclusive caring, moral courage, and positive bystandership both on the societal level and on the level of smaller groups—for example, children's peer groups, where they can inhibit bullying. I will also discuss the developmental roots of such processes and how they can be fostered.

I will then discuss an essentially unexplored but seemingly highly important avenue to helpful, altruistic behavior, which I call *altruism born of suffering*. Following victimization and other types of trauma, which greatly frustrate basic psychological needs, many

Reprinted with permission and minor changes from Staub, E. (2005). The roots of goodness: The fulfillment of basic human needs and the development of caring, helping and nonaggression, inclusive caring, moral courage, active bystandership, and altruism born of suffering. In G. Carlo and C. Edwards (Eds.), *Moral Motivation through the Life Span: Theory, Research, Applications*. Nebraska Symposium on Motivation. Lincoln: Nebraska University Press.

children (and adults) tend to become self-protective and/or aggressive. However, some do become caring and helpful people, even highly committed altruists. I will propose that experiences such as healing, support, and human connection can lead children or adults who have been victims of harsh treatment, abuse, or violence or have suffered in other ways to devote themselves to helping others or prevent others' suffering (see also Chapters 10 and 11 in this book).

This chapter presents material that is connected to my early work on the determinants and development of caring, helping, and altruism. It makes only limited explicit reference to my work on the origins and prevention of violence between groups, such as genocide and mass killing, healing from victimization, and reconciliation between groups (see, e.g., Staub, 1989a, 1998, 1999a, 2003; Staub & Pearlman, 2001; Staub, Pearlman, Gubin, & Hagengimana, 2005; Staub, Pearlman, & Miller, 2003). Nonetheless, it draws heavily on that work, both in posing issues and questions (such as inclusive caring, moral courage, and altruism born of suffering) and in addressing them.

Motivations, Psychological Processes, and Personal Characteristics in Helping (and Nonaggression)

Researchers and theorists have identified several psychological processes, and characteristics of individuals out of which such processes arise, that provide motivations for helping. People can help others for *selfish* reasons, motivated by real or hoped-for rewards. They may want to gain approval or to avoid disapproval, punishment, ostracism, or other negative consequences that follow from not doing what social norms prescribe, such as helping people in need (Berkowitz, 1972). They may also try to gain benefits, expecting that those whom they have helped will reciprocate, as a result of powerful and seemingly universal norms of reciprocity (Mauss, 1954). They can also act to maintain their positive mood or help to alleviate their own distress (Carlson & Miller, 1987).

People can also help others for *moral* reasons, guided by values, beliefs, and principles that they have internalized and/or developed and that lead them to promote others' welfare. One such belief is enlightened self-interest. While enlightened self-interest may seem the least moral of moral beliefs, since the motivation is to create a world in which one will be helped in turn, it may be a core belief out of which much of morality develops. The motivation here arises from the existence, awareness, or knowledge of and belief in the human proclivity for reciprocity, including "generalized reciprocity" (see Chapter 2). The latter is the notion that if one helps another person, this person is not only more likely to help oneself in return, but also more likely to help some other person in need. Thus, by helping others, one contributes to creating a world in which people in general will be helpful to oneself as well as to important people in one's life. The belief in enlightened self-interest can, and in the course of the evolution of morality in society is likely to, develop into the belief that one should help other people and that people ought to help each other. These, as well as justice and the sanctity of human lives, are among important moral beliefs.

I see motivation as moral when to some substantial degree its focus is to fulfill or live up to a moral belief, value, or principle. One limitation of such motivation is that its focus can become adherence to the norm or principle itself rather than the human welfare that it tries to protect or advance. It can, therefore, lead to distortions, such as justice not mitigated by mercy. Children may be punished to serve an adult's conception of justice in ways that make them into less caring people. In the end, the purpose of the moral value or principle, to serve human welfare, is subverted, possibly both at the moment and in the long run. Another possible distortion is a primary focus on living up to one's view of oneself as a moral person rather than on the welfare of the people whom the moral principles aim to serve (Karylowski, 1976).

Altruistic motivation, the desire to benefit someone in need, to reduce a person's distress or enhance his or her well-being, is more directly focused on the person rather than on a belief or principle. It can arise from affective connections to a person or people that make empathy or sympathy possible and more likely. It can also arise from certain types of moral beliefs or values, such as a belief in one's responsibility for others' welfare. It probably often arises from some combination of the two.

Altruistic motivation is likely to have at least two related but not identical roots. One is affective: *empathy,* or the vicarious experience of others' feelings. The kind of empathy that generates *sympathy* has been found especially important in motivating helpful action. Sympathy includes both feeling with and concern about a person (Batson, 1990; Eisenberg, 2002; Eisenberg & Fabes, 1998; Hoffman, 1975a, 1975b; a feeling of sorrow or concern for the distressed or needy other [Eisenberg, 2002, p. 135]). In contrast *personal distress*—when someone's distress generates distress that is seemingly empathic but that is focused on the self (Batson, 1990; Eisenberg, 2002; Eisenberg et al., 1989)—gives rise to motivation to reduce one's own distress. It leads to helping when that is the best way to reduce one's own distress, but not when some other action, like leaving the situation, is a relatively easy way to reduce one's distress.

Another form of altruistic motivation is what I have called *prosocial value orientation.* This orientation is related to helping people in either physical distress (Erkut, Jaquette, & Staub, 1981; Staub, 1974) or psychological distress (Feinberg, 1978; Grodman, 1979; Staub, 1978, 1980; see also Carlo, Eisenberg, Troyer, Switzer, & Speer, 1991; Shroeder, Penner, Dovidio, & Piliavin, 1995). In these studies prosocial orientation was measured by a combination of existing measures. (For statistically minded readers, these were factor analyzed, with the scores on a first, dominant factor used as indicators of prosocial orientation.) For subsequent studies a measure of prosocial orientation that I developed was used (Staub, 1989b, 2003). Scores on this measure were related to self-reports of varied forms of helping (Staub, 1995, 2003). Prosocial orientation was also positively related to constructive patriotism, which combines love of country with the willingness to oppose policies that are contrary to humane values, and negatively related to blind patriotism, a tendency to be uncritical of one's country, to not consider whether its policies or practices are "right or wrong" (Schatz, Staub, & Lavine, 1999; Schatz & Staub, 1997; Staub, 1997).

As we measured it, the three primary aspects of a prosocial value orientation were a positive view of human beings (i.e., a positive evaluation and, hence, valuing), a concern for people's welfare, and a feeling of personal responsibility for others' welfare (see Feinberg, 1978; Grodman, 1979; Schatz et al., 1999; Staub, 1974, 1989b, 1995, 2003). Although a prosocial value orientation has been measured "cognitively," in a questionnaire, it appears to be an affective, sympathetic orientation to people combined with a conscious concern about people's welfare and a belief in one's own responsibility for others' welfare. Empathy, and especially sympathy, embody concern for others, which presumably requires a positive evaluation of or orientation to human beings. A feeling of personal responsibility may, however, be an important additional motivational component, making action in behalf of people in need more likely.

When moral values or a prosocial orientation or a tendency to respond with empathy and sympathy are activated by circumstances such as others' need for help or distress, it is likely that they will give rise to motivation to help. As research with prosocial value orientation indicates, and as one would expect, people inclined to respond with such altruistic motivation to others' needs are helpful under a wide range of conditions.

The literature on aggression also differentiates among motivations for harming others. The most prominent distinction has been between *hostile* aggression, motivated by the desire to harm, and *instrumental* aggression, which aims to gain benefits for oneself and uses aggression as a means to that end (Berkowitz, 1993). *Defensive aggression,* which aims to protect the self (from real or imagined harm)—a common form of aggression (Dodge, 1993; Toch, 1969)—may be differentiated from other forms of instrumental aggression. But in this as well as in other kinds of aggression, hostile and instrumental motives frequently join (Staub, 1996b). Recently a distinction has been made between physical aggression and relational aggression (such as excluding others, or spreading rumors about them, or harming their reputation in other ways). The former has been described as more characteristic of boys, the latter of girls (Crick, 1997).

One would expect that values and emotional orientations that give rise to moral or altruistic motivation for helping would also reduce aggression. This has been explored to a somewhat limited extent. Feshbach and Feshbach (1969), for example, found that very young children who were more empathic were not less aggressive, but somewhat older children who were more empathic were less aggressive. In a number of studies Eisenberg has found that children who respond to others' need with sympathy tend to be less aggressive (Eisenberg et al., 2006). Kohlberg and Candee (1984) found that adults who had higher responsibility scores at various stages of moral reasoning were less likely to continue to obey the experimenter and administer electric shocks in a Milgram obedience study. Spielman and Staub (2000) found that seventh- and eighth-grade boys who were less aggressive, as measured by teacher ratings and in-school detentions, had higher prosocial value orientation scores on an adolescent version of the measure.

In addition to characteristics directly relevant to the motivation to help, other characteristics are required to give rise to the motivation and lead to its expression in action. I have called these *supporting characteristics* (Staub, 1980). One of these is a feeling of efficacy (Midlarsky, 1971; Staub, 1980, 1995, 2003), which makes it likely that the motivation for helping is transformed into action and probably even that the motivation arises. Another is the capacity for role taking, for understanding how others' circumstances would affect them or how others actually feel (Eisenberg & Fabes, 1998; Staub, 1979). This is especially important when the need for help is not obvious.

Basic Human Needs, Altruism, and Aggression

Varied psychological theories include assumptions about central psychological needs. Some theorists (Erikson, 1959; Maslow, 1968, 1987; Murray, 1938; and, more recently, Burton, 1990; Kelman, 1990; Pearlman & Saakvitne, 1995; Staub, 1989a, 2003) have proposed the existence of universal human needs. If there are universal, basic, psychological needs, they must play a substantial role in human life. I have been suggesting that the frustration of basic needs is central in the development of hostility and aggression, and that their fulfillment is central in the development of caring about other people's welfare and altruism (see Staub, 1989a, 1996b, 1999b, 2003).

The needs on which I have focused, which overlap with needs that others have proposed, are those for security, for a positive identity, for effectiveness and control, for a positive connection to other human beings, for autonomy, for a comprehension of reality, for life satisfaction, and for transcendence of the self (for definitions and detailed discussion, see Chapter 4). Apart from transcendence, I see all these needs as present at birth. Possibly the need for security is more basic than the others, and the needs for life satisfaction and for transcendence (the need to go beyond the self, which can be satisfied by helping others or by connecting to nature or to spiritual entities) are more advanced, deriving from and following the satisfaction of the other needs. But even at a very early age children are often in transcendent states, in which there is absorption in something beyond the self—seemingly an element or component of later transcendence (Staub, 2003).

Basic needs are powerful. They press for satisfaction. When they are not fulfilled in constructive ways in the course of normal experience, people will develop destructive modes of need satisfaction. *Destructive need satisfaction* means that a person fulfills one need in a way that frustrates his or her other needs (if not immediately, then in the long run) or that he or she fulfills needs in a way that frustrates other people's fulfillment of their basic needs.

For example, the need for effectiveness and control is the need to feel that one can influence events and, especially important, that one can protect oneself from harmful events and fulfill important goals. When this need is greatly frustrated, and especially when the frustration is the result of traumatic experience, the hallmark of which is lack of control over extremely stressful events that feel life threatening (Herman, 1992; Pearlman & Saakvitne, 1995; Staub, 2003), then a child (or an adult) may attempt to exercise control over all events, including the behavior of other people. This leads to constant vigilance, or hypervigilance, which is stressful.

The excessive need for control limits the range of the individual's behavior and interferes with the development of his or her own self and, thereby, the satisfaction of his or her need for a positive identity. It will also frustrate the needs of other people whom the individual seeks to control (e.g., their need for effectiveness and autonomy) and evoke reactions that will frustrate the individual's need for positive connection to others. For example, a child may try to constantly direct the activities of friends, including the extent and nature of their relationships to other children. This makes the child less attentive to and less engaged with other things. It also negatively affects the friends, possibly even leading them to terminate the friendship.

Difficult, stressful conditions of life may frustrate the basic needs of whole groups of people, leading to destructive modes of need fulfillment. A group may scapegoat some other group, for example, a subgroup of society, blaming it for the difficulties of life. It may create an ideology (a vision of social arrangements) that is destructive, in that it identifies some people as enemies who must be destroyed to fulfill the "positive" vision of the ideology. These psychological/social practices may help fulfill basic needs by making members of the group feel that they are not at fault for life problems, by giving them a feeling of effectiveness in working to fulfill the ideology, by creating connection among those who scapegoat or are part of an ideological movement. But they fulfill basic needs destructively, in that the group's psychological and social processes do not address the real problems and, over time, tend to lead to violent actions against others (Staub, 1989a). They ultimately often lead to the defeat, humiliation, and psychological traumatization of the group that has engaged in violence. Creating hopeful visions of the future that are inclusive, that bring everyone together to address life problems, can help fulfill basic needs constructively (Staub, 1989a, 2003).

Socialization Practices and Experiences That Promote Caring, Helping, Altruism, and Nonaggression

Affection and Nurturance Versus Neglect and Harsh Treatment

Temperamental characteristics of children enter into the development of altruism and aggression (Coie & Dodge, 1998; Eisenberg & Fabes, 1998). However, impulsiveness, which has been linked to boys' aggression, and other temperamental characteristics that may predispose a child to aggression, are affected by experience. Their nature and expressions are shaped by harsh versus nurturant treatment, and the lack of or appropriate caring, support and guidance by parents and other people. Similarly, temperamental dispositions appear to play a role in the development of empathy in conjunction with early socializing experiences (Zahn-Waxler & Radke-Yarrow, 1990). Surrounding social conditions, like poverty, also play an important role, but appear to exert influence primarily by affecting how parents relate and guide children (McLoyd, 1990). Here I will focus on childrearing practices.

Becoming a caring, helpful, altruistic person, or a hostile, aggressive one, is the result of combinations or patterns of childrearing (Staub, 1979, 1996a, 2003). Parents responding to their infants' needs and their continuing nurturance, warmth, affection, and sensitivity to their children are the core socializing practices and experiences for the development of helpful tendencies in children (Eisenberg, 1992; Eisenberg & Fabes, 1998; Hoffman, 1970a, 1970b, 1975a; Shaffer, 1995; Staub, 1971, 1979, 1996a, 1996b, 2003; Yarrow & Scott. 1972). In contrast, parents neglecting or harshly treating their children—rejection, hostility, the extensive use of physical punishment, and physical or verbal abuse—are the core socializing practices and experiences that contribute to the development of aggression (Coie & Dodge, 1998; Eron, Walder, & Lefkowitz, 1971; Huesmann,, Eron, Lefkowitz, & Walder, 1984; Lykken, 2001; Staub, 1996a, 1996b, 2003; Weiss, Dodge, Bates, & Pettit, 1992; Widom, 1989a, 1989b).

Warmth, affection, and nurturance mean that adults are responsive to the needs of the child. Responsiveness to the infant's and young child's physical and social needs fulfills the basic needs for security and connection. Parents' sensitive responding to the infant's signals also satisfies the child's need for efficacy and control. Responding to signals and satisfying needs also affirm the child and begin to develop the rudiments of a positive identity. Such sensitive parental responding is associated with the development of secure attachment (Ainsworth, Bell, & Stayton, 1974; Bretherton, 1992; Shaffer, 1995; Thompson, 1998; Waters, Wippman, & Sroufe, 1979). In turn, secure attachment is associated with helping peers when children are 3½ years old (Waters et al., 1979) and with empathy and prosocial behavior in preschool (Kestenbaum, Farber, & Sroufe, 1989).

As children get older, love, affection, and caring about a child's welfare can take varied forms. For example, an essential characteristic of the parents of boys who have high self-esteem appears to be that they care about their children's welfare, which makes the children feel cared about. But this caring is expressed by them in many ways and not necessarily through physical affection (Coopersmith, 1967). Sensitivity in caring about and responding to the child's feelings and needs, to who the child is, will fulfill all basic needs. It will develop connection to important adults, which in turn is a source of positive orientation toward people in general.

That this is the case is suggested by research findings that show that securely attached children are also capable of *creating* positive connections. Such children have positive relationship to peers in the early school years (Waters et al., 1979). They are able to create non-aggressive interactions in preschool with children who were found avoidantly attached at a younger age and whose interactions with anxiously attached and other avoidantly attached children are aggressive (Troy & Sroufe, 1987). Furthermore, unpublished research that I conducted with Don Operario suggests that college students who rate their parents as affectionate and caring also have a positive view of human beings and express concern about and feelings of responsibility for others' welfare. As noted earlier, such a prosocial value orientation is related to varied forms of helping. Warm parenting is also linked to children's empathy.

In contrast, severe negative effects result from neglect and the ineffectiveness of the child's signals (such as crying) to bring about the satisfaction of essential biological (and social) needs. Research some decades ago has shown that infants in institutions characterized by poor caretaking became depressed and died in significant numbers. Those who survived later showed deficiency in their capacity for human connection and in other domains (Shaffer, 1995; Thompson & Grusec, 1970). The conditions in such institutions frustrated infants' basic needs for security, connection, and effectiveness/control. Because of inadequate staffing, infants were fed and cared for on a rigid schedule and when it was their turn, not when they were in need. Their crying brought no response, and they had no significant connection to their caregivers.

Neglect beyond infancy also has extreme negative consequences. Emotional neglect and inattention to the child as a person and to his or her efforts to gain connection and affirmation appear to have at least as severe consequences as harsh treatment (Erickson & Egeland, 1996). Harsh treatment also frustrates basic needs, increasingly so as it becomes more severe and abusive. When it is unpredictable, it creates insecurity. When it is inescapable, it creates a feeling of helplessness. It diminishes the child and breaks connection with important people. It creates a view of people and the world as hostile and dangerous, which interferes with the ability to develop connections to people.

Aggressive boys, as well as men, may come to use their aggression as a destructive mode of fulfilling needs for security, efficacy, positive identity, and even connection. They come to interpret others' behavior toward themselves as hostile (Dodge, 1980, 1993) and see aggression as normal, appropriate, and even inevitable (Huesmann & Eron, 1984). When boys are victimized, also have aggressive models, and people who coach them or encourage them in aggression—a situation that has been referred to as *violentization*—they may become intensely aggressive (Rhodes, 1999).

Guidance and Discipline

Warmth and affection fulfill basic needs and provide the basis for caring about others' welfare, but they do not develop caring in the child unless accompanied by parental guidance. Parental permissiveness, which is the absence of guidance, has been associated with aggression by adolescents independent of the extent the parents were warm versus hostile (DiLalla, Mitchell, Arthur, & Pagliococca, 1988). Warmth and affection are *not* associated with at least one form of prosocial behavior, generosity, when parents are permissive (Eisenberg, 1992; Eisenberg & Fabes, 1998; Staub, 1979).

Positive guidance itself fulfills basic needs. Guidance provides structure and order in children's lives and makes it easier to gain understanding of the world and develop self-guidance, control, and self-regulation. By teaching children how to act in order to be successful in their efforts, guidance contributes to the development of a sense of efficacy and positive identity. Parents of high-self-esteem children set high but achievable standards for them (Coopersmith, 1967). Guidance can help children set standards for themselves that make self-reinforcement possible.

Positive guidance uses and further develops the potentials/inclinations developed by the fulfillment of basic needs. In contrast, inherent in harsh treatment is negative guidance—the tendency to use force rather than verbal communication and the modeling of aggression. In such parenting, guidance is not separate from discipline and represents a harsh rather than a moderate form of discipline. The frequent use by parents of their power, in denying or withdrawing privileges, makes the development of caring and helping less likely and of aggression more likely (Coie & Dodge, 1998; Eisenberg & Fabes, 1998; Hoffman, 1970b; Staub, 1996a, 2003).

Positive guidance consists of adults setting rules for children, but doing so in a democratic manner. Parents can exercise firm control—so that children will act according to important rules—while still being responsive to their children's reasoning, that is, expressing what they think and want (Baumrind, 1971, 1975). Adults who practice positive guidance also explain reasons for rules. Induction—pointing out to children the consequences of their behavior for others—has been found useful in promoting empathy and prosocial behavior (Eisenberg & Fabes, 1998; Hoffman, 2000; Zahn-Waxler & Radke-Yarrow, 1990). Reasons and explanations, when combined with a positive orientation to other people provided by the fulfillment of basic needs, help children understand others' internal worlds, develop empathy, and the feeling of responsibility to help and not harm others (Staub, 1979). Providing examples of positive behavior toward other people is another important form of guidance, accomplishing similar goals. Through such guidance children learn both the values of caring, empathy, and sympathy and the actions that benefit other people.

When values, rules and explanations that structure and help children understand reality are lacking, then personal experiences, such as interactions that fulfill or frustrate basic needs, and the examples of models become even more powerful. However, explanations that conflict with or are contrary to powerful negative experiences with people—like abuse—will have little positive effect. Verbally guiding children to think about others' needs while they are the objects of abuse or other harmful behaviors is unlikely to be effective. Children who feel uncared for cannot be effectively instructed to care about others.

Adults who verbally promote caring values, while treat children harshly or abusively, will have limited success in developing caring (see, however, the discussion below of altruism born of suffering). Such behavior represents hypocrisy. Even milder forms of hypocrisy—for example, when an adult tells a child that he should donate a certain number of the rewards that he has won but then herself donates fewer—lead children to ignore the adult's guidance, to not do what the adult said. The children themselves learn hypocrisy. They act as the adult did but give younger children the instructions to be generous the adult gave them (Mischel & Liebert, 1966).

Guidance may frequently not be explicit, verbal, or even intentional. The reactions of adults to events can guide and teach children. Eisenberg's research shows that parents' facial expressions in response to emotionally arousing film sequences are related to children's capacity to regulate their feelings, and to their sympathy for others. Facial expressions and other bodily reactions to members of devalued groups, a parent's grip tightening on the child's hand when they pass by a seedy-looking homeless person, an adult's joy or distress, all provide information and create emotional reactions in the child. They tell the child the meaning and affective value of events.

Natural Socialization and Learning by Doing

Helping others increases children's later helping behavior (Staub, 1975, 1979, 2003; see Chapter 5). There is also evidence from research with adults that harming others increases later harmful and aggressive actions (Buss, 1966; Goldstein, Davis, & Herman, 1975). Children and adults, as well as whole groups of people (Staub, 1989a, 2003), learn by doing. Adults can engage in "natural socialization" (Staub, 1979), giving children meaningful responsibilities to help at home or at school (Grusec, Kuczynski, Rushton, & Simutis, 1978; Whiting & Whiting, 1975), or guiding them to engage in helpful actions in relation to peers, adults, or the community. In contrast, parents who allow aggressive behavior by children are likely to promote the development of aggressive/violent tendencies.

Children or adults who harm others and have no negative reactions to their actions from other people, or other constraints on their actions, are likely to justify what they do by both increasingly devaluing those whom they have harmed and finding good reasons for their actions. This makes new and greater harmdoing possible and probable. At the group level as well, lesser harmdoing against members of another group changes individuals, group norms, and even institutions and furthers the motivation for and allows the development of increasingly harmful actions. Intense violence like genocide evolves in this manner. The actions of witnesses, of "bystanders," in exerting positive influence to halt this evolution, individuals or groups, is crucial (Staub, 1989a, 2003).

The constraints on the development of aggressiveness can sometimes be internal, coming from already developed characteristics of a person. One of my students described in a paper his anger at a "friend" who stole a significant amount of money from him. He beat up this friend, giving him a bad nosebleed. But he was so horrified by his action that he became very nonaggressive. However, when values and emotional orientations like sympathy, which can function as internal controls, have not yet developed, the constraints need to be external.

Learning "by doing" is an important way for becoming a helpful person. If the experience of engaging in helpful action has positive cultural meaning (as is often the case, except in certain subcultures) and leads to others' improved welfare, it fulfills basic needs for positive identity, effectiveness, and positive connection both to the people helped and to the larger community. Seeing the benefits of their actions is especially effective in leading children both to value others' welfare and to see themselves as helpful persons (Eisenberg & Cialdini, 1984; Grusec et al., 1978; Staub, 1979, 2003).

In a series of studies with fifth- and sixth-grade children, my students and I have found (reviewed in Staub, 1979, 2003; and Chapter 5) that engaging children in helping others tends to increase their later helping. Children who were led to make toys, either for hospitalized children (especially, in the case of girls, when the benefits of their actions were pointed out to them) or in order to help an art teacher prepare materials, tended later to be more helpful, as were children who had opportunities to teach younger children to make puzzles or to use first-aid techniques.

The benefits of these helping experiences vary depending on particular procedures, on the gender of the children, and on the way they are assessed. For example, fifth- and sixth-grade boys apparently do not write letters—they did not write letters to hospitalized children as a way of helping them. But they showed the effects of learning by doing on an envelopes test, in which they were asked to gather pictures, poems, and other interesting materials for hospitalized children. When boys made puzzles to help poor hospitalized children, they did not show the effects of puzzle making on an immediate posttest. I interpreted this as the result of "psychological reactance" (Brehm, 1966), a negative reaction by boys to the perception that their freedom was limited by the influence exerted on them to do something "good," to be helpful. However, they did show positive effects on a delayed posttest, 2 to 3 weeks later, when presumably the reactance had diminished. The effects of teaching younger children were greater when the interaction between the older child and the younger child he or she taught was more positive.

When aggressive actions are not halted by negative consequences, they lead to more aggression because they fulfill basic needs and, as an aspect of that, affirm the actor's strength and power. However, aggression fulfills basic needs destructively. It may create a feeling of effectiveness and control and affirm identity. But it creates disconnection from the people harmed and, except in violent subcultures, also from the community. It tends to create rejection by others.

Many aggressive youths are unpopular among their peers. However, they are unaware of their unpopularity. This is probably in part because they usually have a few friends similar to themselves, in part because others are afraid to show their dislike and in part because, owing to their personality, they do not process the cues available to them. But as a result they become increasingly aggressive over time (Zakriski, Jacobs, & Coie 1997).

Peer Socialization of Caring and Altruism Versus Aggression

Positive relations between peers have tremendous value in fulfilling basic needs, developing caring values, and helping develop prosocial skills and modes of relating to people. As Piaget has suggested, children learn reciprocity in peer relations. As both Piaget and Kohlberg have emphasized, they learn to take each others' roles. As in their interaction with adults, if they are well treated and also treat others well, they learn to see other people as benevolent and themselves as worthy individuals and effective in positive ways (Staub, 1979). All these are important preconditions for and rudiments of caring about other people and their well-being.

Cross-cultural research has shown that, in all cultures, girls are less aggressive than boys and that girls do substantially more caretaking of younger children than do boys. There is also evidence that boys who do more such caretaking are more prosocial (Whiting & Edwards, 1988), perhaps an example of learning by doing. Caring for younger children requires attention to their needs and is a form of helping—both of the younger child and of the parents.

In contrast, being the recipients of negative behavior from peers is likely to have the opposite effect, leading children to feel insecure and less worthy and to see other people and the world as hostile and dangerous. This may lead to aggression and is likely, at least without healing (see below), to reduce caring for and helping others. Children who are bullied are often deeply affected, in their self-confidence, trust in other people, willingness to initiate relationships, and well-being (Olweus, 1993; Ross & Ross, 1988; Staub, 2003).

Harassment, intimidation, and bullying in schools have negative effects, not just on the victims but on everyone. Peers as well as adults in schools are often passive bystanders in the face of such actions, with passivity by peers *increasing* with age (Staub, 2003). Across grade levels, active response by peers to protect a target of bullying is less common than peers joining in the bullying (Staub, 2003). As a result, not only victims but passive bystanders as well learn that others are dangerous and that one must be careful in one's relationships with people. To reduce empathic distress, created by witnessing the distress of a victimized peer while remaining passive, children and adolescent are likely to distance themselves psychologically from victims—that is, from people in need (Staub, 1989a). Victims suffer, aggressors are likely to become more aggressive, and passive bystanders are likely to become less empathic. The system in which bullying is frequent contributes to the development of a negative view by children probably not only of other people but also of themselves. All this makes the development of caring and helping less likely.

These conditions indicate that, for the development of caring and helping rather than aggression, it is important to guide children to behave in positive ways toward each other. Adults helping develop positive modes of interaction between siblings in the home and peers in the neighborhood or in school is an essential aspect of positive socialization. Children are much more likely, however, to live by rules that promote positive peer interaction if they have had the positive socialization experiences with adults described earlier.

Children are also much more likely to act positively toward peers if they feel included in the peer group or classroom as a community. Children are harmed not only by bullying but also by exclusion—other children not interacting with them. Excluded children have even fewer positive feelings about their lives at school than do children who are victimized by peers (Staub, 2003). It is essential, therefore, to find ways to include all children in the community, even those who are academically less skilled or for other reasons tend to be excluded and made marginal either in the classroom community or in other peer-group settings. (On caring schools, and on ways to create positive peer relations in schools, see Staub, 2003.)

Basic Needs and the Evolution of the Self

A number of socialization practices that fulfill basic human needs, and then build on the tendencies thus created to foster affective orientation and values, join together to develop helpful, altruistic tendencies in children. Warmth, affection, and adults sensitively responding to their needs, to their temperament and personality, are crucial. Nurturance must be sensitive to be experienced as such. A parent offering what the child does not need may not be perceived as loving. Positive guidance is also crucial, particularly forms of guidance that promote caring values, sympathy, and the effectiveness/competence that leads to their expression in action. Such guidance includes setting rules, with a dominance of prescriptive (doing what is right or beneficial) rather than proscriptive (prohibiting what is undesirable) rules, and the explanation of rules in terms of values, as well as induction, modeling, and natural socialization which leads to learning by doing. Such modes of relating to the child and guidance will promote the child's ability to regulate feelings and guide herself or himself.

Evolution in the psychological sense is a core process in the development of caring, helping, altruism and personal characteristics that promote these. The psychological changes in the course of a positive evolution involve increasing concern about those who need help, the extension of that concern to people beyond one's group, and a view of oneself as helpful. In the evolution of aggression, it is increasing devaluation of those harmed and the extension of that devaluation to more people, and a view of oneself as willing to use aggression.

The experiences in the course of such socialization shape and form basic needs. They become cognitive/emotional constructions, which limit or expand ways that needs can be fulfilled. Since aggressive men (Toch, 1969) come to see toughness and strength as masculine ideals, they have to be tough and strong to fulfill their need for a positive identity. The tendency to feel empathy and concern for people (except perhaps some intimates) will not fulfill their need for a positive identity. An increase in empathy will not be a desirable "expansion of the self." When a child devalues another child, when a group of peers or an ethnic or religious group devalues another group, it becomes unlikely that individuals can and will fulfill their need for connection by friendship with the devalued person or with members of the devalued group. Perpetrators learn to deal with consequences of their actions by closing themselves off to the feelings of their victims, by learning to become less empathic (Staub, 1989a; Staub & Pearlman, 2001; Staub, Pearlman, & Miller, 2003). Over time, their capacity to form connections to people in general may diminish.

In the course of the evolution of helping and aggression, the cognitive/emotional construction of basic needs is likely to evolve in ways that contribute to further evolution in the same direction. Individuals—both children and adults—progressively engage in *self-socialization*. This can take the form of actions that bring forth particular reactions, or of the selection of associates, peers, and environments, both of which further shape the direction in which they have been developing.

The Development of Inclusive Caring

Even among people who have learned to care about others' welfare, caring can be limited to people in their own group. There is a human tendency to differentiate between "us" and "them" and to devalue "them," a tendency rooted in, among other things, the cognitive process of categorization (Fiske & Taylor, 1991) and differences in reactions to the familiar and the unfamiliar (Staub, 1989a). Some groups, especially when they are the victims of discrimination and violence, can be devalued to such an extent that they are excluded from the moral realm (Opotow, 1990; Staub, 1989a). People do not see them as deserving moral consideration and do not feel empathy and caring for them. To create a nonviolent, caring world, to create goodness, extending the boundaries of "us" is essential. Inclusive caring, the extension of caring to the "other," ideally to all human beings, develops through words and images that humanize all people, through the example of models who show caring for people regardless of their group membership, and through one's own experience of connection to varied people (Staub 2002a, 2002b).

Many "rescuers"—Christians in Nazi Europe who during the Holocaust endangered themselves and often their families as well by attempting to save the lives of Jews—had been raised in families that promoted both caring, and inclusive caring. They were socialized in a way that was highly consistent with the socialization process described earlier as important in developing altruism. They received more love and affection and positive guidance than did others who were in similar situations but did not help. They had parents who, in cultures where physical punishment was common, used explanation instead. They were exposed to helpful models, often parents who embodied moral values in their actions. They had parents who engaged more in interaction with, and maintained positive social relations with, people outside their own group, including Jews. They heard their parents make fewer negative statements, if any, about Jews—a group devalued in Germany and in other European countries occupied by or under the influence of Nazi Germany—than did comparison persons who were in a position to help but did not do so (Oliner & Oliner, 1988).

Experiences of significant connection to people who are outside one's group and who are generally devalued are important in developing inclusive caring. Social psychologists have long hypothesized that contact between members of different groups helps overcome devaluation, prejudice, and hostility (see, among many others, Allport, 1954; Deutsch, 1973; Pettigrew, 1997, 1998; and Staub, 1989a). A meta-analysis of a very large number of studies confirms that this is so (Pettigrew & Tropp, 2006). Even though the experience of interaction and engagement was limited in many of the studies, it reduced negative attitudes toward members of the other group.

The deeper the contact, and the more it involves shared goals that people work for, the greater the likely benefit. One method of creating such contact in schools has been through cooperative-learning methods. Specifically, in one procedure, six children who are members of different groups—white and minority children—work together. To accomplish their task each must learn some material and teach it to the others (Aronson, Stephan, Sikes, Blaney, & Snapp, 1978). In the course of being both teachers and learners, children are drawn into significant engagement with each other. Such cooperative-learning procedures have led to more positive interaction between white and minority children and improved the academic performance of minority children (see Staub, 2002a, 2002b, 2003).

Learning by doing can also be an avenue to inclusive caring. In the case of aggression by groups toward other groups, the range of victims usually expands. In the case of helping others, the commitment to those who are helped usually deepens, and the range of those who are helped may expand. Rescuers who had initially agreed to help a particular person in a limited way became more engaged and helped more. They may have initially agreed to hide some people for a few days but ended up hiding them for years. Or, if they had succeeded in moving some people to a safer place, they then initiated helping others (Oliner & Oliner, 1988; Staub, 1989a). Rescuers who agreed to help a Jew who was a former friend or associate often decided to help others who were strangers.

Concern can also expand from one group to other groups and to all humanity. At the time of the disappearances in Argentina, the Mothers of the Plaza del Mayo demonstrated, marching every day in the centrally located Plaza del Mayo in Buenos Aires. In spite of intimidation, harassment, and even abduction, they continued to protest the disappearance of their children. But over time their concern expanded, to include other disappeared people as well as people who were persecuted and victimized outside Argentina (Ehlstein, 1986).

Culture and education can promote inclusive caring for all human beings, regardless of group membership. This can be done by humanizing—describing in not devaluative but respectful, caring ways—every group (Staub et al., 2005; Staub et al., 2003). It can also be done by eliminating discrimination, which expresses and promotes devaluation. It can be done by creating social systems in which people belonging to different groups have equal rights, whether in the classroom or in other settings in society, thereby fostering positive relations characterized by mutual respect (Staub, 2003).

The Development of Moral Courage

Moral courage is of great importance for a nonviolent, caring world. The term *moral courage* refers to the *courage to express important values in words and actions, even in the face of opposition, potential disapproval, and ostracism or a violent response*. Moral courage may require physical courage, but often it requires only what may be called *psychological courage* (see Chapter 23).

Is courage in behalf of any kind of belief or value a moral courage? In the perspective that I am proposing, the courage required to act in the face of opposition is moral only if the beliefs or values (including affective reactions like empathy) that motivate it involve protecting or promoting human welfare. For example, young men who joined and persisted in supporting the Nazi movement or joined the SA, the stormtroopers of the Nazi movement, during the 1920s, well before Hitler came to power, often faced opposition from and disapproval by members of the community (Merkl, 1980). Members of violent gangs and violent ideological movements, including terrorists, also face opposition (although receive support from others in their group). Their actions do not constitute moral courage.

Identifying courage as moral only if the values and beliefs involved are moral makes it a more difficult matter to judge when people express moral courage. When harmful actions are ideologically motivated, the perpetrators often claim, and probably often believe, that their beliefs and values are moral and that their actions are for the good of their group or of all human beings. Often they believe that they are acting for a higher morality (Staub, 1989a, 2003). To determine whether their actions, the actions of actors in general, are moral requires an "external" judgment. This judgment may be based on the combination of information available about the actors' beliefs and intentions, the form of the actions themselves (do they appear to be actions that would create benefit, harm, or neither?), the potential or actual consequences of the actions, and the preceding conditions that gave rise to them.

It is more difficult to be morally courageous when acting alone than when acting in a group, for example, a child acting to stop the bullying of another child. Members of movements—whether acting in a moral or in an immoral cause—get support and encouragement from other members, who have become their primary reference group. Speaking out within a group or movement against harmful action by the group requires special moral courage.

The importance of support from like-minded others can be found in many instances. For example, even when abolitionists in the United States were acting alone, facing hostile groups while advocating the abolition of slavery, they were supported by their feelings of connection to other abolitionists (Tompkins, 1965). People may also find support from internalized, imagined others—and the ideals that those others set for them.

The Socialization of Moral Courage

What might be the roots of moral courage in children's experience? Some of the socialization experiences described earlier as involved in the development of moral and caring emotions and values also play an important role in the development of moral courage. For example, the parents of many young civil rights activists in the United States who went to the South in the 1960s to advance desegregation by participating in marches and sit-ins modeled moral concern, engagement, and courage. They demonstrated against injustice and for justice. Some of the fathers fought in the Spanish Civil War. The combined influence of varied experiences is shown in that young activists who had both such moral parental models and unconflicted positive relations with their parents were more committed to, more persistent in their civil rights activities than were those who had moral parents toward whom they felt ambivalence (Rosenhan, 1970).

Providing children with opportunities and encouraging them to express their thoughts, beliefs, and values can be important. Baumrind (1971, 1975) has reported that *authoritative* parents tended to listen to their children's arguments about what they wanted to do, even if what the children wanted was contrary to some rule or to what they had originally been asked to do, and that they sometimes yielded. (However, they would not yield to whining or demanding.) This is likely to encourage children to express themselves.

Teachers in schools may have students participate in making rules for the classroom. This can provide a context in which students learn to engage in discussion, to speak out, and to become comfortable with expressing views that are not necessarily accepted by others (see Staub, 2003, chaps. 15, 20). Parents can do the same in the home. This way children can learn to trust their voice and its potential influence.

This is especially difficult to bring about, but especially important, in societies where children are taught not to question or challenge authority and where they do not normally develop their own perspective and voice. When parents, teachers, and other adults encourage students to be "active bystanders" as they witness harmful actions toward individuals, when they affirm their speaking out against cruelty or injustice or simply their expressing beliefs or points of view that are contrary to those of others (not necessarily agreeing with the content but simply affirming the expression of their views), they are helping to develop moral courage (see also Chapter 23).

The Relationship Between the Self and the Group

Teaching children to think not in terms of abstractions and absolutes but in terms of concrete human welfare is also important. An example of this might be the distinction between *blind* and *constructive* patriotism. Blind patriots support their country and its actions unconditionally. Constructive patriots express about the same degree of love for their country as blind patriots. However, they believe that their love of their country requires them to speak out against policies and practices that are contrary to important human values as well as against policies and practices that they see as contrary to the essential values of their country (Staub, 1997). Constructive patriots score higher on prosocial value orientation, are more willing to criticize their country, and report that they spend more time gathering political information and are more politically active (Schatz et al., 1999).

The types of selves that children develop may be important for moral courage. Psychologists have long been interested in the differences between collectivist and individualist cultures (Triandis, 1994). A number of psychologists, inspired by differences found between those two types of cultures in the construction of identity, have proposed that there are differences within Western, individualist cultures in the identities that women and men develop. While terminologies have differed, some have proposed that women have more relational selves, men more autonomous selves (Sampson, 1988; Surrey, 1985).

I have suggested a further differentiation among relational selves. While the connections to others and the orientation to community that collectivist cultures generate have great benefits, they can also pose problems. Individuals would have difficulty separating themselves from their group and, when important from the moral/caring standpoint discussed here, opposing their group. Individuals with what I have called *embedded selves,* which embody both feelings of connection and strong dependence, will have difficulty separating themselves from and opposing others, whether individuals or the group as a whole. In contrast, individuals with *connected selves,* which embody feelings of connection to other individuals and/or the group but also sufficient independence to stand alone if necessary, will be more likely to take morally courageous actions (Staub, 1993). What seems important for the development of the latter kind of self, in addition to what I have already discussed in the context of the development of "goodness" and moral courage, is granting children appropriate autonomy. That is, while guidance and what Baumrind (1971, 1975) has called *firm control* have great value, it is also important to allow children, in the context of adherence to essential rules, values, and principles, the maximum autonomy that is appropriate for their age.

Not being embedded in a group makes an independent perspective possible. A fair percentage of rescuers of Jews during the Holocaust were in some way marginal to their communities (Tec, 1986). Marginality was often a function of their social situation, for example, having a foreign-born parent or having a different religion—a Catholic in a Protestant community. But it could also be a function of their personality, the nature of their identity, a history of being "different." Their marginality may have enabled them to separate themselves from their communities, which often supported the persecution of Jews, and thereby maintain an independent perspective. Constructive patriots in contrast to blind patriots also seem to have a separate-enough perspective to question the problematic policies and practices of their group.

A "critical consciousness" seems crucial (Staub, 1989a). In order to act on one's values, it is necessary to realize the relevance of those values to particular events or policies and practices in a group. This often entails using one's own judgment about the meaning of events, rather than accepting the meaning that others explicitly or implicitly communicate about them. For example, there was much public discussion in the United States preceding the beginning of the war against Iraq in 2003 about the connection between Iraq and the September 11 attacks. The Bush administration asserted that such a connection existed. However, CIA reports and all other sources, including discussion in the media, have indicated the absence of evidence for it. Still, polls showed that over 50% of the American public believed that Iraq was involved in the attacks, a seeming lack of a critical consciousness. (The woundedness and insecurity that resulted from the attacks may have created both a strong need to know where the violence originated and an increased reliance on the words of leaders.) Some of the practices already discussed as important for the development of moral courage are also likely to help in the development of critical consciousness.

We must learn more about the origins of moral courage and create conditions that help such courage develop. Morally courageous people who are active bystanders can make a crucial difference, in many settings, at important moments, as individuals or as members of groups opposing harmful or violent social policies and practices or promoting helpful ones. Morally courageous actions can be important at particular times, in response to specific events. But, beyond that, morally committed and courageous people can join to overcome the inertia of social systems, activate other bystanders, and work on creating societies and an international community that promote harmony and caring in human relations (Chapter 28).

Trauma and Healing, Resilience, Need Fulfillment, and Altruism Born of Suffering

Research on the development of caring, helping, and altruism in children has focused on positive roots in socialization and experience, as described so far in this chapter. However, observation and many self-reports and case studies indicate that people who have suffered from victimization and other trauma often come to devote themselves to helping others. My attention first focused on this when I prepared a questionnaire assessing prosocial value orientation and helping for *Psychology Today* (Staub, 1989b; see also Staub 2003) that over 7,000 readers filled out and returned. Many of them, in response to my request, also wrote letters with additional information about themselves. Some of those who wrote reported that their own suffering, early in their lives, led them to help others, especially to try to prevent such suffering by other people.

Research and clinical observation has focused on the traumatic effects of victimization and suffering (Herman, 1992; McCann & Pearlman, 1990). It has also been shown that bad treatment, neglect, and abuse, both physical and verbal, contribute to aggression in children. Some of this research was described earlier. Other research has shown that people who were abused as children are more likely to abuse their own children (Kaufman & Zigler, 1987) and that, among violent criminals, the great majority had experiences of victimization at home or in their community (Gilligan, 1996; Rhodes, 1999; Widom, 1989a, 1989b). According to newspaper reports, at least, many of the school shooters were victimized by peers.

People who have been the object of violence at the hands of others, whether those others acted as individuals or as members of a group, are likely to feel diminished. They will tend to feel that something must be wrong with them, that they must somehow have deserved to be treated that way. They will tend to see the world as dangerous and feel vulnerable. They will be more likely to see, therefore, threat, danger, and potential attack and feel the need to defend themselves, even when there is no real threat (Staub, 1998, 2003; Staub & Pearlman, 2001).

However, not everyone who is victimized becomes aggressive. Many children and adults from difficult backgrounds show resilience—effective functioning in spite of their background (Butler, 1997; Masten, 2001; Rutter, 1987; Werner, 1987; Werner & Smith, 1992). And some people who have greatly suffered as children become caring and helpful people who devote themselves to the welfare of others. O'Connell Higgins (1994) described adults severely abused as children, some mercilessly beaten by parents, who have become deeply caring people, devoting their lives to helping people in need or to protecting people from suffering the way they themselves have suffered. Valent (1998) noted that many child survivors of the Holocaust are in service professions or work for positive social change.

Some people who have experienced great suffering and the frustration of basic needs that this entails—the need for security, for effectiveness and control, for a positive identity, for a positive connection, and for comprehension of reality—may lack corrective, transformative experiences. Their environment may not provide them. Or they may have developed such an intensely defensive stance against a hostile world, or an intensely hostile stance, that they cannot use opportunities to ameliorate their hostile orientations. They may not be able to perceive or use opportunities for significant, caring human connections or other healing experiences. However, other people who have been victimized may both have opportunity for and make use of corrective experiences.

I assume that, if they are to become caring, altruistic people, victimized children require that their basic needs be fulfilled, to some degree at least, either before or after their victimization, or both, and that the psychological wounds created by their victimization heal to some degree. Prior need fulfillment may protect them to some extent from the effects of victimization. For example, one of the protective elements for children who come from difficult environments and are resilient seems to be early secure attachment to a caretaker (Werner & Smith, 1992). Subsequent need fulfillment may enable them to see hopeful possibilities in life, the possibility of security, of dignity, and of positive, loving connections between people.

Healing from past trauma involves gaining renewed trust in people. Connection to caring people, adults as well as children, is especially important in this. Resilience in children is usually facilitated by interest and support from and positive connection to one or more persons—teachers, counselors, relatives, neighbors (Butler, 1997; Werner & Smith, 1992). Temperament also contributes to resilience (Rutter, 1987). It may be the case, in part at least, that children who are more outgoing make active efforts to connect with potentially supporting others.

Healing, in part through positive connections to people and the fulfillment of basic needs, enables people who have suffered to become open to the pain of others. This openness to others, combined with a more caring world that they may now be able to envision may, given their own experiences, lead them to strong feelings of empathy and sympathy and even to a feeling of responsibility to help those in need. Identification with those who suffer may lead to increasing engagement and the development of the intense motivation to help others that some of these altruists describe.

Connection to other children can also help wounded children heal. Freud and Dann (1951) described a group of young children who survived Auschwitz together. Taken to England afterward, they were extremely resistant to adults but fiercely loyal to and supportive of each other. According to Freud and Dann, their deep connections to each other enabled them to begin, over time, to develop connections to adults. Suomi and Harlow (1972) found that monkeys isolated in the first 6 months of their lives were highly inappropriate in their social and sexual interactions with their peers. The only treatment that was reasonably effective was pairing them with normal infant monkeys, who would cling to them. The former isolates would carry these infant monkeys around. Presumably, this helped them change both in the kind of emotions that they experienced and in emotional self-regulation. As the growing infants began to develop social skills, the isolates would learn along with them. Research with children has shown that socially ineffective children's social interactions improved after they spent time supervising/interacting with younger children (Furman, Rahe, & Hartup, 1979).

In the case of survivors of genocide, many of them had their basic needs fulfilled through close, loving connections to their families and their group before the genocide and to other survivors afterward. In addition, many survivors were helped by other people. Many also engaged in courageous action to help themselves. This was true of survivors of the Holocaust: even young children often engaged in amazing acts of initiative to help themselves or their families (see Chapter 11). Such experiences fulfill, in the midst of horrible circumstances, needs for connection, effectiveness, and identity and a comprehension of reality that provides hope and makes caring for others possible.

Some of these considerations about the roots of altruism born of suffering are supported by case histories provided by my students. For about the last 15 years of my teaching courses I asked students to write papers in which they apply psychological research and theory to their own experiences, to an exploration of the connection between their life experiences and the people they have become.

One of my students, a bright, attractive young woman, had a terrible year in the eighth grade. There was a boys' clique that dictated the rules by which the girls were to behave. In addition to sexual teasing, they would touch the girls—their breasts, their buttocks. They engaged in many degrading actions, which most of the girls endured, and which some even acted as if they welcomed. Because she did not go along with this, my student was viciously teased and ostracized, not only by the boys but by the girls as well. The teachers witnessed all this but did nothing, even making comments to her like, "Boys will be boys." She suffered all this without yielding but suffered greatly.

In her home life, however, she had received a great deal of love and affection before this and much love and support while this was happening. She also saw her parents as moral, spiritual people, instilling in her both an understanding of others (she came to interpret the behavior of the boy who was the main gang leader as a child of busy socialites who paid little attention to him) and a sense of independence. She believes that it was the combination of her suffering that year and her background and the support that she received that led her to engage in her many and varied activities to help others: volunteering with mentally and physically disabled children; spending time helping rebuild a town in a poor area of the country after a disaster; serving as a peer mention, as a tutor, and as a counselor for emotionally disturbed girls; volunteering at many charities and organizations; being the kind of person to whom others turn for consolation; and more. An interesting aspect of this situation, perhaps having to do with moral courage, perhaps with concern for their daughter, is that, while the parents were highly supportive of her, they were passive in relation to the school, not taking action to stop the bullying.

Another student described a great deal of criticism by her parents, which made her feel diminished and helpless. Perhaps because of this she dropped out of and reentered college several times. One of these times a teacher in a community college showed special interest and caring, not just for my student but for all her students. My student was able to experience and was deeply affected by her caring and benevolence and by her trust in her ability. Later she worked as an intern in a school with mentally less developed children. Being distressed by the way the teachers treated the children, she was both strongly motivated and able to engage in what she felt were supportive and helpful interactions with the children. She felt that both these experiences, the benevolence of her teacher and her own helpful actions, gave her hope and strength and led her to go on to a four-year college and do well there.

Positive connections to and support by other people are important to the healing of victimized children and adults and to the fulfillment of previously deeply frustrated basic needs. They affirm the self, fulfill the need for connection, and offer a more hopeful view of the world. However, other processes of healing are also important. One of these is engagement with painful experiences, in combination with empathy and support from other people. This helps a person realize that the past is not the present and see the present as safe and more hopeful.

With children this may be facilitated by reading and discussing literature that is relevant to their difficult and painful experiences (Staub, 2003). Such indirect engagement may be safer but still helpful. Writing about personal experiences may also be helpful, as it has been found to be in research with college students (Pennebacker & Beall, 1986). If done under the right supportive conditions, talking about personal experiences can be highly beneficial for children. Parents who have divorced have reported to me, for example, that their children gained self-confidence and reassurance from participating in school in group discussions with other children whose parents have divorced.

Another avenue to healing from victimization is understanding how the perpetrators came to do what they did. In Rwanda, discussing with people how genocide comes about (Staub & Pearlman, 2001; Staub et al., 2003; Staub et al., 2005; on the origins of genocide, see also Staub, 1989a), with examples of other instances of genocide, seemed to have highly beneficial effects. Coming to see genocide as an understandable even if a tragic and horrible human process, rather than incomprehensible evil, seemed to help both survivors and bystanders feel more "human," rather than outcasts from the human fold. (While members of both groups, Tutsis and Hutus, participated, perpetrators were not included.) In addition, during the course of the discussion people realized that, if they understood how it happened, they could take action to prevent it from happening again. A formal evaluation of an intervention in which the exploration of the roots of genocide was one of several components showed reduction in trauma symptoms and a more positive orientation by members of the groups involved toward each other (Staub, 2003; Staub et al.,2005; for extensive discussion see Chapters 18 and 19).

In her case histories of resilient adults, O'Connell Higgins (1994) also reports that understanding can be useful. In one of the chapters we learn about Dan, who was an object of his father's rage and frequently and severely beaten by him. He was also given enemas by his mother to make him a better child. Later he found that understanding the source of his parents' behavior—for example, seeing in his mind's eye his father, who was severely neglected by his parents, stand in his crib screaming and shaking it, with nobody responding, this giving rise to his rage—helped him to some degree accept who his father was. Dan himself has become a successful person whose work involves helping others, in efficient and effective ways.

There is substantial evidence that altruism born of suffering is a real and important phenomenon. While I have suggested here some of the experiences that are likely to contribute to its evolution, both the extent to which people who have suffered victimization and other traumas become altruists and the conditions required for this to happen ought to be a focus of concentrated study (see Chapter 10 for detailed discussion of altruism born of suffering).

Conclusions: Optimal Human Functioning and the Good Society

In conclusion, I want to stress two important matters. First, the fulfillment of basic human needs is not just an individual matter, that is, a matter of the circumstances of a particular person, but to a great extent a cultural/societal matter. Second, the fulfillment of these needs contributes not only to goodness but also to individuals' continued development or growth, to their fulfillment of their human and personal potentials—to what may be called *optimal human functioning* (Staub, 2003).

Starting with the second issue, I have suggested that an important avenue to goodness is through the constructive fulfillment of basic needs, in combination with guidance that develops sympathetic emotions and caring values. However, as basic needs are fulfilled, they also provide the base for continued personal growth (see Chapter 4). They undergo transformation, become less pressing, and evolve into personal goals (Staub, 1980), the desire to bring about particular valued outcomes. The outcomes that people value will differ, depending on their life experiences. Realms of effectiveness, sources of positive identity, the nature of connections people seek to others or to a larger community will all vary.

While people whose needs have been fulfilled will differ, they are likely to have in common an openness to experience (since they perceive other people and the world as reasonably benevolent), a capacity for processing their experience and self-awareness (since, given their positive identity and feelings of effectiveness and control, they do not need to protect themselves because of who they are or what they think and feel), as well as other important characteristics that contribute to continued personal growth (Maslow, 1987). Given a sense of effectiveness in the work realm, they will be open to new knowledge and creative endeavors. They are, thus, likely to continue to develop both in the personal and in the work realms. According to the conception of personal goals with which I have been working (Staub, 1989a, 1996b, 1999b, 2003), when other needs are fulfilled, the need for transcendence, to go beyond the self, emerges or becomes more dominant. Thus, people whose basic psychological needs have been constructively fulfilled are able to focus less on themselves and more on other people, the world, and spiritual matters.

What might be the relation between altruism born of suffering and optimal human functioning? It is possible that, even though people who have suffered and whose basic needs have been frustrated can become true altruists under certain conditions, their continued personal growth and evolution will be hindered and made more difficult by the painful experiences that they have had. It is also possible, however, that their caring and altruistic orientation becomes for them an avenue to continued personal growth (Colby & Damon, 1992; O'Connell Higgins, 1994).

With regard to the first issue, the actions of members of families, adults in schools, and peers fulfill or frustrate basic needs. However, families, schools, and peers are located in a society. How they act is affected by the characteristics of that society: beliefs about how children are to be treated; the devaluation of and discrimination against members of particular groups; and so on. Poverty, which varies by society and subgroups in it, creates stress and negatively affects parenting (McLoyd, 1990), frustrating children's needs. Teenage single mothers, especially if they are poor, are likely to have their own needs frustrated by their circumstances and to have difficulty fulfilling the needs of their children. Unless they receive support from others, they are much more likely to abuse their children than are other mothers (Garcia-Coll, Hoffman, & Oh, 1987). When a society helps its members fulfill basic needs constructively, there is likely to be more belief in enlightened self-interest and more generalized reciprocity in people helping each other. It would make great sense to evaluate the goodness of societies in terms of the ease or difficulty of fulfilling basic human needs and to identify desirable social changes in terms of their probable contribution to the fulfillment of basic material and psychological needs.

References

Ainsworth, M. D. S., Bell, S. M., & Stayton, D. J. (1974). Infant–mother attachment and social development: Socialization as a product of reciprocal responsiveness to signals. In M. P. M. Richards (Ed.), *The integration of the child into a social world*. London: Cambridge University Press.

Allport, G. W. (1954). *The nature of prejudice*. Reading, MA: Addison-Wesley.

Aronson, E., Stephan, C., Sikes, J., Blaney, N., & Snapp, M. (1978). *The jigsaw classroom*. Beverly Hills, CA: SAGE.

Batson, C. D. (1990). How social an animal? The human capacity for caring. *American Psychologist, 45*, 336–347.

Baumrind, D. (1971). Current patterns of parental authority. *Developmental Psychology, 4*, 1–101.

Baumrind, D. (1975). *Early socialization and the discipline controversy*. Morristown, NJ: General Learning.

Berkowitz, L. (1972). Social norms, feelings, and other factors affecting helping behavior and altruism. In L. Berkowitz (Ed.), *Advances in experimental social psychology* (Vol. 6, pp. 63–108). New York: Academic.

Berkowitz, L. (1993). *Aggression: Its causes, consequences, and control*. New York: McGraw-Hill.

Brehm, J. W. (1966). *A theory of psychological reactance.* New York: Academic.

Bretherton, I. (1992). The origins of attachment theory: John Bowlby and Mary Ainsworth. *Developmental Psychology, 28,* 759–775.

Burton, J. W. (1990). *Conflict: Human needs theory.* New York: St. Martin's.

Buss, A. H. (1966). The effect of harm on subsequent aggression. *Journal of Experimental Research in Personality, 1,* 249–255.

Butler, K. (1997, March/April). The anatomy of resilience. *Family Therapy Networker, 22–31.*

Carlo, G., Eisenberg, N., Troyer, D., Switzer, G., & Speer, A. K. (1991). The altruistic personality: In what contexts is it apparent? *Journal of Personality and Social Psychology, 61,* 450–458.

Carlson, M., & Miller, N. (1987). Explanation of the relation between negative mood and helping. *Psychological Bulletin, 102,* 91–108.

Coie, J. D., & Dodge, K. A. (1997). Aggression and antisocial behavior. In W. Damon (Series Ed.), N. Eisenberg (Vol. Ed.), *Handbook of child psychology: Vol. 3. Social, emotional, and personality development* (5th ed., pp. 779–862). New York: Wiley.

Colby, A., & Damon, W. (1992). *Some do care.* New York: Free Press.

Coopersmith, S. (1967). *Antecedents of self-esteem.* San Francisco: Fremont.

Crick, N. R. (1997). Engagement in gender normative versus non-normative forms of aggression: Links to social-psychological adjustment. *Developmental Psychology, 33,* 610–617.

Deutsch, M. (1973). *The resolution of conflict: Constructive and destructive processes.* New Haven: Yale University Press.

DiLalla, L. F., Mitchell, C. M., Arthur, M. W., & Pagliococca, P. M. (1988). Aggression and delinquency: Family and environmental factors. *Journal of Youth and Adolescence, 73,* 233–246.

Dodge, K. A. (1980). Social cognition and children's aggressive behavior. *Child Development, 51,* 162–170.

Dodge, K. A. (1993). Social cognitive mechanisms in the development of conduct disorder and depression. *Annual Review of Psychology, 44,* 559–584.

Ehlstein, J. (1986, December). *Reflections on political torture and murder: Visits with the mothers of the Plaza del Mayo.* Invited talk, Department of Psychology, University of Massachusetts, Amherst.

Eisenberg, N. (1992). *The caring child.* Cambridge, MA: Harvard University Press.

Eisenberg, N. (2002). Empathy-related emotional responses, altruism, and their socialization. In R. J. Davidson & A. Harrington (Eds.), *Visions of compassion.* New York: Oxford University Press.

Eisenberg, N., & Cialdini, R. B. (1984). The role of consistency pressures in behavior: A developmental perspective. *Academic Psychology Bulletin, 6,* 115–126.

Eisenberg, N., & Fabes, R. A. (1998). Prosocial development. In W. Damon (Series Ed.), N. Eisenberg (Vol. Ed.), *Handbook of child psychology: Vol. 3. Social, emotional, and personality development* (5th ed., pp. 701–778). New York: Wiley.

Eisenberg, N., Fabes, R. A., Miller, P. A., Fultz, J., Mathy, R. M., Shell, R., & Reno, R. R. (1989). The relations of sympathy and personal distress to prosocial behavior: A multimethod study. *Journal of Personality and Social Psychology, 57,* 55–66.

Eisenberg, N., Fabes, R. A., & Spinrad, T. L. (2006). Prosocial development. In W. Damon (Ed.), *Handbook of child psychology: Vol. 3. Social, emotional, and personality development* (5th ed., pp. 646–718). New York: Wiley.

Erickson, M., & Egeland, B. (1996). The quiet assault: A portrait of child neglect. In J. Briere, L. Berliner, S. Bulkley, C. Jenny, & T. Reid (Eds.), *The handbook of child maltreatment* (pp. 4–20). Newbury Park, CA: SAGE.

Erikson, E. H. (1959). *Identity and the life cycle: Selected papers* (Psychological Issues, Vol. 1, No. 1, Monograph 1). New York: International Universities Press.

Erkut, S., Jaquette, D., & Staub, E. (1981). Moral judgment–situation interaction as a basis for predicting social behavior. *Journal of Personality, 49,* 1–44.

Eron, L. D., Walder, L. O., & Lefkowitz, M. M. (1971). *Learning of aggression in children.* Boston: Little, Brown.

Feinberg, J. K. (1978). *Anatomy of a helping situation: Some personality and situational determinants of helping in a conflict situation involving another's psychological distress.* Unpublished doctoral dissertation, University of Massachusetts.

Feshbach, N. D., & Feshbach, S. (1969). The relationship between empathy and aggression in two age groups. *Development Psychology, 1,* 102–107.

Fiske, S. T., & Taylor, S. E. (1991). *Social cognition* (2d ed.). New York: McGraw-Hill.

Freud, A., & Dann, S. (1951). An experiment in group upbringing. In R. Eissler et al. (Eds.), *The psychoanalytic study of the child* (Vol. 6, pp. 127–163). New York: International Universities Press.

Furman, W., Rahe, D. F., & Hartup, W. W. (1979). Rehabilitation of socially withdrawn children though mixed age and same age socialization. *Child Development, 50,* 915–922.

Garcia-Coll, C. T., Hoffman, J., & Oh, W. (1987). The social ecology and early parenting of Caucasian adolescent mothers. *Child Development, 58,* 955–963.

Gilligan, J. (1996). *Violence: Our deadly epidemic and its causes.* New York: Putnam.

Goldstein, J. H., Davis, R. W., & Herman, D. (1975). Escalation of aggression: Experimental studies. *Journal of Personality and Social Psychology, 31,* 162–170.

Grodman, S. M. (1979). *The role of personality and situational variables in responding to and helping an individual in psychological distress.* Unpublished doctoral dissertation, University of Massachusetts, Amherst.

Grusec, J. E., Kuczynski, L., Rushton, J. P., & Simutis, Z. M. (1978). Modeling, direct instruction, and attributions: Effects on altruism. *Developmental Psychology, 14,* 51–57.

Herman, J. (1992). *Trauma and recovery.* New York: Basic.

Hoffman, M. L. (1970a). Conscience, personality, and socialization technique. *Human Development, 13,* 90–126.

Hoffman, M. L. (1970b). Moral development. In P. H. Mussen (Ed.), *Carmichael's manual of child psychology* (3d ed., Vol. 2, pp. 261–359). New York: Wiley.

Hoffman, M. L. (1975a). Altruistic behavior and the parent-child relationship. *Journal of Personality and Social Psychology, 31,* 937–943.

Hoffman, M. L. (1975b). Developmental synthesis of affect and cognition and its implications for altruistic motivation. *Developmental Psychology, 11,* 607–622.

Hoffman, M. L. (2000). *Empathy and moral development.* New York: Cambridge University Press.

Huesmann, L. R., & Eron, L. D. (1984). Cognitive processes and the persistence of aggressive behavior. *Aggressive Behavior, 10,* 243–251.

Huesmann, L. R., Eron, L. D., Lefkowitz, M. M., & Walder, L. O. (1984). Stability of aggression over time and generations. *Developmental Psychology, 20,* 1120–1134.

Karylowski, J. (1976). Self-esteem, similarity, liking, and helping. *Personality and Social Psychology Bulletin, 2,* 71–74.

Kaufman, J., & Zigler, E. (1987). Do abused children become abusive parents? *American Journal of Orthopsychiatry, 57,* 186–192.

Kelman, H. C. (1990). Applying a human needs perspective to the practice of conflict resolution: The Israeli-Palestinian case. In J. Burton (Ed.), *Conflict: Human needs theory* (pp. 283–297). New York: St. Martin's.

Kestenbaum, R., Farber, E. A., & Sroufe, L. A. (1989). Individual differences in empathy among preschoolers: Relation to attachment history. *New Directions in Child Development, 44,* 51–64.

Kohlberg, L., & Candee, L. (1984). The relationship of moral judgment to moral action. In W. M. Kurtines & J. L. Gewirtz (Eds.), *Morality, moral behavior, and moral development* (pp. 52–73). Mahwah, NJ: Wiley.

Lykken, D. T. (2001). Parental licensure. *American Psychologist, 56,* 885–894.

Maslow, A. H. (1968). *Toward a psychology of being* (2d ed.). New York: Van Nostrand.

Maslow, A. H. (1987). *Motivation and personality* (3d ed.). New York: Harper & Row. (Original work published 1954)

Masten, A. S. (2001). Ordinary magic: Resilience processes in development. *American Psychologist, 59,* 227–238.

Mauss, M. (1954). *The gift: Forms and functions of exchange in archaic societies.* Glencoe, IL: Free Press.

McCann, I. L., & Pearlman, L. A. (1990). *Psychological trauma and the adult survivor: Theory, therapy, and transformation.* New York: Brunner Mazel.

McLoyd, V. C. (1990). The impact of economic hardship on black families and children: Psychological distress, parenting, and socioemotional development. *Child Development, 61,* 311–346.

Merkl, P. H. (1980). *The making of a stormtrooper.* Princeton: Princeton University Press.

Midlarsky, E. (1971). Aiding under stress: The effects of competence, dependence, visibility, and fatalism. *Journal of Personality, 39,* 132–149.

Mischel, W., & Liebert, R. M. (1966). Effects of discrepancies between observed and imposed reward criteria on their acquisition and transmission. *Journal of Personality and Social Psychology, 3,* 45–53.

Murray, H. A. (1938). *Explorations in personality.* New York: Oxford University Press.

O'Connell Higgins, G. (1994). *Resilient adults overcoming a cruel past.* San Francisco: Jossey-Bass.

Oliner, S. B., & Oliner, P. (1988). *The altruistic personality: Rescuers of Jews in Nazi Europe.* New York: Free Press.

Olweus, D. (1993). *Bullying at school: What we know and what we can do.* Oxford: Blackwell.

Opotow, S. (1990). Moral exclusion and injustice. *Journal of Social Issues, 46*(1), 1–20.

Pearlman, L. A., & Saakvitne, K. W. (1995). *Trauma and the therapist: Countertransference and vicarious traumatization in psychotherapy with incest survivors.* New York: Norton.

Pennebacker, J. W., & Beall, S. K. (1986). Confronting a traumatic event: Toward an understanding of inhibition and disease. *Journal of Abnormal Psychology, 95,* 274–281.

Pettigrew, T. F. (1997). Generalized intergroup contact effects on prejudice. *Personality and Social Psychology Bulletin, 23,* 173–185.

Pettigrew, T. F. (1998). Intergroup contact theory. *Annual Review of Psychology, 49,* 65–85.

Pettigrew, T., & Tropp, L. (2006). A meta-analytic test of intergroup contact theory. *Journal of Personality and Social Psychology, 90,* 751–783.

Rhodes, R. (1999). *Why they kill.* New York: Knopf.

Rosenhan, D. (1970). The natural socialization of altruistic autonomy. In J. Macauley & L. Berkowitz (Eds.), *Altruism and helping behavior* (pp. 251–268). New York: Academic.

Ross, D., & Ross, S. (1988). *Childhood pain: Current issues, research, and management.* Baltimore and Munich: Urban & Schwarzenberg.

Rutter, M. (1987). Psychosocial resilience and protective mechanisms. *American Journal of Orthopsychiatry, 57,* 316–331.

Sampson, E. E. (1988). The debate on individualism. *American Psychologist, 47,* 15–22.

Schatz, R. T., & Staub, E. (1997). Manifestations of blind and constructive patriotism. In D. Bar-Tal & E. Staub (Eds.), *Patriotism in the lives of individuals and groups* (pp. 229–245). Chicago: Nelson-Hall.

Schatz, R. T., Staub, E., & Lavine, H. (1999). On the varieties of national attachment: Blind versus constructive patriotism. *Political Psychology, 20,* 151–175.

Shroeder, D. A., Penner, L. A., Dovidio, J. F., & Piliavin, J. A. (1995). *Psychology of helping and altruism: Problems and puzzles.* New York: McGraw-Hill.

Shaffer, D. R. (1995). *Social and personality development.* Monterey, CA: Brooks-Cole.

Spielman, D., & Staub, E. (2000). Reducing boys' aggression: Learning to fulfill basic needs constructively. *Journal of Applied Developmental Psychology, 21,* 165–181.

Staub, E. (1971). The learning and unlearning of aggression: The role of anxiety, empathy, efficacy, and prosocial values. In J. Singer (Ed.), *The control of aggression and violence: Cognitive and physiological factors* (pp. 93–125). New York: Academic.

Staub, E. (1974). Helping a distressed person: Social, personality, and stimulus determinants. In L. Berkowitz (Ed.), *Advances in experimental social psychology* (vol. 7, pp. 203–242). New York: Academic.

Staub, E. (1975). To rear a prosocial child: Reasoning, learning by doing, and learning by teaching others. In D. J. DePalma & J. M. Foley (Eds.), *Moral development: Current theory and research* (pp. 113–135). Hillsdale, NJ: Erlbaum.

Staub, E. (1978). *Positive social behavior and morality: Vol. 1. Social and personal influences.* New York: Academic.

Staub, E. (1979). *Positive social behavior and morality: Vol. 2. Socialization and development.* New York: Academic.

Staub, E. (1980). Social and prosocial behavior: Personal and situational influences and their interactions. In E. Staub (Ed.), *Personality: Basic aspects and current research* (pp. 237–294). Englewood Cliffs, NJ: Prentice-Hall.

Staub, E. (1989a). *The roots of evil: The origins of genocide and other group violence.* New York: Cambridge University Press.

Staub, E. (1989b, May). What are your values and goals? *Psychology Today,* 46–49.

Staub, E. (1993). The psychology of bystanders, perpetrators, and heroic helpers. *International Journal of Intercultural Relations, 17,* 315–341.

Staub, E. (1995). How people learn to care. In P. G. Schervish, V. A. Hodgkinson, M. Gates, et al. (Eds.), *Care and community in modern society: Passing on the tradition of service to future generations* (pp. 51–67). San Francisco: Jossey-Bass.

Staub, E. (1996a). Altruism and aggression in children and youth: Origins and cures. In R. Feldman (Ed.), *The psychology of adversity* (pp. 115–147). Amherst: University of Massachusetts Press.

Staub, E. (1996b). The cultural-societal roots of violence: The examples of genocidal violence and of contemporary youth violence in the United States. *American Psychologist, 51,* 117–132.

Staub, E. (1997). Blind versus constructive patriotism: Moving from embeddedness in the group to critical loyalty and action. In E. Staub & D. Bar-Tal (Eds.), *Patriotism in the lives of individuals and nations* (pp. 213–228). Chicago: Nelson-Hall.

Staub, E. (1998). Breaking the cycle of genocidal violence: Healing and reconciliation. In J. Harvey (Ed.), *Perspectives on loss* (pp. 231–238). Washington, DC: Taylor & Francis.

Staub, E. (1999a). The origins and prevention of genocide, mass killing, and other collective violence. *Peace and Conflict: Journal of Peace Psychology, 5,* 303–337. (Lead article, followed by commentaries)

Staub, E. (1999b). The roots of evil: Personality, social conditions, culture, and basic human needs. *Personality and Social Psychology Review, 3,* 179–192.

Staub, E. (2002a). From healing past wounds to the development of inclusive caring: Contents and processes of peace education. In G. Salomon & B. Nevo (Eds.), *Peace education: The concepts, principles, and practices around the world* (pp. 73–89). Mahwah, NJ: Erlbaum.

Staub, E. (2002b). Preventing terrorism: Raising "inclusively" caring children in the complex world of the 21st century. In C. E. Stout (Ed.). *The psychology of terrorism* (pp. 119–131). New York: Praeger.

Staub, E. (2003). *The psychology of good and evil: Why children, adults, and groups help and harm others.* New York: Cambridge University Press.

Staub, E., & Pearlman, L. (2001). Healing, reconciliation, and forgiving after genocide and other collective violence. In S. J. Helmick & R. L. Petersen (Eds.), *Forgiveness and reconciliation: Religion, public policy, and conflict transformation.* Radnor, PA: Templeton Foundation Press.

Staub, E., Pearlman, L. A., Gubin, A., & Hagengimana, A. (2005). Healing, reconciliation, forgiving and the prevention of violence after genocide or mass killing: An intervention and its experimental evaluation in Rwanda. *Journal of Social and Clinical Psychology, 24*(3), 297–334.

Staub, E., Pearlman, L. A., & Miller, V. (2003). Healing and roots of genocide in Rwanda. *Peace Review, 15*(3), 287–294.

Suomi, S. J., & Harlow, H. F. (1972). Social rehabilitation of isolate-reared monkeys. *Developmental Psychology, 6,* 487–496.

Surrey, J. (1985). *Self-in-relation: A theory of women's development.* Wellesley, MA: Stone Center, Wellesley College.

Tec, N. (1986). *When light pierced the darkness: Christian rescue of Jews in Nazi-occupied Poland.* New York: Oxford University Press.

Thompson, R. A. (1998). Early sociopersonality development. In W. Damon (Series Ed.), N. Eisenberg (Vol. Ed.), *Handbook of child psychology: Vol. 3. Social, emotional, and personality development* (5th ed., pp. 25–104). New York: Wiley.

Thompson, W. R., & Grusec, J. (1970). Studies of early experience. In P. H. Mussen (Ed.), *Carmichael's manual of child psychology* (3d ed., Vol. 2, pp. 565–656). New York: Wiley.

Toch, H. (1969). *Violent men.* Chicago: Aldine.

Tompkins, S. (1965). The constructive role of violence and suffering for the individual and for his society. In S. S. Tomkins & C. E. Izard (Eds.), *Affect, cognition and personality: Empirical studies* (pp. 148–171). New York: Springer.

Triandis, H. C. (1994). *Cultural and social behavior.* New York: McGraw-Hill.

Troy, M., & Sroufe, L. A. (1987). Victimization among preschoolers: Role of attachment relationships. *Child and Adolescent Psychiatry, 26,* 166–172.

Valent, P. (1998). Child survivors: A review. In J. Kestenberg & C. Kahn (Eds.), *Children surviving persecution: An international study of trauma and healing.* New York: Praeger.

Waters, E., Wippman, J., & Sroufe, L. A. (1979). Attachment, positive affect, and competence in the peer group: Two studies in construct validation. *Child Development, 50,* 821–829.

Weiss, B., Dodge, K., Bates, J. E., & Pettit, G. S. (1992). Some consequences of early harsh discipline: Child aggression and a maladaptive social information processing style. *Child Development, 63,* 1325–1333.

Werner, E. E. (1987). Vulnerability and resiliency in children at risk for delinquency: A longitudinal study from birth to young adulthood. In J. D. Burchard & S. N. Burchard (Eds.), *Primary prevention of psychopathology: Vol. 10. Prevention of delinquent behavior* (pp. 16–43). Newbury Park, CA: SAGE.

Werner, E. E., & Smith, R. S. (1992). *Overcoming the odds: High risk children from birth to adulthood.* Ithaca: Cornell University Press.

Whiting, B. B., & Edwards, C. P. (1988). *Children of different worlds: The formation of social behavior.* Cambridge, MA: Harvard University Press.

Whiting, B. B., & Whiting, J. W. M. (1975). *Children of six cultures: A psychocultural analysis.* Cambridge, MA: Harvard University Press.

Widom, C. S. (1989a). Does violence beget violence? A critical examination of the literature. *Psychological Bulletin, 106,* 3–28.

Widom, C. S. (1989b). The cycle of violence. *Science, 224,* 160–166.

Yarrow, M. R., & Scott, P. M. (1972). Limitation of nurturant and nonnurturant models. *Journal of Personality and Social Psychology, 8,* 240–261.

Zahn-Waxler, C., & Radke-Yarrow, M. (1990). The origins of empathic concern. *Motivation and Emotion, 14,* 107–130.

Zakriski, A., Jacobs, M., & Coie, J. (1997). Coping with childhood peer rejection. In S. A. Wolchik & I. N. Sandler (Eds.), *Handbook of children's coping: Linking theory and intervention* (pp. 423–451). New York: Plenum.

4

Basic Psychological Needs, Caring and Violence, and Optimal Human Functioning

One of the deepest concerns of psychologists and others interested in understanding human life has been about the springs of human action. What moves us to action, and what determines the directions in which we move? In other words, what are our motives: our needs, desires, aims, and aspirations? Our needs and desires, aims or goals, influence our actions, including our helpful and aggressive acts. But their fulfillment or lack of it also deeply affects our inner life, our experience of ourselves and of the world, and whether we feel happy or not.

In the course of their lives different people develop different motives. But we human beings also have universal, shared needs, which are part of our evolutionary heritage. These needs must be fulfilled to some degree for people to be able to lead effective, constructive, satisfying lives. The degree they are fulfilled, and how they are fulfilled, have profound consequences on us. Other psychologists and social thinkers have also proposed that human beings have fundamental needs, with reasonable consistency in their views and mine about what these needs are (Maslow, 1971; Kelman, 1990; Pearlman & Saakvitne, 1995). What are these needs, what is their nature, and what kinds of socialization by parents and schools fulfill them in children's lives? What are the consequences of their frustration or fulfillment for caring, helping, altruism—and aggression?

Basic needs have an imperative quality; they press for fulfillment. If they are frustrated and cannot be fulfilled constructively they will be fulfilled destructively, by hook or crook, so to speak. Their constructive fulfillment brings continued growth. It makes caring about and helping others possible and probable. Their progressively higher level fulfillment leads to optimal functioning or the fulfillment of our human potential. Their frustration or destructive fulfillment limits the ability to function in the world and limits happiness. It generates hostility and violence. Developing our own individual purpose and meaning in life depends on the constructive fulfillment of our basic needs.

Basic human needs are psychological, not biological. Of course we have biological needs. Our need for food, water, air, and elimination are the most imperative needs, which must be fulfilled for survival. Many millions of people are moved to action by their unfulfilled biological needs. But even how we go about fulfilling biological needs is greatly affected by our experience with the fulfillment of our basic psychological needs.

The Need for Security

This is a psychological need based on biological requirements for survival. I define it as *the need to know or believe that we are and will continue to be free of physical and psychological harm (physical attacks on our body and attacks on our self-respect and dignity) and that we are and will be able to satisfy our essential biological needs (for food, etc.) and our need for shelter.* This is the most basic of basic needs.

Early experiences in a child's life can satisfy or frustrate several basic needs. When a caretaker feeds an infant or changes the infant's diaper and eliminates discomfort, the infant begins to develop a feeling of security or, as Erik Erickson proposed, basic trust, in people and in the world. The infant learns that he or she can bring this caretaking about, by crying, then by making sounds or giving other signals, then by asking. This begins to fulfill a basic need for efficacy and control. The faster an infant's caretakers respond to crying, the less the infant cries by one year of age and the more he or she expresses hunger, pain, or other needs in less intrusive ways. Good caretaking helps to create an experience of the world as a benevolent and therefore safe place. As a feeling of security evolves, it contributes to the infant's capacity for good relationships with people.

In the 1940s and 1950s researchers found that in some orphanages and hospitals infants got depressed and died in large numbers. First, driven by psychoanalytic theory they thought it was due to lack of a single mother figure. But continued observation and research led to the conclusion that it was due to lack of attention and stimulation, and to helplessness and giving up when in understaffed institutions crying brought no response, no relief from hunger or pain (Thompson & Grusec, 1970). Both the need for security and the need for effectiveness were profoundly frustrated.

An intense need for security contributes to abused children blaming themselves. Violent parents tell their children that they are bad. And people who are victimized or even mistreated to a less extreme degree usually feel that they must have somehow deserved this. Especially young children would not have the capacity to see their parents as bad. But if they did, this would lead them to feel even more in danger. As long as they don't think that their parents are vicious and violent, it seems possible to avoid punishment, by figuring out how to act.

People who are innocent of wrongdoing blaming themselves is one of the destructive ways to fulfill a basic need. The fulfillment of a basic need is destructive when it frustrates other basic needs or harms other people. Believing in one's own badness frustrates the basic need for a positive identity. In later life, for people violently treated as children, feeling bad about themselves can interfere with the initiative required to fulfill their goals. Feeling insecure, diminished by their bad treatment, and unable to protect themselves, they may withdraw from people and life. Or they may learn to use power and force over people to gain security, a feeling of effectiveness, and a positive identity (Rhodes, 1999). When they do the former they frustrate their own needs; when they do the latter they frustrate others' basic needs. Since reciprocity is a powerful principle in human relations, it is nearly certain that those others will respond to them in negative ways, so that in the long run they end up frustrating their own needs as well.

Abusive parents are often arbitrary and unpredictable, so that the child cannot find a way to avoid abuse. One person said to me that he lost optimism about life about the age of seven, due to his parents' violence against him. The beatings he received from his father were not so bad. His father would take him out to the shed and whip him with a belt. He knew exactly what to expect. But beatings by his mother were much worse. Her rage would flare up and anything could happen. He was afraid that her wild slapping of him would escalate and never stop. In other words, he felt extremely insecure.

Security provides comfort and even joy. The two and a half year old daughter of one of my colleague's witnesses another child's parents shout at her. At the dinner table that night she asks her father to shout at her and repeats her request until he grants it. She stands up while he is shouting and then sits down with a happy smile on her face. When a child feels secure in being loved, such experimentation is exciting and enjoyable.

The Need for Effectiveness and Control

This is *a need to believe and feel that we have the capacity to protect ourselves from harm (danger, attack, etc.) and to fulfill our important goals.* Later it gives us confidence that we can lead purposeful lives and have the potential to impact our community and the world. (The experience of and a "belief" in control is important for all organisms. In a widely known demonstration, when rats were put into hot water and then lifted out, when they were put into hot water again, they jumped out and saved themselves. They have learned that getting out is possible. Rats that are put into hot water and not taken out stay there and die.)

Infants strive for and delight in having an impact, in creating change. Their delight in playing peek-a-boo presumably derives from the ability to both predict and influence others' behavior. The ability to predict events makes effective action and control possible. Infants will suck hard on a pacifier when that brings on a light in front of them. I once observed a toddler spend a half an hour knocking a napkin holder full of napkins off a table, then replacing it and the napkins in it, then knocking it down and replacing it again, repeating this over and over. This child was learning about the world and her ability to manipulate it. Such activities are satisfying in themselves, without rewards and sometimes in spite of punishments they bring.

Curiosity, interest in everything new, and enjoyment in manipulating things help young children learn about the world and about themselves as effective agents in the world. As feelings of efficacy and control increase, we are more able to protect ourselves and fend off harm, which brings increased feelings of security. We are also more able to successfully fulfill our goals, which brings increased well-being.

While an interest in the world and in acting on the world are part of us, as with other human proclivities their fate, to what extent and in what form they develop, depends on our experience. A child who is supported in exploring and experimenting will maximize this potential. A child who is obstructed by parental disapproval or a greatly impoverished physical environment may lose some of this potential—and develop destructive ways of its fulfillment. Providing the child with stimulating materials, for painting, math, making and building things, and a stimulating social environment can develop and shape the direction of the child's curiosity, constructive manipulative tendencies, and effectiveness.

Overly great concern for the safety of the child, for orderliness, or for saving time can inhibit this evolution. For example, very young children are often interested in feeding or dressing themselves, but in doing so they create a mess or take more time. Initially the total effort required from the parent is greater, but so is the child's feeling of effectiveness and control and continued interest. The more children are allowed or encouraged to act, the more their interest and desire for independent action develops. However, unreasonable expectations for effective action beyond the child's capacity can also frustrate the need for effectiveness and control.

An important realm for developing or frustrating feelings of effectiveness is social interaction with people. In a fascinating series of studies Ed Tronick (Tronick & Beeghly, 2011) had mothers sit opposite their infants and observed what happens, repeating such observations over an extended period of time. There is usually affectionate gazing, smiling, and other positive acts for a period of time. Then infants need a time out—they look away, turn away for a period of time. Many mothers wait until the infant looks back and the affectionate interaction resumes. But some mothers shift their position to maintain eye contact and interaction. Perhaps they cannot tolerate the breaking of the connection. Over a period of months such infants seem to become less lively, even seemingly depressed. Presumably the tendency of these mothers to force interaction is also present in everyday life, limiting for the child a most basic form of agency or control.

On the other hand, the roots of empathy project (Gordon, 2009) facilitates children's understanding of basic needs, as well as constructive need fulfillment. A mother and infant come into a classroom every week, usually for 10 weeks. An instructor meets with the children both before and after each visit. The infant lies on a green cloth in the middle. The children observe the interaction between infant and mother, the instructor fostering empathy by helping children identify the feelings of the infant and reflect on their own feelings and the feelings of other students. The students learn about the infants' needs, how their satisfaction can be facilitated by people around them, how the infants' competencies increasingly develop, and the infants' openness to people and capacity for loving connections. They then talk with each other, with the guidance of an adult, about their own feelings, relationships, and issues.

The children can also hold the infant, sometimes with powerful emotional effects. Gordon (2009) describes, for example, a boy who witnessed the murder of his mother when he was four, who was then in various foster homes. He had many problems both academically and in his relationships to others. Holding the infant, completely engaged in his interaction with the infant, he then wondered whether someone who has never been loved can become a good father. Thus the children's learning is both vicarious, through their connection to and understanding of the infant, as well as direct, as they potentially fulfill several psychological needs in interaction with the infant and mother, and then use what they have learned to engage with each other. Evaluation studies show positive effects, such as decrease in bullying.

Children are curious, ready to experiment, and this can lead to the development of feelings of effectiveness in varied domains. It can lead to skills and comfort with using one's hands in building things, with artistic activities, with intellectual pursuits. It can lead to setting goals and purposefully guiding oneself in their pursuit. Providing the child with stimulating and responsive social interaction can develop interest and feelings of effectiveness in the social realm and lead to interest and satisfaction in building relationships. A person whose needs for effectiveness and control are fulfilled in varied realms is likely to develop creativity not only in special realms but also in living life.

The enjoyment of learning and doing well in school, of helping others, or engaging in antisocial activities, including bullying, are the result of different influences. But they are likely to have some shared origins in the need for efficacy and control. When the constructive fulfillment of this need is obstructed, whether actively or due to lack of opportunity, it may be fulfilled in antisocial ways. A person who is able to constructively and effectively fulfill this (and other) needs is likely to be open to others, to care about others, and to express caring in action.

The Need for Positive Identity

This need is more than just to feel good about ourselves. *Its fulfillment requires a well-developed and positive conception of who we are and who we want to be, with faith in our ability to become who we want to be. It requires us to gain experience and progressively expand our identity.* A positive identity requires self-awareness without self-preoccupation and accepting ourselves, including our limitations. It also requires some coherence among the different parts of ourselves.

Having many and varied experiences can lead to an evolved self. Parents can expose children to many or few people, places, books and experiences. The child whose experiences make him secure and effective will be comfortable in entering new situations, in engaging with different kinds of people, in creating new experiences.

When my two sons were young, we had friends and were involved in the community in ways that provided them with exposure to people. But at the same time when I was alone with either one or both of them I did not invite other people in with us. I did not want our contact to be diluted by the presence of other people.

I believe this was the result of my own life experience. I survived the Holocaust as a young Jewish child, in the midst of tremendous danger, in Budapest. I escaped from Hungary, at age 18, with two friends, after the revolution there was crushed by Soviet tanks. My parents and sister stayed in Budapest. I lived in Vienna then came to the United States alone at 21. My friends also planned to come but then for various family reasons changed their minds. I did not see my parents and sister for 10 years, until I became a US citizen and could safely go back to visit. All this made me want more connection and intimacy with my children.

The line I drew around my family loosened with time. While my children were young, we never had a stranger stay with us who needed a place for an extended time. I also rarely picked up hitchhikers while I was with them, not due to concern for our safety in the peaceful town of Amherst, Massachusetts, but because I wanted to be alone with them. After my older son left home for college, during the four years my younger son was still at home, we had a woman from Costa Rica stay with us for two weeks, then a young woman from El Salvador stay with us for several weeks. Both were in Amherst for educational programs.

I assume that these experiences had something to do with my younger son deciding to spend a summer in a community service program in Costa Rica and later to spend half a year in Bolivia. He ended up spending three months out of this half year traveling on his own, at age 17, in South and Central America. We were anxious, but survived with the help of his weekly phone calls. He became more interested in and open to people from different backgrounds and nations, and I believe more secure in the world.

I was not aware of my exclusiveness. I knew that I liked to be just with my children, but I did not observe it, did not have a third eye looking and commenting "this is what I am doing." As a result, I could not examine why I did it this way, what the roots of it were in my experience and its potential consequences, and could not make an effort to change it.

Such self-awareness is very valuable. To know ourselves and to accept ourselves are essential aspects of a positive identity. But acceptance does not mean that we do not strive to change. Knowing ourselves, and accepting that we are a certain way now, can make change more possible. Just as it is true in moving from one geographical place to another, so it is true in psychological and behavioral change: it is best to know where we are if we are to journey to some other place. Knowing and accepting who we are, we can still have ideals and aspirations for who we want to be.

Part of a positive identity is valuing ourselves. Ideally we have a positive although not too unrealistic, overly superior image of ourselves. A feeling of inferiority may mean that we feel ineffective, unintelligent, morally inadequate, uninteresting, or in general not good enough. A feeling of superiority may mean that we deny incompleteness in ourselves. This may represent lack of self-awareness, or denial of undesirable qualities in ourselves, or a compensation for feelings of inferiority. Perhaps in rare cases a person with outstanding qualities who has been widely celebrated by parents, teachers, and peers may authentically feel "superior." But life is complicated, none of us are perfect, and this is not too probable. Feeling good about ourselves with humility is likely to serve us best.

Sometimes a feeling of superiority can be the result of skills that are highly valued in a particular environment, such as outstanding athletic ability. This may bring problems later on, if easy popularity made it unnecessary for a child or teenager to learn the openness, understanding of people, empathy, and caring normally required for responding to others' needs and for friendship and love relationships. Or led to not learning that it requires work to create and maintain relationships.

We develop as persons and learn about ourselves through our experiences. Some of this learning is direct; we can see that we are better or worse than others in hammering in a nail. But even when we can make such direct comparisons, their meaning substantially depends on the reactions of people in our environment and the values they express. In some cultures, for example, Japan, standing out, being visibly better than others, has been traditionally frowned upon.

We learn about ourselves and develop an image of ourselves by the way others reflect us back to ourselves. Others provide us with mirrors in which we see ourselves. But depending on who they are, people can be different mirrors. Even a teacher telling us whether our answer to a question was right or wrong, and especially how the teacher tells us, depends not only on our answer but also on the teacher and our relationship. Parents and other people can mirror a young child to himself or herself as lovable and capable, or as incompetent, morally deficient, bad. This is likely to be as much or more a function of who the parents are than who the child is. The former image fulfills, and the latter deeply frustrates the need for a positive identity.

The norms and standards in our environment also are bases for evaluating ourselves. Parents, teachers, and others tell the child what actions are expected and good and what actions are undesirable or bad. Norms and standards can be supportive and encouraging, or demanding, harsh, and punitive. Performance can be evaluated on the basis of set standards and by comparisons to others, or children can be evaluated in terms of their own capacities and encouraged to do better than their own past performance.

Whether caretakers encourage, allow, or inhibit the expression of different thoughts, feelings, or desires also greatly affect children's growth. A child may learn that anger is bad, may stop expressing anger, or may even stop feeling and recognizing anger and ultimately deny the existence of it in himself or herself. Or depressed, traumatized, serious parents may frown upon a child expressing joy. Since children want to please parents, the child stops showing joy, which then diminishes the capacity for experiencing it. Children's identities can become, through all this, more expanded or restricted, with a greater or lesser range of feelings, thoughts, and actions. Children can develop more or less acceptance, awareness, and liking of themselves.

We all have certain ways of being (I spend a lot of time thinking, writing, doing research, and lecturing on psychology; I talk to my children on the phone; I swim for exercise; I spend time with my grandchildren; I travel to work at different places around the world). We see ourselves and evaluate ourselves in particular ways (I am a good psychologist, I have become somewhat depressed realizing that other than academic rewards my work on understanding and preventing violence between groups has not had observable effect in the real world—a kind of self-evaluation—but felt better after I began to work with real people in Rwanda and thought that I was able to offer some actual help; I have been a committed father; and so on). Most of us also have images of how we should be or would like to be and how this differs from who we actually are. Since helping or harming others are the outgrowth of three elements—me, other people, and my relationship to others—who I am, how I see myself, how I evaluate myself, and what my self-ideals are affect my helpful and harmful actions toward others.

The Need for Comprehension of Reality

This is a need to understand people and the world (what they are like, how they operate) and our own place in the scheme of things. It requires a worldview to make sense of the world and of our relationships to people, places, institutions, and life as a whole. Our comprehension of reality helps us create meaning in our lives by bringing ourselves and the world into alignment. We need to have a view of the world in order to have a vision of how we want to live life.

It is not possible to function without a "usable" worldview that provides at least a minimum comprehension of reality. Even a view of the world as dangerous and hostile, which creates insecurity, is better than the experience of confusion, chaos, and incomprehension of people, institutions, and how the world operates. But unless we live in a dangerous world in which we must constantly protect ourselves, a view of the world as benevolent serves us better. Children or adults who see the world as hostile and dangerous will feel insecure even in potentially benevolent environments. Their behavior, in turn, tends to create a self-fulfilling prophecy, eliciting reactions that confirm their view. The same is true of groups, including nations (see also Campbell & Vollhardt, 2013).

Aggressive boys see other people as hostile, especially toward themselves. But our views of the world guide our actions, which create reactions. When aggressive boys are put into a new group, after a while their peers become hostile toward them (Dodge & Frame, 1982; Dodge, Bates, & Pettit, 1990). In contrast, seeing the world as reasonably benevolent enables children to create satisfying relationships, which fulfill the need for connection and promotes continued growth.

We need comprehension and ideally our comprehension will be veridical, true to the circumstances, and when the circumstances allow it also trusting, although not gullible. Such a comprehension of reality makes it possible to be open to and consider others' understanding of the world. Openness requires that we have limited prejudice and that we are able to see, or become aware of, our prejudices against certain people. Such an understanding of reality requires developing self-awareness. For many people it also requires healing from painful past experiences that shape worldviews and limit self-awareness (see later chapters).

The Need for Positive Connection

People need to have close relationships to individuals and groups: intimate friendships, family ties, and relationships to communities. Because the need for connection, like all basic needs, is intense, when positive connections are not available people often maintain abusive connections, whether couples in relationships, or grown children with abusive parents, or parents with abusive children. This is especially the case when children grow up in an environment that teaches them that causing and receiving pain, through physical or psychological abuse, are natural (and, in the children's limited experience, inevitable) aspects of relationships.

Children who are badly treated by their parents are sometimes especially intensely tied to the parents. Harsh treatment creates insecurity. Young children will have no one else to turn to and will, paradoxically, may turn to their parents for protection from the insecurity that the parents create. They will also turn to parents to satisfy their need for connection. Older children may also hang on to unloving, rejecting parents.

Positive connections and helping are intimately related. Both require the ability to see others' needs, understand others, and feel empathy. Our past history of connections strongly enters into our proclivity to help or harm others. Helping others is a form of positive connection; harming others is the result of negative connection or disconnection and can be a destructive way of fulfilling the need for connection. This is evident in some cases of bullying among children when a bully has a persistent, ongoing relationship with a victim. Sometimes torturers also have a "connection" to their victim (Staub, 2011), which may be their destructive way of fulfilling this need. There is a good fictional example of this in Orwell's book, *1984*; O'Brien, the torturer, needs a relationship with his victim.

Our past history of connections and disconnections come to be built into the nature of our identity. We can develop a connected self, our identity open to and easily connected to others, or a disconnected self, so that we are walled off from others and find it difficult to enter into connection. A potentially useful approach to help children fulfill a number of needs, including the need for positive connection, is to provide them with knowledge about their families. Children who know their family's history, events and people in the family, are better able to resist challenges and are more resilient. Children who are exposed to the story of the family, which makes them feel more part of it as a community, are emotionally better off. It is also likely to help with the development of their identity, and even with understanding the world and their place in it.

Engaging with the past is especially important in families that have a history of victimization. In some Holocaust survivor families, and most likely families that survived other horrors, the children know that terrible things have happened. But members of the older generation often do not talk about their painful experiences, and "knowing but not knowing" has adverse psychological consequences on children. Without overdoing it, talking to children about the painful past—but also about survival and how people have moved forward in life—is of benefit to them.

The Need for Independence or Autonomy

This refers to the ability to be not only connected, but also sufficiently separate to make one's own decisions, one's own choices. Young children already work hard to assert their will. The famous terrible twos is an expression of this need, as is the often intense and at times hostile efforts of adolescents to separate from parents to some degree. Cultures shape the expressions of psychological needs, and in more independence-oriented cultures, such as the United States, the need for adolescents to separate themselves may be greater and more manifest.

The Need for Long-Term Satisfaction

I regard this as a secondary but still basic need. *This is the need to believe that things are well in our lives and that our life is progressing in a desirable way, together with a feeling of well-being that accompanies this.* People seek satisfaction, joy, and happiness. Long-term satisfaction is, in part, a summation of these short-term states, but not completely. It is also in part trust in future satisfaction and happiness. Pain, sadness, grief arising from loss are inevitable in human life: a friend moves away, a teacher we love is no more a part of our lives, we have a humiliating experience, someone does not return our love, a parent dies. The experience or belief in one's long-term satisfaction in life makes significant periods of pain or distress easier to bear.

It might seem that long-term satisfaction becomes relevant as we move into adolescence and adulthood, since children have a limited time perspective. But a toddler who recovers fast from temporary losses, like the distress of a parent leaving him or her at a daycare setting, may already manifest long-term satisfaction. This child's accumulated experience creates self-reliance and trust in the future. This makes it easier to deal with losses in the present.

Long-term satisfaction is to a large extent a byproduct of the fulfillment of basic needs. It is a result of our accumulated experiences in life and not primarily present circumstance. Presumably the fulfillment of basic needs creates long term satisfaction, and optimism or trust that good things will happen—that we will be able to create them—in the future. Psychologists have shown that optimistic people are more likely to take action in pursuing their desired goals and less likely to be depressed. The more effective and capable people feel influencing what happens in their lives and the more positive (but still realistic) their self-esteem, the greater the likelihood of their happiness.

Basic Needs and Higher-Level Functioning

I regard two more needs as secondary basic needs. Their fulfillment represents higher human functioning. These needs become especially important in later life, but the groundwork for their satisfaction is laid all through life. One of them is the *integration of the self*. We have many different parts, which need to be integrated to gain coherence and inner harmony. This integration enables us to lead purposeful lives with a sense of meaning. Motives pulling us in contradictory directions and lack of self-awareness and self-acceptance interfere with integration. An unexplored question is whether developing a caring and helpful orientation to people in one's own group, but lack of caring and hostility toward people outside one's group, interferes with psychological integration in later life. Do people whose caring is not inclusive mature less well?

To achieve high-level, optimal functioning, we must also fulfill our need for *transcendence of the self*. This is a need to go beyond the self. It tends to become important when other basic needs have been reasonably fulfilled. We can do this through the experience of connection with nature, or through spiritual experiences, or connection to spiritual entities, or by devoting ourselves to the welfare of others, like directly helping people or working for positive social change.

Sometimes people attempt to escape from difficulties in their lives and frustrated basic needs by what I call *pseudo-transcendence*—giving themselves over to higher ideals, of spirituality, causes, or ideologies. Occasionally, while working for their cause, people can fulfill their basic needs, and pseudo-transcendence becomes real transcendence. More often, their engagement becomes destructive to self or others, or both, for example, by adopting destructive ideologies like racial purity or intense nationalism as their higher ideals and participating in the actions of destructive ideological movements.

The Roots of the Theory of Basic Needs

The ideas of other psychologists (especially Maslow, 1971), and my observations of children have all shaped my ideas about basic human needs. But the main starting point for these ideas has been my study of groups that experience intensely difficult life conditions (Staub, 1989, 2003, 2011). These can be severe economic deterioration in a country, like inflation, or depression and unemployment, as in Germany after the First World War that brought Hitler to power. Or they can be intense political conflict and uncertainty within a society or group, as in the former Yugoslavia after communism collapsed. In Rwanda, in addition to such conditions there was also a civil war (Staub, 2011). Or it can be very great, rapid social change, like changes in technology and jobs, changes in social mores, changes in the relationships within families and among people in general. To some degree this has taken place in the United States over several decades. Sometimes these different types of difficulties occur together and create social chaos and disorganization.

When a society goes through difficult times, people's feelings of security, positive identity, effectiveness, connections to each other, and understanding of reality can all be challenged and frustrated. (The same is true of families; being laid off a job can by itself create frustration, disconnection, challenge identity and effectiveness, and create negative family experiences for children.) Especially when these difficulties are very intense, and when the culture has certain characteristics (see Chapter 22), people may turn to some group to satisfy such needs.

Often no constructive groups are available, and people turn to destructive ideological movements. Such groups tend to adopt destructive beliefs and views in difficult times, which do not normally improve the actual conditions of life, but can serve to fulfill basic psychological needs. These include devaluing and scapegoating some group for life problems and turning to ideologies that offer hope but are destructive, in that they promise a better future for a group but identify enemies. Nationalism, racial purity, and other visions affirm the group, while turning it against other groups that presumably limit the greatness of the nation or represent impurity.

The group's reactions elevate the group relative to others and reduce its members' feeling of responsibility for life problems, thereby protecting or rebuilding their positive identities. They create connection and feelings of effectiveness through shared hostility to the scapegoat and ideological enemy, and joint pursuit of the ideological vision. Even as people do not know how to deal with the actual problems, working to fulfill the ideology and especially attending to the task of destroying its supposed enemies gives them a sense of effectiveness and control. The ideology also offers a new comprehension of reality. An important challenge in limiting violence between individuals and groups, promoting helpful behavior, and building peaceful societies is creating constructive ways to fulfill psychological needs in difficult times (see Chapters 22 and 21).

Societal Variations in the Fulfillment of Basic Needs

The theory of basic needs, which assumes universal human characteristics, is contrary to a strong view of cultural relativity, the view that everything about human beings is determined by socialization and experience and therefore the culture out of which they arise. As a corollary it is also contrary to the view that cultures can only be judged from the inside, and practices within a culture only need to be inherently consistent. Cultures vary in the extent to which they facilitate or inhibit the constructive fulfillment of basic needs and promote morality, caring, and helpfulness.

While all human beings have basic needs, they can be fulfilled in varied ways. Different societies can offer different constructive ways of fulfilling them. However, some cultures have developed ways of life that do not fulfill or only destructively fulfill basic needs, at least for some segment of the population. One perspective from which we can examine a society is whether it provides the conditions required to fulfill not only the material needs but also the psychological needs of its members.

Certain practices can fit well with and support the societal system but interfere with the fulfillment of psychological needs. For example, in many countries, including the United States, childrearing in the 19th and the beginning of the 20th century stressed strong respect for authority and obedience in children. The focus on authority and obedience was very strong in Germany as well, where these characteristics were idealized. To create obedience almost any and all practices were acceptable, including severe physical punishment (Miller, 1983; Staub, 1989). Until the not-that-distant past, the emphasis on children's obedience was great in many places, including Britain and the United States.

Raising children in these ways restricts the growth of their identity. While children and adolescents in authoritarian families can gain security through strict obedience, the rules are unilaterally laid down by parents. They allow little questioning, discussion, or experimentation. They provide little leeway (Baumrind, 1971, 1975—in contrast to this is *authoritative* parenting, also studied by Baumrind; see also Larzelere, Morris, & Harrist, 2013). Although children can learn to be effective within the constraints of the rules, it will be difficult for them to face changing conditions, to deal with novelty. Their ability to function in difficult times will be impaired. A culture that stresses very strong respect for authority also contributes to the likelihood of violence in difficult times, including genocide, since people are less ready to challenge destructive leaders. This was the case in the Holocaust, in the genocide in Rwanda, and other instances of mass violence (Staub, 1989, 2011).

Culturally prescribed roles and characteristics of men and women can also limit the fulfillment of needs and the development of identities, and limit personal growth. When the domains in which girls and women are allowed participation is limited, and the kind of relationships they are allowed to have with other people restricted (e.g., friendship with boys/men in Muslim countries and until recently leadership roles in Western countries), the nature of their identity, effectiveness, and need for autonomy are all frustrated. Without support by males, financial or otherwise, their circumstances can make them intensely insecure.

Cultural prescriptions and ideals about what men should be like can have similarly restrictive effects. In spite of cultural change in the past several decades, in the West feelings of vulnerability, emotional dependence, and needing other people are still challenging for many men. Cultural ideals of maleness still place value on strength and power—more in some subcultures than others—and at many places around the world. In Rwanda, where we were told men never cry, once leading a workshop I had tears in my eyes. I afterward asked some associates whether I thereby discredited myself. They said no—because I was an outsider.

The need to be strong and powerful, to not be emotionally dependent, soft, or "weak," creates a potential for violence. Interviews with men incarcerated for violence show that many of them were motivated by the need maintain a feeling of strength within, and the image of strength and power in the eyes of others (Gilligan, 1996; Rhodes, 1999; Toch, 1969). Having difficulty with vulnerability also limits the capacity for deep positive connections.

Some needs are more difficult to fulfill and have to find more subtle modes of fulfillment, depending on culture. This is true of the need for connection in societies that focus on independence, and the need for independence in communally oriented societies. Societies differing on these and other dimensions offer diverse avenues for fulfilling needs. For example, an essential element of effectiveness and control is the belief in one's ability to influence important events in one's life, a feeling of agency. In the United States, agency means action that fends off undesirable outcomes and brings about desired ones. In Japan, people have traditionally gained a feeling of effectiveness and control by being part of the group or by aligning themselves with powerful others. They also have gained such feelings by interpreting events in ways that provide the experience of control. When people go to therapists with problems in living, in the West the focus has been on eliminating symptoms, in Japan on accepting them. These cultural emphases are relative. Certainly most people in both cultures use all these avenues to some degree for feeling effective and in control (Weiss, Rothbaum, & Blackburn, 1984). Flexibility in the way people fulfill basic needs may be the best cultures can offer.

The ways children are socialized shape the different approaches to exercising effectiveness and control. For example, in the United States children are "grounded" as punishment, not allowed to go outside. The punishment is that they cannot be independent, autonomous, or active. In Japan children are punished by not being allowed into the house. The punishment is that they are deprived of connection to significant others (Weiss et al., 1984).

Social Conditions and the Fulfillment of Basic Needs

Apart from culture, the conditions of life in a society can make it easier or more difficult to fulfill psychological needs. As I have already noted, intensely difficult life conditions that deeply frustrate basic needs have been the starting point for genocide (and also violent conflict—Staub, 2011) in a number of societies. The tremendous societal changes currently in the world also frustrate basic needs. Both social disorganization and rapid change makes it difficult to understand the world and one's place in it, to know how to be effective and in control of one's life, even to know who one is.

In societies where the culture stresses independence, like the United States, people usually address great changes on their own. But parents trying to figure out how to live life and how to guide their children as they are buffeted by changes in technology, jobs, culture, and society may feel deeply frustrated. Ideally people would come together to work on constructive, positive visions for living life under changing conditions. They can do this in groups connected to schools, civic institutions, churches, or voluntary organizations they create. Research shows that single, poor women are much better parents when they have support from others in the community. Everyone else can also benefit from connection, support, and the exchange of ideas in difficult times.

Extreme poverty frustrates the need for security and usually other needs as well. Even when less extreme, especially in equalitarian societies that proclaim the value of fairness and a belief in the equality of human beings, poverty can make people feel less worthy. If they are a minority, they may also feel disconnected from the rest of society. The experience of relative deprivation—poverty in the midst of plenty—and inequality in opportunity can make people angry and hostile. For people to become caring and helpful, we must work on creating caring societies (Chapter 28).

Basic Needs and Personal Goals

Out of various roots we develop personal values, or goals, which specify desirable outcomes. One of the roots is the manner in which we have fulfilled our psychological needs. For one person, intellectual activity may come to fulfill the need for effectiveness, can be a basis for positive identity, and can even be a primary way to develop positive connections. For another person social relations, and empathic engagement with other people, may serve the same needs. Although not all values, goals, or motives necessarily directly develop out of basic needs, many do, or at least they have significant connections to basic needs. For example, a strong commitment to the principle of justice may have roots in socialization and experience, as parents advocate it, call a child's attention to examples of injustice, guide the child to be just in his or her behavior, and as the child experiences both just and unjust treatment. Fulfilling needs such as effectiveness, connection, positive identity, autonomy, and comprehension of reality in the course of responding to and following parental guidance, and life experience become intertwined as justice becomes an important personal value or goal.

Helping others, becoming wealthy, social relations, or intellectual engagement all can be important goals or outcomes that particular persons are motivated to reach. For each person, personal values/goals can be arranged in a hierarchy, according to their importance. However, such a hierarchy is not static. Conditions in the environment can activate values or goals lower in the hierarchy and raise their position, making them dominant over others that are normally higher in the hierarchy. Working in one's office, parenting one's children, relaxing at the beach, or facing some threat can all activate different values/goals and the desired outcomes associated with them. When they are satisfied, they in turn also fulfill basic needs. The combination of basic needs theory and personal goal theory (Staub, 1978, 1980, 2013, 2011 see especially Chapter 22) can help us understand a great deal of human behavior.

References

Baumrind, D. (1971). Current patterns of parental authority. *Developmental Psychology, 4*, 1–101.

Baumrind, D. (1975). *Early socialization and the discipline controversy.* Morristown, NJ: General Learning Press.

Campbell, M., & Vollhardt, J. R. (2013). Fighting the good fight: The relationship between belief in evil and support for violent policies. *Personality and Social Psychology Bulletin, 40*(1), 16–33.

Dodge, K. A., & Frame, C. L. (1982). Social cognitive biases and deficits in aggressive boys. *Child Development, 53*, 620–635.

Dodge, K. A., Bates, J. E., & Pettit, G. S. (1990). Mechanisms in the cycle of violence. *Science, 250*, 1678–1683.

Gilligan, J. (1996). *Violence: Our deadly epidemic and its causes.* New York: Putnam.

Gordon, M. (2009). *Roots of empathy: Changing the world, child by child.* New York: The Experiment.

Kelman, H. C. (1990). Applying a human needs perspective to the practice of conflict resolution: The Israeli-Palestinian Case. In J. Burton (Ed.), *Conflict: Human needs theory* (pp. 283–297). New York: St. Martin's Press.

Larzelere, R. E., Morris, A. S., & Harrist, A. W. (2013). *Authoritative parenting: Synthesizing nurturance and discipline for optimal child development.* Washington, DC: American Psychological Association.

Maslow, A. H. (1971). *The farther reaches of human nature.* New York: Viking.

Miller, A. (1983). *For your own good: Hidden cruelty in child-rearing and the roots of violence.* New York: Farrar, Straus, Giroux.

Pearlman, L. A., & Saakvitne, K. W. (1995). *Trauma and the therapist: Countertransference and vicarious traumatization in psychotherapy with incest survivors.* New York: W. W. Norton.

Rhodes, R. (1999). *Why they kill.* New York: Knopf.

Staub, E. (1978). *Positive social behavior and morality: Personal and social influences.* (Vol. 1). New York: Academic Press.

Staub, E. (1980). Social and prosocial behavior: Personal and situational influences and their interactions. In. E. Staub (Ed.), *Personality: Basic aspects and current research* (pp. 237–294). Englewood Cliffs, NJ: Prentice-Hall.

Staub, E. (1989). *The roots of evil: The origins of genocide and other group violence.* New York: Cambridge University Press.

Staub, E. (2003). *The psychology of good and evil: Why children, adults and groups help and harm others.* New York: Cambridge University Press.

Staub, E. (2011). *Overcoming evil: genocide, violent conflict and terrorism.* New York: Oxford University Press.

Staub, E. (2013). Building a peaceful society: Origins, prevention, and reconciliation after genocide and other group violence. *American Psychologist, 68*(7), 576–589.

Thompson, W. R., & Grusec, J. (1970). Studies of early experience. In P. H. Mussen (Ed.), *Carmichael's manual of child psychology* (Vol. 2, 3rd ed.). New York: Wiley.

Toch, H. (1969). *Violent men.* Chicago: Aldine.

Tronick, E., & Beeghly, M. (2011). Meaning making and infant mental health. *American Psychologist, 66*(2), 107–119.

Weiss, J. R., Rothbaum, F. M., & Blackburn, T. C. (1984). Standing out and standing in: The psychology of control in America and Japan. *American Psychologist, 39*, 955–969.

5

Learning by Doing and Natural Socialization

The Evolution of Helping and Caring (and Violence) Through One's Own Actions

Helping others may be one of the most effective ways for children (and adults) to become caring and helpful people. People learn from the experience of their own actions and its effects. This seems a profound principle, in varied realms, of developing the motivation, emotional orientations, and values, skills, and habits that lead to later actions. Through experience people can develop interests, goals, commitment, and a sense of effectiveness. This is true even when the exposure is through games, even more so when actions have real-life effects. It is true in intellectual realms such as math or in the play of the imagination.

This form of learning is highly important in helping—and harmdoing. As children help others, they come to value the welfare of other people more and come to see themselves as helpful persons. As they harm others, they come to value others' welfare less and see themselves as willing to harm people. I have called guiding children to engage in helping others *natural socialization*. Rather than directly teaching, rewarding, or punishing the child, the parent guides the child to share, help, or do some form of service to others, with the experience of these actions and their consequences changing the child.

Everyday interactions provide many opportunities for unstructured guidance. Children play, and the play becomes aggressive. In play the opportunity for sharing toys, candy, or other goods presents itself. Another child can be allowed to join or is excluded. Someone is in distress or is hurt in an accident. It is good for children to work out their problems with each other, but whether at an early age or later, if in their interaction children begin to do physical or psychological harm to each other, adult guidance is needed. If children are allowed to act aggressively, to take toys from others by force, to say verbally damaging things, or to hit others, they are likely to learn aggression by doing. If they are led to be generous, to share, to console or help a distressed person, they are likely to become more caring (Whiting & Whiting, 1975; Staub, 1979, 2003).

Many parents do such guidance, discouraging children from hurting other children and encouraging them to share and help. But natural socialization can be more structured, leading to regular involvement in helping. Children can be given responsibilities or provided opportunities for helping. John and Beatrice Whiting, two distinguished social anthropologists at Harvard, conducted a study of six cultures in the 1960s. They found that in some cultures (Kenya, Mexico, and Philippines) children were more altruistic (they made more responsible suggestions to others, were more helpful and generous, e.g., offering food and toys), while in others (Okinawa, India, and the United States) they were more selfish or egoistic (they sought more help for and attention to themselves; Whiting & Whiting, 1975).

The six cultures differed in many ways, including technological development and forms of social organization. However, what was most strongly related to and in the researchers' view responsible for the differences in children's altruism-egoism was the degree to which children participated in activities that contributed to the maintenance of their families and group. The children who tended animals, took care of younger siblings, or were given other significant responsibilities were more altruistic.

The children were most egoistic in a "Yankee" town in the United States, which Whiting and Whiting (1975) called Orchardtown, located in the Northeast. The children's obligation in the family consisted of keeping order in their own rooms. This seems unlikely to give youth much of a feeling that they are contributing to their family's welfare and much of a sense of importance for their helpful actions.

Researchers have found that one of the important contributors to the development of empathy and prosocial behavior is induction, pointing out to children the consequences of their behavior on other people (Hoffman, 2000). Most research has focused on pointing out the negative consequences of harmful behavior on others' feelings and well-being, but pointing out positive consequences of helpful behavior is also important (Staub, 1979). However, in the cultures that Whiting and Whiting (1975) studied, where children helped extensively, parents did not use "induction" or gentle persuasion. Rather, they exerted influence in a straightforward manner. The prosocial tasks were simply part of children's role. If in the life of a group children contributing to the welfare of a family or the group is a basic, naturally occurring aspect of life, explanations may not be required. The need for the actions and the value underlying them will not be questioned. The participation of children in maintaining the family or group is taken for granted, and it confers importance on the child as a group member.

Research and Life Examples of Learning by Doing/Participation

While Whiting and Whiting's (1975) research is highly informative, we cannot conclusively say that it was engagement in helping that brought about "altruism," or that the absence of such engagement fostered "egoism." The six cultures differed in many ways, and some of the other differences may have created the difference in altruism and egoism. For example, in poorer and more collectivist societies people may rely more on each other, and children may see more helping around them and be influenced more by examples or models of helping, than in a richer and more individualist society like the United States. Nonetheless, the explanation makes sense, and I and my students conducted research to show that it is the experience of helping and "learning by doing" that increases children's later helping (Staub, 1979). We were also interested in promoting helping toward strangers, rather than only members of the children's family or even a limited community (see also Eisenberg, Spinrad, & Eggum, in press).

In one of our studies children made toys for poor hospitalized children. Whole classrooms of fifth and sixth grade children spent four class periods making a variety of toys for children, who because of some illness were in hospitals. We gave them materials prepared beforehand. They received instruction on how to make the toys, then proceeded to make them. The children were told that they were making the toys for hospitalized children whose parents were poor and could not provide toys for them.

Children in other classrooms participated in the same activity, making toys but simply to learn how to do it, their actions only benefiting themselves, to the extent that they learned skills to make toys such as puzzles or pogo sticks. They were not told about hospitalized children. We had children in these "control" groups in order to show that it was making toys for hospitalized children that affected later helping, not the activity of making toys itself, or the attention children received in the course of it, or learning a skill, which were all equal in the "learning by doing" and control groups.

In some experimental conditions the participating children were also told about benefits to children in the hospitals, in particular that the toys would give the children something to do and that they would feel good that someone cared about them. After the first toys were finished, the toymakers were also told that upon delivering the toys to the hospital they indeed had these beneficial effects. This is what I referred to earlier as "induction."

In another study, fifth and sixth grade children taught something to second or third grade children. Teaching is an inherently helpful activity, and therefore I expected the older children to learn by doing. In some cases the teachers taught first-aid skills, which the younger child could then use to help others. In other cases they simply taught them to make a puzzle.

While there were variations in specific details, the studies found that children who participated in helping others were later more helpful. They were provided with varied opportunities to help. One of them was writing letters to hospitalized children. Girls in the learning-by-doing condition did this more than girls in the control condition. Boys' helping could not be measured this way, because with rare exceptions fifth and sixth grade boys simply did not write letters. But both boys and girls who participated in helping spent more effort preparing packages for hospitalized children consisting of pictures, stories, and poems that they cut out of magazines or copied out of books. Describing to children the benefits created by their activity increased later helping more. (Distressingly, in spite of our repeated efforts, we found out in the course of the study that, for privacy reasons, the area hospitals would not allow us to engage with the children there—to deliver toys or letters to them.)

A very old study found that children who had pets acted more sympathetically toward their peers (Murphy, 1937). It may be that more sympathetic children are more interested in having pets, but in light of the discussion so far it makes sense that taking care of animals would lead to learning by doing and develop empathy, sympathy, and helping. This is not surprising in light of findings of a later study that 7- to 10-year-old children named on the average two pets when they listed the 10 most important individuals in their lives, and in another study about half of the five-year-olds mentioned their pet when asked who they turned to when they were sad, angry, or happy (described in Siebert, 2010).

In some of my research, children who were the oldest siblings were the most helpful upon hearing distress sounds coming from an adjoining room, while children *of the same age* who were the youngest in their families were the least helpful (Staub, 1970). Those who were the oldest presumably had responsibilities at home, whether helping around the house or taking care of siblings, and became more helpful as a result. The youngest children may have had the least responsibility.

Diane Baumrind (1971, 1975; see also Larzelere, Morris, & Harrist, 2013) reported that "authoritative" parents had friendly and sociable children. The parents were affectionate and used reasoning, but also exercised firm (but not harsh) control. They also assigned household duties to their children. Other researchers found somewhat more helping by children who had some household duties (Grusec, 1982).

Young children who have been well treated seem to enjoy helping in their home. Contributing to the family can make them feel important. To expand caring and helping it is useful to provide children with experiences that develop connections to and emotional engagement with other people and help them become aware of others' needs. A graduate student in one of my classes described his father taking him to Kenya on a business trip, before he started fourth grade. Visiting native villages, he saw with wonder how others lived. He realized that even as a child he had more possessions than most of the people there. Fourteen years later he returned to Africa, as a Peace Corps volunteer in Uganda, both to help and to learn more about other people and cultures.

Once in Uganda, he saw the vast needs of people there. AIDS was at a peak, the education system was still recovering from years of civil war, torture victims were daily written about in newspapers, and poverty was all around. He learned that at the very least, he could help in small ways to make the lives of a few people better:

> I started paying school fees for a local girl, I organized competitions between local
> schools to win soccer balls and educational supplies, and I focused my efforts on
> helping to train unqualified teachers. Doing things that made others happy was
> a very rewarding experience . . . as I begin to finish my doctorate, I hope to return
> to Africa and continue to make a difference in (people's) lives. I believe I will be in
> Africa because my father believed that I would learn best about the world around me
> if I experienced it for myself. (Lee, class presentation/paper, 2005)

Adults also change and evolve as a result of their actions. People who rescued Jews in Nazi Europe, whether they agreed to help a person or a family in response to a request, or initiated help, often agreed to help in a limited way, like hiding people in a cellar for a short time. They usually ended up hiding them for a very long time, sometimes taking in additional people to hide. At times the people who were hidden could be moved to a safer place. By this time many "rescuers" had become committed to helping. Even though this endangered their own and their families' lives, they looked for further opportunities to help. Many joined with others; some participated in underground railroads that saved lives by moving people to less dangerous regions or countries (Oliner & Oliner, 1988; Staub, 1989; see Chapter 7).

In Argentina, the Mothers of the Plaza del Mayo changed through their actions. These were the mothers of the disappeared, people who were kidnapped, tortured, and most of them killed. The Mothers began to march around the Plaza del Mayo, a central square in Buenos Aires. In spite of the prohibition by the military government, harassment, and even the murder of some of their members, they continued to march. At first they were only concerned about their children, demanding information. But progressively they became concerned about all the disappeared, and then about human rights in general both at home and abroad.

How Does Helping Others Shape Children—and Adults?

Why do helpers become more helpful? As we help, our attention focuses on the people we help. As we engage with them we feel connected to them and come to value them. As we become fully aware of their distress, suffering, or even the need for help to accomplish a positive goal, such as getting a good grade on an exam, our empathy expands. Hiding a family in a cellar that others plan to kill because they belong to a particular group, seeing the anxiety of children who are in such danger, the concern of the parents for their children and the sacrifices they are willing to make for them, are experiences that can enlarge empathy and sympathy. The same can happen under less dramatic circumstances—for example, when a child sees and consoles an upset peer or a distressed puppy. As we successfully help, we see our power to protect or help. We come to feel both more effective as persons and more responsible to help.

Helping others changes the way we see ourselves. In a number of studies children were guided to do something positive—to cooperate, or to be neat. In one study, Grusec, Kuczynski, Rushton, and Simutis (1978) told children afterward: "the way you acted shows that you are a cooperative (or neat) person." Having been labeled this way, these children were later more cooperative or neater. When children or adults help others, they are likely to implicitly think of themselves as being helpful, caring, or kind, and later this motivates them to live up to this image of themselves. Something similar may have happened in studies in which children played a bowling game, won rewards, were instructed to share a specific amount of what they received, and did so (for a review, see Staub, 1979). They later continued to share, even when the sharing was private. Being instructed to share without actually sharing did not have the same effect.

As I mentioned in Chapter 2, many people who volunteer report pleasurable feelings and greater energy while helping. Helping others not just on a single occasion but more frequently or consistently appears to be associated with greater well-being and happiness (Luks & Payne, 1992). Carolyn Schwartz and her associates had one group of multiple sclerosis patients regularly call members of another group of patients to provide support. After three years they found that the helpers' self-worth and mood had greatly improved. They talked about how "helping other people transformed their experience of multiple sclerosis from something that victimized them to something that enabled them to be a positive force in the world" (described in Svoboda, 2013, p. 96; see also Seppala, 2013, about the benefits of helping to the helper).

In my *Psychology Today* study mentioned in earlier chapters, the people in the 2,000 questionnaires we analyzed reported feeling good after they helped. People who helped more felt even better. And helpers who had strong caring values (a prosocial value orientation) felt especially good. People may feel good as they get vicarious satisfaction from someone's increased well-being, from living up to personal or social values (since helping is valued in most societies and most religions), or from feeling empowered. People who unselfishly, altruistically help someone may experience a moment of transcendence as they go beyond themselves, as they forget about their own interests and concerns, as they are liberated from their normally limited horizons. No wonder (unselfish) helping can be deeply satisfying and leads people to be later more helpful.

Helping can also be healing. Past disconnection, pain, and trauma may be healed as helping connects a person to others. This is an aspect of what I have called altruism born of suffering (Staub, 2003; Staub & Vollhardt, 2008; see Chapters 10 and 11). In the studies of Harry Harlow and his associates (Suomi & Harlow, 1972), monkeys isolated in the first months of life became more normally functioning after they were put together with infant monkeys, who clung to them. They responded to the need of the infant monkey and in turn received affectionate connection. Their behavior became less bizarre, their emotions more regulated. Their social skills developed. They learned from the younger monkeys as they began to mature and exhibit appropriate social behavior.

An evolution in the course of which their own actions change them into increasingly caring persons can be traced in the lives of altruists who devote themselves to helping people who are poor, sick, or minorities, or work to bring about social change. Ann Colby and William Damon (1992) studied a substantial number of such caring people. The life of some of them was completely devoted to helping others. Others had highly successful careers as businesspeople, professionals, professors, or university presidents, combined with service to people in need or work for positive social change. These people usually started with small acts of caring. Some entered difficult situations that helped them better understand others' need. One university president lived on the streets as a homeless person for a while. At many choice points they enlarged their engagement. Increasingly, helping others became an essential part of them. They were not sacrificing themselves; helping became a source of deep fulfillment for them.

One woman in Colby and Damon's (1992) study, who grew up in a racist environment, later became a committed civil rights activist, who by her actions exposed herself and her family to ostracism and danger. As a young child, her favorite playmates were the Black children of her family's servants. At age seven, told that she could not invite these children to her birthday party, she had a temper tantrum, and her parents had a separate party for them. But by the time she started at Wellesley College, she was deeply insulted when a Black girl was assigned to her dinner table.

She changed step by step. Accidental events and circumstances exposed her to opportunities to act. At a young age, in a women's organization that included Eleanor Roosevelt, she met women who were concerned about the rights of African Americans. She chose to engage with them, follow their lead, and participate in meetings and protests. Her choices led to experiences which led to her to enter more situations that moved her to act in the service of civil rights.

Will children or adults who help others always become more caring and helpful? When early efforts at helping are ineffective, unsuccessful—which can happen no matter how good a person's intention or great his or her effort—and especially when early actions are punished or result in harm to the helper, they are unlikely to lead to greater helping. Learning by doing may also not happen when a person helps purely to gain some benefit, through reciprocation or by getting material or social rewards, especially if these benefits are not forthcoming. But when already committed people, with strong empathy or prosocial value orientation are thwarted in helping, they may engage in renewed efforts.

Participation/Responsibilities as Exploitation

Helping will not lead to greater or more frequent helping, or at least will lead to ambivalence about helping, if children or adolescents are asked to do too much so that it becomes a burden and the demands placed on them feel unjust, both in terms of how much others in the family do and what their peers do. A study of 100 large families (Bossard & Boll, 1956) found that older children were often put into the role of caring for younger ones, administering discipline to them, and running the household. Some of these children, often the oldest girl in the household, were described by the researchers as having developed a "responsible" personality type.

Such a role can be appropriate and reasonable up to a point and, depending on circumstances, may develop caring and responsibility. But children or adolescents can be unfairly burdened. They may be used and exploited by parents who neither do their fair share nor ask the other children to help. A young person who is given many tasks, sees parents not living up to their obligations, and compares herself to her peers may feel greatly overburdened. This is not likely to develop genuine caring. These issues are exemplified in the statement of a girl who was the oldest of eight children:

> By the time I was in third grade, I was always helping mother, while the others played with neighboring children. This made me old beyond my years, serious, quite responsible for all that went on in the household. . . . Each Saturday my mother went into the city six miles away for the groceries and stayed for the day. In the evening she

and dad visited friends and came home about midnight. From age fifteen to nineteen, I found myself responsible for seeing that the housework was finished, cooking lunch and dinner for children, and caring for the newest baby. At night I bathed six children, washed their heads, and tucked them into bed. Saturday nights continued like this until I rebelled. I wanted to have time for dates like other girls. (Bossard & Boll, 1956, pp. 159–160)

Adolescents who are treated this way may opt out of care-taking roles and become unhelpful. Other serious consequences may also follow. In some families with father–daughter incest, the mother is a "parentified" child (Gelinas, 1983). In this situation the mother, in her family of origin, may have had extensive care-taking responsibilities, in place of the parents, and became very responsible. When she meets a man who is dependent, ineffective in social relationships, and needs care taking, they are a perfect match. They get married and have children. At some point the mother, overwhelmed by a lifetime of responsibility and caretaking, rebels, in some form or another. Sometimes she becomes sick. Other times she simply withdraws, from the husband sexually and from her family both emotionally and as a caretaker.

One of the daughters gradually assumes the caretaker role, and she and the father begin to get close. She cooks for him, cares for him, perhaps watches TV with him. At some point the father, who does not know how to take reasonable action to fulfill the emotional and sexual needs frustrated by his wife's withdrawal, breaks the moral barrier and engages the daughter sexually (Gelinas, 1983; Groth, 1982). This is one type of incest, perpetrated by a needy, dependent man (Staub, 1991). The daughter herself may have emotional needs due to the mother's withdrawal that are fulfilled by closeness to the father. Nonetheless, incest is likely to have traumatic effects on her with severe, long-term consequences.

Children can be exploited by too much work in the home and by sexual abuse, child labor, or prostitution. While child labor may be due in some places to desperate poverty, it obviously limits children's development. Under normal conditions caring about children and using good judgment can go a long way to stop adults from overburdening children with responsibilities. But the social context, like poverty and cultural practices, can make the life of children more difficult.

Role-Playing or "As If" Participation: Learning Helping and Unlearning Aggression

Children can also learn from role-playing, which I think of as somewhere between imagining action and actually taking action, or "as if" participation. We have evidence of the power of imagination. For example, getting people to imagine meeting a member of another group on a train and engage in an extensive, friendly interaction with this person leads to a more positive attitude toward members of this person's group (Crisp & Turner, 2009).

Role-playing can be a very lifelike experience. In one of our studies, pairs of kindergarten children role-played scenes in which one child provided help to another: to reach something on a shelf, to get out of the path of an oncoming bicycle, by consoling the other child after someone knocked off a tower he or she was building, by helping after the other fell off a chair. After enacting each scene, children exchanged roles. Afterward, boys shared more of the candy they received as rewards with a needy child, while girls responded more when they heard sounds of another child's distress coming from an adjoining room, than children in control conditions (Staub, 1971).

Among the things that can be learned through role-playing are skills in helping and cognitive empathy, seeing the other's perspective, and standing in the other's shoes. Exchanging roles, being both the person in need and the helper, should contribute to role-taking. Emotional empathy may also increase as the child sees another's need, knows that he or she will help (after all, that is the role), and actually helps. Perhaps a feeling of responsibility also develops. To some degree children's concern about others' welfare and a self-concept as a helper may develop.

Michael Chandler (1973) had delinquent boys role-play and film scenes they developed about real-life situations involving persons of their own age. They were to repeat each scene until each participant played every role. They reviewed the videotape at the end of each set to look for ways to improve what they were doing. In comparison to appropriate control groups, this increased the role-taking capacity of the boys (it decreased their egocentrism). In addition, comparison of police records for the 18 months before and after this experience showed a substantial decrease in offenses by participants, in comparison to those in control groups.

One of my students, Darren Spielman and I (Spielman & Staub, 2000) used an elaborate procedure to reduce aggression by aggressive boys. Our assumption was that these boys have learned to fulfill their basic needs destructively, by using aggression. We wanted to help them become aware of this and learn to use constructive, positive ways to fulfill their needs and the everyday goals that arise from them (being with friends, acceptance in a group, inclusion in games, being well treated by a teacher).

We had them enact everyday situations that can lead to conflict and aggression. We suggested the first scene and when necessary suggested and/or helped to develop others, but participants were mostly able to design their own scenes. The first scene was about a boy who put his bag down at the table where he and his friends usually eat lunch at school. Then he remembers that he left something in the classroom and goes back for it. By the time he returns someone else has sat down at "his" place and the table is full. In another scene boys are playing basketball. Another kid wants to join them, but one of the boys objects because that will make the number uneven. In later sessions, boys also generated scenes in which they had conflicts with teachers.

We encouraged our seventh grade participants to first do in each scene what was customary for them—which often led to conflict and aggression. In the first scene the boy may have started off by demanding that the other kid get up and leave, or verbally if not physically attack him. Roles of perpetrator, victim (who would often also become aggressive), and bystander were rotated among the participants. They videotaped their role-play, then looked at and discussed the tape.

Then we had them plan and enact scenes in ways that would minimize conflict and avoid aggression. In the first scene, upon his return the boy might in a reasonable manner describe how he left his bag there and why he left. If the other boy does not want to give back the seat they might find a way for everyone to sit at the table. After the role-play, we had them watch and discuss the video of this constructive resolution.

Beginning already in the first session, we introduced the idea of basic psychological needs. We described one or two needs in each session. As we progressed we had the boys consider whether and how their aggressive actions fulfilled their needs to feel secure, to feel good about themselves, to feel effective and in control, to feel connected to other people—specifically their friends. Then we discussed how their needs can be fulfilled in constructive, prosocial ways. We also had them discuss how aggression affected others and in turn others' reactions to them. They were surprised to learn that instead of making kids popular, being forceful and aggressive tends to lead to dislike by peers (Coie & Dodge, 1997).

The effect of participation was to make boys less likely to interpret the ambiguous behavior of others as hostile. Each boy was asked about the intention of actors in ambiguous situations, for example, when a boy while playing soccer and trying to dribble away the ball kicks another boy, or when several kids are throwing a baseball around a boy hits another boy in the back. Aggressive boys, after participating in our procedure, were like nonaggressive boys in seeing such actions as accidents, rather than intentional, hostile acts. Aggressive boys who did not participate in our procedure saw such actions as hostile and thought that the right response was to take revenge. In one of the two schools, participation also reduced in-school suspensions of aggressive boys. In this school teachers seemed quite harsh with students. Suspensions by aggressive boys who did not participate in our study increased in the course of the year but not by aggressive boys who did participate. In the other school, with a more benevolent atmosphere, both groups of boys received fewer suspensions as the year progressed.

Both the research and my practical experiences with having kids and adults role-play indicates to me that role-playing can be useful for both conceptual and emotional learning. It can develop both skills in social interaction and empathy. When adults engage young people in role-play, the characters should not be one-dimensional, preaching goodness like elementary school readers in the 1950s to 1970s in which children were always helpful and generous. Learning by doing through "as if" participation can happen as children and youth enact complex human relationship in which the characters make choices that are respectful of others and responsive to their needs.

Learning Violence by Participation

Children, adults, and whole societies become more aggressive by engagement in harmful, aggressive, violent actions. In a once quite frequent type of psychological study, some people were told that they are "teachers." Each teacher is paired with a "learner." Teachers are to give an electric shock each time the learner makes a mistake on a task.

In the famous obedience experiments of Stanley Milgram (1974), participants put into the role of teachers were told to increase the level of shock after each mistake by a "learner," up to a maximum level, which marked on the machine indicate were highly dangerous. Under the urging of the person in charge, a large percentage of them administered what they had reason to believe were the most dangerous and painful shocks. (The learners did not actually receive the shocks.) The percentage who proceeded to the most intense shocks depended in part on how close the learner was to them. The greater the proximity (the learner was in the adjoining room; there were sounds of distress and protests of the shocks by the learner coming from the adjoining room; the learner was in the same room; the teacher had to put the learner's hand on the shock apparatus), the lower the percentage of teachers who administered the most intense shocks. These percentages ranged from almost 70% to about 30%. Depending on their characteristics, people were more likely to continue to administer shocks (those with an "authoritarian orientation"—Elms & Milgram, 1966) or less likely (those whose moral reasoning that focuses on responsibility—Kohlberg & Candee, 1984).

Learning by doing is one likely influence on the behavior of the participants in this study. By administering lower intensity shocks first, the teachers changed, and it became easier for them to administer higher intensity shocks. Milgram (1967) reported that teachers devalued the learners along the way and quite commonly said things like, "He was stupid and stubborn and deserved to be shocked" (p. 7). I have proposed that such devaluation is one of the ways that people learn by doing and change in the course of the progression toward or evolution of genocide (Staub, 1989, 2011). In a study by Buss (1966), the teachers set the intensity of the electric shocks themselves. They were not told to increase shock levels as they administered shocks in response to mistakes. But as learners made mistakes, teachers increased the intensity of the shocks.

The increasing aggressiveness of the son of a childhood friend in Hungary can also be understood as a result of learning by doing. The parents were (unnecessarily) concerned about his eating and health when he was an infant (perhaps because of their losses during the war and Holocaust—my friend's father was killed) and were extremely permissive. When the child picked up a salt shaker in a restaurant and began to spread salt all over the table, they said and did nothing. When the child kicked one of them, they remained passive. By his adolescent years this boy seriously hit the parents and the grandmother who lived with the family.

Intense abuse by a spouse or partner also develops step by step. While it is women who are usually physically abused by men, and the damage is usually greater, at times the opposite happens. Richard Rhodes (2000) described how not only he and his brother were very cruelly treated by his stepmother but that she frequently hit their father as well. Men who engage in intense acts of partner abuse tend to start out with verbal attacks, which over time intensify and at some point turn into physical aggression. This is then repeated and becomes more intense over time (Beck, 2000). Often the man is hypersensitive, sees criticism and attacks on himself, even when they do not exist, and responds to conflict intensely.

Extreme violence by groups, like genocide, also evolves step by step. Usually it starts with discrimination against a group of people, then moves to increasingly harmful, violent acts. In Nazi Germany, leading up to the Holocaust, people boycotted Jewish stores. Jews were thrown out of the military and government jobs and increasingly were replaced in other jobs by non-Jewish Germans. Later Jews were forced to sell their businesses for little money, or these were confiscated. People stopped having contact with Jewish friends. Jews had to wear a yellow star. There were limited acts of violence against them (Staub, 1989). Along the way, the norms and standards of the society changed, allowing behavior that would have been inconceivable before. In the end, extreme violence became possible.

Similarly, in Rwanda there was a long history of discrimination against the Tutsis. There was violence against them, occasionally even mass killings, with thousands killed. Then, as economic conditions deteriorated, political chaos increased, and there was a civil war, a genocide began (Staub, 2011).

In both Germany and Rwanda, even though the authorities at the time inspired and even dictated such actions, people still have to justify them to themselves. In addition, to reduce their own suffering that would result from feeling empathy with people treated this way, they distance themselves from victims. Both perpetrators and passive bystanders devalue the victims even more than they initially did, seeing them as less good, less human. The attitude of the population, their passivity and various degrees of complicity makes it possible for leaders to start, continue with, and increase killings. Such evolution has occurred in most cases of ethnic and genocidal violence, often over a long historical period (Staub, 1989, 2011).

Do people always become more aggressive after an aggressive act? Certainly not. As I discussed in previous chapters, a person can harm another, feel bad and guilty and stop, even expressing regret and attempting to compensate the person he or she harmed. This can happen if a person has previously acquired caring values and a disposition for empathy.

Some Conditions Under Which Helping Does Not Increase Later Helping

Helping is unlikely to increase later helping when it obviously has no beneficial effects for the recipients of help. Whether children who are given responsibilities become more helpful is likely to be affected by whether they see their actions as a contribution to the family's or other people's well-being. Learning by doing is also unlikely if attempts to help have negative consequences for the helper. Negative consequences to aggression, for example, through the reactions of active bystanders, can also inhibit the evolution of aggressiveness—by both individuals and groups.

In our studies of learning by doing, when older children taught younger children, one of two adults instructed them in this activity. Learning by doing "worked" only with the supervising adult who seemed a warmer, more affectionate person. Older children who participated under the supervision of this person were later generally more helpful. In addition, the more responsive the younger child was to instruction—the more harmonious the interaction between the fifth and sixth grade teachers and the mostly second grade children they instructed—the more helpful the "teachers" were afterward. Presumably, the positive interaction made teaching the younger child a satisfying experience, providing a sense of effectiveness. This greater harmony may have been the result of the characteristics of the younger children, or the skill, empathy, and already existing caring by the older child, or a combination.

The force exerted in inducing someone to help also can make a difference. Some high schools and colleges now require students to participate in community service programs in order to graduate (see more later in this chapter). In general, volunteering increases the intention to volunteer in the future. This is consistent with learning by doing. But what is the effect of being required to "volunteer"?

Piliavin and Callero (1991) found that first-time blood donors who were pressed into donating intended to donate less in the future than those who were not pressured or coerced. Stukas, Snyer, and Clary (1999) expected, consistent with this and with research showing that external pressure, whether through reward or coercion, undermines people's intrinsic motivation, that requirement to volunteer would undermine the future intention to volunteer. They indeed found that volunteering did not increase the intention to later volunteer for students who felt that their volunteering was coerced (that it was under external control). In another study, students were either required to volunteer (reading textbooks for the blind) or had the choice to do it or not do it but were persuaded to do it. Those who had initially lower intention to volunteer had less intention to volunteer in the future when they were required to volunteer than when they had a choice. Those who initially felt more likely to volunteer were not significantly affected by having a choice or not. Stukas et al. concluded that the requirement to volunteer lessened the future intention to volunteer "only of those individuals who currently do not feel free to volunteer (perhaps for a variety of reasons, which may involve interest or available time and resources)" (p. 63).

However, even people not inclined to initiate helping, if they are moved to repeatedly and persistently engage in some form of helping under the pressure of some circumstance, may over time develop the motivation and habits to do so. This was apparently the case in some rescuers who, while they had enough motivation to help when asked, did not initiate the helping (Oliner & Oliner, 1988). It is also relevant that continued experience as a blood donor led to being a donor becoming a central part of people's self-concept (Charng, Piliavin, & Callero, 1988).

It is possible that many people who have just helped someone would help less soon after. This is likely to depend on both personal characteristics (see Chapter 22) and how great another person's need is. I proposed a theory of *hedonic balancing* (Staub, 1978) according to which people consider others' needs relative to their own needs. Having just helped, the desire to attend to one's own needs and concerns may increase, and helping someone who is not in intense need becomes less likely. Hedonic balancing also applies to illegitimate demands for persistent helping, for example, by parents who give children too many responsibilities.

Participation in Life: Learning by Doing in School or Guided by School

Exposing children to varied environments and experiences enlarges what they know and how they see themselves, their interest in the world, their realms of effectiveness. It expands their identity. Becoming accustomed to change, they learn to cope with a wide range of circumstances. Feeling more confident and effective they are more likely to initiate help in complex situations. It is important to respect children's temperament and developing inclinations, helping them to both act on their inclinations and expand their horizons.

Like adults, children sometimes have to face complex and highly challenging life situations. Dori Laub (2012) described such a situation. A Jewish family was hiding in The Netherlands during WWII to escape deportation. Their young son, about four years old, was playing outside. A man in German uniform walked by and asked the boy (overheard by a woman inside, the family's rescuer): "Where is your father?" The child responds: "One month ago, people in uniform like you, came into our house and took him away. We haven't heard from him since" (Laub, 2012, p. 66). The German moved on and the boy continued his play. No one instructed the child in such an action, but at his young age he understood the situation and was able to improvise a response to protect his father in hiding. His action was likely to give him a sense of effectiveness and be a building block for altruism born of suffering (see Chapters 10, 11).

Schools have many opportunities to develop caring through learning by doing. Children can help within the school or in the community. One junior high school teacher told me about a boy who had many discipline problems. As the boy returned to school after one of his suspensions, the teacher had him write something on the board every morning, a task usually the teacher had done. The boy's behavior improved. Another teacher told me about a boy who in the past stole from others. One morning the children were to bring contributions for a charity. Someone was to go to every classroom to collect the money. This boy was extremely eager to do it. The teacher, after some hesitation, agreed. The boy fulfilled this task very responsibly. His behavior also improved, the teacher thought because he felt more trusted and more important.

Having a responsible activity or role can make children feel better about themselves and more connected to their peers, classroom, and the school. This is especially important for children who are on the fringes, excluded by other kids (or excluding themselves), whether due to low academic skills, being a member of a minority group, antisocial behavior, or just being different. Such children are unhappy in school (Staub & Spielman, 2003), and becoming more connected to the school and their peers can make a great difference in their lives.

It is a natural activity for older children to tutor younger children. Many schools use some form of peer tutoring, primarily because they believe that it helps the child who receives the teaching. But it probably helps just as much the tutors, who come to know better the material they teach. In addition, as my research has suggested, teaching can develop caring and helping in the teachers.

Children and adolescents can also help people in the community. They can make toys for poor children. They can, as individuals or a group, provide help for old people—running errands, shoveling driveways, or just visiting. They can initiate and participate in activities that bring students, teachers, and members of the community together in community cleanup, sports teams, or collecting money for charities.

In Amherst, Massachusetts, the community came together to build a new playground at one of the elementary schools. For four days many people, including high school and university students, local residents, and police officers, worked, talked, and ate together. This was such a satisfying experience that some people who came for a four-hour shift continued to come back until the end. The project gave them permission and provided an opportunity to be part of a community. Such an experience can make people more helpful and change their relationship to people in their town.

> An outgrowth of this community effort was a larger scale collaborative effort at a nearby campus of the University of Massachusetts. The graduating class cleaned, repaired and painted one floor of the library building. The project was initiated by the director of the university's physical plant, who had participated in building the playground. (A year later) students, faculty, administrators and staff members, and some Amherst residents, under the leadership of volunteers from the physical plant, repaired in four days the remaining 23 floors of the huge library. (Staub, 1989, p. 275)

I participated in this event. It was not only fun, but for years afterward I felt a special tie to students and the one other faculty member from the psychology department who participated in it. Such joint activities can create connections both within groups and between different and even antagonistic groups (see Chapter 22).

Schools can inspire students to work for positive social change. School personnel can stimulate ideas and action. Students can inform themselves about issues and engage in advocacy with state and congressional representatives, or participate in the work of human rights organizations. The more they engage in positive action to benefit both their own and other groups, the more their inclusive caring and active bystandership as responsible citizens and human beings develop.

One of the benefits of a small school is that many students participate in extracurricular activities—whether sports, theater, chess clubs, or other groups. They are not just an audience. Participation creates habits of action and engagement, as well as connection among students. Creating wide participation in larger schools is especially important since students can feel lost, disconnected, unsupported. A student who has no loving support at home and receives no attention from teachers and peers will suffer. In our study evaluating peer interaction in a whole school system, excluded students, who had the least behavior directed at them, whether positive or negative, had the least positive feelings about their lives at school (Staub & Spielman, 2003). Some such students may turn to antisocial peers or gangs for connection.

Many high schools have begun to create community service programs. Some give students credit for community service. Others require community service for graduation. To revisit the earlier discussion, it is true that if parents, teachers, schools (or even peers) induce positive behavior using power, threat, or punishment, so that children feel forced, they may comply without learning the values adults want to impart. But this is less likely if over time the activities children and youth engage with come to have appeal for them, or their outcome—such as the benefits they produce—feel rewarding. Moreover, as in the Stukas et al. study (1999), students can be guided and persuaded to "choose" to participate. When adults guide children to share valued possessions, or not hit another child, or help at home, they often use some form of influence. The less forceful the influence, the better. But initially children, especially those least inclined to share or help, may have to be moved to engage in positive actions.

With some forms of participation, like household work, children may simply be required by parents to do it, at least initially. If it starts early enough, and is presented as a natural part of family life, children may easily enter into it and then feel pride in it. Children may be introduced to doing community service in a similarly natural way. Participation in such activities can become a way of life and satisfying.

For example, in Metro High School in St. Louis, doing for others has been an integral part of education. The approximately 250 students selected for the school, 65% Black and 35% White, were required to work as volunteers in the community. As early as 1983, they were to work 60 hours a year at some nonprofit agency. According to Ernest Boyer (1983), students received far more than they gave:

> One young man with longish hair, tight and faded blue jeans, and a street wise expression on his face spoke movingly of what he learned while working on the "graveyard shift" (midnight to 7 a.m.) in the emergency room of the medical center. "I learned a lot this past summer. I learned how to deal with my own feelings. I learned to cry. That was a big step. When a little three-year-old girl goes into seizure and they found out she had meningitis and died that morning, you learn to feel for people." (p. 213)

In cultures that prize individual choice like the United States, required service is bound to create some resistance, especially among young people who have not previously learned concern about others' welfare (and who are not interested in adding to their resume for college admission). Whatever pressure or inducement is used to engage them should be gradually withdrawn, so that the activity becomes dominant. But without inducement, those who need most to develop caring will participate in and learn least by doing.

It is important that service be genuinely helpful. A number of my college students fulfilled high school social service requirements with work that they did not perceive as beneficial to people. One of them worked in a library, spending much of her time restocking books. Many of them did not receive preparation that would have shown them the value of social service.

Adults must also be aware that in many peer cultures boys have learned that being helpful, seeming to be a good person, is not cool. It is not part of the ideal image of an adolescent boy. As in one of our studies I reported earlier, getting boys to participate in a helpful activity can activate opposition, at least initially. Having done something helpful made fifth and sixth grade boys less helpful soon afterward, but it increased their helping when they had opportunities to help several weeks later. In spite of initial resistance, they learned by doing.

Children and youth develop interests in different activities and most likely concern about different types of need—physical, material, or emotional. To be able to choose service that speaks to them is important (Wade, 1997), as is the opportunity afterward to examine the experiences they have had. Helping old people in a nursing home, they may learn about characteristics and challenges of old age. Such experiences may lead to commitment to work in behalf of causes, such as old people obtaining the services they need.

References

Baumrind, D. (1971). Current patterns of parental authority. *Developmental Psychology, 4*, 1–101.

Baumrind, D. (1975). *Early socialization and the discipline controversy.* Morristown, NJ: General Learning Press.

Beck, A. T. (2000). *Prisoners of hate.* New York: HarperCollins.

Bossard, J. H. S., & Boll, E. S. (1956). *The large family system.* Philadelphia: University of Pennsylvania Press.

Boyer, E. (1983). *High school: A report on secondary education in America.* New York: Harper & Row.

Buss, A. H. (1966). The effect of harm on subsequent aggression. *Journal of Experimental Research in Personality, 1*, 249–255.

Chandler, M. J. (1973). Egocentrism and antisocial behavior: The assessment and training of social perspective-taking skills. *Developmental Psychology, 9*, 326–332.

Charng, H., Piliavin, J. A., & Callero, P. L. (1988). Role identity and reasoned action in the prediction of repeated behavior. *Social Psychological Quarterly, 51*, 303–317.

Coie, J. D., & Dodge, K. A. (1997). Aggression and antisocial behavior. In W. Damon (Ed.), N. Eisenberg (Vol. Ed.), *Handbook of child psychology: Vol. 3. Social, emotional, and personality development* (5th ed.). New York: Wiley.

Colby, A., & Damon, W. (1992). *Some do care.* New York: Free Press.

Crisp, R. J., & Turner, R. N. (2009). Can imagined interactions produce positive perceptions? Reducing prejudice through simulated social contact. *American Psychologist, 64*(4), 231–240.

Eisenberg, N., Spinrad, T. L., & Eggum, N. D. (in press). The development of prosocial behavior. In D. A. Schroeder & W. Graziano (Eds.), *Oxford handbook of prosocial behavior.* New York: Oxford University Press.

Elms, A. C., & Milgram, S. (1966). Personality characteristics associated with obedience and defiance toward authoritative command. *Journal of Experimental Research in Personality, 2*, 282–289.

Gelinas, D. (1983). The persisting negative effects of incest. *Psychiatry, 46*, 312–331.

Groth, N. A. (1982). The incest offender. In S. M. Sgrio (Ed.), *Handbook of clinical intervention and child sexual abuse* (pp. 215–239).Lexington, MA. D.C. Heath.

Grusec, J. E. (1982). The socialization of altruism. In N. Eisenberg (Ed.), *The development of prosocial behavior* (pp. 139–166). New York: Academic Press.

Grusec, J. E., Kuczynski, L., Rushton, J. P., & Simutis, Z. M. (1978). Modeling, direct instruction, and attributions: Effects on altruism. *Developmental Psychology, 14*, 51–57.

Hoffman, M. L. (2000). *Empathy and moral development.* New York: Cambridge University Press.

Kohlberg, L., & Candee, L. (1984). The relationship of moral judgment to moral action. In W. M. Kurtines & J. L. Gewirtz (Eds.), *Morality, moral behavior, and moral development* (pp.52–73). New York: Wiley.

Larzelere, R. E., Morris, A. S., & Harrist, A. W. (2013). *Authoritative parenting: Synthesizing nurturance and discipline for optimal child development.* Washington, DC: American Psychological Association.

Laub, D. (2012). Testimony as life experience and legacy (pp. 59-81). In N. R. Goodman & M. B. Meyers (Eds.), *The power of witnessing: Reflections, reverberations, and traces of the Holocaust.* New York: Routledge.

Luks, A., & Payne, P. (1992). *The healing power of doing good: The health and spiritual benefits of helping others.* New York: Fawcett.

Milgram, S. (1967). The compulsion to do evil. *Patterns of Prejudice, 1*(6), 3–7.

Milgram, S. (1974). *Obedience to authority: An experimental view.* New York: Harper & Row.

Murphy, L. B. (1937). *Social behavior and child personality: An exploratory study of some roots of sympathy.* New York: Columbia University Press.

Oliner, S. B., & Oliner, P. (1988). *The altruistic personality: Rescuers of Jews in Nazi Europe.* New York: Free Press.

Piliavin, J. A., & Callero, P. L. (1991). *Giving blood: The development of an altruistic identity.* Baltimore: Johns Hopkins University Press.

Rhodes, R. (2000). *A hole in the world: An American boyhood.* Lawrence: University Press of Kansas.

Seppala, E. (2013). The compassionate mind. *Observer, 26*(5), 20–24.

Siebert, C. (2010, June 11). The animal cruelty syndrome. *The New York Times Magazine*, pp. 44–51.

Spielman, D., & Staub, E. (2000). Reducing boys' aggression. Learning to fulfill basic needs constructively. *Journal of Applied Developmental Psychology, 21*(2), 165–181.

Staub, E. (1970). A child in distress: The influence of age and number of witnesses on children's attempts to help. *Journal of Personality and Social Psychology, 14*, 130–140.

Staub, E. (1971). The use of role playing and induction in children's learning of helping and sharing behavior. *Child Development, 42*, 805–817.

Staub, E. (1978). *Positive social behavior and morality*: Personal *and social influences*. (Vol. 1). New York: Academic Press.

Staub, E. (1979). *Positive social behavior and morality: Socialization and development* (Vol. 2). New York: Academic Press.

Staub, E. (1989). *The roots of evil: The origins of genocide and other group violence*. New York: Cambridge University Press.

Staub, E. (1991). Psychological and cultural origins of extreme destructiveness and extreme altruism. In W. Kurtines & J. Gewirtz (Eds.), *The handbook of moral behavior and development* (pp. 425–447). Hillsdale, NJ: Lawrence Erlbaum.

Staub, E. (2003). *The psychology of good and evil: Why children, adults and groups help and harm others*. New York: Cambridge University Press.

Staub, E. (2011). *Overcoming evil: genocide, violent conflict and terrorism*. New York: Oxford University Press.

Staub, E., & Spielman, D. (2003). Students' experience of bullying and other aspects of their lives in middle school in Belchertown: Report summary. In E. Staub, *The psychology of good and evil: Why children, adults and groups help and harm others* (pp. 227–240). New York: Cambridge University Press.

Staub, E., & Vollhardt, J. (2008). Altruism born of suffering: The roots of caring and helping after experiences of personal and political victimization. *American Journal of Orthopsychiatry, 78*, 267–280.

Stukas, A. A., Snyder, M. E., & Clary, G. (1999). The effects of "mandatory volunteerism" on intentions to volunteer. *Psychological Science, 10*, 59–64.

Suomi, S. J., & Harlow, H. F. (1972). Social rehabilitation of isolate-reared monkeys. *Developmental Psychology, 6*, 487–496.

Svoboda, E. (2013). *What makes a hero? The surprising science of selflessness*. New York: Current/Penguin Group.

Wade, R. C. (1997). *Community service learning: A guide to including service in the public school curriculum*. Albany, NY: SUNY Press.

Whiting, B. B., & Whiting, J. W. M. (1975). *Children of six cultures: A psycho cultural analysis*. Cambridge, MA: Harvard University Press.

6

Passivity

Bystanders to Genocide

The passivity of bystanders significantly increases the likelihood of genocide. Frequently, genocide evolves as a process that starts with discrimination and limited acts of violence against members of a victim group, which change individual perpetrators, institutions and social norms, and over time greater violence becomes possible and probable.

Bystanders are individuals and groups, including nations, that are witnesses to events. They are in a position to know, even if sometimes through psychological maneuvers or other ways they avoid knowing. I have distinguished between internal bystanders, members of the perpetrator group or society but not themselves perpetrators, and external bystanders, who are outside individuals and groups. Both types of bystanders usually remain passive or in various ways support perpetrators.

Preceding the Holocaust, very few Germans protested the increasing, intense persecution of Jews. Most Germans cooperated with Nazi authorities and boycotted Jewish stores, stopped relationships with Jewish friends and lovers and took over Jewish businesses and jobs. Over time, many initially passive bystanders joined the perpetrators. In other instances as well, like the genocide of the Armenians in Turkey, the population remained passive or in various ways supported the perpetrators.

External bystanders also remain passive or, by continuing with business as usual, even support perpetrators. Thus, in 1936 the nations of the world participated in the Berlin Olympics, thereby affirming Germany. US corporations were busy conducting business in Germany in the 1930s. As the genocide of the Armenians progressed, Germany, Turkey's ally in the war, remained passive. When Iraq used chemical weapons to destroy Kurdish villages, many countries continued to provide Iraq with arms and economic aid.

The bystanders' passivity and complicity affirms and encourages perpetrators. Hitler and the Nazis were surprised by the cooperation of the German people with their early

Reprinted with permission and minor changes from Staub, E. (2000). Bystanders to genocide. In I. Charny (Ed.), *The encyclopedia of genocide*. Santa Barbara, Denver, and Oxford: ABC-CLIO.

anti-Jewish acts. When the community of nations at the Evian Conference refused to take in Jewish refugees from Germany, Goebbels, the Nazi propaganda minister, wrote in his diary that the whole world wants to do to the Jews what the Germans were doing but does not have the courage.

There are several likely reasons why internal bystanders remain passive. One of them is that with the group selected as victim usually historically devalued in their society, and influenced by the ideology and propaganda of the perpetrators, they support what perpetrators are doing. In Argentina, in the late 1970s, because the military government that overturned the democratically elected one was fighting terrorists, for a long time many people approved the disappearances of their neighbors. They were slow to realize that the military and allied paramilitary groups, which tortured many thousands of people, dropped people from helicopters into the sea and engaged in other atrocities, abducted people on the basis of slightly left-leaning political views, or even stole their property, and that they themselves may be the next victims.

Fear of authorities is a significant reason for passivity. However, Germans did act against the euthanasia killings of other Germans. Frequently, genocide begins or a genocidal system comes to power in difficult times, when the need for connection to the group is strong and risking ostracism by going against it is especially threatening. The victim group being a historically devalued group further reduces the motivation to act. Finally, as bystanders remain passive, they reduce their guilt and empathic distress by further devaluing victims and thereby further distancing themselves from them, which makes action by them even less likely.

Passivity and complicity by nations comes in part from their pursuit of national interest defined as power, wealth and influence. In addition, most nations have not historically regarded themselves as moral agents who are responsible for the welfare of those outside their borders. Diffusion of responsibility contributes to the passivity of all bystanders.

The potential power and therefore responsibility of bystanders is great. As violence against a victim group evolves, many of the perpetrators become intensely committed to their guiding ideology and the specific goal of destroying the victims, whom they see as the enemy of their group and of the fulfillment of their vision of a better world, their ideology. As a result, only bystanders can halt the evolution.

Although bystanders rarely act, even individual bystanders, groups and nations have great potential power. What one person says or does in an emergency when someone is in great need due to an accident or illness greatly affects how other bystanders behave. In Le Chambon, the Huguenot village in France, the heroic actions of the villagers in helping Jewish refugees influenced some perpetrators, who then helped the villagers. The unusual instance of coordinated boycotts and sanctions against South Africa helped bring its apartheid system to an end. The limited military intervention by NATO in Bosnia stopped the ongoing violence.

Actions by bystanders can reaffirm the humanity of victims. They can make perpetrators afraid of, or actually experience, the negative consequences of their actions to themselves. Early actions, before strong commitment develops to an ideology or the destruction of a group, have the potential of bringing violence to a halt without the use of violence.

Preventive actions can aim at overcoming devaluation of victims and promoting reconciliation between historically antagonistic groups. Helping previously victimized groups heal makes it less likely that they respond to threat with violence. Helping to create or strengthen democracy also makes genocide less likely, partly by bringing about culture change such as decreasing devaluation, partly by empowering people and making active bystandership more likely.

In order for "bystander nations" and the international community to act, it is essential to develop international standards for when action should be taken, by whom, and what kinds of action. It is essential to develop effective institutions for early warning, activation of response and prevention. It is also essential for citizens to exert influence on their governments in bystander nations, so that they will create the necessary institutions and take necessary actions.

References and Recommended Reading

Latane, B., & Darley, J. M. (1970). *The unresponsive bystander: Why doesn't he help?* New York: Appleton-Crofts.

Staub, E. (1989). *The roots of evil: The origins of genocide and other group violence.* Cambridge, UK: Cambridge University Press.

Staub, E. (1996). Preventing genocide: Activating bystanders, helping victims and the creation of caring. *Peace and Conflict: Journal of Peace Psychology, 2*(3), 189–201.

Staub, E. (1997). The psychology of rescue: Perpetrators, bystanders and heroic helpers. In J. Michalczyk (Ed.), *Resisters, rescuers and refugees: Historical and ethical issues.* Kansas City: Sheed & Ward.

Staub, E. (2011). *Genocide, violent conflict and terrorism.* New York: Oxford University Press.

7

The Psychology of Rescue
Perpetrators, Bystanders, and Heroic Helpers

The Holocaust, like every genocide, had perpetrators. It had passive bystanders, people within Germany and in the rest of the world, who knew along the way that Jews were being harmed, and in the end that they were being killed. They could have acted, but remained passive. It had victims, and survivors who have been deeply impacted by their experience. Even members of a victim group who, because of geographic location or other reasons, are not directly targeted are still deeply impacted by the experience of their group and carry that impact within themselves. There were also resistors, mainly rescuers who endangered their lives to help victims.

I will briefly consider the role and psychology of perpetrators and bystanders, and then focus on rescuers, as well as child-rearing practices that may increase resistance to the evolution of extreme violence. We must remember what happened; we must have an understanding of how these things can happen; and we must take action to stop genocides based on our understanding of what might do so, even if it requires commitment and persistence. (Staub, 1996).

The Origins of Perpetration

I will briefly discuss here the influences that lead to genocides that are especially relevant for our understanding of the social and psychological obstacles rescuers have to overcome (see Chapter 22 for a more detailed discussion of origins). A starting point for genocide is usually extremely difficult conditions of life in a society. People could deal with life problems by joining together, working together to solve them, to overcome them. Instead, very frequently one group points at another as responsible for the life problems and makes it into a scapegoat, which happened in Germany, Turkey, Cambodia, Rwanda, and elsewhere

Reprinted with permission and minor changes from Staub, E. (1997). The psychology of rescue: Perpetrators, bystanders and heroic helpers. In J. Michalczyk (Ed.), *Resisters, rescuers and refugees: Historical and ethical issues* (pp. 137–147). Kansas City, MO: Sheed & Ward.

(Staub, 1989b, 2011). The group creates a vision, an ideology that offers a better future, a blueprint for a future that gives them hope. Unfortunately, this blueprint often identifies the scapegoated group as the enemy of the better future it promises. Finding a scapegoat and creating a destructive ideology lead the group—a majority or the government—to turn against a designated victim group.

This is more likely to happen in societies with certain characteristics. One is a history of devaluating a group of people. We humans, unfortunately, have an easy capacity, and even an inclination, to create divisions between "us" and "them" and to devalue and, under certain circumstances, turn against "them." It is this inclination that we have to overcome, to work against. In genocidal societies the devaluation of a whole group has usually become a part of the culture and is carried in the culture. Anti-Semitism in Germany, for example, had deep and continuing historical roots. In difficult times, the devalued group becomes the designated scapegoat and the ideological enemy. In Rwanda, Hutus were devalued and badly treated before 1959. In 1962 they came to power and devalued and discriminated against the Tutsis.

Devaluation and discrimination are followed by limited acts of violence. People who harm others change, whether individuals or a whole society. Unless there are countervailing forces, an evolution begins that leads step by step to genocide. Frequently this evolution, this progression on a continuum towards destruction, begins before the group committing genocide comes to power. It often has deeply rooted historical origins. With regard to the Holocaust, apart from general anti-Semitism in Europe, in Germany in the Middle Ages there was especially great violence against Jews (Dimont, 1962). During the evolution the dominant group and its members devalue the victim group more and more. In the end, they exclude the victims from the human and moral realm, no longer treating them as human beings (Staub, 1989a, b, 1990).

Another beginning point for extreme violence is conflict between groups. Material conflict, over land and other resources, usually also turns into psychological conflict: devaluation of the other, seeing the other as immoral, or as a great threat. Material conflict has turned into psychological conflict between Israelis and Palestinians (Staub, 2011). In Germany there was no actual conflict between Germans and Jews, but in the minds of the Nazis there was very great conflict.

The Passivity of Bystanders

The only individuals and groups who could stop this evolution are the so-called bystanders. I call *internal* bystanders those who are part of the same population as the perpetrators and victims. They live in the same country and observe, or know about, harm done to the victims, or at least have sufficient information to know about it, even if they choose to close their eyes. They usually remain passive; the Germans remained passive. Often it is more than remaining passive. In Germany, for example, the internal bystanders were what I call semi-active participants (Staub, 1989b). They boycotted Jewish stores, stopped interacting with Jews, and said good-bye to Jewish friends and lovers, thus cooperating with and affirming the Nazi system. In this way bystanders are often in complicity with perpetrators.

When they are passive, bystanders themselves begin to change. When people see others' suffering and do nothing, they usually begin to distance themselves from those who suffer, even if at first they felt for the suffering victims. They do this to protect themselves from suffering, due to sympathy or guilt. They begin to distance themselves partly by justifying the violence against the victims. As the bystanders evolve, some in the end join the perpetrators. For example, a group of Berlin psychoanalysts moved through various stages, from being passive bystanders to Nazi sympathizers. Some of them became active perpetrators, first in the euthanasia program, the killing of mentally or physically handicapped Germans, and then in the extermination of the Jews (Staub, 1989a).

External bystanders—other nations or external individuals and groups—have also been usually passive. At times they have supported perpetrators. Nations have not traditionally seen themselves as moral agents, with moral obligations for the life and well-being of those outside their borders. They usually define national interest in terms of power, wealth and influence. The whole world went to the Berlin Olympics in 1936, affirming Germany, when much of the nature of the Nazi system was already evident. Without being asked, out of consideration for the host nation, the U.S. replaced two Jewish runners on an outstanding relay team—which in its original composition set a new world record soon after the Olympics. In the 1930s, American corporations were very busy in Nazi Germany drumming up business (Simpson, 1993). Bystander nations often distance themselves from victims; they did so before the Holocaust. Government officials and leaders may diminish the victims, justifying their inaction to themselves.

The Psychology, Childhood Experience, and Evolution of Rescuers

Following the evolution that led to intense violence by Nazi Germany, and in the midst of the passivity of bystanders, some people took action to help Jews. It was extremely difficult, not only because of the danger to their lives. Both in Germany and many of the European countries that Germany occupied or were allied with Germany, the population as a whole abandoned the Jews. People find it profoundly difficult, especially in difficult times, in the midst of chaos, to separate themselves from their own group, to stand apart, to oppose, and thereby at the very least to risk ostracism. And many rescuers, even if not identified and punished by Germans during the war, brought ostracism on themselves. Oscar Schindler, a German who saved more than 1,000 Jews in Poland, when he went to live in Germany after the war suffered abuse, as did other rescuers. This was at a time when the evil of the Nazi system should have been clear to everyone.

During the war, rescuers were at times denounced to the Germans. Rescuers both endangered their lives and engaged in a profoundly difficult psychological process. In the midst of chaos and difficulties, they dared to act contrary to the general spirit and direction of their group.

What were some characteristics of the rescuers? They had a variety of characteristics, a combination of influences acting on them, and became engaged in diverse ways. Interviews with rescuers and with people they helped indicate that many of them possessed one of three kinds of moral inclination. These correspond to what research in the United States and elsewhere has found in people who help others. The first is empathy, an emotional response to the suffering of others. The second is what some researchers have called caring, and I have called a prosocial value orientation (Staub, 1978). This mostly means empathy combined with a feeling of responsibility for the welfare of other human beings. The feeling of responsibility is a very important addition. Not only should people be helped; it says *I* am responsible to help another person who suffers. Prosocial value orientation seems the most significant motivator of people helping others. The largest percentage of rescuers in the most elaborately researched study had this characteristic (Oliner and Oliner, 1988). The third moral characteristic is the belief in certain basic principles of morality, such as justice and viewing what was happening to the Jews as profoundly unjust.

Rescuers also tended not to make as strong a differentiation between their own group and Jews and did not devalue Jews as did nonrescuers—people who were in a position to help, who could have been rescuers but did not rescue. Even those rescuers who described their parents making negative remarks about Jews, reported them expressing less intense negative feelings than parents of nonrescuers:

> Before the war, my father worked for a Jew. The Jew was a dealer. My father didn't say anything special about Jews. Sometimes he used to say—about those he didn't like—that they were misers.
>
> POLISH RESCUER

> My father said Jews as business people had excessive influence.
>
> GERMAN RESCUER

> I heard about the Dreyfus affair at home. My parents thought that he was guilty. Other than the Dreyfus affair my father didn't talk about Jews very much. He said that Jews had a sense for business.
>
> FRENCH RESCUER

> I never heard anything bad about Jews in West Poland—the worst anti-Semitism was in central Poland.
>
> POLISH RESCUER

In contrast, a nonrescuer said,

> I don't mean this in a bad way, but Jews were considered rather a cowardly people. They would rather talk themselves out of anything than fight. Jews were too smart to fight. Also any time that you dealt with a Jew (I hate the word "Jew," it sounds so rotten), but if you were buying or selling to them, you knew beforehand that you would be cheated because they were smarter than you.
>
> DUTCH
> OLINER AND OLINER, *1988, pp. 151–152*

Many rescuers reported that in their families they heard good things about Jews, not bad things, that the family had relationships with Jews, and that they did not learn to devalue people who were not their own kind, whatever that kind was in their eyes.

Many rescuers described a moral parent who influenced them by his or her generosity, caring, or good actions in the community. Some reported that this parent sometimes took them along on activities helping others. In general, what rescuers said about how they were raised is very similar to what research finds with children who become caring and helpful (Eisenberg, 1992; Staub, 1979, 1992; see Chapter 3). In families of helpful and caring children, parents don't set rules in an authoritarian manner and there is little physical punishment or strong use by parents of their power over the child. There is discipline of a softer kind, with reasoning, in a more caring context. Parents explain to children the rationale for rules and the way their behavior impacts other people. Affection and caring for the child, guidance, and discipline in the context of reasoning—not forceful and punitive discipline—are core elements in raising caring children.

Caring, however, has to extend beyond one's own group. People can come to care about other human beings, but only those in their own group. Children need to have experiences that point to the humanity of the other, such as education, exposure to others' cultures, and, very importantly, interactive experiences. Many rescuers reported familiarity with Jews, in contrast to nonrescuers.

We have profound difficulty separating ourselves from our group. Much of the time we go along with things that happen, accept the words of our leaders, and do not oppose destructive practices of our group. To avoid this, children have to learn two things at an early age. One is *critical consciousness,* making our own judgments about events. The other I call *critical loyalty,* a commitment to the long-term welfare of our group, but also the willingness to oppose what happens in the group at a particular time in order to promote that long-term welfare (Staub, 1989b, 1997; Schatz and Staub, 1997). To develop critical consciousness and critical loyalty, which can add up to moral courage, the school and the home have to allow children to participate in decision making from an early age. Children have to learn to use their voices and gain confidence in themselves.

For rescuers, not only moral characteristics were relevant. Some rescuers had what some researchers describe as *marginality.* While rescuers usually were connected to other human beings, some of them were less embedded in their community. A parent may have been born in another country, or they may have had a different religion from the community in which they lived, or they were different in other ways (London, 1970; Tec, 1986). Thus they more easily took a different perspective from the people around them in relation to Jews, exercised a critical consciousness, and showed critical loyalty. Schindler, for example, was a German who grew up in Czechoslovakia, a Sudeten-Deutsch. Born in a Protestant village, he went to a neighboring village and married a Catholic woman. In these ways he was different from the average German (Keneally, 1983).

How did rescuers become active? Some of them witnessed horrible mistreatment of Jews, which evoked feelings of empathy or activated a moral principle. One saw an infant smashed to death as Jews were being thrown into a truck. Such events so affected and out-raged them that they felt they had to do something, and looked for opportunities. Many res-cuers were approached; someone they knew, or an intermediary, asked them for help. Many agreed to help someone for a limited time. But after hiding a person or a family for a day or a few days in a cellar, they may have ended up hiding them for the rest of the war. Or they may have decided to help more people and actively looked for others to help. Or when the people they were hiding were moved on to some safe area, they became connected to other rescuers and joined in shared rescue activities.

Just as perpetrators evolved and just as bystanders evolved from being passive to some-times becoming perpetrators, so, too, after rescuers began to help in limited ways, they fre-quently became more and more helpful. Many of them totally committed themselves to help Jews survive (Staub, 1989, 1993). It affords us hope, that when people get involved in helping others, even to a small extent, they often move to progressively greater concern and involve-ment. This is what happened to Schindler, who was humane enough to engage with Jews as human beings. In the end, he became totally committed and gave up a dream of wealth that led him to Poland.

The activation of rescuers is complicated. Raoul Wallenberg, who saved my life in Hungary when I was a young child, might never have become the Wallenberg we know if not for circumstances. He was a poor member of a very wealthy and influential fam-ily. His grandfather, who was his supporter, wanted him to work for the family bank, but Wallenberg did not want to at that time. After the grandfather died, Wallenberg changed his mind, but he was not allowed to join the bank. He became a partner in an export-import business with a Hungarian Jew. He visited Hungary on business, came to know Budapest, and met his partner's relatives.

Through his partner, Wallenberg was approached and asked to go to Hungary to try to help Hungarian Jews after the summer of 1944, when almost 500,000 Jews were trans-ported to Auschwitz, most of them killed immediately. Wallenberg was rather dissatisfied with his life and was restless. Had he been strongly committed to some self-interested activ-ity, he might have been less likely to undertake such a mission. He also hated the Nazis. He agreed to go and, with great ingenuity and total commitment, saved probably tens of thousands of lives.

Hannah Arendt (Arendt, 1963), watching the trial of Eichmann, proposed the con-cept of the banality of evil. She left the trial early and missed testimony that showed that Eichman was a committed Nazi, rather than what she believed—that he was just a bureau-crat. She was also wrong describing evil as banal. Neither evil nor goodness is banal. Both arise, however, out of *ordinary psychological and human processes* that are carried to an extreme: in one case to the extreme of the destruction of lives and in the other to the extreme of a willingness to endanger oneself and one's family to save other human beings. We must understand these ordinary psychological and human processes in order to know how to raise children in schools and in the home and how to change social systems in such as way that we promote goodness and inhibit evil.

A final issue I wish to stress is the great power of bystanders. In one of my studies, what one person said in response to sounds of distress from another room powerfully affected how another person responded (Staub, 1974). Bystanders can affect the behavior of other bystanders, and also of perpetrators. In the Huguenot village of LeChambon the villagers hid- and saved- a couple of thousand people, many of them children (Hallie, 1979). After a while they began to receive telephone calls in the presbytery from the local Vichy police (the police of the government allied with Germans) announcing that a raid was coming. This enabled them to temporarily move people they were hiding into the nearby forest.

The heroic behavior of the villagers apparently influenced some members of the police. The village doctor was executed for his help in hiding people. But, a German major was so influenced by the deeds and words of the doctor at his trial that he persuaded a German colonel not to destroy the village. Our potential power as bystanders is great; we can choose to exercise it by our words and by our actions and example.

References

Arendt, H. (1963). *Eichmann in Jerusalem: A report on the banality of evil*. New York: Viking Press.

Dimont, M. I. (1962). *Jews, God and history*. New York: Signet Books.

Eisenberg, N. (1992). *The caring child*. Cambridge, MA: Harvard University Press.

Hallie, P. P. (1979). *Lest innocent blood be shed. The story of the village of Le Chambon, and how goodness happened there*. New York: Harper & Row.

Keneally, T. (1983). *Schindler's list*. New York: Penguin Books.

London, P. (1970). The rescuers: Motivational hypotheses about Christians who saved Jews from the Nazis. In J. Macaulay & L. Berkowitz (Eds.), *Altruism and helping behavior*. New York: Academic Press.

Oliner, S. B., & Oliner, P. (1988). *The altruistic personality: Rescuers of Jews in Nazi Europe*. New York: Free Press.

Schatz, R. T., & Staub, E. (1997). Manifestations of blind and constructive patriotism: Personality correlates and individual-group relations. In D. Bar-Tal & E. Staub (Eds.), *Patriotism in the life of individuals and nations*. Chicago: Nelson Hall.

Simpson, C. (1993). *The splendid blond beast*. New York: Grove Press.

Staub, E. (1974). Helping a distressed person: Social, personality, and stimulus determinants. In L. Berkowitz (Ed.), *Advances in experimental social psychology* (Vol. 7). New York: Academic Press.

Staub, E. (1978). *Positive social behavior and morality: Social and personal influences* (Vol. 1). New York: Academic Press.

Staub, E. (1979). *Positive social behavior and morality: Socialization and development* (Vol. 2). New York: Academic Press.

Staub, E. (1989a). Steps along the continuum of destruction: The evolution of bystanders—German psychoanalysts and lessons for today. *Political Psychology, 10*, 39.

Staub, E. (1989b). *The roots of evil: The origins of genocide and other group violence*. New York: Cambridge University Press.

Staub, E. (1990). Moral exclusion, personal goal theory, and extreme destructiveness. In S. Opawa (Ed.), Moral exclusion and injustice. *Journal of Social Issues, 46*, 47–65.

Staub, E. (1992). The origins of caring, helping, and nonaggression: Parental socialization, the family system, schools, and cultural influence. In S. Oliner, P. Oliner, L. Baron, & L. Blum (Eds.), *Embracing the other: Philosophical, psychological, and historical perspectives on altruism*. New York: New York University Press.

Staub, E. (1993). The psychology of bystanders, perpetrators, and heroic helpers. *International Journal of Intercultural Relations, 17*, 315–341.

Staub, E. (1996). Preventing genocide: Activating bystanders, helping victims, and the creation of caring. *Peace and Conflict: Journal of Peace Psychology 2*, 189–200.

Staub, E. (1997). Blind versus constructive patriotism: Moving from embeddedness in the group to critical loyalty and action. In D. Bar-Tal & E. Staub (Eds.), *Patriotism in the lives of individuals and nations.* Chicago: Nelson Hall.

Staub, E. (2011). *Overcoming evil: Genocide, violent conflict and terrorism.* New York: Oxford University Press.

Tec, N. (1986). *When light pierced the darkness: Christian rescue of Jews in Nazi-occupied Poland.* New York: Oxford University Press.

8

Psychology, Morality, Devaluation, and Evil

Psychological forces can overwhelm or subvert moral principles and emotions. I define morality as principles, values, emotional orientations, and practices that maintain or promote human welfare. With the increasing awareness of our interconnected existence and the increasing spirituality in the world, *human welfare* could be replaced with the *welfare of all beings*. Rather than a code of conduct in a particular society or group, moral principles, values, and ways of relating to others—and the very essence of morality, human welfare (or the welfare of all beings)—are universal considerations. Ultimately, it is *actions* that are moral or immoral. Principles and values are moral or immoral to the extent that they guide behavior in a moral or immoral direction.

Traditionally, philosophers and moral psychologists such as Kohlberg (1976) have classified actions as moral or immoral as a function of a person's intentions or reasoning about them. But as I wrote in *Overcoming Evil* (Staub, 2011),

> this judgment cannot be based *only or primarily* on the intentions of actors, especially their stated intentions. They themselves may not know what internal psychological or outside forces lead them to their actions, and if they do, what they say may not express their motives but provide justifications for them.... [When people act violently,] they may incorrectly perceive the need for self-defense, or act with unnecessary violence in the name of self-defense. They may be guided by ideals and visions that aim to benefit their group or to improve the world, but have developed the belief that any means are acceptable to serve these ideals. (pp. 32–33)

Reprinted with permission, a brief segment from Staub, E. (2012). The psychology of morality in genocide and violent conflict: perpetrators, passive bystanders, rescuers. In M. Mikulincer & P. Shaver (Eds.), *The social psychology of morality*. Washington, DC: American Psychological Association Press.

Guided by these beliefs, they engage in harmful action against people who have not done or intended to do harm to them.

In light of these considerations, and of others such as the fact that individuals—and societies—change as a result of their own actions, I view judging actions good or evil, moral or immoral, as requiring a consideration of intentions, the nature of the acts, their probable consequences, their actual consequences, the degree of environmental pressure on a person to act, and even their effects on the actors' further behavior. It requires consideration of universal principles (e.g., sanctity of life, justice) and the principles of utilitarianism, the greatest good for the greatest number (Staub, 2011).

Usually, discussions of morality focus on principles or codes of conduct. However, moral action can be the result either of principles, values, and related norms that dictate certain action, or of emotional orientations such as caring about other people and empathizing or sympathizing with them. *Caring* means genuine concern for the welfare of others. It is an outgrowth of feelings of connection to other people and feelings of empathy or sympathy. Emotional orientations such as empathy, sympathy and compassion, and moral principles such as justice or the sanctity of life, can lead to moral action or inhibit immoral action. A person can even help another whom he or she sees in a negative light, guided by principles such as justice, as in the case of some anti-Semitic Christians who rescued Jews during the Holocaust (Oliner & Oliner, 1988). A person can also harm others on the basis of principles, such as punishment for wrongdoing or reciprocity for harm, or refrain from harming others because of empathic feelings.

We can use the word evil when actions that are not self-defense and not a response to extreme provocation create extreme harm. The concept of evil suggests an extreme form of immorality. In an immoral society, where actions that harm people who have themselves done no harm have become normal, as under slavery in the United States, or in Nazi Germany or during the genocide in Cambodia in the late 1970s, for people to act morally they must deviate from the standards or codes of conduct of that society. A leadership group, much of a society (often the population is implicated as they remain passive or support the perpetrators), or a small terrorist group can develop beliefs, values, and practices that normalize violence against all members of another group.

I have referred to genocide as evil because it involves extreme destructiveness (Staub, 1989). By the aforementioned criteria, killing a whole group of people in genocide, which invariably includes killing people who have done no harm, such as young children—against whom no defense is required and against whom violent retaliation, even if one considers that moral, is not appropriate—would always be judged immoral. Group conflict is part of human life. Unfortunately, it can resist resolution, become intractable and violent, and lead to mass killing in which many people are killed indiscriminately.

Even though there are many societal, cultural, and institutional forces at work, the proximal influences leading to genocide or mass killing are psychological. Psychological forces can overwhelm or subvert moral principles and emotions. Both genocide and other mass violence are the outcomes of normal, ordinary psychological processes that come together to create extreme and immoral actions and outcomes. While I do not like Hannah Arendt's (1963) term, "the banality of evil," the *processes* leading to extreme group violence are not extraordinary. They are ordinary psychological and social processes such as identification with a group, scapegoating another group, and creating visions of a better life for one's group, that is, ideologies, that identify some group as an enemy.

As the participants undergo a grim evolution, progressing along a "continuum of destruction" (Staub, 1989), moved by psychological and social forces, moral principles and orientations are subverted. As people respond to these forces, they may undergo a progressive transformation. As the evolution progresses, many of them may not even struggle with the immorality of their thoughts, feelings, and actions (see Chapter 7 and, for a more detailed discussion of the origins of genocide, Chapter 22).

A core influence in people harming others is devaluation, or a negative view of a group and its members. Devaluation is one ways that morality is undermined. We usually only harm people, whether individuals or members of a group, if we see them in a negative light. As we harm them, we justify what we do with increased devaluation. In cases of genocide and mass killing, the victims are greatly devalued (Staub, 1989, 2011). Bandura, Underwood, and Fromson (1975) showed that when people overhear derogatory comments about someone, they punish this person more; when they hear positive comments, they punish less. In the case of the Janjaweed, Arab horseman who attacked Black Africans in Darfur, survivors' reports indicated a relationship between shouting more derogatory comments in the course of their attack and the intensity of violent actions (Hagan & Rymond-Richmond, 2008).

Morality can take a punitive form: people who are bad—who are immoral or who want to harm us—deserve punishment. Justice is an important aspect of morality in every moral system and punishment is an aspect of most moral systems. Just-world thinking (Lerner, 1980) is a kind of morality; it involves the belief that the world is a just place, and its corollary is that to uphold a just world, people who are bad ought to be punished. A group and its members can move from punishing bad actions to punishing those they believe are likely to engage in bad actions and then those whose supposed nature is bad.

We might regard the devaluation of people—a negative judgment of an entire group that is frequently not based on the actual behavior of members of the group and certainly not the behavior of all members—as inherently immoral. It is a cognitive–emotional orientation that diminishes people and is likely to lead to harmful actions. This would also mean that the justification of harmful actions against others, by increased devaluation of them, is also immoral.

A significant aspect of morality is good judgment, a correct or veridical assessment of events, including both what is happening and the meaning of what is happening. Classical Greek philosophers thought that prudence, or good judgment, was one of the major virtues. To be moral requires the ability to assess whether particular claims are true or false. It requires a critical consciousness—not accepting what leaders, the media, or other people say, or even what one's culture teaches, without examining it and judging it for oneself. This is, of course, profoundly demanding. Children simply absorb their culture. Socializers, parents and teachers, only rarely foster the tendency to critically evaluate what the culture teaches. But to be a moral person, one must ask about devaluation: Is what is being said about these people true? Is this view justified, and in the rare cases when it is, what is a reasonable course of action in relation to these people? A society advances morality when it prepares its citizens for such critical examination and good judgment.

References

Arendt, H. (1963). *Eichmann in Jerusalem: A report on the banality of evil*. New York: Viking Press.

Bandura, A., Underwood, B., & Fromson, M. E. (1975). Disinhibition of aggression through diffusion of responsibility and dehumanization of victims. *Journal of Research in Personality, 9*, 253–269. doi:10.1016/0092-6566(75)90001-X

Hagan, J., & Rymond-Richmond, W. (2008). *Darfur and the crime of genocide*. New York: Cambridge University Press.

Kohlberg, L. (1976). Moral stages and moralization: The cognitive developmental approach. In T. Lickona (Ed.), *Moral development and behavior* (pp. 31–53). New York: Holt.

Lerner, M. (1980). *The belief in a just world: A fundamental delusion*. New York: Plenum Press.

Oliner, S. B., & Oliner, P. (1988). *The altruistic personality: Rescuers of Jews in Nazi Europe*. New York: Free Press.

Staub, E. (1989). *The roots of evil: The origins of genocide and other group violence*. New York: Cambridge University Press.

Staub, E. (2011). *Overcoming evil: Genocide, violent conflict, and terrorism*. New York: Oxford University Press.

9

Helping Psychologically Wounded Children Heal

What are some sources of psychological wounds in children? A primary source is physical, sexual, or psychological abuse in their homes, or severe neglect. Bessel van der Kolk wrote in 2009 (p.455) that in the United States, "each year three million children . . . are reported by Child Protective Services for abuse and neglect." Certainly many more are not reported. Physical deprivation is also wounding, especially if others around a child have sufficient food and material goods, while the child is deprived of these. Psychological neglect, the absence of warmth, affection, or interest in a child by parents and other people in his or her environment is intensely wounding, often even more than physical abuse, which can be occasional, while neglect can be constant and pervasive. Being physically or verbally harassed or excluded by peers can also be greatly wounding, especially if it is intense and persistent.

A genocide or other intense violence can lead to severe psychological wounds. Children who have survived such violence had often been in great danger, or actually victimized. This is true of children who survived the Holocaust in hiding or after living in camps such as Auschwitz. In Rwanda the parents or other relatives of many of the Tutsi children who survived were killed. Most children, whether members of the victim or the perpetrator group, witnessed great violence. But even the children who were not alive at the time of a genocide or mass violence can be wounded, as wounded adults raise them in sometimes harsh, sometimes extremely overprotective, sometimes other problematic ways. Children may be affected by the violence they have seen, experienced, and by being raised in families of wounded people. But even children, and adults, who have had no such experiences, can be wounded by "life injuries"—a loved one dying, the closest friend of a child moving away.

Children, human beings in general, are resilient. Most of us manage to function—have jobs and families—in spite of traumatizing and painful experiences. But many people who have had such experiences are emotionally affected. Satisfaction, joy, and

This chapter is a revised and expanded version of a *Psychology Today* blog, published on February 11, 2013. Its original version was prepared for an organization in Rwanda. Some of its content was also presented at a meeting of the International Society for Political Psychology, Lund, Sweden, July 2004.

happiness are challenging to find, and relationships to other people may be far from optimal. Healing can help improve our emotional life, our relationships, and thereby other people's lives around us.

Engagement with painful experience as an avenue to healing. For most people it is useful to engage with rather than avoid memories of such experiences. Since a central element of trauma is the inability to control what happens to oneself, this ought to happen under conditions that allow a person to control the degree and speed of engagement with painful experience (Saakvitne et al., 2000), and with support by and in connection to people who offer acknowledgment of suffering and empathy. This is what happens in good therapies. But this can also happen person to person, in interactions between people in everyday life. In our educational radio drama in Rwanda we have provided examples of how people can support traumatized persons by empathic listening (see Staub, 2011, and Chapter 19). That, by itself, can contribute to healing.

Engagement with experience can also happen in schools. Children can be exposed to stories that describe experiences that are less intense, and possibly somewhat removed, from the traumatizing experiences they have had. Reading such stories, talking about them, writing about them, together empathically examining the experience of the characters in them, can contribute to healing. Later students may initiate stories of their own. While teachers can grant students choice and control—over the topics they write about and the extent and ways they talk about the stories they read or write—they can also provide safety by initially guiding them away from intense, traumatizing content. Over time they can help them create stories of hope.

Young children can enact experiences following the long-standing practice of play therapy, with materials to draw and play with. The specifics of practices should be appropriate for the age and developmental level of children. It should also be appropriate for the culture—of a country or particular community. Teachers require some training for these practices, especially in supporting and helping to modulates feelings that arise.

It is widely recognized that healing is advanced when people can make meaning out of their suffering. Creating a story that describes one's experience, and to the extent possible makes sense of and creates meaning out of it, helps with healing (Pennebaker, 2000). But how can one create meaning out of horrendous events, like abuse in one's own home or genocide? Or even out of being persistently bullied, persecuted by other children?

Some meaning can come from understanding the roots of violence, the influences that lead to it. Working with adults in Rwanda, my associates and I found that helping people develop such understanding was highly beneficial (Staub, 2011; also Chapters 18 and 19). Providing information about the origins and impact of genocide, and having participants apply such information to their own experience of the genocide there, led to more positive attitudes by members of the former victim and perpetrators groups toward each other, fewer trauma symptoms, and other benefits. Understanding can benefit even young children, for example, that children and adults can learn to think badly of others they don't even know, which can lead to harmful actions.

One way to derive meaning from suffering is through commitment to help prevent others' suffering. Learning how to be an active bystander who stops the bullying of a peer, for example, is both meaningful and empowering (see Chapter 16). Altruism evolving out of past suffering is itself an avenue to healing (see Chapters 10, 11).

Affectionate human connections are an essential source of healing. A primary source of healing for people is good relationships—in the case of children with parents, teachers, and peers. Trauma diminishes people, makes the world seem dangerous, and creates vulnerability and mistrust. It tends to create disconnection from other people. Research on resilience in children and adults who come from difficult environments or have had intensely painful experiences but function well in spite of this shows that they often had loving and supportive people in their lives (Masten, 2001; Staub & Vollhardt, 2008—see Chapter 10).

Warmth and affection are core elements of raising caring and not-violent children. They can transform experiences that otherwise might lead to aggressiveness, withdrawal, or ineffectiveness. Research by Harry Harlow and his associates (e.g. Suomi & Harlow, 1972) has shown that monkeys who have been isolated from others in the first six months of their lives were very disruptive in their social and sexual behavior. They were greatly helped by affectionate body contact, after they were put together with infant monkeys who embraced them and clung to them. Socially ineffective children were also helped by being paired with younger children (Furman, Rahe, & Hartup, 1979).

Warm, affectionate relations between parents and children, and between teachers and students in schools, can help heal wounds. Classrooms in which students have positive connections with each other provide healing. According to Anna Freud (Freud & Dann, 1951), the capacity of very young children who survived together in Auschwitz, who were initially wild and uncooperative with adults, to develop normal relationships was due to their deep connection to each other. This maintained their humanity. Love, affection, and positive connections to other people help previously wounded children (and adults) see the world as at least potentially benevolent. To be consistently loving with wounded people who may enact their woundedness in a variety of ways can be challenging. But consistent connections to other people can rebuild security, develop feelings of effectiveness and power to exercise control over important events in one's life, and over time can lead to an understanding of reality that is primarily positive rather than scary.

References

Freud, A., & Dann, S. (1951). An experiment in group upbringing. *The Psychoanalytic Study of the Child, 6*, 127–168.

Furman, W., Rahe, D. F., & Hartup, W. W. (1979). Rehabilitation of socially withdrawn children though mixed age and same age socialization. *Child Development, 50*, 915–922.

Masten, A. S. (2001). Ordinary magic: Resilience processes in development. *American Psychologist, 59*, 227–238.

Pennebaker, J. W. (2000). The effects of traumatic disclosure on physical and mental health: The values of writing and talking about upsetting events, In J. M. Violanti, D. Paton, & C. Dunning (Eds.), *Posttraumatic stress intervention* (pp. 97–114). Springfield, IL: Charles Thomas.

Saakvitne, K. W., Gamble, S. G., Pearlman, L. A., & Lev, B. T. (2000). *Risking connection: A training curriculum for working with survivors of childhood abuse.* Lutherville, MD: Sidran Press.

Staub, E. (2011). *Overcoming evil: Genocide, violent conflict and terrorism.* New York: Oxford University Press.

Staub, E., & Vollhardt, J. (2008). Altruism born of suffering: The roots of caring and helping after experiences of personal and political victimization. *American Journal of Orthopsychiatry, 78,* 267–280.

Suomi, S. J., & Harlow, H. F. (1972). Social rehabilitation of isolation-reared monkeys. *Developmental Psychology, 6,* 487–496.

Van der Kolk, B. A. (2009). Afterword. In C. A. Curtois & J. D. Ford (Eds.), *Treating complex traumatic stress disorders* (pp. 455–466). New York: Guilford.

10

Altruism Born of Suffering

The Roots of Caring and Helping After Victimization and Other Trauma

ERVIN STAUB AND JOHANNA VOLLHARDT

Experiencing violence often shakes the very foundations of a person's beliefs and can create, in individuals and whole communities, a sense of living in a meaningless and threatening world. Many individuals (and groups), feeling vulnerable and seeing other people as dangerous, become hostile and aggressive. Others show difficulties in functioning, or mental health problems. Yet some who have suffered from violence reclaim meaning and turn towards others, becoming caring and helpful, a phenomenon that has been referred to as *altruism born of suffering* (ABS) (Staub, 2003, 2005). In this article we will discuss this phenomenon with a focus on experiences and related psychological processes that bring about changes that may transform past suffering into altruism.

Over the past 40 years, a substantial body of research on helping behavior and altruism has focused almost exclusively on the positive roots of prosocial feelings, values, and actions. This research has examined how a loving, supportive environment and positive guidance can lead to personal characteristics and psychological processes that give rise to helping (e.g. Eisenberg, Fabes & Spinrad, 2006; Staub, 1979, 2005; see Chapter 3). Conversely, research on the effects of trauma and victimization has until recently focused on the enduring negative consequences of such experiences. Studies with victims of physical or sexual abuse, and of ethno-political violence have shown that these experiences often give rise to violent behavior, withdrawal, social maladjustment, and a host of clinical problems such as depression and post-traumatic stress disorder (Gilligan, 1996; Herman, 1992; McCann & Pearlman, 1990; Widom, 1989).

Reprinted with permission and minor revisions from Staub, E., & Vollhardt, J. (2008). Altruism born of suffering: The roots of caring and helping after experiences of personal and political victimization. *American Journal of Orthopsychiatry, 78*, 267–280.

In actuality, however, only a relatively small percentage of those who have had traumatic experiences as individuals (in contrast to members of victimized groups) develop PTSD or other severe symptoms of trauma (Bonanno, 2004; Tedeschi, 1999). Moreover, theory and research has also come to focus on resilience after trauma, and on post-traumatic growth (PTG). This literature also mentions empathy and altruism as potential growth outcomes (see Tedeschi, Park, & Calhoun, 1998). The concept of an alternative "survivor mission" has also been proposed, referring to a deep commitment by victims of violence to prevent future suffering (Lifton, 1967, 2003). Moreover, case studies (O'Connell Higgins, 1994), autobiographical writings (Noble & Coram, 1994), the history of important public figures including Nobel Peace Laureates Eli Wiesel and the Dalia Lama, anecdotal evidence (e.g., letters from some of the over 7,000 people who have completed a questionnaire on "Values and Helping" published by the magazine *Psychology Today*—Staub, 1989b, 2003), as well as limited empirical evidence that we review here indicate that some people who have suffered do act in caring, loving, altruistic ways. In letters responding to the "Values and Helping" questionnaire, some people specifically noted that they want to help others because of the suffering they had endured.

People suffer for many reasons. Some suffering is simply part of life, such as grief due to the death of loved ones, or harm caused by natural disasters. Other suffering is the result of human agency, but without the intention to cause harm and without harm doers being blameworthy, such as in many divorces and car accidents. However, often suffering is the result of intentional human acts. People are victimized by rape or physical assault. Many children are persistently victimized in their families, through physical and emotional neglect or acts that create physical, sexual, or emotional harm. Many people are also greatly victimized as members of identity groups that become the target of devaluation, discrimination, persecution, and violence, including extreme violence such as genocide.

While we are concerned with altruism arising out of the whole range of human suffering, we will focus especially on altruism following persistent, intentional victimization. This is because even when it does not lead to significant trauma symptoms, intentional victimization is likely to create psychological wounds and transformations that turn people away from, and at times against others. It is likely to make people feel diminished and vulnerable, and to see other people and the world as dangerous. This can lead them to perceive others' actions as threatening or hostile, and to respond with "defensive violence," even when aggressive self-defense is unnecessary (Dodge, 1993; Staub, 1998, 2011; Staub & Pearlman, 2006). Victims then become perpetrators, and a cycle of violence and revenge can evolve (Mamdani, 2002), especially as people's violent actions lead to changes in them and increase the likelihood that they commit further violence (Rhodes, 1999; Staub, 1989a). This distinction between the impact of victimization and other types of suffering is also supported, for example, by research in which "childhood sexual abuse, childhood physical abuse, adult physical abuse, and domestic violence were all significant predictors of child abuse potential in adult caregivers. . . . On the other hand, exposure to disasters, experiencing motor vehicle accidents, and the death of a loved one were not significant predictors of child physical abuse potential. . . ." (Craig & Sprang, 2007, p. 302).

Many people around the world endure persistent harm-doing and violence. If a large percentage of them developed in the way described here, we would have to despair for the future of humanity. Our interest in understanding the development of altruism born of suffering arose from our concern with reducing violence. The psychological processes that give rise to altruism tend to make aggression less likely (Feshbach & Feshbach, 1969; Spielman & Staub, 2000; Staub, 2003). Moreover, through ABS, trauma can be transformed not only into a personal asset, but into a community asset (see Bloom, 1998). Thus, developing theory and research on altruism born of suffering will not only expand our knowledge about the roots of altruism, and contribute to the understanding of resilience and post-traumatic growth. It can also lead to practices and interventions that promote altruism born of suffering, and thereby reduce violence between individuals and groups while enhancing caring, helping others in need and harmonious relations. The article aims to address the following questions:

(1) What are the *experiences,* and the resulting psychological *changes,* through which people who have suffered, especially from significant victimization, may come to care about and help others?
(2) How might altruism born of suffering (ABS) be promoted?
(3) What are the limitations of previous research, and what kind of future research is needed to study ABS?

To answer these questions we draw on research in clinical psychology, especially on resilience and post-traumatic growth, research in developmental and social psychology on helping behavior, and on work in postconflict settings with survivors of mass victimization (particularly in Rwanda: Staub, 2006; Staub & Pearlman, 2006; Staub, Pearlman, Gubin & Hagengimana, 2005). In the first part of this article, we discuss the concepts of trauma, resilience, post-traumatic growth, provide a brief characterization of the research on these topics, and differentiate and define the concept of ABS. We then review the relevant evidence about prosocial behavior both at the time of and in the aftermath of suffering, which provides empirical support of the ABS concept.

In the second part of the article we discuss what is likely to promote ABS. This includes: (a) experiences that promote a positive cognitive and emotional orientation to self and others (healing after suffering, which includes truth and justice processes; understanding the origins of the perpetrator's actions); (b) the supportive and guiding influence of others (help received at the time of victimization; support and loving connections; altruistic role models); (c) the individual's own actions (taking action in one's own or others' behalf in the face of victimization; and helping others in the aftermath, which may become an avenue to personal change); and (d) psychological processes that presumably arise from these experiences and give rise to ABS, such as increased awareness of suffering, empathy, perceived similarity and identification with other victims, and a greater sense of responsibility to prevent their suffering. The issue of methods and future research are discussed in both parts of the article and summarized in the conclusion.

Trauma, Resilience, Post-Traumatic Growth, and Altruism Born of Suffering

The Negative Impact of Family and Political Violence

There is a large body of research and clinical literature detailing the negative impact of trauma. Its effects are well documented and include PTSD, probably the most commonly studied effect (see *Diagnostic and Statistical Manual of Mental Disorders*, fourth edition; American Psychiatric Association, 1994), a defensive, fearful stance toward the world (McCann & Pearlman, 1990), and negative views of the self as helpless and unworthy (Herman, 1992; Janoff-Bulman, 1992). When people are the objects of harm-doing, normal human assumptions that the world is benevolent and meaningful are shattered (Janoff-Bulman, 1992). Basic human needs for security, connection and trust, positive identity, comprehension of reality, and feelings of effectiveness and control are deeply frustrated (McCann & Pearlman, 1990; Pearlman & Saakvitne, 1995; Staub, 1998, 2003). Particularly in human-induced trauma, there can be an overriding feeling of betrayal, a sense of abandonment, and a view of people as malevolent and the world as a dangerous place (Dodge, 1993; Martens, 2005).

Consequently, having been the target of harmful actions often leads to the need for defense, and also to hostility, and can motivate revenge. Thus, past victimization can fuel violence (Dodge, Bates, & Pettit, 1990; Staub, 1989a), whether people have been victimized as individuals or as group members. Even the experience of ostracism often leads to aggression and decreased prosocial behavior (Twenge & Baumeister, 2005). Most school shooters in the U.S. had been bullied by peers (Leary, Kowalski, Smith, & Phillips, 2003). Among violent criminals, the great majority had experienced significant victimization (Gilligan, 1996; Rhodes, 1999; Widom, 1989).

The experience of violence can make people more readily perceive later threat (Staub, 2011). Boys who had been harshly treated tended to see actions by others as hostile when their peers did not, and responded to perceived provocation with aggression (Dodge, 1993). The same appears to be true of people who have experienced discrimination and violence because they are members of an ethnic, religious, political, or other identity group. While varied experiences can mitigate this, in the face of new threats individuals and groups with such past experiences are more likely to engage in preemptive, violent "self-defense", thereby becoming perpetrators. Thus, past victimization appears to be one of the influences that contribute to the evolution of mass violence (Mamdani, 2002; Rouhana & Bar-Tal, 1998; Staub, 1998, 2011; Staub & Pearlman, 2006; Volkan, 1998).

Resilience

However, some individuals who have had adverse and traumatic experiences exhibit "positive adaptation within the context of significant adversity," which has been defined as resilience (Luthar & Cicchetti, 2000; see also Masten, 2001; Masten & Coatsworth, 1998). Research on resilience has identified numerous protective factors that buffer the effects of risk factors

(Christiansen & Evans, 2005) and enable the development of "behaviorally manifested social competence" (Luthar & Cicchetti, 2000). In theoretical writings on resilience, altruism and prosocial behavior are also listed among the proposed characteristics of resilient, socially competent individuals (Charney, 2004; Southwick, Vythilingham, & Charney, 2005).

Three types of protective factors were found to contribute to resilience (e.g. Luthar & Cicchetti, 2000; Werner & Smith, 1992). (1) *Individual characteristics* include high self-esteem, internal locus of control (the belief that one can influence events), self-efficacy, social expressiveness, easy-going temperament, optimism and humor, high problem-solving and learning skills, and good intellectual functioning (see Southwick et al., 2005; Masten & Coatsworth, 1998; Werner & Smith, 1992). Because these characteristics were assessed in individuals who are identified as resilient, some of them may be the result of experiences that promote resilience, rather than pre-existing protective factors. Moreover, in addition to any direct protective influence, some personal characteristics, such as positive temperament, may attract support and create positive experiences during or after traumatic events.

(2) *Family characteristics* promoting resilience include positive parenting practices, characterized by warmth and discipline that uses reasoning (Serbin & Karp, 2004), parental monitoring (Christiansen & Evans, 2005), a close bond with at least one competent care-giver (Rutter, 1990), as well as a family that encourages perspective-taking and empathy (Eisenberg et al., 2006). (3) *Characteristics of the wider social environment,* in particular systems and individuals providing support. They include bonds to prosocial adults outside the family and connections to prosocial organizations (Masten & Coatsworth, 1998; Werner & Smith, 1992), positive peer influence (Werner, 1987), and neighborhood cohesion (Christiansen & Evans, 2005). For example, a single person can help by organizing children for regular soccer games; the Big Brother-Big Sister programs have promoted better functioning in neglected children (Butler, 1997).

These factors may help people cope with adverse events and limit their negative impact (Westphal & Bonanno, 2007). Or they may help transform their meaning and change the negative psychological orientation to self and others that often arises from adverse experiences. However, the definition of resilience is minimalist, focusing on normal functioning and the absence of problems in people at risk for varied reasons, ranging from poverty, to social disorganization and violence. The literature mentions prosocial behavior as a possible, but not as a necessary defining characteristic of resilient individuals. In contrast, central to our concern is *unselfish caring and helping* by individuals who have experienced *substantial suffering*, especially through *victimization*.

Altruism requires a focus beyond the self. It is reasonable to assume that to develop altruism in the context or aftermath of suffering experiences beyond those that foster resilience are necessary. Thus, the experiences we propose as conducive to ABS overlap with, but also extend beyond, those that have been identified as promoting resilience.

Post-Traumatic Growth

As already noted, an emerging field of theory and research has explored personal growth following trauma (see Hobfoll et al., 2007; Linley & Joseph, 2004; Tedeschi et al., 1998). When positive changes occur, they tend to go together with negative effects of traumatic experience—which is likely to be also true of altruism born of suffering. Seemingly guided by the view that the rebuilding of disrupted schemas is essential to healing from trauma (Janoff-Bulman, 1992; Tedeschi, 1999), the research on post-traumatic growth (PTG) has focused on cognitive changes, or changes in thinking, especially in three domains: perception of self, relationship to others, and philosophy of life (Tedeschi & Calhoun, 1995, Tedeschi et al., 1998).

Post trauma growth is assumed to depend not on the nature of the events themselves, but on how people appraise or interpret them. The perception of threat to life, an existential struggle surrounding the events, and their assessment that creates meaning—of experiences that appear meaningless (Herman, 1992; Pearlman & Saakvitne, 1995; Pennebacker, 2000)—are all assumed essential to post-traumatic growth (Westphal & Bonanno, 2007). Growth-producing assessment has mostly been attributed to personal characteristics similar to those promoting resilience mentioned earlier, such as self-confidence, locus of control, and optimism (Tedeschi, 1999; Woodward & Joseph, 2003). While the role of *experiences* that can transform the meaning of past suffering has not been a focus of attention, researchers have noted the importance of receiving and providing social support. In one interview study, traumatized people reported that experiences such as the role of a caring teacher, working with and helping children, or other connections that made them feel nurtured, liberated or validated, were sources of growth (Woodward & Joseph, 2003).

Among other authors, Tedeschi et al. (1998) have identified compassion and altruism as likely aspects of post-trauma growth:

> when people recognize their own vulnerability, they may be better able to feel
> compassion and that some trauma may be a kind of empathy training. Out of this . . .
> may come a need to help. . . . This is likely to occur after certain time has passed.
> (p. 12f.)

From the research mentioned on aggression after victimization it is apparent, however, that for many people time alone does not lead to compassion and the desire to help others. In this article, we propose that certain experiences that occur after victimization and other trauma, experiences at the time of trauma, as well as experiences preceding trauma, will jointly contribute to the growthful effects we refer to as altruism born of suffering (ABS).

Post-traumatic growth is a relatively new area of research and theory, and there are complexities and inconsistencies in research findings (Westphal & Bonanno, 2007). For example, while the majority of individuals who have experienced stressful life events report positive changes, in one study such self-reports were not correlated with a greater sense of well-being (Frazier & Kaler, 2006). Moreover, in a study of Jews' and Arabs' reactions to violence and terrorism in Israel during the second Intifada, reports of PTG were associated with heightened PTSD (Hobfoll et al., 2007). This relationship was especially strong for people with low self-efficacy. PTG was also associated with greater "ethnocentrism, authoritarianism, and support for extreme political violence" (Hobfoll et al., 2007, p. 352). These researchers suggest that the positive cognitions people report on post-traumatic growth questionnaires may be defensive in nature. However, the ongoing threat and danger during the Intifada may have also contributed to their findings (Butler, 2007; Tedeschi, Calhoun, & Cann, 2007).

Hobfoll et al. (2007) also suggest that genuine growth only occurs when cognitive changes are transformed into action. They studied Israeli settlers in Gaza who, presumably guided by their beliefs, chose to stay and oppose their evacuation when the settlements were demolished. In their case, higher levels of PTG were associated with reduced PTSD symptoms. It is possible that *choosing* to face adversity, and the strong beliefs that motivated this choice, jointly promoted PTG and lessened PTSD. Thus, motivations, the actions they give rise to, and the meanings attached to them may all be crucial in determining whether growthful outcomes arise from seemingly stressful and potentially dangerous experiences. Limited actions that can have positive psychological meaning are often possible even under overwhelming conditions. For example, in German extermination camps slave laborers could help others through small acts, and at the very least it helped them maintain their feeling of dignity (Frankl, 1984; Kahana, Kahana, Harel, & Segal, 1985).

In contexts where action is not possible, the way we interpret and assign meaning to events can be of profound significance by itself (Tedeschi et al., 2007). However, it is important to note that while, for example, empathy may change a person's psychological experience of events and also make aggressive behavior less likely, it has a quite different meaning (and impact) than helpful action. Action may often be a hallmark of true change as well as promote further change as individuals learn by doing (Eisenberg et al., 2006; Staub, 1979, 1989a).

Conceptual Explorations: Resilience, Post-Traumatic Growth, and Altruism Born of Suffering

While altruism born of suffering overlaps with resilience and PTG, we regard it as an important concept and domain of theory and research in its own right. It is distinctive with regard to at least three foci: its focus on *victimization* (i.e., intentional harm-doing), on the *prevention of violence*, and on the generation of positive psychological changes that lead to helpful *action*. The extent to which resilient individuals exhibit ABS has not been examined in the literature; neither has the question whether those who do exhibit ABS have had experiences different from people who do not. PTG theory and research, while noting the importance of social support, has focused on personal characteristics that lead to interpretations that bring about positive cognitive changes after traumatic events. In this article we emphasize certain social *experiences* as a source of ABS; these may also be important to promote PTG.

Thus, our theoretical focus is on experiences after, during, and to some degree before suffering that foster the psychological orientations which, under appropriate eliciting conditions, give rise to altruism. This involves change in the orientations to self (Karylowski, 1976) and others (Staub, 2003) that tend to result from victimization. We are concerned with two types of changes. First, people who have been victimized must come to see other human beings in a positive light, so that what happens to them matters. They also have to experience the self as strong enough so that attention and care can shift from the self to others in need; and they must feel empowered enough to act on others' behalf. These processes are likely preconditions for a second type of change, namely increased perspective-taking and empathy (Eisenberg & Miller, 1987; Eisenberg et al., 2006) and an increase in "prosocial value orientation" (Staub, 1978, 2003, 2005; see also Feinberg, 1978; Spielman & Staub, 2000). These are important sources of the motivation to act in others' behalf.

In considering altruism born of suffering it is reasonable to distinguish conceptually between preexisting altruism that is *maintained in spite of suffering* and altruism that *arises* after suffering. This is a meaningful but empirically difficult distinction. Certain experiences preceding victimization, such as nurturant caretaking and positive human connections, may both contribute to the initial development of altruism, and protect people from pervasive psychological after effects of victimization, thereby helping to maintain altruism. However, instead of being maintained through these protective factors, preexisting altruism may also be renewed or recreated as a result of the experiences—during or subsequent to victimization—that we propose as contributors to ABS. To assess altruism in spite of suffering requires researchers to document altruism preceding the suffering, through information gathered from people in a person's life space. To understand how altruism is maintained or renewed, researchers might compare individuals who have experienced similar traumatic events and had been altruistic before, but differ in post-trauma altruism. Do they also differ in the extent to which they had experiences that we propose might contribute to both the renewal and generation of altruism?

Empirical Support for Altruism Born of Suffering

Research on altruism born of suffering is difficult to conduct, because suffering cannot be experimentally imposed in order to study its effects. It is also difficult to plan longitudinal studies comparing behavior before and after suffering, since suffering cannot be easily predicted. When it can be, the focus has to be on prevention. Nevertheless, we will suggest some ways to study temporal changes in individuals who are undergoing significant adversity. In addition to the inherent limitations of conducting research on this phenomenon, a fair number of relevant studies have additional methodological limitations, partly because most of the research was not explicitly designed to examine altruism born of suffering. Thus, the relevant findings we review were often incidental in research addressing other questions.

A good number of the studies are correlational, lack control groups, and have small sample sizes. Even in more systematic studies, the data are often self-reports of past events and experiences. Nonetheless, this body of research helps to identify some of the dimensions of this important phenomenon and provides encouraging initial support. We will highlight it when the methodology give studies more credibility, and propose research questions and methodologies for future research, especially in the course of evaluating interventions to promote ABS.

One group of studies demonstrates helping behavior at the time of and in response to adverse conditions, including both natural disasters and human-induced suffering. Although our primary concern is altruism in the aftermath of suffering, these studies are relevant because one of the experiences we propose as promoting ABS is helping oneself or others at the time of suffering. Research on "learning by doing" (see later section) demonstrates that people who have helped under situational influences are subsequently more likely to help. We also review another group of studies that shows helping *after* victimization and suffering. This body of research demonstrates the phenomenon of ABS, but lacks information about experiences that may have promoted it. We then focus on the experiences we consider important to promote ABS, along with the resulting psychological changes we expect, and review relevant research.

Altruism and Prosocial Behavior at the Time of Suffering
Human-caused suffering

Several studies have documented how human beings who are undergoing harm inflicted by others, such as genocide, war, or terrorist attacks, exhibit helpful behavior. In interviews, Holocaust survivors reported that "helping was a prevalent, potent, and essential aspect of the experience of survivors, one which emerged as a necessary condition of their survival" (Kahana et al., 1985, p. 363). Among a sample of 100 Holocaust survivors, 82% reported that they had helped other prisoners in concentration camps. They reported sharing food and clothing and providing emotional support, a large majority describing their motive as altruistic (Kahana et al., 1985). In a large interview study of civilians from 12 war-torn countries, although the researchers did not ask about helping behavior, a content analysis of the interviews revealed many reports of altruistic and prosocial behavior, even towards members of the enemy group (Leaning & Briton, 2004). The motivations respondents described were classified as group affiliation, perceived self-efficacy, the hope for reciprocity, and the desire to maintain moral identity in war.

Natural disasters and other non-human caused suffering

"Increased compassion" was reported as a frequent growth outcome among those who have experienced a spinal-cord injury (McMillen & Cook, 2003), or other illnesses or bereavement (McMillen & Fisher, 1998). In these studies, the data consists of self-reported feelings, not actions. High levels of altruism and prosocial behavior have also been documented at times of natural disasters. Some scholars have written about the emergence of an "altruistic community" in the aftermath of hurricanes, floods, or earthquakes, characterized by "higher than usual levels of solidarity, fellowship, and altruism" (Kaniasty & Norris 1995a, p. 94). A structured interview study with a sample of 500 victims of Hurricane Hugo, and an equally large control group, found that victims reported more prosocial behavior than non-victims, in particular tangible support (Kaniasty & Norris, 1995b).

The research we reviewed on helping at the time of suffering has not assessed whether long term changes follow from people helping others, or from experiencing mutual help. However, given that people helped at a time when their own need might have led them to focus on themselves, and that helpful actions tend to increase later helping (Eisenberg et al., 2006; Staub, 1979, 2003), it is likely that their actions would promote their later altruism.

Altruism and Prosocial Behavior
in the Aftermath of Victimization

Because the studies in this section provide information about altruism after victimization, and because their methodologies include control groups or a longitudinal design, they provide a stronger basis for the interpretation that they demonstrate altruism born of suffering. While some studies assess motivation, often it is on the basis of post-hoc self-reports.

Studies with control groups

Control groups make it possible to compare the extent to which previously victimized and non-victimized people help. In a correlational, cross-sectional study, undergraduate students in the United States were asked about their own past victimization and suffering. Those who reported that they had suffered from interpersonal violence, group-based violence, or a natural disaster reported significantly more feelings of empathy for, as well as personal responsibility to help victims of the tsunami in South East Asia than a control group of students who reported no such suffering (Vollhardt & Staub, 2011, Study 2). They also volunteered to help more, by signing up to join a tsunami relief group and collect money.

That the average helping by those who suffered in varied ways was greater than by those who have not suffered suggests that ABS may be more common than would be expected on the basis of the literature on victimization and its effects. In another correlational study that examined prosocial behavior in everyday life, students who had suffered from traumatic life events reported significantly more often than their peers who had not suffered that they participate in volunteer activities. The activities they participated in more tended to involve direct contact with others in need (elderly, sick, disabled, homeless; Vollhardt & Staub, 2011, Study 2).

A structured interview study (Macksoud & Aber, 1996) explored the psychological adaptation of a sample of 224 Lebanese children, age 10 to 16, who had been directly affected by violence. They had been separated from parents, witnessed the intimidation of family members by militia forces, or had seen community members killed or injured. Contrary to the authors' expectations, these children scored higher on a self-report measure of prosocial behavior than children in a control group not directly affected by the violence.

Longitudinal studies

The assessment of change in altruistic attitudes or behaviors from before to after suffering is important as evidence of altruism born of suffering. It is rare, however, that such information is available. In a study that was started prior to the war in the early 1990s in Croatia, teachers rated 5- and 6-year old children higher on a measure of prosocial behaviors (e.g., sharing sweets and toys or feeling sorry for other children in need) after a period in which the city was heavily targeted by air-raids, compared to before the war (Raboteg-Šaric, Žužul, & Keresteš, 1994). In contrast, ratings of aggressive behavior had not changed. The researchers also included a group to control for possible changes with age alone.

Explicit measures of motivation

Survivors of a terrorist attack in Israel reported that in their life after the attacks, "help[ing] those who feel pain like I do" (Kleinman, 1989, p. 53) reduced their survivor guilt and gave them new meaning in life. A number of studies have suggested a relationship between helping and past experiences of ostracism and social rejection. This has been referred to as "positive marginality" (Unger, 2000) and was found in interview studies with people working in organizations benefiting minority groups and refugees (Borshuk, 2004) as well as among rescuers of Jews during the Holocaust (London, 1970; Tec, 2003). In some of these studies the investigators drew conclusions about the relationship between past suffering and the motivation for helping. In others, helpers reported it. These retrospective studies do not, however, establish the actual motives at the time of helping.

Positive correlations between degree of suffering and prosocial behavior

In line with the altruism born of suffering hypothesis, at times of natural disasters greater suffering was associated with more helping of other victims, even when controlling for relevant variables such as group size, life events, race, sex, age, marital status and education. Specifically, greater physical harm, material loss, and perceived life threat were associated with providing more tangible and informational support (Kaniasty & Norris, 1995b). Similarly, among a sample of 416 adults who had experienced various adverse life events, self-reported compassion was higher among participants who reported that they had experienced more upsetting and harmful events (McMillan & Fisher, 1998). In research conducted in the U.S. after 9/11, participants who reported higher stress reactions, that is, suffered more subjectively, also reported donating and volunteering more than those who reported less suffering (Schuster et al., 2001). Similarly, donating and volunteering after 09/11 were predicted by survivor guilt and grief, which can also be viewed as indicators of suffering (Wayment, 2004). These findings are correlational, and we cannot exclude the possibility that they are expressions of personal characteristics, such as greater sensitivity to stressful events and greater disposition for empathy, rather than suffering leading to more caring.

Experiences Promoting Altruism Born of Suffering

In the following, we discuss the conditions and experiences after victimization or other significant suffering that we regard as important in leading people to caring actions (see Figure 10.1), and note some ways to foster ABS. Just as experiencing a greater number of adverse conditions makes later psychological and behavioral problems more likely (e.g. Monroe & Simons, 1991), we assume that the greater the number and extensiveness of positive experiences before, at the time of, and in the aftermath of victimization, the more likely it is that people who have suffered become altruistic. The psychological changes that may result from these experiences include a change from vulnerability, mistrust and the perception of others as dangerous to a stronger sense of self and seeing the world and other human beings in a more positive way. As these changes take place, one's own past suffering can become a source of intense empathy/sympathy for others in need, and of an increased prosocial orientation, a central aspect of which is a feeling of personal responsibility for others' welfare.

Traumatized people differ in the extent to which they have had experiences that foster psychological recovery after the trauma, or in contrast, experiences that exacerbate the

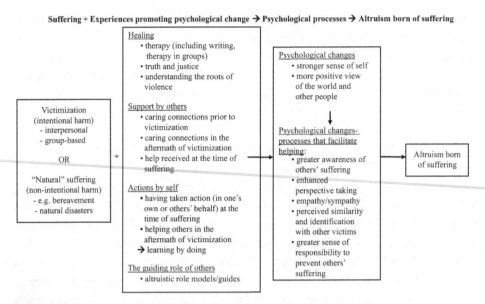

FIGURE 10.1 Experiences and psychological changes leading to altruism born of suffering.

negative impact of suffering. Because of victimization and preceding or subsequent experiences, some people may develop such an intensely defensive stance against a hostile world that they cannot recognize or use opportunities that might result in cognitive and emotional changes and are potentially healing (Martens, 2005; Staub, 2005).

Healing or Psychological Recovery
After Intense Suffering

Healing from trauma is crucial for the development of ABS. It can open people to other ABS-promoting experiences, and lead to actions that further enhance ABS. A number of the ABS-promoting experiences we describe later in the chapter that have other positive functions are also likely to contribute to healing. Among the experiences that can promote healing are therapy (Herman, 1992), including creative writing or writing about painful experiences (Pennebaker, 2000), finding social support and significant human connections (Kishon-Barash, Midlarsky, & Johnson, 1999) and learning about the causes and consequences of violence (Staub, Pearlman, Gubin, & Hagengimana, 2005; Staub & Pearlman, 2006).

While there may be exceptions, such as people who have been referred to as "repressors" (Bonanno, 2004), engaging with memories of painful past experiences rather than avoiding them, and finding or creating meaning in the course of it, has been identified both by therapists (Herman, 1992; Pearlman & Saakvitne, 1995) and researchers (e.g. Janoff-Bulman, 1992; Pennebaker, 2000; Staub et al., 2005) as important aspects of healing. As people engage with their experiences, among other benefits, they can come to believe that they themselves should not have been victimized and that other human beings should not be victimized either. Their painful experiences can acquire meaning by acting to prevent victimization and by helping people who have suffered or are suffering (Herman, 1992; Lifton, 2003; Staub, 2005).

Healing from trauma fosters the fulfillment of basic psychological needs that have been frustrated during periods of suffering. People's feeling of security, their belief in their ability to influence events, their self-concept, their feelings of connections to others, their sense of autonomy and choice, and their comprehension of reality and understanding of their place in the world (Staub, 1989a, 2003; see also Kelman, 1990; Maslow, 1968, Pearlman & Saakvitne, 1995) can all improve. As basic needs are fulfilled, the need for transcendence, that is, the need to focus beyond oneself, may emerge (Staub, 2003, 2005; see also Chapter 4). Promoting others' welfare through altruistic actions may be one way this need can be fulfilled.

Some correlational studies have demonstrated a positive relationship between healing and altruism in traumatized and victimized populations. In a study of 100 Vietnam Veterans, lower PTSD was associated with more altruistic intention to help (Kishon-Barash et al., 1999). In a study of Holocaust survivors, prosocial behavior was among the variables most highly correlated with well-being (Kahana, Harel, & Kahana, 1988).

Possible interventions

Huge numbers of people are victimized throughout the world, many of them through severe repression or mass violence. Even if there were sufficient resources for individual therapy, healing in groups, promoted by shared activities, is likely to be more effective (Herman, 1992), especially when the culture is collectivist and the violence was experienced together with other group members (Staub & Pearlman, 2006). Healing and ABS may also be promoted by having people write about relevant experiences. They may start with emotionally less intense material, such as reading and then writing about other people's painful experiences, and continue at first with their own, less painful experiences. Positive reactions to the writing by others in the group can provide valuable support. People writing in groups and sharing what they have written has been a seemingly effective technique in working with disadvantaged groups (Chandler, 2002). Additional topics can be introduced in a controlled manner, relevant to other experiences that we discuss later, such as fostering understanding, and exposure to altruistic models.

Such interventions would also make systematic study of ABS possible. Control groups can be included of people who have not suffered and of people who have suffered in a comparable way, but have not received the intervention. Moreover, such interventions allow the study of the evolution of altruism born of suffering, of the psychological and behavioral changes over time following the introduction of ABS-promoting experiences. In Rwanda, interventions to promote reconciliation had slightly negative effects in the short run, but significant positive effects in reducing trauma symptoms and creating positive orientation toward the "other" a few months later (Staub et al., 2005).

Truth, justice, and the assumption of responsibility by perpetrators

Truth and justice processes may further contribute to healing after both interpersonal and societal violence. People who have been the object of great harm-doing have a profound need to have their suffering be acknowledged (Byrne, 2004; Staub, 1998, 2006, 2011). Therapists help clients, in part, by empathically listening to their truth. However, perpetrators of serious victimization rarely acknowledge their responsibility (Staub, 2006, 2011). Establishing the truth, for example, as it has occurred through the truth and reconciliation commission in South Africa, even if painful to those who testify about their experiences (Byrne, 2004), contributes to societal reconciliation (Gibson, 2006).

Truth is essential for justice, which is also a central need for victimized people. It helps fulfill survivors' basic needs—for example, for a positive identity as well as security—by showing that what was done to them is not accepted by the world (Proceedings, 2002). An important form of justice is restorative justice, which aims to restore the relationship between victims and perpetrators (Maiese, 2003). In restorative justice processes, the needs of victims are of primary consideration. Victims and perpetrators meet and talk, usually in the presence of people important in their lives. Apology, which acknowledges the victim's suffering and contributes to forgiveness (Strang et al., 2007), is frequent. Accordingly, participation in a restorative justice program has been found to improve psychological and physical health of victims as well as perpetrators (Rugge, 2007). Participation in various restorative justice programs was associated with substantially less fear and anger by victims, and more sympathy for perpetrators in comparison to control subjects (Strang et al., 2007). By contributing to healing, promoting a more positive attitude toward perpetrators, and helping victimized people begin to let go of anger, restorative justice programs are likely to both strengthen the self and create a more positive attitude toward human beings in general, thereby promoting ABS.

Understanding the roots of one's suffering

Both case studies of individuals abused in their families (O'Connell Higgins, 1994) and research with genocide survivors (Staub, 2006; Staub et al., 2005) indicate that understanding the influences that have led perpetrators to their actions can promote healing. Such understanding contributes to a sense of meaning (Bloom, 1998) and makes it less likely that people who have suffered become perpetrators. Understanding can be gained, for example, through exploration of the harm doer's history (O'Connell Higgins, 1994) or education about the origins of genocide (Staub et al., 2005).

In Rwanda, fostering both knowledge of the psychological impact of violence and understanding of the influences that lead perpetrators of mass violence to their actions reduced trauma symptoms. It also led to a more positive view of the other group among members of both victim and perpetrator groups, as well as to "conditional forgiveness" (Staub et al., 2005). Discussion of the roots of violence also led to comments such as "so what happened to us was not God's punishment" and that "understanding what led to violence enables us to take action to prevent it." Understanding what led perpetrators to their actions provides comprehension and thereby meaning, creates empowerment, and reinstates a person's feeling of humanity. Moreover, changing the view of perpetrators as simply evil, and differentiating perpetrators from other members of their group, fosters a more positive view of human beings in general (Staub, 2006, 2011; See Chapters 18 and 19). Facilitating such understanding may, therefore, be important for promoting altruism born of suffering after any type of victimization.

Supportive and Guiding Influence of Others

Loving connections and social support
before or after victimization

Early positive experiences that fulfill psychological needs for connection and security may protect individuals from the effects of victimization. Generally, social support, both emotional and tangible support, promotes positive outcomes in the development of youth and protects people from adverse consequences of difficult life events (Benard, 1991; Coie et al., 1993). Accordingly, Werner and Smith (1992) found in a longitudinal study—a study conducted over many years—that early secure attachment was associated with resilience. Victimized, traumatized children receiving support has also been associated with resilience (Rutter, 1987). With regard to prosocial behavior, a study among Croatian children found that positive parenting buffered the negative effects of exposure to war on prosocial behavior (Kerestes, 2006). Thus, social support prior to victimization served a protective function.

Experiencing caring by other people in the aftermath of suffering can also be profoundly important. In a study of Vietnam Veterans who were suffering from PTSD, support received after the war was positively related to helping (Kishon-Barash et al., 1999). In a case study of Israeli survivors of terrorism, participants who reported altruistic actions also indicated that they had received support from others who had suffered, including Holocaust survivors. The participants reported that the other survivors "understood" them like nobody else in their social network (Kleinman, 1989). Some case studies suggest that people who are victimized can even gain significant benefit from relationships with caring others with whom they have only limited contact (O'Connell Higgins, 1994).

Help received at the time of one's suffering

Receiving help or support at the time of one's suffering may reduce feelings of insecurity and vulnerability and help maintain a positive view of human beings. In the previously described study of reactions to the tsunami, participants' reports of help received at the time of their traumatic life experiences were positively correlated with their perceived personal responsibility to help tsunami survivors (Vollhardt & Staub, 2011, Study 1). Similarly, in a qualitative interview study, Holocaust survivors in Israel who actively worked for better treatment of Palestinians reported that they had received help in the course of their survival, in comparison to survivors who were not involved in working for peace (Marsa, 2007). One of the survivors reported that German soldiers allowed her and her family to escape from German-held to Russian-held territory in Poland.

Receiving help at the time of victimization can help maintain a belief in human goodness and the possibility of caring and love. The actions of rescuers who endangered themselves to save the lives of potential genocide victims (see Tec, 2003; Oliner & Oliner, 1988), older siblings endangering themselves to protect younger ones from abusive parents, and even kind acts by neighbors toward children who are badly treated at home may have such effects.

Providing and receiving help can also be a mutual process *during* a traumatic event. For example, a study among victims of natural disasters revealed correlations as high as .71 between providing and receiving help (Kaniasty & Norris, 1995b). People may respond to each other's need guided by reciprocity norms (Gouldner, 1960), by good feelings that result from others' actions, and by the example of others as altruistic role models (see Kaniasty & Norris, 1995b). We would expect their experience of receiving and giving help at a time of great need to contribute to subsequent helping by them.

Altruistic models or guides

When people receive help at the time of victimization, they are exposed to models of helping which can result in identification with helpers, rather than with aggressors, and the imitation of the helpers' actions (see Raboteg-Saric et al., 1994). This is in line with a large body of research, ranging from experiments that show how altruistic models can increase helping (see Eisenberg et al., 2006), to studies of rescuers during the Holocaust who reported the influence humane and prosocial parents had on them (Oliner & Oliner, 1988). By communicating prosocial values and providing knowledge of how to help, the presence of altruistic models before, during, or after an individual's victimization is likely to facilitate the development of altruism born of suffering. Others who have suffered and act altruistically are presumably especially powerful models in the development of ABS.

In addition to real-life models, caring and helpful models can be introduced in stories, as we have proposed earlier. In such stories it is important to indicate the challenges that can be involved in helping. One of them is competence, not only in terms of the ability to perform certain actions, but also in terms of the creativity required to generate responses to challenging situations. Another is the requirement of moral courage, the willingness to act on one's values in the face of potential or actual opposition and danger. People telling the stories of their suffering, and in general children and adults finding their "voice," can contribute to moral courage (Staub, 2005).

Individuals' Own Actions

Having taken action in one's own or others' behalf at the time of suffering

People who have been able to take effective action to help themselves or others at the time of their victimization may feel empowered to take action on behalf of others in the future. In case studies, combat soldiers and psychiatric patients reported that help they performed in response to requirements of a situation ("required helpfulness"), and under danger, improved their perceived competence to help (Rachman, 1979). Helping others is also likely to result in a perception of oneself as helpful, increase caring for the people one has helped, and over time generalize to other people in need (Eisenberg et al., 2006; Staub, 1979, 1989a).

The Holocaust survivors who were peace activists in Israel reported, in comparison to non-activists, not only that they received help, but also that they and their families had taken significant actions to help them survive (Marsa, 2007). In a case described by O'Connor Higgins (1994), a girl abused by her mother tried to protect her younger siblings from abuse, and was later cared for by nuns. The combination of having been helped, and having helped oneself or others, may be especially powerful in preparing the psychological ground for altruism born of suffering.

Helping as an avenue to healing and personal or societal change

As we have noted, one of the ways to derive meaning from suffering is to help others. Engaging in altruistic acts can also help restore shattered assumptions about the benevolence of the world, as well as about the value and worthiness of the self (Janoff-Bulman, 1992). Helping others increases self-efficacy (Midlarsky, 1991) and fulfills the need both for effectiveness and positive connection. Helping has been described in the literature as an effective coping mechanism (Midlarsky, 1991) and a possible pathway to healing (Tedeschi et al., 1998). We assume that some prior healing and other experiences we have described create the initial ability and motivation to help others.

The literature provides some examples of this positive relation between altruism and healing. For example, Hernandez (2001, 2002) interviewed eight Colombians who had been significantly affected by political violence. Their way of making sense of their experience included working with other victims of political violence. Their active engagement helped them connect to the community, rebuild personal identity, and heal the wounds of trauma. Thus, actions that contribute to personal healing may also foster positive social change. Bloom (1997, 1998) describes many ways in which trauma is transformed in a social context, both through individual relationships and actions, as well as group actions. These include education, self-help groups, witnessing and seeking justice, political action and rescue, many of which contribute to both personal and societal change.

The potential of altruism to contribute to healing has also been utilized in therapeutic intervention programs both with people who had traumatic experiences, such as Vietnam Veterans (Johnson, Feldman, Southwick, & Charney, 1991; Kishon-Barash et al., 1999), torture victims (Mollica, 2004), survivors of the Cambodian genocide (Mollica, Cui, McInnes, & Massagli, 2002), children who had been exposed to community violence (Errante, 1997), as well as at-risk youth (Canale & Beckley, 1999). These structured and guided opportunities to help others are not only likely to promote healing, but also to further altruism and prosocial behavior through "learning by doing" (Eisenberg et al., 2006; Staub, 1979) that results in increased self-efficacy and competence, a changed self-concept as someone who helps, and increased concern for people in need.

The Psychological Effects of ABS Promoting Experiences

Along with experiences expected to promote ABS, we have discussed psychological changes expected to result from these experiences involving, briefly stated, a more positive sense of self and view of others. We will now focus on psychological changes that may increase the motivation to help in the aftermath of victimization (see also Figure 10.1).

Greater salience and awareness of suffering

In order for individuals to become motivated to help, the need of others must be noticed and interpreted as requiring help (Latane & Darley, 1970). Because of their experience with and presumably sensitivity to situations of need, individuals who have suffered themselves may become more easily aware of the suffering of other people. Accordingly, people who had suffered from traumatic life events were more aware of the news about the tsunami, which in turn contributed to the positive relation between suffering and the perceived responsibility to help tsunami victims (Vollhardt & Staub, 2011, Study 2). In another example, children of manic-depressive parents were found to be more sensitive to parents' facial expressions of distress than a control group of children with healthy parents. The authors describe this as a "preoccupation . . . with the suffering of others" (Zahn-Waxler, Cummings, McKnew, & Radke-Yarrow, 1984, p. 112).While these children were not directly victimized, they were exposed to suffering and presumably unpredictable adults, and may have lacked reliable caretaking. Their sensitivity to distress cues may indicate empathy, or a tendency for personal distress (see later section), or may be defensiveness.

Increased perspective-taking, empathy, and sympathy

Taking the role or perspective of another person can lead to feelings of empathy and sympathy with those who suffer or need help (Batson & Oleson, 1991; Eisenberg, 1992; Eisenberg et al., 2006; Staub, 1979). One's own experiences of suffering can lead to a greater ability to understand how people who have suffered would feel. For example, women who had experienced rape reported more empathy with other rape victims—who were shown on videos— than women without these experiences did (Barnett, Tetreault, Esper, & Bristow, 1986). However, no differences were observed in empathy for people with other problems (Barnett, Tetreauld, & Masbad, 1987). Likewise, people who had experienced traumatic life events were more likely to spontaneously express empathy with tsunami victims than those who had not suffered (Vollhardt & Staub, 2011, Study 2). Empathy also mediated the relationship between suffering and perceived responsibility to help, whereas personal distress did not (see later discussion about the relation between personal distress and empathy).

Perceived similarity and identification with other victims. Perceptions of common fate lead to increased helping behavior, especially in high-stress situations (Dovidio & Morris, 1975). We therefore expect that individuals who have suffered, and had some of the proposed facilitating experiences, will tend to perceive similarity to and identify with others in need. The perception of similarity, and of a superordinate (shared) group membership increase the probability of helping (Dovidio et al., 1997). Identification with others who have suffered is one possible mechanism of altruism born of suffering. Civilians in war-torn countries reported that shared group affiliation, including refugee status, was one of their motivations to help outgroup members during the war (Leaning & Briton, 2004). The awareness of shared victimization across group lines is a particularly important process in explaining the rare, but very important, occurrences of altruism born of suffering that also benefits outgroup members (Vollhardt, 2009).

Greater sense of responsibility for others' suffering

Theory and research have indicated that perceived responsibility for others' welfare makes helping more likely (Berkowitz & Lutterman, 1968; Latane & Darley, 1970; Staub, 1978, 2003). Experiences of victimization combined with the positive and corrective experiences we have described are likely to lead to an increased feeling of responsibility to alleviate or prevent others' suffering (see also Lifton, 2003). This view is supported by the finding that people who had suffered felt more responsibility to help tsunami victims (Vollhardt & Staub, 2011, Study 2).

Discussion and Conclusions

We have proposed that a number of conditions and experiences may promote the development of altruism after experiences of intense suffering (see Figure 10.1). These positive experiences include *healing; establishing truth and justice* and *understanding the influences* that led to the actions of harm doers, both of which foster healing; *significant connections* to and *care and support* by people before and after victimization; *altruistic models and guides; help and support by bystanders* at the time of suffering; people having effectively *helped themselves or others at the time of victimization*; and once they are prepared for this by some of these experiences, *helping to prevent others' victimization or helping in its aftermath*. While we have referred to the effects of such experiences as transformational, given the significant impact of victimization and trauma the transformation they bring about is likely to be progressive and cumulative.

The concept of altruism points to action motivated by caring and the unselfish desire to benefit others (Batson, 1991; Leeds, 1963). Altruistic action can result in good feelings for the actor, but this is a byproduct, not the primary motivation for action. However, little of the research we have reviewed explicitly examined the motivation involved in helping. Helping can be self-focused, motivated by moral norms that make a person feel obligated to help and an associated desire to feel good about oneself, or by wanting to gain benefits through reciprocation or social approval (Staub, 1978).

People who have suffered may develop varied motives for helping. We have focused on altruism, because it is the most stable motivation for helping. Reciprocity or social approval motivate helping primarily when benefits to the self can be expected (but see Chapter 2 for a discussion of generalized reciprocity and enlightened self-interest). While establishing motivation is difficult, relating personal dispositions such as empathy and prosocial orientation to helping (Staub, 1978, 2005), and measuring psychological states at the time of helping (Batson, 1991), are useful in inferring motives.

The proximal influences and motivations for helping by people who have suffered, such as awareness of others' need, perspective taking, empathy and prosocial value orientation might be the same as in the case of altruism that develops through positive socialization. However, once the psychological changes take place that we suggest are necessary to shift from a defensive orientation to concern about others, a person's own suffering can become a source of especially pronounced awareness of human suffering, empathy with others in need, and feelings of responsibility for their welfare, resulting in strong commitment to helping. For example, perspective taking leads a person to understand another's state, their thoughts and feelings, but does not inevitably lead to empathy. But perspective taking by people who have suffered may give rise to deeper understanding of someone's actual or potential suffering (Staub, 1979), and in turn to empathy or sympathy as well as feelings of personal responsibility that enhance helping.

But will the motivation to help be inclusive, extending to people who have suffered in varied ways or have varied needs, as well as to outgroup members? We have so far limited findings on this point. In the study of responses to the victims of tsunami, both people who had experienced natural disasters and those who had suffered from interpersonal or group-based victimization were more empathic, felt more responsible, and volunteered more frequently to help members of groups living in a different part of the world, compared to people who had not suffered. Israeli Holocaust survivors engaged in behavior aimed at helping Palestinians. However, in another study, rape victims were more empathic than control subjects only with other rape victims, and not with people who had different problems.

These findings leave open the question, and require further research about to what extent and under what conditions will altruism born of suffering be inclusive, extending to people who have suffered in different ways, and who belong to different groups. Most past research did not specify whether help was directed at ingroup or outgroup members. It may be that suffering of *similar* kinds may override prior group boundaries and lead to altruism toward outgroup members, and that certain kinds of suffering will result in less generality in altruism than other kinds. An additional issue for future research is how relevant (preexisting) individual characteristics and facilitating experiences combine as sources of ABS. Preexisting characteristics relevant to altruism may affect the inclusiveness of altruism born of suffering.

Victimization and trauma leave significant psychological marks, and when people subsequently help others, the nature of their motivation and action tendencies can sometimes be problematic, to the recipients of help or to the helper. One such motivation to which we alluded is a preoccupation with others' suffering. Belief in one's moral duty to help can be a positive motivator, but may also create distress for the helper, especially if it is not accompanied by genuine caring. A person's history of distress can also lead to false empathy, based on misperception or the assumption of distress on the basis of circumstances, even when there is no actual distress.

Researchers in both social and developmental psychology have also distinguished between empathy and personal distress as motivations of prosocial behavior. The latter looks like empathy, but is a distress reaction to another's distress, rather than the vicarious experience of or a sympathetic reaction to this person's distress. People motivated by personal distress will help when it is the only way to lessen their own distress, but will escape from the situation without helping when that is possible (Batson, 1991).

While personal distress has been studied as a consequence of parental socialization and guidance (Eisenberg et al., 2006), a person's own past suffering is another likely source of personal distress, through memories of painful experiences that are triggered by witnessing others in similar situations. This may result in overarousal and decrease in prosocial behavior (Fabes, Eisenberg, & Eisenbud, 1993; see also Carlson & Miller, 1987). Thus, healing and the increased self-regulation presumably associated with it are both important in determining whether one's past suffering results in personal distress, or empathy and sympathy. The role of empathy, in contrast to personal distress, in altruism born of suffering was also indicated in our study that assessed both and found that after suffering only empathy was associated with greater prosocial orientation (Vollhardt & Staub, 2011, Study 2).

Unhealed wounds of the past may also give rise to destructive motivations that lead to unnecessary, intrusive, or inadequate helping. Some people who have suffered give themselves over to destructive causes or ideological movements which they believe will improve society or the world. What combination of personal characteristics, background, past or current suffering, and experiences after suffering lead to such negative outcomes—rather than 'genuine' and constructive forms of ABS—is important to study.

Throughout the article, we have noted varied directions for further research. Research on interventions to promote ABS provides the best opportunity to establish the causal role of the experiences we proposed. Other important issues that should be addressed in future research include: demonstrating the cognitive and emotional changes that we have proposed as the result of ABS-promoting experiences; exploring similarities and differences in personal dispositions and motivations leading to help as a result of positive socialization versus past suffering; exploring further the surprising findings in some studies that on average people who have suffered help more than people who have not; and studying how the extent and type of trauma (interpersonal versus collective violence, victimization versus naturally occurring traumatizing events, or prolonged exposure versus isolated incidences of violence) affects subsequent caring and altruism.

Developing interventions based on theory, and evaluating them in research can guide parents, teachers, therapists, peers, or people working in post-conflict settings to promote caring, helping, and altruism in people who have suffered. Such interventions could include cognitive elements such as understanding the roots of violence, fostering engagement with and creating meaning of one's experience, and information that increases perceived similarity with other individuals who have suffered. It may also help people who have suffered to realize the extent that many other people have suffered. In Rwanda, learning about other genocides seemed to reinstate people's experience of their own humanity (Staub, et al., 2005). Interventions could also include behavioral elements, such as the provision of opportunities for individuals who have suffered to help others. Even in the absence of protective experiences during victimization, we expect appropriate subsequent experiences to promote altruism. Understanding the importance of support may inspire people to be active bystanders who help others when they are victimized, support them in the aftermath, and become active in preventing victimization.

With a great deal of suffering in the world, helping people who have suffered to turn towards others and act altruistically, rather than turn away from or against other people, is an important way to increase both their well-being, and the well-being of the rest of the community. Altruism born of suffering can improve individual lives and contribute to the creation of caring, harmonious and peaceful communities. Beyond practical and theoretical benefits, it has moral meaning to show that people who have suffered are not condemned to indifference, passivity, inhumanity and violence, and that members of the community can make important contributions to the well-being of those who have suffered.

References

American Psychiatric Association. (1994). *Diagnostic and statistical manual of mental disorders* (4th ed.). Washington, DC: American Psychiatric Association.

Barnett, M., Tetreault, P., Esper, J., & Bristow, A. (1986). Similarity and empathy: The experience of rape. *Journal of Social Psychology, 126*, 47–49.

Barnett, M., Tetreault, P., & Masbad, I. (1987). Empathy with a rape victim: The role of similarity of experience. *Violence and Victims, 2*, 255–262.

Batson, C. (1991). *The altruism question: Toward a social-psychological answer*. Hillsdale, NJ: Lawrence Erlbaum.

Batson, C. D., & Oleson, K. C. (1991). Current status of the empathy-altruism hypothesis. In M. S. Clark (Ed.), *Prosocial behavior* (pp. 62–85). Thousand Oaks, CA: SAGE.

Benard, B. (1991). *Fostering Resiliency in Kids: Protective Factors in the Family, School, and Community*. Portland, OR: Western Center for Drug-Free Schools and Communities.

Berkowitz, L., & Lutterman, K. G. (1968). The traditional socially responsible personality. *Public Opinion Quarterly, 32*, 169–185.

Bloom, S. L. (1997). *Creating sanctuary: Toward the evolution of sane societies*. New York: Routledge.

Bloom, S. L. (1998). By the crowd they have been broken, by the crowd they shall be healed: The social transformation of trauma. In R. G. Tedeschi, C. L. Park, & L. G. Calhoun, (Eds.). *Posttraumatic growth: Positive transformations in the aftermath of crisis* (pp. 179–214). Mahwah, NJ: Lawrence Erlbaum.

Bonanno, G. A. (2004). Loss, trauma, and human resilience: Have we underestimated the human capacity to thrive after extremely aversive events? *American Psychologist, 59*, 20–29.

Borshuk, C. (2004). An interpretive investigation into motivations for outgroup activism. [Electronic version]. *The Qualitative Report, 9*, 300–319. Retrieved from http://www.nova.edu/ssss/QR/QR9-2/borshuk.pdf

Butler, K. (1997). The anatomy of resilience. *The Family Therapy Networker, 21*, 22–31.

Butler, L. D. (2007). Growing pains: Commentary on the field of posttraumatic growth and Hobfoll and colleagues' recent contribution to it. *Applied Psychology: An International Review, 56*, 367–379.

Byrne, C. (2004). Benefit of burden: Victims' reflections on TRC participation. *Peace and Conflict: Journal of Peace Psychology, 10*, 237–256.

Canale, J., & Beckley, S. (1999). Promoting altruism in trouble youth: Considerations and suggestions. *North American Journal of Psychology, 1*, 95–102.

Carlson, M., & Miller, N. (1987). Explanation of the relation between negative mood and helping. *Psychological Bulletin, 102*, 91–108.

Chandler, G.E. (2002). An evaluation of college and low-income youth writing together: Self-discovery and cultural connection. *Issues in Comprehensive Pediatric Nursing, 25*, 255–269.

Charney, D. (2004). Psychobiological mechanisms of resilience and vulnerability: Implications for successful adaptation to extreme stress. *American Journal of Psychiatry, 161*, 195–216.

Christiansen, E. J., & Evans, W. P. (2005). Adolescent victimization: Testing models of resiliency by gender. *Journal of Early Adolescence, 25*, 298–316.

Coie, J. D., Watt, N., West, S., Hawkins, J., Asarnow, J., Markman, H. J., . . . Long, B. (1993). The science of prevention: A conceptual framework and some directions for a national research program. *American Psychologist, 48*, 1013–22.

Craig, C. D., & Sprang, G. (2007). Trauma exposure and child abuse potential: Investigating the cycle of violence. *American Journal of Orthopsychiatry, 77*, 296–385.

Dodge, K. A. (1993). Social cognitive mechanisms in the development of conduct disorder and depression. *Annual Review of Psychology, 44*, 559–584.

Dodge, K. A., Bates, J. E., & Pettit, G. S. (1990). Mechanisms in the cycle of violence. *Science, 250*, 1678–1683.

Dovidio, J. F., Gaertner, S. L., Validzic, A., Matoka, K., Johnson, B., & Frazier, S. (1997). Extending the benefits of recategorization: Evaluations, self-disclosure, and helping. *Journal of Experimental and Social Psychology, 33*, 401–420.

Dovidio, J. F., & Morris, W. N. (1975). The effects of stress and commonality of fate on helping behavior. *Journal of Personality and Social Psychology, 31*, 145–149.

Eisenberg, N. (1992). *The caring child*. Cambridge, MA: Harvard University Press.

Eisenberg, N., Fabes, R. A., & Spinrad, T. L. (2006). Prosocial development. In W. Damon (Series Ed.), R. M. Lerner (Series Ed.), & N. Eisenberg (Vol. Ed.), *Handbook of child psychology: Vol. 3. Social, emotional, and personality development* (6th ed., pp. 646–718). New York: Wiley.

Eisenberg, N., & Miller, P. (1987). The relation of empathy to prosocial and related behaviors. *Psychological Bulletin, 101*, 91–119.

Errante, A. (1997). Close to home: Comparative perspectives on childhood and community violence. *American Journal of Education, 105*, 355–400.

Fabes, R., Eisenberg, N., & Eisenbud, L. (1993). Behavioral and physiological correlates of children's reactions to others in distress. *Developmental Psychology, 29*, 655–663.

Feinberg, J. K. (1978). Anatomy of a helping situation: Some personality and situational determinants of helping in a conflict situation involving another's psychological distress (Doctoral dissertation, University of Massachusetts, Amherst). *Dissertation Abstracts International, 39*(1-B), 357–358.

Feshbach, N. D., & Feshbach, S. (1969). The relationship between empathy and aggression in two age groups. *Developmental Psychology, 1*, 102–107.

Frankl, V. (1984). *Man's search for meaning.* New York: Pocket/Simon & Schuster. (Originally published in 1958)

Frazier, P. A., & Kaler, M. E. (2006). Assessing the validity of self-reported stress-related growth. *Journal of Consulting and Clinical Psychology, 74*, 859–869.

Gibson, J. (2006). The contribution of truth to reconciliation: Lessons from South Africa. *Journal of Conflict Resolution, 50*, 409–432.

Gilligan, J. (1996). *Violence: Our deadly epidemic and its causes.* New York: Putnam.

Gouldner, A. (1960). The norm of reciprocity: A preliminary statement. *American Sociological Review, 25*, 161–178.

Herman, J. (1992). *Trauma and recovery.* New York: Basic Books.

Hernandez, P. (2001). A personal dimension of human rights activism: Narratives of trauma, resilience and solidarity. (Doctoral dissertation, University of Massachusetts, Amherst). *Dissertation Abstracts International, 61*(7-B), 3846.

Hernandez, P. (2002). Resilience in families and communities: Latin American contributions from the psychology of liberation. *The Family Journal, 10*, 334–343.

Hobfoll, S., Hall, B., Canetti-Nisim, D., Galea, S., Johnson, R., & Palmiari, P. (2007). Refining the understanding of traumatic growth in the face of terrorism: Moving from meaning cognitions to doing what is meaningful. *Applied Psychology: An International Review, 56*, 345–366.

Janoff-Bulman, R. (1992). *Shattered assumptions. Towards a new psychology of trauma.* New York: Free Press.

Johnson, D. R., Feldman, S., Southwick, S., & Charney, L. (1991). The concept of the second generation trauma program in the treatment of PTSD among Vietnam veterans. *Journal of Traumatic Stress, 8*, 283–299.

Kahana, B., Harel, Z., & Kahana, E. (1988). Predictors of psychological well-being among survivors of the Holocaust. In J. Wilson, Z. Harel & B. Kahana (Eds.), *Human adaptation to extreme stress: From the Holocaust to Vietnam* (pp. 171–192). New York: Plenum.

Kahana, B., Kahana, E., Harel, Z., & Segal, M. (1985). The victim as helper: Prosocial behavior during the Holocaust. *Humboldt Journal of Social Relations, 13*, 357–373.

Kaniasty, K., & Norris, F. (1995a). In search of altruistic community: Patterns of social support mobilization following Hurricane Hugo. *American Journal of Community Psychology, 23*, 447–477.

Kaniasty, K., & Norris, F. (1995b). Mobilization and deterioration of social support following natural disasters. *Current Directions in Psychological Science, 4*, 94–98.

Kerestes, G. (2006). Children's aggressive and prosocial behavior in relation to war exposure: Testing the role of perceived parenting and child's gender. *International Journal of Behavioral Development, 30*, 227–239.

Karylowski, J. (1976). Self-esteem, similarity, liking and helping. *Personality and Social Psychology Bulletin, 2*, 71–74.

Kelman, H. C. (1990). Applying a human needs perspective to the practice of conflict resolution: The Israeli-Palestinian case. In J. Burton (Ed.), *Conflict: Human needs theory.* New York: St. Martin's Press.

Kishon-Barash, R., Midlarsky, E., & Johnson, D. R. (1999). Altruism and the Vietnam War veteran: The relationship of helping to symptomatology. *Journal of Traumatic Stress, 12*, 655–662.

Kleinman, S. (1989). A terrorist hijacking: Victims' experiences initially and 9 years later. *Journal of Traumatic Stress, 2*, 49–58.

Latane, B., & Darley, J. (1970). *The unresponsive bystander: Why doesn't he help?* New York: Appleton-Crofts.

Leaning, J., & Briton, N. (2004, May). *Altruism and compassion in war.* Paper presented at the Compassionate Love Research Conference of the Institute for Research on Unlimited Love and the Fetzer Institute, Washington, DC.

Leary, M. R., Kowalski, R. M., Smith, L., & Phillips, S. (2003). Teasing, rejection, and violence: Case studies of the school shootings. *Aggressive Behavior, 29,* 202–214.

Leeds, R. (1963). Altruism and the norm of giving. *Merrill-Palmer Quarterly, 9,* 229–240.

Lifton, R. J. (1967). *Death in life. Survivors of Hiroshima.* New York: Vintage.

Lifton, R. J. (2003). *Superpower syndrome. America's apocalyptic confrontation with the world.* New York: Thunder's Mouth Press/Nation Books.

Linley, P. A., & Joseph, S. (2004). Positive change following trauma and adversity: A review. *Journal of Traumatic Stress, 17,* 11–21.

London, P. (1970). The rescuers: Motivational hypotheses about Christians who saved Jews from the Nazis. In J. Macaulay & L. Berkowitz (Eds.), *Altruism and helping behavior* (pp. 241–250). New York: Academic Press.

Luthar, S., & Cicchetti, D. (2000). The construct of resilience: A critical evaluation and guidelines for future work. *Child Development, 71,* 543–562.

Macksoud, M., & Aber, J. (1996). The war experiences and psychosocial development of children in Lebanon. *Child Development, 67,* 70–88.

Maiese, M. (2003). Restorative justice. In G. Burgess & H. Burgess (Eds.), *Beyond intractability.* Boulder: University of Colorado, Conflict Research Consortium. Retrieved from http://www.beyondintractability.org/essay/restorative_justice/

Mamdani, M. (2001). *When victims become killers: Colonialism, nativism, and the genocide in Rwanda.* Princeton, NJ: Princeton University Press.

Marsa, A. M. (2007, February). *Jewish-Israeli peacebuilders and the Holocaust: Perceptions, national myths, meaning and actions.* Paper presented at the conference "Peacebuilding and Trauma Recovery: Integrated Strategies in Post-War Reconstruction." Denver, CO.

Martens, W. H. J. (2005). Multidimensional model of trauma and correlated antisocial personality disorder. *Journal of Loss & Trauma, 10,* 115–129.

Maslow, A. H. (1968). *Toward a psychology of being* (2nd ed.). New York: Van Nostrand.

Masten, A. S. (2001) Ordinary magic: Resilience processes in development. *American Psychologist, 56,* 227–238.

Masten, A. S., & Coatsworth, J. D. (1998). The development of competence in favorable and unfavorable environments: Lessons from research on successful children. *American Psychologist, 53,* 205–220.

McCann, I. L., & Pearlman, L. A. (1990). *Psychological trauma and the adult survivor: Theory, therapy, and transformation.* New York: Brunner/Mazel.

McMillen, J., & Cook, C. (2003). The positive by-products of spinal cord injury and their correlates. *Rehabilitation Psychology, 48,* 77–85.

McMillen, J., & Fisher, R. (1998). The perceived benefit scales: Measuring perceived positive life changes after negative events. *Social Work Research, 22,* 173–186.

Midlarsky, E. (1991). Helping as coping. In M. Clark (Ed.), *Prosocial behavior: Review of personality and social psychology* (Vol. 12, pp. 238–264). Thousand Oaks, CA: SAGE.

Mollica, R. (2004). Surviving torture. *New England Journal of Medicine, 351,* 5–7.

Mollica, R., Cui, X., McInnes, K., & Massagli, M. (2002). Science-based policy for psychosocial interventions in refugee camps: A Cambodian example. *Journal of Nervous and Mental Disease, 190,* 158–166.

Monroe, S. M., & Simons, A. D. (1991). Diathesis-stress theories in the context of life stress research. Implications for depressive disorders. *Psychological Bulletin, 110,* 406–425.

Noble, C., & Coram, R. (1994). *Bridge across my sorrows.* London: John Murray.

O'Connell Higgins, G. (1994). *Resilient adults overcoming a cruel past.* San Francisco: Jossey-Bass.

Oliner, S. B., & Oliner, P. (1988). *The altruistic personality: Rescuers of Jews in Nazi Europe.* New York: Free Press.

Pearlman, L. A., & Saakvitne, K. W. (1995). *Trauma and the therapist: Countertransference and vicarious traumatization in psychotherapy with incest survivors.* New York: W. W. Norton.

Pennebaker, J. (2000). The effects of traumatic disclosure on physical and mental health: The values of writing and talking about upsetting events. In J. Violanti, D. Paton, & C. Dunning (Eds.), *Posttraumatic stress intervention* (pp. 97–114). Springfield, IL: Charles Thomas.

Proceedings of Stockholm International Forum. (2002, April). *A conference on truth, justice and reconciliation.* Stockholm: Regeringskanliet.

Raboteg-Šaric, Z., Žužul, M., & Keresteš, G. (1994). War and children's aggressive and prosocial behaviour. *European Journal of Personality, 8,* 210–212.

Rachman, S. (1979). The concept of required helpfulness. *Behaviour Research and Therapy, 17,* 1–6.

Rhodes, R. (1999). *Why they kill.* New York: Knopf.

Rouhana, N., & Bar-Tal, D. (1998). Psychological dynamics of intractable ethnonational conflicts. The Israeli-Palestinian case. *American Psychologist, 53,* 761–770.

Rugge, T. (2007). The impact of restorative justice practices on participants. *Dissertations Abstracts International, 67*(10-B), 6076.

Rutter, M. (1987). Psychosocial resilience and protective mechanisms. *American Journal of Orthopsychiatry, 57,* 316–331.

Rutter, M. (1990). Psychosocial resilience and protective mechanisms. In J. Rolf, A. Masten, D. Cicchetti, K. Nuechterlein, & S. Weintraub (Eds.), *Risk and protective factors in the development of psychopathology* (pp. 181–214). Cambridge, MA: Cambridge University Press.

Schuster, M., Stein, B., Jaycox, L., Collins, R., Marshall, G., Elliott, M., . . . Berry, S. A. (2001). A national survey of stress reactions after the September 11, 2001, terrorist attacks. *New England Journal of Medicine, 345,* 1507–1512.

Serbin, L. A., & Karp, J. (2004). The intergenerational transfer of psychosocial risk: Mediators of vulnerability and resilience. *Annual Review of Psychology, 55,* 333–363.

Southwick, S., Vythilingam, M., & Charney, D. (2005). The psychobiology of depression and resilience to stress: Implications for prevention and treatment. *Annual Review of Clinical Psychology, 1,* 255–291.

Spielman, D., & Staub, E. (2000). Reducing boys' aggression. Learning to fulfill basic needs constructively. *Journal of Applied Developmental Psychology, 21,* 165–181.

Staub, E. (1978). *Positive social behavior and morality: Personal and social influences* (Vol. 1). New York: Academic Press.

Staub, E. (1979). *Positive social behavior and morality: Socialization and development* (Vol. 2). New York: Academic Press.

Staub, E. (1989a). *The roots of evil: The origins of genocide and other group violence.* New York: Cambridge University Press.

Staub, E. (1989b). What are your values and goals? *Psychology Today, 23,* 46–49.

Staub, E. (1998). Breaking the cycle of genocidal violence: Healing and reconciliation. In J. Harvey (Ed.), *Perspectives on loss* (pp. 231–238). Washington, DC: Taylor & Francis.

Staub, E. (2003). *The psychology of good and evil: Why children, adults and groups help and harm others.* New York: Cambridge University Press.

Staub, E. (2005). The roots of goodness: The fulfillment of basic human needs and the development of caring, helping and nonaggression, inclusive caring, moral courage, active bystandership, and altruism born of suffering. In G. Carlo & C. Edwards (Eds.), *Nebraska Symposium on Motivation: Vol. 51. Moral motivation through the life span: Theory, research, applications.* Lincoln: University of Nebraska Press.

Staub, E. (2006). Reconciliation after genocide, mass killing or intractable conflict: Understanding the roots of violence, psychological recovery and steps toward a general theory. *Political Psychology, 27,* 867–895.

Staub, E. (2011). *Overcoming evil: Genocide, violent conflict and terrorism.* New York: Oxford University Press.

Staub E., & Pearlman, L. (2006). Advancing healing and reconciliation. In L. Barbanel & R. Sternberg (Eds.), *Applications of psychological knowledge to real world problems* (pp. 213–243). New York: Springer.

Staub, E., Pearlman, L., Gubin, A., & Hagengimana, A. (2005). Healing, reconciliation, forgiveness and the prevention of violence after genocide or mass killing: An intervention and its experimental evaluation in Rwanda. *Journal of Social and Clinical Psychology, 24,* 297–334.

Strang, H., Sherman, L., Angel, C., Woods, D., Bennett, S., Newbury-Birch, D., & Inkpen, N. (2007). Victim evaluations of face to face restorative justice conferences: A quasi-experimental analysis. *Journal of Social Issues, 62,* 281–307.

Tec, N. (2003). *Resilience and courage: Women, men, and the Holocaust.* New Haven, CT: Yale University Press.

Tedeschi, R. G. (1999). Violence transformed: Posttraumatic growth in survivors and their societies. *Aggression and Violent Behavior, 4,* 319–341.

Tedeschi, R. G., & Calhoun, L. G. (1995). *Trauma and transformation: Growing in the aftermath of suffering.* Thousand Oaks, CA: SAGE.

Tedeschi, R. G., Park, C. L., & Calhoun, L. G. (Eds.). (1998). *Posttraumatic growth: Positive transformations in the aftermath of crisis.* Mahwah, NJ: Lawrence Erlbaum.

Tedeschi, R. G., Calhoun, L. G., & Cann, A. (2007). Evaluating resource gain: Understanding and misunderstanding posttraumatic growth. *Applied Psychology: An International Review, 56,* 396–407.

Twenge, J., & Baumeister, R. (2005). Social exclusion increases aggression and self-defeating behavior while reducing intelligent thought and prosocial behavior. In D. Abrams, M. Hogg, & J. Marques (Eds.), *The social psychology of inclusion and exclusion* (pp. 29–46). New York: Psychology Press.

Unger, R. (2000). The 1999 SPSSI presidential address: Outsiders inside: Positive marginality and social change. *Journal of Social Issues, 56,* 163–179.

Volkan, V. D. (1998). Tree model: Psychopolitical dialogues and the promotion of coexistence. In E. Weiner (Ed.). *The handbook of interethnic coexistence.* New York: Continuum.

Vollhardt, J. (2009). The role of victim beliefs in the Israeli-Palestinian conflict: Risk or potential for peace? *Peace and Conflict: Journal of Peace Psychology, 15*(2), 135–159.

Vollhardt, J., & Staub, E. (2011). Inclusive altruism born of suffering: The relationship between adversity and prosocial attitudes and behavior toward disadvantaged outgroups. *American Journal of Orthopsychiatry, 81,* 307–315.

Wayment, H. (2004). It could have been me: Vicarious victims and disaster-focused distress. *Personality and Social Psychology Bulletin, 30,* 515–528.

Werner, E. E. (1987). Vulnerability and resiliency in children at risk for delinquency: A longitudinal study from birth to young adulthood. In J. D. Burchard & S. N. Burchard (Eds.), *Prevention of delinquent behavior* (pp. 16–43). Newbury Park, CA: SAGE.

Werner, E. E., & Smith, R. (1992). *Overcoming the odds. High risk children from birth to adulthood.* Ithaca, NY: Cornell University Press.

Westphal, M., & Bonanno, G. A. (2007). Posttraumatic growth and resilience to trauma: Different sides of the same coin or different coins? *Applied Psychology: An International Review, 56,* 417–428.

Widom, C.S. (1989). Does violence beget violence? A critical examination of the literature. *Psychological Bulletin, 106,* 3–28.

Woodward, C., & Joseph, S. (2003). Positive change processes and post-traumatic growth in people who have experienced childhood abuse: Understanding vehicles of change. *Psychology and Psychotherapy: Theory, Research and Practice, 76,* 267–283.

Zahn-Waxler, C., Cummings, E. M., McKnew, D. H., & Radke-Yarrow, M. (1984). Altruism, aggression, and social interactions in young children with a manic-depressive parent. *Child Development, 55,* 112–122.

11

The Heroism of Survivors

Survivors Saving Themselves and the Impact on Their Lives

The majority of the small percentage of European Jews who survived the Holocaust were helped by people who endangered their lives, and often the lives of their families, to save these persecuted people. In the last three decades such rescuers received a great deal of well deserved attention. Their motivation, personality, and childhood experience have been studied, their heroic actions described and commemorated (Oliner & Oliner, 1988; Tec, 1986). In the midst of human cruelty so great that it easily brings despair, their actions provide hope.

Bystanders, members of an ethnic, religious, or political group who are not themselves perpetrators, are often passive while their group inflicts increasing harm on some subgroup of their society. However, when such harmdoing evolves into genocide, as in the Holocaust so in other instances also rescuers have emerged who endangered themselves to save lives (Staub, 1989, 1999). This has been true during the genocide of the Armenians in Turkey (Hovanissian, 2003), and of the Tutsis in Rwanda (African Rights, 2002; see Chapter 7).

But another kind of heroism also deserves attention and study. Many who survived the Holocaust (and also many who have survived other genocides), demonstrated great courage and decisiveness in saving their own lives and the lives of family members. Parents often saved children, or their whole family, by making difficult decisions and acting with great courage to carry them out. Young children often responded to sudden danger with calm, initiative, maturity, courage, and the capacity to make the right judgment. They responded with actions almost inconceivable given their age, to save themselves or protect family members.

Often heroic actions by survivors and rescuers were intertwined, in a number of ways. For example, those who survived often helped themselves by seeking out people who might

Reprinted with permission and minor revisions from Staub, E. (2008). The heroism of survivors: Survivors saving themselves, its impact on their lives, and altruism born of suffering. In D. C. Berliner & H. Kupermintz (Eds.), *Fostering change in institutions, environments, and people: Festschrift in honor of Gavriel Salomon*. Mahwah, NJ: Lawrence Erlbaum Associates.

help them. The helpers, in turn, were often drawn into helping by being asked to help. In the largest study of rescuers, by Sam and Pearl Oliner (1988), about 50 percent of the rescuers reported that they first helped after they were approached and asked to help either by a person who needed help or by an intermediary (who most likely was approached by the person needing help). People are changed by their actions, and many rescuers who helped continued to help and extended their rescue activities to more people (Staub, 1989). Thus, survivors who helped themselves by asking for someone's help often ended up helping other people as well.

I knew that those who survived often engaged in determined, courageous action, in part, from my own experience. In Budapest, in 1944, my mother and my aunt succeeded, through determined efforts, to get into the Swedish embassy and to obtain "letters of protection" created by the Swede, Raoul Wallenberg, which helped save many lives, including our lives. My father escaped during an overnight stay in Budapest when, from a forced labor camp, his group was being taken to Germany. He was the only survivor of that group.

To learn more about survivors helping themselves, for a number of years informally in conversations, and at times more formally by asking people to write down their experiences, I have collected stories of survivors of the Holocaust. I asked some survivors at a yearly conference of child survivors to describe how they survived and to mention "Any decisions and actions by members of your family, including yourself, that helped you or others in your family to survive." The information I have collected amounts to a pilot study, with 19 written statements and a dozen of what may be called "conversations," in that they were not formal interviews.

Most of my informants were child survivors, which has been defined as a child less than 13 years of age at the time the Holocaust began. Most of them wrote about their own actions. When they described their experiences they usually showed little awareness, or celebration, of their own or their family's heroism. When they wrote about their own actions, my questions have sometimes elicited appreciation of their initiative and decisiveness, astounding in some cases given their youth. I will provide a few examples here of actions taken by children.

Many of these children had to assume a false identity, to act out a role, often for years. One person's parents were taken away in 1942, when she was 11 years old and her sister 6 and a half. Her grandmother, who then cared for them, died soon after. A friend of their parents, before he escaped from Paris with his family, placed them in a boarding school, where they spent the next three war years pretending to be Catholic.

Another person who gave me written answers to my questions about her and her family's experience during he Holocaust lived in Amsterdam. She was 7 years old in the fall of 1942. Her father was already taken away. She was walking home from visiting a friend when the Nazis blocked both ends of the street, and started to round up people. She rang the doorbell of the house nearest to her. Someone called down to her "come on upstairs." The people in the upstairs apartment acted as if this was a normal visit and offered her tea and cookies.

This same child the night the rest of her family was rounded up and taken to a collection center (from which people were sent to extermination camps) fell ill with scarlet fever. She was taken to a hospital. Her mother and sister were allowed to wait for her—not put in a "transport" to a concentration/extermination camp—until she got better. She remained in the hospital, which offered some safety, after she was no longer ill. She wore a nightgown. One night a neighbor came to visit and brought her a complete set of clothes. The neighbor hid the clothes under the mattress and told her to use it when needed.

One day shortly after that trucks pulled up outside, filled with Nazis. It was rumored that Nazi doctors would examine everyone to determine "who was sick and who was not. I knew I was no longer ill, so I put on my clothes and this little 7-year-old walked down the stairs into a large downstairs hallway. It was filled with all sorts of people and lots of them in military uniforms. I passed right through them and walked out of the door and walked to the neighbor's house, who lived approximately 10 blocks away. She almost fainted when she saw me." During that time her mother was approached by an underground organization that offered to hide her two daughters, and she agreed. The parents of children who survived often made the courageous decision to separate from their children in the hope of saving their lives. In this case, the mother also found a hiding place and survived.

Another person wrote "My survival tactics were heavily psychological. As I was shuffled from family to family, what seemed to work is to look and act cute—so I did as best as I could. The other tactic to help me survive was unfortunately to cut off my feelings, which I have been spending my life trying to undo."

One more example is that of a Polish child who survived the war in the USSR. The family was separated from the father, then reunited. The USSR occupied the Eastern part of Poland. When the Germans invaded, the factory in which the father worked was to be transported further into the USSR. The mother, whose family lived in the area decided to stay. This 12 year old child, after accusing the father of leaving them again and being told that it is the mother who does not want to go, went home and said to her surprised mother "Pack the bags immediately, we are going with Dad." She packed, they went and survived.

Not surprisingly, the traumatic experiences of persecution, great danger and deprivation often had continuing psychological effects on survivors. The nature of these effects varied, depending on many factors. The exact nature of their experience during the Holocaust was important. But so was the nature of their experience afterwards, for example, in the case of child survivors whose parents also survived, whether they avoided talking about the past, were preoccupied by it, or had some other way of relating to it. Probably temperamental characteristics of the child were also important.

The continuing impact of the Holocaust was probably greatest in finding inner peace and a sense of well being, not so much in the realm of effectiveness. The actions taken by parents, and the children themselves, which saved their lives, had to shape their personality and later behavior. This may at least partly account for the high energy and effectiveness of many survivors of the Holocaust. Many of the child survivors are successful people who lead effective professional lives. Many of them are in service professions, or engage in volunteer activities, devoted to helping others (Valent, 1998). It is likely that this is at least partly the result of what they have learned as they witnessed their parents' decisive judgment and determined and persistent actions in the face of overwhelming odds, and/or as they themselves participated in or initiated actions that furthered their own and, at times, their family's survival.

Their experience of being helped by rescuers, by people who cared enough to endanger their lives for them, was also likely to have highly beneficial effects.

From Survival Heroism to Altruism Born of Suffering

Research on people who have been victimized has focused on their difficulties in functioning and/or their aggressiveness, while research on aggressive/violent people has found that a large percentage of such people have experienced early victimization (Dodge, 1993; Gilligan, 1996; Widom, 1989a, 1989b). However, anecdotal evidence and beginning research indicates that some people who have suffered become highly altruistic (Staub, 2003, 2005; see Chapter 10). As I noted, many child survivors are in professions that serve people's needs (Valent, 1993). In Rwanda, in the course of my experience of working there on reconciliation in the aftermath of the genocide of 1994 (e.g. Staub, 2011; Staub and Pearlman 2006; Chapter 18 and 19), I have found that many survivors of the genocide are at the forefront of working on reconciliation between Hutus and Tutsis.

Trauma is usually defined as lack of control in the face of events that threaten survival or are experienced as endangering one's life (Herman, 1992; Pearlman & Saakvitne, 1995). Trauma, especially when it arises out of victimization, profoundly frustrates basic human psychological needs (see Staub, 1989, 2003, 2011). The intended victims of genocide will have these basic needs intensely frustrated—the needs for security, a feeling of effectiveness and control over important events, a positive identity, feelings of connection to other people, the need for autonomy (the ability to make important decisions for oneself) and the need for a comprehension of the world one lives in and of one's own place in the world. The heroic survivors of genocide I am writing about here had their lives in great danger, but learned from their own actions and the actions of important others that it is possible to take effective action and survive. This had to enhance their feeling of effectiveness and control, and probably contributed to a positive identity. It was likely to increase their belief in their ability to protect themselves, thereby contributing to the fulfillment of their need for security.

If they received help from others, this was likely to fulfill, to some degree, their need for connection to other people, deeply frustrated by their persecution, as well as by abandonment of them and their group by much of the world, which had remained passive. All these experiences together were also likely to create a more constructive comprehension of reality—rather than seeing the world and human beings as dangerous, they could also see the potential for and possibilities of human goodness.

I have proposed a number of experiences as contributing to altruism born of suffering. These are healing from past trauma, having received help at the time of one's victimization and suffering, care and support by and significant connections to other people before (such a loving families) and very importantly after the traumatic experience, having helped oneself (and/or others) at the time of victimization, as well as altruistic models and guidance (Staub, 2003, 2005; Staub & Vollhardt, 2008; see Chapter 10). A number of these were inherent to the experience of heroic survivors, especially in the case of those who have both helped themselves and were helped by other people.

For heroic survivors, in the midst of great trauma, their own and their families actions (and often also the actions of rescuers) served to ameliorate the trauma, or to provide protection that would later help build resilience. To put it a different way, these experiences helped heal wounds to some degree even as they were created. This does not mean that the great persecution, danger to their lives, and loss of relatives that most of them experienced did not have deep and lifelong effects. But especially for those who have had the experiences I posit as important for altruism born of suffering, their suffering could become a source of empathy and caring for other people.

Case studies of victimized people (O'Connell, 1994), autobiographies (e.g., Noble & Coram, 1994) and other material (Staub & Vollhardt, 2008; described in Chapter 10) support the concept of altruism born of suffering, and provide some evidence that the experiences listed above contribute to it. Further supporting research, which can be in the form of interventions to promote altruism born of suffering (see Chapter 10), should enable parents, teachers, and caring adults in general to help children (as well as adults) who have suffered to move from being cut off from or turned against people, to see the possibilities of caring and love, and transform their own past suffering into empathy, compassion, and feelings of responsibility to help others.

References

African Rights (2002). *Tribute to courage*. London: Author.

Dodge, K. A. (1993). Social cognitive mechanisms in the development of conduct disorder and depression. *Annual Review of Psychology, 44*, 559–584.

Gilligan, J. (1996). *Violence: Our deadly epidemic and its causes*. New York: Putnam and Sons.

Herman, J. (1992). *Trauma and recovery*. New York: Basic Books.

Hovannisian, R. (Ed.). (2003). *Looking backward, moving forward*. New Brunswick, NJ: Transaction.

Noble, C. with Coram, R. (1994). *Bridge across my sorrows*. London: John Murray.

O'Connell Higgins, G. (1994). *Resilient adults overcoming a cruel past*. San Francisco: Jossey-Bass.

Oliner, S. B., & Oliner, P. (1988). *The altruistic personality: Rescuers of Jews in Nazi Europe*. New York: Free Press.

Pearlman, L. A., & Saakvitne, K. W. (1995). *Trauma and the therapist: Countertransference and vicarious traumatization in psychotherapy with incest survivors*. New York: W. W. Norton.

Staub, E. (1989). *The roots of evil: The origins of genocide and other group violence*. New York: Cambridge University Press.

Staub, E. (1999). The roots of evil: Personality, social conditions, culture and basic human needs. *Personality and Social Psychology Review, 3*, 179–192.

Staub, E. (2003). *The psychology of good and evil: Why children, adults and groups help and harm others*. New York: Cambridge University Press.

Staub, E. (2005). The roots of goodness: The fulfillment of basic human needs and the development of caring, helping and nonaggression, inclusive caring, moral courage, active bystandership, and altruism born of suffering. In G. Carlo & C. Edwards, (Eds.), *Moral motivation across the life span*. Nebraska Symposium on Motivation. Lincoln: Nebraska University Press.

Staub, E. (2011). *Overcoming evil: Genocide, violent conflict and terrorism*. New York: Oxford University Press.

Staub E., & Pearlman, L. (2006). Advancing healing and reconciliation. In L. Barbanel & R. Sternberg (Eds.), *Applications of psychological knowledge to real world problems*. New York: Springer Verlag.

Staub, E., & Vollhardt, J. (2008). Altruism born of suffering: The roots of caring and helping after experiences of personal and political victimization. *American Journal of Orthopsychiatry, 78*, 267–280.

Tec, N. (1986). *When light pierced the darkness: Christian rescue of Jews in Nazi-occupied Poland*. New York: Oxford University Press.

Valent, P. (1998). Child survivors: A review. In J. Kestenberg & C. Kahn (Eds.), *Children surviving persecution: An international study of trauma and healing.* New York: Praeger.

Widom, C.S. (1989a). Does violence beget violence? A critical examination of the literature. *Psychological Bulletin, 106*(1), 3–28.

Widom, C.S. (1989b). The cycle of violence. *Science, 224,* 160–166.

12

Heroes and Other Committed Individuals

The actions of single individuals sometimes have wide-ranging consequences. A number of Westerners who stayed in Nanking after the Japanese invasion of China in World War II acted with determination and courage to save lives during the massacre of much of the population of the city. One woman missionary, the dean of a girls' college, transformed the college into a sanctuary for the Chinese. A German businessman, a member of the Nazi party, hid 600 people in his home. He was also instrumental in establishing a safe zone, a large area in the city, in which tens of thousands of Chinese survived. He continuously protested the killings at the Japanese embassy. After he returned to Germany, he wrote to Hitler with dismay about what happened in Nanking. But Japan was Germany's ally, the Germans were even more violent, and the Gestapo came to his house and told him to not talk about it again (Chang, 1998; see also www.irischangthemovie.com).

Armin Wegner was a volunteer medical nurse in the German army in World War I. He heard about the killing of Armenians and during a leave traveled to areas where the genocide of the Armenians was taking place. In spite of strict orders of both the Turks and the German army, he took many photos—of women and children marching to their death, of dead Armenians, and of orphaned children. He was arrested, many of his pictures taken away, but he hid and smuggled others to Germany and the United States. His photos were of great value in calling attention to the fate of the Armenians. In the 1930s, he spoke out against the persecution of Jews. He was detained and tortured, but he survived and went into exile in Italy (see http://www.armenian-genocide.org/wegnerbio.html).

Major Schmelling, a German, persuaded a superior not to destroy the village of La Chambon and saved the lives of thousands of refugees. Although he acted alone, he may have felt confident because of his relationship to a leading general (Hallie, 1979).

Reprinted with permission and minor changes from Staub, E. (2011). *Overcoming evil: Genocide, violent conflict and terrorism*. New York: Oxford University Press, pp. 396–399.

Joe Darby, the guard who put a disk with the Abu Ghraib pictures in Iraq under a superior's door, also acted alone, although he first sought the advice of a friend, and his former, trusted commander. Aware of the ostracism and danger he faced, he sought their advice in a veiled manner, by describing to them a hypothetical situation (Thalhammer et al., 2007). The abuse of prisoners was widespread in American prisons in Iraq. The shocking pictures and subsequent investigations of Abu Ghraib, at the very least lessened the abuse in these prisons and prevented the evolution of greater violence.

Ron Ridenhour was a U.S. soldier in Vietnam. He was not at My Lai, where several hundred civilians were killed by American soldiers who attacked a group of villages expecting to find enemy fighters but found none, but learned about it from fellow soldiers he trained with. He completely invested himself in finding out what happened at My Lai from other soldiers and friends who were there. He searched out a soldier who was reputed to have been there but not to have participated in the shooting. He found him in a hospital. According to the soldier, his superiors, aware of his nonparticipation, kept him at the front and constantly sent him on dangerous missions. They did not allow him to leave even though he had jungle rot, a serious condition, but he hopped on a nearby helicopter and had himself taken to a hospital (see http://www.law.umkc.edu/faculty/projects/ftrials/mylai/Myl_hero.html#RON).

After he collected all possible information, Ridenhour consulted relatives and friends at home, who advised him to forget about it. It was not his business. Instead, he wrote many letters to Congress about My Lai. In one letter, explaining his reason for writing, he quoted Winston Churchill, "A country without a conscience is a country without a soul, and a country without a soul is a country that cannot survive." (See the letter at http://www.law.umkc.edu/faculty/projects/ftrials/mylai/ridenhour_ltr.html.) He did not rest until one Congressman, Mo Udall, held hearings on the massacre. Then journalist Seymour Hersh wrote about it in the *New York Times*. Public knowledge about My Lai, and the trial of Lt. William Calley in charge of the troops there, were important in making such actions less likely and affecting attitudes toward the Vietnam War.

Another courageous resister—a much more appropriate term than "whistle blower"—was Daniel Ellsberg, who passed the Pentagon Papers, the top-secret government history of U.S. involvement in Vietnam, to the *New York Times*. They revealed the extent to which several presidents had misled the nation about their intentions in the war. While he had help, he made the decision and took action. What these heroic individuals did had important social consequences.

Institutions, and their members, often protect their own even if they act contrary to proclaimed values of the institution, or even the nation they serve. But they turn against their own if they perceive them as harming the institution. Darby and Ridenhour became the targets of anger by other soldiers. General Taguba, who was appointed by the army to provide the first report on the Abu Ghraib abuse of prisoners and wrote a truthful report, apparently ruined his career by doing so. The army and defense secretary Rumsfeld wanted a whitewash, not the truth (Zimbardo, 2007).

Another courageous person, Matthew Diaz, was part of the Navy judicial system, the JAG corps. He sent the list of prisoners at Guantanamo Bay, which the government kept secret, to a human rights lawyer. He dearly paid for this—the lawyer gave it to a judge, who sent it to the military. Dias was court-martialed, spent six months in jail, and had difficulty finding a job afterward. The psychological challenge, in acting as he did, is indicated by contrasting statements he made. At his trial he said he was ashamed of his actions. After his release, when he received an award for what he did, he said he was guided by the U.S. Constitution, by a Supreme Court ruling that the inmates had a right to representation, and by his ethical/moral compass (NPR, 2008). Different values, morality, and the rule of law versus loyalty, were apparently activated by the different social contexts.

The story of Leyman Gbowee of Liberia was told in the documentary film *Pray the Devil Back to Hell* and described by columnist Bob Herbert in the *New York Times* in January 2009. The film shows the horror of the Liberian war between the dictatorial president Charles Taylor and a brutal rebel army, with civilians running from gunfire, children "paralyzed with fear by nearby explosions; homes engulfed in flames" (Herbert, 2009).

A single individual can inspire many people to act together. Leyman Gbowee first inspired the women at her Lutheran church to pray for peace, then she organized them for action involving both other Christian churches and Muslim women. To prayer they added demonstrations, involving more people and becoming the movement Liberal Mass Action for Peace. Thousands of women joined them to demonstrate for peace at the marketplace, which was their headquarters, in response to their call broadcast over Catholic radio stations. As their public support grew, first Charles Taylor and then the rebel leaders met with them. Their actions contributed to pushing the parties to negotiate. When the peace talks held in Ghana seemed to break down, about 200 of the women staged a sit-in at the site of the talks. Their continued engagement had a role in bringing about at first a tentative peace, and then Charles Taylor's exile from the country. The women remained active. In 2006 Liberia elected the first woman president of an African country (Herbert, 2009).

Ralph Lemkin, an attorney and a Jewish refugee from Poland, worked tirelessly for many years to create what became the U.N. Genocide Convention. At the start he was a lone voice in the wilderness; slowly he gained the support of influential people, including Eleanor Roosevelt (Lemkin, 1944). In a number of other instances a few individuals managed to create institutions to protect human rights. Amnesty International and Human Rights Watch were started by a few dedicated people.

The empowerment of people under difficult conditions who feel helpless, diminished, frustrated in both their material and psychological needs, is especially valuable in preventing violence. Otherwise, like the men in the Congo, they empower themselves through violence. Social entrepreneurs, effective social change agents, are people who, with ingenuity and commitment, generate activities in communities that build connections and create opportunities. As one example, a woman in Poland, Dagmara Bienkowska, engaged with people in a highly divided community. One part of the community has taken "possession of all the economic assets . . . the other left without any financial capital"(Praszkier, Nowak, & Coleman, 2010), a real-world version of the story in our radio drama in Rwanda (see Chapter 19). She lived in the community for 1 month, talking to people. She learned that two groups in particular were excluded from the life of the community, senior citizens and aggressive "wayward" youth, "local bullies." She involved the two groups in a joint undertaking: the young people gathering recipes of regional dishes from the old people, and putting them together in a cookbook. The unedited version of this was a great success. A professional edition that followed was even more successful.

Through further entrepreneurial activities of the youth group, their County experienced substantial economic development. Social change agents like Bienkowska are heroes of a different kind, as they use their substantial creativity for the social good.

The role of individual actors within a society is also of great importance in preventing mass violence. However, during the evolution of increasing destructiveness in a society there is frequently limited opposition and resistance, little if any active bystandership. But if a genocide begins, often a small number of people take action to save lives. To change the course of a destructive evolution in a society, it is necessary for people to begin to act early, and to join together for action (see other chapters, particularly 22).

References

Chang, I. (1998). *The rape of Nanking*. Penguin Books.

Hallie, P. P. (1979). *Lest innocent blood be shed: The story of the village of Le Chambon, and how goodness happened there*. New York: Harper and Row.

Herbert, B. (2009, January 21). A crazy dream. *The New York Times*, p. 19.

Lemkin, R. (1944). Axis rule in occupied Europe: laws of occupation—Analysis of government: Proposals for redress, Washington, DC: Carnegie Endowment for International Peace

NPR. (2008, April 10). Ex-Navy lawyer explains Guantanamo leak. *All Things Considered*. http://www.npr.org/templates/story/story.php?storyId=89538109&ft=1&f=1001

Praszkier, R., Nowak, A., & Coleman, P. T. (2010). Social entrepreneurs and constructive change: The wisdom of circumventing conflict. *Peace and Conflict: Journal of Peace Psychology, 16*, 153–174.

Thalhammer, K. E., O'Loughlin, P. L., Glazer, M. P., Glazer, P. M., McFarland, S., Shepela, S. T., & Stoltzfus, N. (2007). *Courageous resistance: The power of ordinary people*. New York: Palgrave Macmillan.

Zimbardo, P. (2007). *The Lucifer effect: Understanding how good people turn evil*. New York: Random House.

13

How Can We Become Good Bystanders—In Response to Needs Around Us and in the World?

We are all witnesses to others' need or suffering. People who need help may be right in front of us, people we see on the street, or they may be part of our life space as family, friends, neighbors, or fellow citizens. Or they may be in faraway places, like Sudan. It creates a safer world for everyone, more trust between people, better communities, and a better world if we take helpful action when we either directly witness or know about other people's need. Research also indicates that people who regularly help others are more satisfied with life and happier. But to help we must overcome barriers that at times can be powerful.

While many of us believe that we ought to do something when we see a child being harmed, a person injured in an accident, an old person in need, or a genocide at faraway places, all too often we remain passive. If we are to act, we must train, teach or transform ourselves to become "active bystanders." Once we do that, we can influence other people to join us as allies, so that we can act together. In some situations this is important for safety; in others it is necessary for successful action. Under most circumstances it can increase our confidence to act. Here are some proposals, based on past research and theory, my own and others', that may help people who care about others and the world to overcome barriers and become active in helping people—and even in working to create harmonious and peaceful societies.

Paying Attention and Taking in What We See

In one of my studies, when a young man, one of my students at Harvard, collapsed as someone was approaching on the other side of the street, sometimes that person immediately rushed over. Others hesitated, but in the end approached. Some walked on slowly, looking back, until someone else helped. But some passers-by after a single glance looked away, continued walking, and never looked back. Some even turned away at the next corner.

Sometimes faced with others' need we almost automatically avoid taking in what is in front of us—we look away, switch the channel. Since often the information is much more subtle than a person collapsing within our view, avoidance is easier. Also, information can be ambiguous. A first requirement for action is to attend to, perceive and come to understand the meaning of events.

In one study participants who had difficulty deciding whether a light had moved were less likely to report a man they saw taking his hand out of a women's handbag as they entered a room. If we have difficulty interpreting events, just becoming aware of this can be helpful. The difficulty of some people may at least in part be due to worry about the responsibility thrust on us by events. Gathering skills, increasing confidence in our ability to judge events as well as what to do, and coming to realize that even in demanding situations we have a choice about how much to engage and what to do can all increase our active bystandership.

Acting (Appropriately) in Spite of Ambiguity About the Meaning of Events

The clearer the need to help, the more people help. But ambiguity is more the rule than the exception. Fear of doing something inappropriate, which is one of the inhibitors of helping, is enhanced by ambiguity. But we may also see events as unclear or misinterpret them to avoid feeling responsible to act. Governments, outside parties, often remain passive in the face of genocide, claiming that it is a civil war, which the parties must themselves resolve.

When I taught a large class at Stanford University in 1974, I described to students a situation in which sounds of distress came from another room, but their meaning, whether it was someone's distress, was ambiguous. This was the situation in some of my research studies. Many of the students thought that it was better not to take action than to be embarrassed by unnecessary or wrong action.

But my personal experience has taught me that people appreciate the underlying intention, even if the action is not needed. One example is the time I heard an angry interaction between a man and a woman that I thought came from the apartment above me, and sounds of the women's distress that made me think she was being hurt. I went upstairs and knocked on the door of the apartment. It was midnight. The man who answered the door was in his undershorts and told me the sounds did not come from there—probably came from the building adjoining ours. When I returned to my apartment I saw a police car pull up next door. My neighbors from upstairs, whom I only greeted in passing before, always warmly greeted me after this, and we developed a casual friendship. If we are to help we must often act on the basis of less than full information. We can start cautiously, so that the situation becomes clearer along the way.

Pluralistic Ignorance, Suffering at Faraway Places, and Using Our Imagination

Researchers who have studied people's reactions to an emergency—an accident or attack of illness—suggested that one reason for passivity is "pluralistic ignorance." People put on a poker face in public. Each person, seeing that others do not react, is likely to decide that there is no reason for concern and that action is not necessary—or appropriate. In my study with children that I mentioned in Chapter 1, pairs of young children talked to each other and then helped. Older children stopped doing this. In a situation where a number of people witness someone's need for help, a single person expressing concern can activate other people.

Often the media ignore or barely attend to human suffering at faraway places, or even in our midst. This inhibits action in two ways. First, people do not have information. Second, with media paying little attention people conclude that there is little reason for concern. When media do pay attention, people tend to act in response to human suffering—the famine in Ethiopia, the tsunami in Asia, Katrina in New Orleans. It helps if in addition to knowing that large numbers of people are suffering, the media present, or people in their imagination engage with the fate of individuals.

Surprisingly, people feel less empathy and are willing to help less when eight or even two children desperately need help than if only one child needs help. When we learn about the victimization or suffering of large numbers of people, we may be able to move ourselves to active bystandership by imagining what it is like for one among the many. What must it be like for a child or an adult in that situation? What would it be like for me? Past research shows that taking the role of other people, imagining what it is like for them, increases empathy most, followed by imagining what it would be like for us to be in their place. Taking an observer or onlooker stance leads to the least empathy.

We can follow up rudimentary information about harmful actions against groups of people with information on the Internet. The international media and nongovernmental organizations usually provide in-depth information about events the US media might only briefly mention. Leaders if they are motivated to learn about events in other countries can also employ personnel at their disposal to gather information. But at the start we all need to engage our imagination, so that we are motivated to explore. Talking about it with other people can also further engage us—and them. Joining some group that works on helping can reduce the feeling that alone one cannot affect the fate of many people.

Beyond Us and Them: Seeing the Humanity of the Other

We all too easily separate people into "us" and "them" and see people who are far away, or even near us but different physically or in their religion, culture, or political orientation as "them." We identify with them less, see their humanity less, and help them less. This can happen even when these other people share our life space, are in the same classrooms, university, workplace, or live in the same neighborhood. Contact helps to overcome such differentiation. But it has to be significant contact that enables us to experience the others' humanity. In addition, when suffering is not the result of natural events but imposed by other humans, we often blame those who suffer, believing that somehow they must have deserved what other people do to them. This is a natural tendency, which leads to inaction. Awareness that very often people innocent of any wrongdoing suffer, or are persecuted and harmed, can counteract this tendency.

Most people have basic material and psychological needs like we do—they need food, shelter, security; they want to feel good about themselves and be connected to other people; they want to protect their children and families. Thinking about this, imagining their situation, and seeing them as people like ourselves can move us to act in their behalf. Members of groups who have themselves suffered from persecution can well remember, or know from their history, how being seen as "them," as the other, led some people to harm them and others to remain passive in the face of their suffering. Past suffering can lead some people to distance themselves from human beings, or even to turn against others. But it can also lead people to use their knowledge of what it is like to suffer and to want to protect and help others.

Overcoming Feelings of Ineffectiveness, in Part by Joining With Others

Another great inhibitor of action is the belief that whatever one does will not make a difference. People who care about others, feel responsible for others' welfare, are more likely to act if they also feel that they have the power to improve others' welfare. Actual competence, and belief in our competence, can move us to help. But it is challenging when it comes to conditions in our society, or in the world, to answer the question, "what can I, a single person, do"?

We know from history, however, that sometimes even a single individual can make a huge difference. Few of us are Gandhis or Martin Luther Kings. But even as we lead our normal, everyday lives, we can make a difference. People who participated in demonstrations around the world that led to an international boycott by corporations contributed to the end of apartheid in South Africa. The business community there, faced with the boycott, supported change. The killings of Bahai's in Iran, which started after Khomeini's revolution, was stopped by Bahai's around the world. They made presentations to the governments of their countries and the United Nations, which then protested to Iran. People can join together and act in behalf of groups with which they only share a common humanity.

To feel effective and be effective, it helps to join with other people. When we see a person harmed in front of us, we can turn to others around us and engage them in joint action. We can join groups that work for causes important to us or that respond to emergencies created by nature—or by human beings. We can work together with friends and neighbors. Social reality is the result of shared understanding by people. We have power to influence each other—how we interpret events and respond to them. In one of my studies, when two people sat together in a room and heard a crash and sounds of distress from another room, what one of them said (a "confederate" who said one of a number of prearranged things) greatly influenced the other person's actions, reducing or increasing helping.

Being part of a group, just knowing that there are likeminded others working for the same cause, has great value. The abolitionists in the United States apparently found strength in knowing about each other, and facing the same dangers, as they advocated against slavery.

Working for a cause people can do a lot on their own. They can write to the president, members of the government or the Congress, the media, people in the government in other countries. For example, China has resisted pressuring Sudan to halt the violence against civilians in Darfur, or the Blue Nile region, or to allow bringing food and other humanitarian aid to refugees, presumably because of its interest in Sudan's oil. Many people writing such letters can influence even leaders of other countries. In the United States many people writing letters to a newspaper, even if few of them are published, can increase coverage by the paper of the issues the letters address.

Feeling Overwhelmed by Life but Making Choices

Most of us carry many responsibilities: our work, family obligations, attending to our children, paying bills, taxes, problems with our house. This affects our attention, our concern, and our actions. In a study by John Darley and Dan Batson, seminary students were to give a sermon. If they were told that they are late, people are waiting for them, and they were to hurry, they were more likely to pass by a person lying on the ground in their path, even if the sermon they were to give was about the Good Samaritan. Most of us are in a hurry much of the time, and even when we are not, we have goals on which we are focused. In addition, we may be overwhelmed by the pain, suffering, and injustice in the world. The combination of preoccupation with our lives and too much need in the world can lead to closing our hearts and minds to others.

Without making choices about what to respond to, we may be paralyzed. With our varied life experiences, we differ in what engages our heart. The guideline I often suggest to people and try to follow myself is to commit to one cause that is close to one's heart and also respond to emergencies in the world. Contrary to my advice, I have two causes—but they are related. One of them is understanding the roots of and working on the prevention of genocide and other mass violence. Genocide should be an emergency for everyone. My other cause is raising caring and nonviolent children who will be active bystanders in the face of others' need.

Creating the Right Institutions

Individuals, politicians, and nations at times respond to great need somewhere, such as apartheid in South Africa or mass killing in Bosnia. But many times they do nothing. Action requires not only caring beliefs and attitudes but also the right institutions. Without them nations may respond one time but not another, depending on the country's leadership at the time or past relationships to an offending country or its leaders.

Governments, including that of the United States, have historically remained passive in the face of persecution and violence against ethnic or political groups in other countries, and at times been complicit by going on with business as usual with offending governments and countries (the Germans during the 1930s) or supporting violent governments (El Salvador, Guatemala, Chile, and elsewhere in the 1970s and 1980s). At the time of the genocide in Rwanda, the US government worked hard to avoid using the term *genocide*, thereby avoiding the obligation to act, and was opposed to the United Nations/international community taking action there. Bosnia and Kosovo were exceptions to the general rule, but the NATO intervention in Bosnia came only after years of violence against Bosnians, and in Kosovo it involved substantial destruction, because it was so late in coming and was then a response to great violence that needed to be immediately stopped.

Early preventive actions may stop the evolution of violence. For early prevention it is essential to establish high-level offices in the State Department and foreign ministries of many countries, which have the responsibility both to collect early warning information and activate preventive response. Without the responsibilities and tasks so established, early action remains highly unlikely—and later response very infrequent. There is now an Atrocities Prevention Board, established by President Obama in 2011, but little evidence of its actions. Part of the problem may be that its members have primary responsibilities in other government agencies. There is need for a group of high-level officials who have responsibility only for atrocity prevention. The motivation by government officials to create the right institutions, and to make them active and effective, is likely to come if concern, interest, and demand is expressed by many people. We also need institutions that will create a responsive, caring society at home, in the United States (see Chapter 28).

The Evolution of Active Bystandership

People who harm others justify their actions by seeing those they have harmed in a more and more negative light. In the end, they exclude them from the moral realm and even see harming them as the right thing to do. The good news is that just as violence evolves, so do caring and helping. Children whom we engaged in helping other children, as part of research projects I have conducted, were later more helpful. The humanitarian concerns of the Mothers of the Plaza del Mayo in Argentina, who marched in opposition to the military dictators, demanding to know what happened to their children who disappeared, progressively expanded. When we help others, we become more committed to their well-being. This often generalizes to other people, so that our caring expands. We also come to see ourselves as caring people. We can then increasingly contribute to a caring world.

14

Understanding Police Violence and Active Bystandership in Preventing It

Rodney King is beaten by Los Angeles police officers

Why do police officers use unnecessary force against citizens, as in the Rodney King case, when after a car chase, while lying on the ground, Rodney King was beaten by a couple of officers using their batons, while other officers stood around watching? What can be done to stop or reduce police violence? I have been addressing these questions in depth due to my involvement with the Commission on Peace Officers Standards and Training (POST), an agency of California's Department of Justice that sets requirements, creates standards, and develops training procedures for all police officers in the state.

A Brief Background

After the Rodney King beating the *Los Angeles Times* (March 28, 1991) published a front-page article on reasons for group violence, aiming to explain police violence based primarily on an interview with me. After this POST contacted me, and I gave a talk at a POST seminar on the unnecessary use of force that September with about 200 participants—chiefs, police instructors, and representatives of police rank and file and of community organizations. In December, 1991, I was contacted by a special consultant whom POST hired to develop recommendations for reducing the use of unnecessary force. POST was especially interested in my prior work and focus on the role of "bystanders," in this instance fellow officers whose intervention can *inhibit or stop the use of unnecessary force.*

I developed a proposal for a course on "Bystandership," or active intervention. I presented this proposal in Sacramento in July 1992 in a two-day workshop with about twenty five participants, ranging from chiefs to field officers from around California,

Reprinted with permission and minor changes from Staub, E. (1992). Understanding and preventing police violence. *Center Review, 6*, 1–7. A publication of the Center for Psychology and Social Change: An affiliate of Harvard Medical School, Cambridge, MA.

to civilians with responsibilities for the functioning of police. Several participants served on the special consultant's Use of Force committee, and several taught at or commanded police training academies. Their tasks were to evaluate the proposal, and then advise POST.

The Sources of Police Violence

My analysis of police violence partly originated in my understanding of the many kinds of group violence described in my book, *The Roots of Evil: The Origins of Genocide and Other Group Violence*. Groups and individuals change as a result of their own actions; they learn by doing. When they harm others, or use force against others, it becomes easier for them to use force again. People justify harming others partly by devaluing their victims, and they perceive themselves as increasingly willing to use force for what they regard as good reasons. This is a problem inherent in police work in that the work sometimes *requires* the use of force, which can be a starting point for the use of unnecessary force and the evolution of police violence.

Once the unnecessary use of force begins, it will expand, unless the response of "bystanders"—people who witness it or know about it—indicates that such actions are inappropriate and unacceptable. These people can be fellow officers, superiors, or community groups and agencies. Both experimental and real-life evidence show that, by what they say and do, people can influence each other, and bystanders can influence perpetrators' actions. Like other uniformed groups engaged in dangerous work, police officers develop strong bonds and an identity deeply rooted in the group. These bonds make it difficult for them to oppose one another's actions and thereby endanger their relationship to fellow officers— even to oppose them in thought, since that can create internal conflict. But when *bystanders* remain silent they affirm the perpetrators, and they themselves change, for example, by joining perpetrators in devaluing victims. Over time there can be a shift in the whole system which will make violence acceptable.

Superior officers can speak out strongly against the use of unnecessary force and create accountability by investigating allegations and punishing perpetrators. When they remain passive bystanders they allow the development of a violent system; this, apparently, was the case in Los Angeles.

The strong bond within police units can create a differentiation between "us" (the police) and "them" (which can potentially include all outsiders, who may come to be seen as potential lawbreakers). And officers will tend to devalue most, and become most violent against, groups devalued by society. Police violence in turn generates anger and the desire to retaliate. Members of a community may withhold support from police officers or engage in hostile actions. A vicious cycle can result, with mutual anger and increasing police violence.

I will only briefly list here other contributors to police violence: lack of verbal and physical skills to effectively deal with interactions with citizens; lack of cultural awareness that would enable officers to understand and effectively communicate with various groups of citizens; the characteristics of some individuals who join the police, such as valuing strength and power, without themselves feeling strong and powerful, and an associated tendency to interpret the behavior of citizens (for instance, Rodney King not stopping his car) as a personal challenge; and, finally, the way some people, including police officers, deal with the impact of difficult life conditions, such as the tremendous social changes and the political and social problems in the United States (see also Staub, 2001).

An Avenue for Reducing Police Violence

What are the central elements of training in bystandership? First an effort must be made to create a change in perspective—from seeing intervention as action against fellow officers to seeing it as effective teamwork, serving the shared goals of police work, protecting the rights of citizens, and keeping fellow officers out of trouble. Second, the issue of disloyalty can be avoided and the effectiveness of intervention increased by training officers to notice when interactions between fellow officers and citizens develop in ways that make the use of unnecessary force probable, and to intervene to shape situations so that unnecessary force is not used. Training is also required for ways to intervene both before, and as unnecessary force is used.

Watching and discussing film clips that depict such situations, along with role-playing and rehearsing interventions, are among the central aspects of the training. Officers can play the roles of potentially violently *acting* officers, *bystanding* (or intervening) officers, as well as citizen-victims. Playing the victim role can help officers understand the perspective—the feelings, thoughts, and actions—of a citizen. Following an intervention officers should discuss what happened, in the course of which they can also resolve negative feelings that arose during the role play.

Ideally, an aspect of positive bystandership would be for officers to speak out when their superior officers remain passive in the face of police violence. The hierarchical culture, however, makes this extremely difficult. It is essential, therefore, to expose top administrative officers to these ideas and practices so that they understand their own role if they allow a violent culture to develop, and their responsibility to support and reward active intervention by officers in the field.

The group assembled in Sacramento strongly supported the idea of police training in bystandership, or active intervention, at all levels—starting with chiefs—not only in relation to the use of force but also in other domains, such as interpersonal conflict or racism within the police. They also supported the central ideas for methods of training. They did not support all suggestions: for example, they thought that creating joint projects for police and community, which I proposed as an avenue for crosscutting relations or deep engagement, should not be part of this training; they also did not support the idea that officers role-play victims; and they were uncertain about the best name for the program.

The Special Consultant's Report to POST

Based on feedback from the committee, personally listening to portions of Dr. Staub's presentation, reviewing his materials, and consulting with POST staff, the following recommendations are made:

> "Bystandership" should be replaced with the term "intervention" or other similar terminology.
>
> Training relative to intervention should be incorporated with other POST courses already developed.
>
> The subject of intervention should be taught to all levels of police officers (Basic Course through Executive Development).
>
> Some of the members from the Bystandership Committee should be reconvened to assist with the integration of intervention into other POST courses.
>
> The police organization must be supportive of officers who employ intervention tactics.

On the basis of these recommendations, it is reasonable to believe that at least some of these ideas and practices will be introduced into police training in California.

Postscript

In late 2012 a group of professionals—retired police officers who now work as consultants, attorneys who have worked with issues of the unnecessary use of force by the police, and others, including me, and partly based on the training I developed in 1992 for the State of California briefly described in this chapter—have worked on creating a new training for police in active bystandership. The aim of this training is both early intervention to prevent harmful behavior by fellow officers, as well as ethical decision making and reporting unlawful behavior when necessary. Members of the group have been introducing elements of the active bystandership training with varied workshops and trainings they do with police, with prison officials, and in other relevant settings.

Reference

Staub, E. (2001). Understanding and preventing police violence. In S. Epstein & M. Amir (Eds.), *Policing, security and democracy*. Huntsville, TX: Office of Criminal Justice Press.

15

Many Students Are Happy, Others Are Bullied, Some Excluded
Active Bystandership Helps

Years ago one of my students described in a paper for a class how she received a phone call and when she picked up the phone, she was listening to a conversation among her up-to-then best friends and some other girls saying terrible things about her. The effect on her was devastating.

Bullying—children and youth intimidating, harassing, verbally degrading, spreading rumors about, destroying the property of or physically harming each other—has received a great deal of attention in recent years. Researchers first in Norway, then in Britain and other countries, and then in the United States have shown that this happens a great deal and can create intense suffering in its targets (see also Chapter 16). Cyberbullying has become an additional form of it.

Usually the victims quietly suffer while it is happening but carry for a long time, sometimes all their lives, the psychological wounds that result from their bad treatment and from the passivity of witnesses to their torment. In rare instances this is a short life, as the victim commits suicide at some point. Also in rare instances victims strike back, sometimes at their tormentors, more often in an indiscriminate manner at anyone who happens to be around them in the school where they have felt abandoned. Research on school shooters has shown that in a substantial percentage of instances the perpetrators were severely bullied.

I and my students have studied the negative and positive behaviors that students direct at each other in a whole school district in western Massachusetts, together with how students feel about their lives at school (Chapters 15 and 16 in Staub, 2003). Students from 2nd through 12th grade report a great deal of positive behavior directed at them and at other students by peers and adults in the school, or that they perform. They report less, but still a substantial amount of negative behaviors within the past week, such as being called names

This chapter is a revised version of a blog that was published in *Psychology Today* on April 29, 2012.

(62%); someone kicking, hitting, or pushing them (42%); and others, with such behaviors directed at many students multiple times in the course of a week. Some students are the recipients of little negative behavior and others a great deal.

Students report a lot of positive feelings about their lives at school: feeling happy, comfortable, accepted, safe, and part of the group. But the more negative acts that are directed at them, the more students have negative feelings about school life. Eighteen percent reported that they feel unsafe or very unsafe from other students and 15% from adults, reporting a variety of other negative feelings as well. But even students who have many negative behaviors directed at them feel less bad about school if other students have intervened in their behalf. And students who report that they have attempted to protect someone who was bullied feel better about their lives at school than those who have not. A striking finding was that the 15% of the students who received the least positive behavior from their peers (zero or one instance during the week) reported even less positive feelings than the 15 percent who received the most negative behaviors.

Bullying diminished by the fourth grade, then increased and remained high through the school years. Fifty percent of the students reported in fifth grade that they had witnessed bullying in the last two weeks, 71 percent in high school. Another striking finding was that *active bystandership decreased over the years*. This was reported by students who were bullied, students observing others' response to someone being bullied, and students reporting their own passivity or action. While 80% of the students in 2nd grade reported that they came to the aid of a bullied peer in the past week, in spite of more bullying in 12th grade less than 30% reported that they did this. Adults in the schools are active bystanders more often than students, but only 45 percent of students who reported that they were bullied in the presence of an adult said the adult came to their aid. Only 32 percent reported that another student was an active bystander, helping them.

When there is substantial negative behavior in a classroom, it affects everyone. When students are harmed by their peers and no one does anything to stop it or to support the person who was harmed, it teaches everyone that this is an unkind world. It also interferes with learning. It is not always easy to know where to draw the line between playful if somewhat negative interactions, letting children deal with their own problems, or taking positive action. We found that some teachers believe in letting children work out their relationships. This is good up to a point; it is relinquishing responsibility as an adult and a socializer beyond that point.

While teachers have important responsibilities, so do students. By turning to and joining with other witnesses and acting together, students could often stop or prevent bullying. They can learn to do this with minimal force. Since people learn from and change through their own actions, and some aggressive children become more aggressive over time, such actions help not only the children who are harmed but also those who do the harm—and everyone else. A classroom culture of caring and active bystandership also means including students in the community who are excluded and receive little positive behavior. Their need is more difficult to notice, but their life in school is painful.

People who are victimized, whether children or adults, tend to feel shame, that something must be wrong with them. As a result, they keep quiet. Parents often do not know what is happening to their child, and, if they do, they often take only limited action, not wanting to make things worse by intervening. But our way of thinking needs to change. While some children are both targets and harmdoers, many who are targeted do not themselves engage in bullying. We must work to create a culture in which children understand their right to be safe and not harmed and are encouraged to look for help, if they have difficulty protecting themselves, and where parents and school personnel join to create environments in which all students can feel safe and thrive.

Reference

Staub, E. (2003). The psychology of good and evil: Why children, adults and groups help and harm others. New York: Cambridge University Press, 2003.

16

Training Active Bystanders in Schools (and Other Settings)

A bystander is a witness, someone who is in a position to know what is happening and is in a position to take action (Staub, 2005; see Chapter 3). This definition includes "a position to know" because, as our research (Staub & Baer, 1974) and the behavior of leaders of countries (Staub, 2011) show, people often avoid information, avoid knowing, presumably to avoid feeling responsible or be blamed for their inaction and others' suffering

A bystander can remain passive or take action. Active bystandership is a normal part of our humanity, a responsibility of every person who witnesses certain situations. The focus of the training active bystanders (TAB) program described in this chapter is to help students in schools become active bystanders, individuals who take positive action when they witness harassment, intimidation, verbal or physical abuse—that is, the bullying of fellow students. However, this training has elements that can promote active bystandership not only in schools but in varied settings. It can be adapted to other situations, whether work settings or conflict situations.

In this chapter I first discuss my own and others' research that provides a background for the components of the training and briefly also mention my experience in developing a bystandership training for use in police academies in California. Then I discuss the problem of bullying. This is followed by an outline of the elements of the training, a brief description of its first use in schools, and the findings of an evaluation study of its impact.

This training bystanders program has a number of aims: understanding what inhibits or can promote active bystandership; understanding harmdoers, victims, and the witnesses/bystanders themselves; developing skills, as well as good judgment, of when intervention is needed, what might be the best types of interventions in particular situations, and how to engage other bystanders for joint action. The best interventions will help stop harmful behavior in the moment, create some long-term beneficial effects, and keep the intervener safe. Another aim may be for bystander actions to help transform, at least to some degree,

The curriculum referred to in this chapter is available at http://www.ervinstaub.com

perpetrator–victim relationships. Finally, an aim is to create a culture in which bullying is not acceptable and active bystandership becomes the norm.

Some Elements of the Research and Conceptual Background of the Training

Most of the elements of the training are based on or derived from prior research and theory, primarily my own but also of others. What follows is a brief and partial overview of research findings and relevant publications.

Darley and Latane (1970), based on their research on helping in emergency situations, developed a conceptualization of how helping is inhibited. They found that the presence of others normally inhibits helping. The larger the number of people who are present or who are believed to know about an event, the less likely any one person will initiate action, the so-called *bystander effect*. One of their explanations is pluralistic ignorance, people not showing their reactions in public. As people look around and they see no reaction by others, they decide that there is no real problem and no need to take action. Another explanation is diffusion of responsibility: with other people present, or knowing that others have information about the situation, each person feels less responsible to act. It is also the case the people often feel self-conscious about stepping forward in a public situation, afraid of criticism of their actions (Staub, 1978). Finally, greater potential cost, in terms of effort or potential negative consequences, also diminishes helping.

Young children (kindergarteners and first graders) do not show a bystander effect. Presumably because when they hear distress sounds from another room they naturally and spontaneously react to them, there is no pluralistic ignorance. They talk to each other when they hear distress sounds and jointly move to take some kind of action. By second grade, children inhibit each other—the bystander effect appears (Staub, 1970c).

Focusing responsibility on children to help, by telling them that they are in charge if anything happens, increases helping by first graders of another child in distress in an adjoining room (Staub, 1970b). In general, when circumstances focus responsibility on a person (e.g., by having special expertise, being in a leadership role, or being the only person present), this person is more likely to help (Staub, 1978; Myers, 2010). Training in active bystandership can lead to greater feelings of responsibility when someone is bullied, for example, by increasing awareness of the distress of the target of the bullying and by providing skills and a feeling of efficacy.

As children get older (by sixth grade), many are inhibited from helping by rules of appropriate behavior (Staub, 1970c). But when seventh graders received prior permission to do what is later required for helping (stop working on their task and go into an adjoining room in a strange environment), over 90% helped. Not receiving such permission had the same effect as a prohibition, when for an irrelevant reason each seventh grader was earlier told not to go into the adjoining room. In both conditions, very few helped (Staub, 1971a). To some extent the training gives students permission to intervene, as well as indicating to them that certain values and rules supersede conventional rules, which for older students especially may include the belief that one should not interfere with others' business. This belief may be one reason that active bystandership in school decreases with increasing age (Staub, Fellner, Barry, & Morange, 2003).

How one witness/bystander defines the meaning of something happening and the appropriate action can greatly affect how other bystanders act, as well as how potential harmdoers act. What a person said in response to sounds of distress in an adjoining room greatly affected (diminished or increased) the likelihood of another person helping. When this person verbally defined the situation as a need for help and the appropriate form of helping, the other person helped every time (Staub, 1974). The training is likely to lead students to define the meaning of harmful actions against other students as a situation in which help is needed and also increases their capacity to formulate appropriate actions. It also empowers them to turn to and engage other bystanders, thereby gaining allies in active bystandership.

The many aspects of circumstances, of which the presence of other people is only one, affects people's behavior differently as a function of their personal characteristics, such as values, beliefs, and competencies. A *prosocial value orientation* was associated with helping others in both physical and psychological distress (Feinberg, 1978; Staub, 1974, 1978) and with constructive in contrast to blind patriotism. (Schatz, Staub, & Levine, 1999). Aggressive boys had less of a prosocial orientation (Spielman & Staub, 2000). The combination of prosocial value orientation and people's feeling that they have the capacity to influence others' welfare was especially strongly related to a variety of self-reported helping behaviors (Staub, 2003, ch. 9). The components of a prosocial value orientation include a positive view of human beings, concern about others' welfare, and a feeling of personal responsibility for others' welfare. To some degree all of these, as well as belief in one's capacity to help others, can be affected by the training.

Inclusive caring—caring that extends to people who are not part of one's group and may be devalued in one's group—and moral courage are both important for helping others under a variety of circumstances. The meaning of *group* can be a religious, racial, or ethnic group—or a particular group in school that a student associates and identifies with. TAB humanizes students who are normally devalued. By giving students a voice in the course of the training, having them participate with ideas and principles, and enact behaviors in role-play situations that normally require moral courage (Staub, 2005; Chapter 3), TAB can increase moral courage to some degree.

In addition to research, I have studied the role of passive and active bystanders in real-world situations such as the evolution of genocide (Staub, 1989, 2003, 2011) and settings like Abu Ghraib, as well as the behavior of rescuers who saved lives in genocide (Staub, 1989, 1997, 2011). In many of these situations it is the passivity of witnesses that allows violence to unfold and intensify. I have also developed a training program for the state of California to use in police academies, to make the use of unnecessary force by police officers less likely. The focus of this program is to lead officers, who normally work in pairs, to become active bystanders to a fellow officer who is engaging in an interaction with a citizen that becomes increasingly heated and likely to lead to violence by the officer, even when this is inappropriate and illegal. That program, to be effective, needs also to lead to culture change, so that in place of unquestioning support of a fellow officer, intervening to head off unnecessary violence comes to be regarded as good teamwork (Staub, 2003, ch. 32; see Chapter 14 in this book). This also is relevant to students in schools, who may unquestioningly support bullying by a friend, a member of a group they identity with, or a popular student.

The Problem To Be Addressed

There is a lot of bullying, harassment, intimidation in schools, and among peers in general. In the course of their years in school, a very large number/percentage of students are targeted. Some are special targets for extended periods, often with severe consequences for them (Olweus, 1993, 1994; Fried & Fried 1996; Rigby, 1996; Staub & Spielman, 2003; Unnever, & Cornell, 2003). For the last 10 to 15 years of my teaching career, I had students write papers in which they applied research and theory to their life experience. One of my students described in a paper how a group of students ganged up on him for a long time and about the difficulty of living with this for many years afterward. Another student described persistent harassment by fellow students and in particular one boy because she was not willing to participate in the mainly verbal sexual games the boys engaged in with the girls in her class (see Chapter 3).

An important related problem is that much of the time witnesses, other students and even teachers who can see or are in a position to know what is happening and could take action to prevent it, remain passive. Some students become complicit, by standing around just observing, and even more by laughing. Some join those who do harm. My conversations with therapists, and also published reports (O'Connell Higgins, 1994), indicate that people who have been physically or sexually abused as children often report that they found it most painful, and some of them felt most affected by the passivity of witnesses—the other parent, or relatives, who knew or were certainly in a position to know what was done to them and should have taken action. Bystander passivity is also likely to have significant impact on students who are bullied. Students who reported that they were victimized but also helped by a bystander reported better feelings about their lives in school than those who were not helped (Staub & Spielman, 2003).

The Consequences of Bullying and Passivity

Passivity encourages perpetrators. They tend to interpret passivity as acceptance of what they are doing, and even as approval. It makes further harmful actions by them more likely. Students who bully sometimes do it for the audience, showing off their power.

For the children/youth who are special targets, the harm done to them combined with the passivity by witnesses can be devastating. The consequences of persistent victimization and lack of protection can include depression, suicidal tendencies with an increased likelihood of actual suicide, long-term effects in negative orientation to other people such as mistrust and seeing other people as a source of danger, reduced functioning (Fried & Fried, 1996; Nansel et al., 2001), and on rare occasions violence (e.g., school shootings; Leary, Kowalski, Smith, & Phillips, 2003). For aggressive boys, the consequences include being disliked by most peers (often hidden, due to fear of them) and increasing aggressiveness over time. For some this tendency for increased aggression continues after the school years and ends in criminal violence (Coie & Dodge, 1997).

Passivity in the face of harmful actions affects the whole community, including the bystanders. It is likely to change, over time, norms of conduct, allowing more aggression. Bullying and passivity can lead to seeing aggression as normal and people as aggressive, with students coming to trust human relationships less. Everybody in school may develop a more self-protective attitude. Not surprisingly, fearing that others look at you critically, see you negatively, and may verbally (or physically) attack you, significantly interferes with the capacity for academic learning. An unsafe school environment reduces students' capacity to learn and teachers' ability to teach.

However, some students who do harm or remain passive feel bad or guilty, either at the time or later when they become more mature, and carry this guilt in later life. Some learn from this not to be passive, at least in their later life. In writing papers in my classes a number of students reported such guilty feelings and later actions that were motivated at least in part by the desire to redeem themselves. Personal values, acquired before or developed later, positive models, and other life experiences can stop learning by doing in a negative direction and lead to such reversals. Training in active bystandership can be such an experience, with immediate rather than delayed effects.

Ideally such training also creates an awareness of and the motivation to engage students who are not the victims of harmful actions but are not included in, or are excluded from the community. Perhaps surprisingly, this is more painful to students than being targets of harmdoing. Students who are the recipients of the least positive behavior are the most unhappy about their lives in school (Staub & Spielman, 2003).

What Is the Desirable State of Affairs?

Harmonious social relationships in general, and in the classroom and school in particular, maximize students' well-being, capacity to learn, and development as persons. One important way to prevent bullying and develop such relationships is active bystandership. TAB aims to promote knowledge, skills, and the motivation by students to take positive, not aggressive, actions to prevent bullying. The actions of each student in protecting others can in turn influence others through modeling, lead to generalized reciprocity, and contribute to positive class and schools norms of behavior.

Acting as bystanders who help others can be of special value to students who have been previously victimized, whether at home, in school, or in other settings. First the training and then their own actions can empower them. Developing a desire to help others and actual helping can give some meaning to their own suffering. It can also further the development in them of altruism born of suffering (Chapters 10, 11).

When should people in general and students in particular be active bystanders? One aspect of training has to be the development of *understanding, judgment, values, and standards and norms about the circumstances that require active bystandership*. In the training of trainers, and in their subsequent training of many students, the discussion by participants of the various aspects of the training is essential. Those in charge can guide the discussion, eliciting ideas from participants and introducing ideas as appropriate and necessary.

Some General Training Issues

Teachers should be involved in the training in some manner, primarily as observers. As silent observers, after a while students are likely not to be distracted by them. Their presence can contribute to understanding themselves as bystanders, supporting students as active bystanders, and helping to create school/class norms of active bystandership. If teachers are negative models and discourage positive bystandership by students, the impact of the training will be greatly reduced.

The training should involve students both in brainstorming and role-plays. After introducing a new element of the training and after discussion, volunteers may role-play in front of the group. It can be valuable to videotape the performance of the initial group and study and discuss the video, and then repeat the role-play with different participants (see Spielman & Staub, 2000). If circumstances allow it, some scenes may be role played by all the students in small groups.

It is useful early in the training to ask participants to tell bystander stories. These are stories about times when they needed help and others did or did not help, when others needed help and people who were present did or did not help, and when others needed help and they themselves did or did not help. It is useful to discuss why people did or did not act.

Primary Elements of the Training

Always when intervention is needed, whether it is bullying in school or the potential for violence between groups, intervening early tends to be less dangerous and more effective. Harmful actions evolve, both in a particular situation as a person begins to harm another and over time in relation to a particular person or people in general. This, fortunately, is true not only of negative behavior but also of positive behavior (Staub, 1989, 1997, 2011).
In the case of mutually harmful actions, all the principles and practices described next apply, augmented by peer–mediator type interventions. Peer mediation aims to help the parties talk things over and enables them to listen to and hear each other.

Why Do Young People (and Adults) Harm Others?

As students address such questions, information should be gradually introduced and discussed (Hazler, Carney, Green, Powell, & Jolly, 1997). It is best to spend a limited period providing new information (such as basic human needs) at each meeting, using stories (including experiments presented as stories) that make the information interesting and accessible.

One reason for harming others has to do with basic psychological needs—needs for security, effectiveness, positive identity, positive connection to other people, some degree of autonomy, and understanding the nature of the world and one's place in it. Students (and adults) who bully may be fulfilling such needs destructively, trying to feel effective, increase their self-esteem, even gain connection to some peers through dominance and force over others. Ways to fulfill these needs by constructive means can then be discussed and role-played (see Spielman & Staub, 2000).

Another reason for harming others may be growing up in families in which aggressive behavior among the family members, or directed at a child, is common. This can make it normal and, from the child's perspective, reasonable to behave aggressively. Also, if children have been victimized, they will tend to interpret others' behavior as hostile and may respond with aggression (Dodge, Bates, & Pettit, 1990; Rhodes, 1999) that they regard as "defensive aggression" or self-defense (Staub, 2011). Students may also project their vulnerability and negative feelings about themselves into other, vulnerable children and, seeing these disliked characteristics in them, turn against them.

Learning About Inhibitors of Active Bystandership and Ways to Address Them

Research shows that learning about inhibitors can itself lead people to become more active in situations when someone is in need (although the research was done about situations when the person's need or distress was not due to being harmed by someone). The first two inhibitors were proposed by Latane and Darley (1970).

- *Pluralistic ignorance.* People do not show their feelings in public and their lack of reactions *defines* the situation as one in which no action is needed.

  Some solutions: A person saying something, even something minimal that calls attention to a situation, can change perceptions (Staub, 1974, 1978). Even a startle response by one person can activate another person.
- *Diffusion of responsibility.* When other people are present the feeling that one is not responsible or less responsible makes actions less likely.

  Some solutions. Awareness that this happens can by itself increase responsibility, as can discussing the responsibility of each person. Research shows that some people have more of a feeling of personal responsibility (Schwartz & Howard, 1984) or a prosocial value orientation that includes beliefs in and feelings of personal responsibility (Staub, 1974, 1978, 2003; Feinberg, 1978), which leads to more helping.

  People are more likely to act when circumstances focus responsibility on them, or when because of their personality/values they feel personally responsible. Education about these matters can contribute to feelings of responsibility. The discussion of responsibility can also increase the likelihood that relevant personal orientations are expressed in behavior when circumstances require it. Also, community norms can develop that make each person responsible. Learning that we are all responsible—a culture and group in which everyone comes to feel responsible—can increase the feeling of and taking on responsibility.
- *Lack of words and actions to indicate that help is needed.* When it is ambiguous whether someone needs help, it is less likely that bystanders help. Because being bullied feels shameful, victims of bullying often make light of it, as if what is done to them is no big deal.

Some solutions: Simply knowing this can help students be aware that there is a need to help (and makes it more difficult to justify one's passivity by claiming that the person who was bullied did not mind). Also, those who are bullied may learn to show their need for help, in whatever way is least humiliating to them, perhaps saying to the harmdoer that what he or she is doing is disturbing, asking him or her to stop, or asking "why are you doing this?" Such actions can activate bystanders. It is useful to brainstorm with participants the best actions.

- *Concern about negative reactions to bystander actions.* Concern about acting inappropriately, looking foolish, or that one does not have the right skills for intervention/helping, and fear of being judged negatively by other people inhibit helping/active bystandership. In the case of bullying, fear of the perpetrator's reactions, as well as the reactions of other bystanders, fear of becoming a victim oneself—at least through exclusion—may all inhibit action.

Some solutions: Involving other bystanders is one way to deal with this, so that one does not act alone. Learning effective modes of intervention and feeling reasonably competent is another way. Over time creating a culture in which intervention is normal, accepted, and appropriate is a third way. Developing good judgment about when it is or is not overly dangerous to intervene is important. However, when the danger is substantial, finding people with authority and power to stop harmdoing is an important way of intervening.

Learning that those who are active bystanders feel better about themselves, and those who receive support from active bystanders feel less badly about having been bullied (Staub & Spielman, 2003), may motivate witnesses to be active. Students who have friends who support them are less likely to be bullied. Being friendly with a person who is others' target (or who is excluded) is a valuable form of active bystandership.

- *Devaluation of potential or actual targets/victims.* Since targets of harmdoing are often people who are seen as the "other," extending caring to others is an important element of the training. The devaluation of groups of students because they belong to minorities, and of particular peers for often trivial reasons such as their clothing or something in their demeanor, reduces caring and empathy for them. For some students it may even make seeing them harmed satisfying.

Some solutions. A primary solution is "humanizing" everyone and promoting inclusive caring. Some chapters in this book provide guidance to ways of humanizing others. They include significant contact, working on shared projects, and teachers and other students emphasizing positive characteristics and behaviors of members of varied groups or of individual students who are vulnerable to becoming or may already be victims (for example, Chapters 3, 22; also Staub, 2011, 2013). These practices, as well as the discussion of devaluation as often based on stereotypes rather than the actual characteristics of a person, can lead students to be active bystanders in relation to other students they initially see as "them." The value of humanizing others goes beyond training in active bystandership. It promotes inclusive caring and thereby positively shapes students.

- *Addressing the belief that people/students should take care of themselves.* The belief that it is best if people (other students) work out problems between themselves can inhibit active bystandership. Possibly such a belief contributes to less active bystandership at later ages, especially around grades 11 and 12 (Staub et al., 2003; Chapter 15). In our study of bullying in a school system, a number of teachers expressed this belief (Staub et al., 2003). It may help to brainstorm with students how to discriminate between playful if somewhat aggressive interactions, and harm done to someone.

Moral Courage as a Promoter of Active Bystandership

Earlier in this chapter I discussed why stopping harmful actions is beneficial to everyone. Exploring this with students can activate feelings of responsibility not only to a target but the whole community. It may also contribute to moral courage.

I defined *moral courage* as "the ability and willingness to act according to one's important values even in the face of opposition, disapproval, and the danger of ostracism" (Staub, 2003, p. 8). At times, acting according to one's values also requires physical courage. The willingness to act on empathy, caring, and moral values, in spite of potential or actual negative consequences, is important if students are to intervene when a fellow student is harmed. Aligning themselves with unpopular peers, active bystanders face potential negative reactions not only from harmdoers but also from other students. Attracting allies is one way to minimize or avoid negative consequences. Brainstorming during the discussion of the elements of the training, which gives students a voice, is one way to increase confidence in one's values and beliefs and contribute to the courage to act on them.

Attempting to Halt Aggressive Actions; Expressing Caring and Empathy for Targets

Examples include offers of help when seeing a problematic interaction ("Can I help in some way?") and expressions of disapproval to the harmdoers ("That does not seem right to me; please stop that"). Support for the person who is picked on can also stop harmdoers ("I am sorry this has happened. Are you all right? Can I help some way? I don't think he/she should have done that." Or simply putting an arm around this student's shoulder).

Showing empathy can be useful both at the time of harmful actions, as well as afterward. Consistent support for targets of harmdoing combined with disapproval can make aggression not pay—or at least eliminate one potential motive for it, to elevate oneself and create connection to the "audience." Seeing the target "elevated" should reduce the motivation to harm. Support can also empower victims and make it more likely that they act in their own behalf, that they (verbally) assert themselves. Victims of bullying tend not to stand up for themselves. The combination of support and self-assertion makes it less likely that a student will be victimized.

Recruiting Other Bystanders

The risks involved in active bystandership are greatly reduced and confidence needed for action can greatly increase when bystanders act together. Saying things to other bystanders, making suggestion or asking questions, like "I don't think he/she should be doing this,"

"This is not all right," "Should we do something?", "What should we do?", "You go and get a teacher and we [including other bystanders] will try to stop it", "We should tell her/him to stop this", can be helpful. Here again, brainstorming and role-plays should be part of the training of both trainers and students.

Combining Actions to Stop "Perpetrators" with Caring and Support for Nonharmful Actions by Them

Interventions will work better if they do not humiliate perpetrators. Empathy for perpetrators may be developed by discussing during the training why students might bully—reasons I discussed earlier and will list later. Since bystandership training includes perpetrators, this is a good way to help them become self-aware and perhaps begin to fulfill needs in more constructive ways. To do this is especially important because aggressive students tend not to be self-aware, at least in that they tend not to know that they are not liked by others (Coie & Dodge, 1997).

Offering help and support to the harmdoer to disrupt harmful actions may be effective, such as asking, "can I help you two resolve some problem?" Using humor (but not ridicule) may also discourage harmful action, like saying to the target: "He does not mean it. He is just kidding. He is not a bad guy but sometimes gets carried away." But it is students themselves, in the course of brainstorming and role-play, who may come up with the best ways of engaging perpetrators.

Transfer to Other Situations

It is worthwhile to promote the transfer of active, positive bystandership to situations other than harassment, intimidation/bullying, and exclusion. This may be done through discussion, identification of other situations where positive bystandership is relevant, and role-plays. It is important, however, to discuss the dangers of attempting active bystandership in situations in which there is substantial potential for harmful consequences to actors, especially outside the school. This can in part be done by discussing differences in the values and norms of the school environment and of other environments in the students' lives, possibly even their homes. However, when bystandership is of special importance to others' welfare, indirect forms—calling authorities or other people who have the capacity to directly address the situation—become important.

Outline of the Elements of the Training

   I. Defining the problem: harassment, intimidation, verbal assault, and violence—bullying
      A. Worldwide nature of these phenomena in schools
      B. What is bullying?
      C. Consequences for
         1. Victims
         2. Harmdoers
         3. Bystanders
         4. School culture and learning

    D. Why students/people engage in such behaviors
        1. Destructive means of fulfilling psychological needs, including elevating the self over others, feeling competent, etc.
        2. Responding to *perceived* hostility of others, which may be real or imagined. When not real, the perception may be the result of past victimization, leading to what the actor believes is self-defense—"defensive aggression."
        3. Having learned that aggression is an appropriate behavior in many situations
            a. In some families children are exposed to substantial aggressive behavior. Also, in some families, members of the family get their way by using force, aggression
            b. What is seen in the media
        4. Projecting negative feelings about oneself into others and then turning against them

II. Define *bystander*
    A. Discuss "position" to know and "position" to act (witnesses with an opportunity)
    B. Describe and define *passive bystandership*
    C. Describe and define *active bystandership*

III. Situational inhibitors of active bystandership
    A. Pluralistic ignorance
    B. Diffusion of responsibility
    C. Ambiguity of the need for help (there is no problem/need; justifications of inaction such as victim wants to take care of himself/herself, does not want to seem needy or weak)
    D. Danger or cost of helping (fear retaliation or amount of effort required)
    E. Fear of disapproval, of taking action in a public situation (not feeling competent, concern about standing out)

IV. Values and beliefs that inhibit helping
    A. People can/should take care of themselves
    B. Absence of empathy
    C. Absence of personal responsibility
    D. Seeing some others as "them" and devaluing them

V. Values and beliefs about helping that students possess and promoting them through discussion, role-playing, and other elements of the training.
    A. Empathy, personal responsibility, inclusive caring, moral values that lead to action (justice, the value of human beings and their welfare)
    B. Beliefs about generalized reciprocity, benefits to the community, etc.
    C. Community values and norms

VI. Competencies that promote active bystandership
    A. Role-taking (ability to understand how others feel)
    B. Competencies/Intervention skills
    C. Skill in engaging other bystanders for joint action: calling attention to the situation, defining the situation as one in which action is needed, defining the appropriate action, engaging others as allies

VII. Considering other realms of active bystandership
   A. Discussing (and role-playing) other situations where active bystandership is appropriate
   B. Considering situations where it is too dangerous to be an active bystander and what to do in those situations

The Application of the Approach in an Actual Training

Using the conception and outline I presented here, working with the staff of a nonprofit community organization, Quabbin Mediation, we elaborated it into a curriculum for TAB and applied it in schools in Orange and Athol, Massachusetts. (This application was supported by a grant from the US Department of Justice.) We added to the principles or dimensions I described communication style such as tone of voice, facial expressions, personal distance, and other nonverbal cues. We also added games to exemplify some principles, such as the exclusion of others.

We developed a collaborative relationship with the school administrations and some teachers. We then trained 8th and 10th grade students from the schools of both towns who were selected to be trainers. The students we selected as trainers included some boys and girls who had limited behavior problems, but in the judgment of teachers had the potential to be good trainers. We trained 12 students from each town and 3 police officers from the two towns, who were to be cotrainers with the students. These were officers who had experience in the schools and in interacting with students.

We provided 18 hours of training. (The length of training can be adapted to practical circumstances.) Classroom management and facilitation techniques were included in the training. As part of the training, trainers taught the material to small groups. Afterward one student and one police officer worked together, in varying combinations, to train the 754 8th and 10th graders in the two towns. The schools gave over health classes for the training. In random observations, observers recorded the actions of the trainers to assess the extent to which the trainings were "internally valid," that they did what they were intended to do. This was the case to a substantial degree. It was a challenge for student trainers and police officers to work together as equal team members, and at some point police officers were replaced with community volunteers—parents, teachers, community members.

Evaluating the Effects of the Training

There were assessments before, immediately after, and several months after the training in "treatment schools" and comparable "control schools" in similar, neighboring cities. Control schools received the same assessments but no training. Harmdoing was assessed by the frequently used Olweus Bully/Victim Scale (1996) questionnaire and by parts of a measure my students and I developed for another, large-scale study (Staub & Spielman, 2003; Staub et al., 2003), which assessed reports by students of behavior directed at them, behavior they saw directed at others, and behavior they reported they directed at others.

The treatment and control schools were highly similar on a variety of dimensions, such as the socioeconomic level of students, student/teacher ratios, and frequency of suspensions. On the initial assessments, on relevant measures of harmdoing the differences between treatment and control schools were less than 2%. There were both quantitative (Gubin, 2007) and qualitative (Habib, 2007) assessments. The latter used open-ended surveys during the training of trainers, observations of training sessions of trainers and later of students they trained, interviews with some trainers and the students they trained as well as with some teachers and school administrators, and diaries in which trainees described their experience after each training session.

Harmdoing in the treatment and control schools was about the same before the training. Harmdoing in schools that received the training diminished from before the training to the delayed posttest about five months after the end of the training, while it increased slightly in the control schools. This was the case with negative behaviors students reported were directed at them, as well as negative behavior they observed directed at others. For example, at the time of the delayed posttest, 45% of students in the treatment schools and 74% in the control schools reported that negative behavior was directed at them in the preceding seven days. The most frequent negative behavior was verbal harassment or abuse, and the largest decline was in such behavior.

Considering that this was the first use of a complex program, with changes along the way—in particular in trainers—this is a substantial change. However, our quantitative assessment found no significant change in students' reports of bystander behavior. This may have been the result of the inadequacy of our measure—although a similar measure in an earlier study found significant relationships between bystander behavior and other measures, such as students' feelings about their lives at school (Staub & Spielman, 2003) and significant changes with age (Staub et al., 2003).

Other than bystander behavior, the decline in harmdoing may have been the result of potential harmdoers understanding themselves better, as well as understanding the harm done by their actions and how their actions are seen by others. Or the training may have created an awareness that others might, or expectation that they would, respond to harmful actions as active bystanders. Both the journals/diaries students wrote at the end of each training session and interviews with a small number of them indicated greater awareness of their actions and roles as harmdoers, victims, and bystanders. However, students also reported both greater readiness to be active bystanders and actually engaging more in active bystandership, which the quantitative evaluation did not find. The training may also have affected the behavior of potential or actual victims, which we did not assess.

While we did not do a quantitative evaluation of the impact of their experience on trainers, there were many indications that being trained and then training others had very positive effects on them. One trainer said, "I realize now that I have been a harmdoer in the past, and I never knew how it affected the target" (the person harmed). Trainers reported increased self-confidence and surprise and pleasure that other students now turned to them rather than to adults to ask questions, for example, after a training session. Since teaching can solidify and expand knowledge—something that at least one trainer commented on—it is an important source of change, and it would be useful to evaluate its effects in the future.

Further Anecdotal Reports of Change

Reports by teachers and students indicated a change in school climates, with greater acceptance of active bystandership by students. Some teachers reported their own greater willingness to be active (Habib, 2007). When students found in the school corridor a list of people someone was thinking of killing, knowing who made the list, after some discussion among themselves they reported it to school authorities. Police and school personnel attributed this to the effects of the TAB training. There was a 43% decrease in dropout rate in Orange, which the superintendent attributed to TAB (Courville, 2008), and a 60% decline in the arraignments of juveniles in court compared to the year before the TAB program in the schools.

In Summary

Training active bystanders seems a promising program that can potentially be adapted to many settings. Information alone can change attitudes and behavior, and enactments of behavior can develop skills and increase the capacity to take others' perspective. In TAB, the information that students received was expanded through brainstorming, rehearsals of actions and role-plays (see Staub, 1970a, 1971b), and games that provided further experiential opportunities. Through these, as well as through students writing diaries at the end of each training session, the information could easily be applied to one's own experience. In our intervention in Rwanda and evaluations of their effects (see Staub, Pearlman, Gubin, & Hagengimana, 2005; Paluck, 2009; Staub & Pearlman, 2009; Staub, 2011; and Chapters 18, 19 in this book) we found that "experiential understanding"—people applying information to their own experience, in that case information about the origins and impact of genocides in general and examples from other countries—had a variety of beneficial effects.

New applications will hopefully replicate and enlarge the effects of the training. Their evaluations can include other measures, for example, of active bystandership by observations of behavior, and clarify the mechanisms through which positive effects come about.

References

Coie, J. D., & Dodge, K. A. (1997). Aggression and antisocial behavior. In W. Damon (Ed.), *Handbook of child psychology: Vol. 3. Social, emotional, and personality development* (5th ed.) New York: Wiley.

Courville, C., prod. (2008). *Training active bystanders* [Video]. Athol-Orange Community Television, Athol, MA.

Dodge, K. A., Bates, J. E., & Pettit, G. S. (1990). Mechanisms in the cycle of violence. *Science, 250,* 1678–1683.

Feinberg, J. K. (1978). *Anatomy of a helping situation: Some personality and situational determinants of helping in a conflict situation involving another's psychological distress* (Unpublished doctoral dissertation). University of Massachusetts, Amherst.

Fried, S., & Fried, D. (1996). *Bullies and victims.* New York: M. Evans.

Gubin, A. (2007). *Training Active Bystanders Quantitative program evaluation*. Belmont, MA: Sun Statistical and Research Consulting.

Habib, D. (2007). *Training active bystanders: Stories of implementation: A report on the findings of qualitative research*. Orange, MA: SOS Education Center.

Hazler, R., Carney, J., Green, S., Powell, R., & Jolly, L. (1997). Areas of expert agreement on identification of school bullies and victims. *School Psychology International, 18*, 5–14.

Latane, B., & Darley, J. (1970). *The unresponsive bystander*. New York: Appleton.

Leary, M. R., Kowalski, R. M., Smith, L., & Phillips, S. (2003). Teasing, rejection, and violence: Case studies of the school shootings. *Aggressive Behavior, 29*, 202–214.

Myers, D. (2010). *Social psychology*. New York: McGraw-Hill.

Nansel, T. R., Overpeck, M., Pilla, R. S., Ruan, W. J., Simons-Morton, B., & Scheidt, P. (2001). Bullying behaviors among U.S. youth: Prevalence and association with psychological adjustment. *JAMA: Journal of the American Medical Association, 285*(16), 2094–2100.

O'Connell Higgins, G. (1994). *Resilient adults overcoming a cruel past*. San Francisco: Jossey-Bass.

Olweus, D. (1993). *Bullying at school: What we know and what we can do*. Oxford: Oxford University Press.

Olweus, D. (1994). Bullying at school: Basic facts and effects of a school based intervention program. *Journal of Child Psychology and Psychiatry, 35*, 1171–1190.

Paluck, E. L. (2009). Reducing intergroup prejudice and conflict using the media: A field experiment in Rwanda. *Journal of Personality and Social Psychology, 96*, 574–587.

Rigby, K. (1996). *Bullying in schools and what to do about it*. Melbourne: Australian Council for Educational Research.

Rhodes, R. (1999). *Why they kill*. New York: Knopf.

Schatz, R. T., Staub, E., & Lavine, H. (1999). On the varieties of national attachment: Blind versus constructive patriotism. *Political Psychology, 20*, 151–175.

Schwartz, S. H., & Howard, J. (1984). Internalized values as motivators of altruism. In E. Staub, D. Bar-Tal, J. Karylowski, & J. Reykowski (Eds.), *The development and maintenance of prosocial behavior* (pp. 229–256). New York: Plenum Press.

Spielman, D., & Staub, E. (2000). Reducing boys' aggression. Learning to fulfill basic needs constructively. *Journal of Applied Developmental Psychology, 21*(2), 165–181.

Staub, E. (1970a). Assertive training, role playing and self control. In D. Upper & D. Goodenough (Eds.), *Behavior therapy in the institutional setting: Proceedings of the First Annual Brockton Symposium on Behavior Therapy*. Nutley, NJ: Roche Laboratories.

Staub, E. (1970b). A child in distress: The effects of focusing responsibility on children on their attempts to help. *Developmental Psychology, 2*, 152–154.

Staub, E. (1970c). A child in distress: The influence of age and number of witnesses on children's attempts to help. *Journal of Personality and Social Psychology, 14*, 130–140.

Staub, E. (1971a). Helping a person in distress: The influence of implicit and explicit "rules" of conduct on children and adults. *Journal of Personality and Social Psychology, 17*, 137–145.

Staub, E. (1971b). The use of role playing and induction in children's learning of helping and sharing behavior. *Child Development, 42*, 805–817.

Staub, E. (1974). Helping a distressed person: Social, personality and stimulus determinants. In L. Berkowitz (Ed.), *Advances in experimental social psychology* (Vol. 7., pp. 203–342). New York: Academic Press.

Staub, E. (1978). *Positive social behavior and morality: Vol. 1. Social and personal influences*. New York: Academic Press.

Staub, E. (1979). *Positive social behavior and morality: Vol. 2. Socialization and development*. New York: Academic Press.

Staub, E. (1989). *The roots of evil: The origins of genocide and other group violence*. New York: Cambridge University Press.

Staub, E. (1997). The psychology of rescue: Perpetrators, bystanders and heroic helpers. In J. Michalczyk (Ed.), *Resisters, rescuers and refugees: Historical and ethical issues* (pp. 137–147). Kansas City, MO: Sheed & Ward.

Staub, E. (2003). *The psychology of good and evil: Why children, adults and groups help and harm others*. New York: Cambridge University Press.

Staub, E. (2005). The roots of goodness: The fulfillment of basic human needs and the development of caring, helping and nonaggression, inclusive caring, moral courage, active bystandership, and altruism born of suffering. In G. Carlo & C. Edwards (Eds.), *Moral motivation through the life span: Theory, research, applications* (pp. 33–73). Nebraska Symposium on Motivation. Lincoln: Nebraska University Press.

Staub, E. (2011). *Overcoming evil: genocide, violent conflict and terrorism*. New York: Oxford University Press.

Staub, E. (2013). Building a peaceful society: Origins, prevention and reconciliation in genocide and other group violence. *American Psychologist, 68*(7), 576–589.

Staub, E., & Baer, R. S. Jr. (1974). Stimulus characteristics of a sufferer and difficulty of escape as determinants of helping. *Journal of Personality and Social Psychology, 30*, 279–285.

Staub, E., Fellner, D. Jr., Berry, J., & Morange, K. (2003). Passive and active bystandership across grades in response to students bullying others students. In E. Staub (Ed.), *The psychology of good and evil: Why children, adults and groups help and harm others* (pp. 240–244). New York: Cambridge University Press.

Staub, E., & Pearlman, L. A. (2009). Reducing intergroup prejudice and conflict: A commentary. *Journal of Personality and Social Psychology, 96*, 588–594.

Staub, E., Pearlman, L.A., Gubin, A., & Hagengimana, A. (2005). Healing, reconciliation, forgiving and the prevention of violence after genocide or mass killing: An intervention and its experimental evaluation in Rwanda. *Journal of Social and Clinical Psychology, 24*(3), 297–334.

Staub, E., & Spielman, D. A. (2003). Students' experience of bullying and other aspects of their lives in middle school in Belchertown: Report summary. In E. Staub (Ed.), *The psychology of good and evil: Why children, adults and groups help and harm others* (pp. 227–240). New York: Cambridge University Press.

Unnever, J., & Cornell, D. (2003). The culture of bullying in middle school. *Journal of School Violence, 2*, 5–27.

17

Education and Training as Routes to Helping, Nonaggression, Compassion, and Heroism

In recent years there have been projects that provide experiences (education and training) to children and especially adults to help them develop a disposition for helpful behavior, even for heroism, compassion, or positive responses to members of a group that has been an enemy, or to reduce aggression. It is socialization that has traditionally been seen as the basis of such characteristics and behaviors. Can educational experiences accomplish such aims? This is a significant matter, since many children are not raised in ways and many adults may not possess the characteristics that generate goodness. I will briefly summarize here some projects that I describe in more detail in other chapters of the book and additional ones.

Most research has focused on childrearing as the roots of personal dispositions to caring and helping—experiences in interaction with parents and teachers and the guidance they provide (see Chapter 3). There has also been interest in experiences with peers and the influence of culture. Sensitivity to the child's needs, warmth and affection, adults emphasizing positive values and leading children to behave according to them, helping children learn ways to modulate intense emotions all contribute to later caring and helping. Engaging children to help others is also important. It leads to "learning by doing," as anthropologists and my research with fifth and sixth graders found, increasing later helping.

Such socialization and experiences lead children to see people in a positive light, develop empathy and a feeling of responsibility for others' welfare. They can also develop competence and skills in helping. The circumstances surrounding the need for help can make helping more or less likely. But even then who we are, the personal characteristics and inclinations we have developed make a difference.

Can training or education, limited in time and extensiveness, also lead to helping in the real world, and can it do so even for people who have not experienced socialization for caring or have experienced negative socialization? The effects of trainings are not always evaluated; the effects of most of those I mention here have been evaluated. Because passivity by some witnesses—or bystanders—to others' need increases passivity by others, and such passivity allows the unfolding or evolution of increasingly harmful actions, I have been using the term *active bystandership* for intervening in a helpful manner.

In the famous Rodney King incident, a couple of police officers in Los Angeles beat Rodney King with their batons as he was lying on the ground while several officers stood around watching. This was captured on video and became infamous. I was asked to develop a training, to be used in police academies in California, aimed to make the use of unnecessary force by officers unlikely. It focused on active bystandership by police officers, who usually work in pairs, to redirect the interaction of their partner with a citizen if it became increasingly heated or to stop violent action if it has already begun. The training intended to bring about change both in officers' thinking, so that they would see halting rather than supporting harmful actions as good teamwork, and in their actions (see Chapter 14).

I have also developed, with associates, a training for students in schools to intervene when fellow students harass, intimidate, and verbally or physically harm—or bully—other students. We provided information based on past research about what inhibits people from helping others, as well as about the powerful impact that bystanders can have on other bystanders. In one of my studies, there was a crash and sounds of distress from another room. Depending on what one person (my confederate) said, the frequency of helping by the real participant—going into the other room—ranged from about 25% to 100%. In the training, students role-played engaging other bystanders as allies in helping. Acting together increases impact and reduces risk. We also worked on skills in intervening in as positive ways as possible. We discussed what past experiences might lead a student to bully others and the impact on the targets of such behavior. In two schools where 8th and 10th graders were trained, harmful behavior decreased by 20%, in comparison to two similar schools where students were not trained. We did not evaluate the impact of the training on those who were probably most affected, student trainers. One of them said: "I used to do such things, and never realized the harmful effects of my behavior" (see Chapter 16).

My associates and I have also worked on reconciliation after the genocide in Rwanda, training groups ranging from the staff of local organizations to national leaders, and creating educational radio programs including a radio drama about two villages in conflict that has been extremely popular since 2004 and is ongoing. We provide information about the origins of violence between groups, the impact of violence on people, avenues to the prevention of violence and reconciliation, and examples of active bystanders resisting leaders who promote violence. Studies evaluating the effects of these programs showed more positive attitudes by Hutus and Tutsis toward each other, less trauma symptoms, and more empathy for survivors of the genocide, as well as bystanders and even perpetrators. Those who listened to our educational radio drama both reported and actually showed, after one year, more willingness say what they believed and were more independent of authorities, both important for less violence in a society. They also engaged in more reconciliation activities, approaching people whose family members they had harmed, possibly killed, or people who had harmed their family (see Chapters 18 and 19, as well as Staub, 2011).

Another training project, initiated by Philip Zimbardo, the Heroic Imagination Project (heroicimagination.org), like our training with students, uses information about what inhibits helping. It also provides examples of people who have engaged in heroic action. It promotes "situational awareness," understanding situations so that people are more likely to appropriately respond to them (described in Svoboda, 2013). The project leaders are aware that initially what they can expect is "active bystandership," but hope that by engaging in helping people "learn by doing" (both my terminology), and become more ready to respond in dangerous situations that require heroism. I have found learning by doing even by rescuers who have saved lives in the Holocaust.

There are also trainings in compassion, using primarily varied meditation practices. In such practices people focus their attention, often on their breath. They observe and then let go of thoughts that emerge. In "loving kindness" meditation they send loving thoughts to other people, themselves, and the world. Research has shown that these trainings generate more positive feelings for the targets of loving feelings in the course of meditation and more hopefulness in children. They also activate empathy-related regions of the brain. In at least one study such a training also led to more compassionate action toward a suffering person (for an overview, see Seppala, 2013).

Neither my associates and I, in our evaluation studies of participants in these projects, nor apparently others, have assessed whether such learning experiences have greater or lesser effects on people with different characteristics, or how such trainings affect children or adults who have developed less capacity for empathy or responsibility for others' welfare. In one project my student Darren Spielman and I (Spielman & Staub, 2000) found that training aggressive boys reduced their aggression. Initially these boys saw people as more hostile and human nature as more negative and felt less responsibility for others' welfare than nonaggressive boys.

The training consisted of role-playing situations that tend to evoke aggression in these boys, such as someone taking the seat where a boy left his bag to sit with his friends at lunch. They enacted these situations first in the way they would usually unfold and then in constructive ways. They videotaped and discussed their role-plays. In the course of a series of sessions we introduced ideas about psychological needs that all people have—for security, for feeling effective, for a positive identity, for positive connection to other people, and for understanding one's world. We discussed fulfilling these needs by destructive actions, as they had been doing (actions that harmed others and also ultimately oneself), or constructive actions. Thus the training provided both a way of thinking and practice and skills in constructive ways of fulfilling needs.

An evaluation study showed that in one school with a supportive environment, both boys who received this training and aggressive boys who did not became less aggressive. In another school with a more challenging environment, aggressive boys who did not receive the training became more aggressive—as judged by teachers and in-school suspensions—but boys who had received the training became slightly less aggressive, with a clear difference between the two groups. Boys who received the training also came to see people as less hostile. It is a negative past that usually leads to hostility and aggression. That certain experiences can lead to transformation is consistent with "altruism born of suffering," that some people who have been victimized, whether in the home or by political violence, devote themselves to preventing harm or helping people who have been harmed.

I have developed another practice that I informally used in workshops with teachers, but that has not been applied in its complete form. This was a blueprint to develop caring schools in which the experiences of children in the classroom generate caring and helping and make aggression less likely (Staub, 2003). The essence of this blueprint or plan was specification of how to apply to the classroom the socialization practices I described in this book (for example, in Chapters 3 and 5). To create such classrooms requires the training of teachers. It is frequent practice, of course, to provide people with training in order that they then guide others. That it is possible to do this effectively is indicated in our work in Rwanda. The formal evaluation of a training that showed many positive effects was done with people we did not directly work with, but whose meetings were facilitated by some of the people who participated in one of our workshops.

It seems that "training," both direct education and public education through media, can help people become more caring, more active as bystanders, as well as less aggressive. The combination of socialization for caring and helping and further learning experiences may be especially powerful. Training, that is, new learning experience, can also counteract prior negative experiences. Education or training that is more extensive and solidified by applications to behavior is likely to be more successful.

References

Seppala, E. (2013). The compassionate mind. *Observer of the Association for Psychological Science, 26*(5). 20–24.

Spielman, D., & Staub, E. (2000). Reducing boys' aggression. Learning to fulfill basic needs constructively. *Journal of Applied Developmental Psychology, 21*(2), 165–181.

Staub, E. (2003). *The psychology of good and evil: Why children, adults and groups help and harm others.* New York: Cambridge University Press.

Staub, E. (2011). *Overcoming evil: genocide, violent conflict and terrorism.* New York: Oxford University Press.Svoboda, E. (2013). *What makes a hero? The surprising science of selflessness.* New York: Current/Penguin.

18

Advancing Healing and Reconciliation—in Rwanda and Beyond

ERVIN STAUB AND LAURIE ANNE PEARLMAN

In this chapter, we describe an approach to promoting post-genocide psychological recovery, reconciliation, the development of positive relations between groups, and a peaceful society. We describe workshops/trainings that we conducted in Rwanda between 1999 and 2006 and the evaluation of the approach we used. We have used its components with the staff of local and international nongovernmental organizations (NGOs) whose work ranges from community-building to reconciliation, leaders and field staff from survivor organizations, journalists, high-level national leaders, trauma counselors, commissioners of the Rwandan National Unity and Reconciliation Commission (NURC), and others.

In the course of describing this work, we discuss some issues important in reconciliation and the prevention of new violence, such as a shared understanding of history (or collective memory). We comment on some current conditions in Rwanda that appear to facilitate or create problems for reconciliation and the building of a peaceful society. We also offer observations along the way about how outsiders or third parties might be most helpful in reconciliation.

Our work has been a response to a fundamental question that arises in the aftermath of genocide or intractable, violent conflict: after such violence, how can groups that continue to live together build a better, nonviolent future? While the approach we describe here was developed and used in Rwanda, it seems applicable to other places where violent conflict, mass killing, or genocide has taken place.

In recent years, especially since the activity of the Truth and Reconciliation Commission in South Africa, the necessity for reconciliation in the aftermath of violence between groups

Reprinted with permission and minor changes from Staub, E., & Pearlman, L. A. (2006). Advancing healing and reconciliation. In L. Barbanel & R. Sternberg (Eds.), *Psychological interventions in times of crisis*. New York: Springer-Verlag.

and ways to promote it have received a great deal of attention (Lederach, 1995, 1997). It has become apparent to many observers that violence between groups often resumes (de la Rey, 2001), even when it has ended with peace treaties and agreements. Segments of one or both of the groups may find the agreements unacceptable, and/or deep feelings of insecurity, hurt, anger and hostility may remain. The resumption of violence seems an even greater danger when genocide ends with victory by the victim group over the perpetrator group, as in Rwanda.

Reconciliation is a change in attitude and behaviors toward the other group. We define it as mutual acceptance by members of groups of each other, and the processes and structures that lead to or maintain that acceptance (Staub & Pearlman, 2001). While structures and institutions that promote and serve reconciliation are important, the essence of reconciliation is a changed psychological orientation toward the other. Reconciliation implies that victims and perpetrators do not see the past as defining the future. They come to accept and see the humanity of one another and see the possibility of a constructive relationship.

Following great violence between groups, especially genocide, reconciliation is a profoundly difficult challenge. It can only develop gradually, with likely setbacks along the way (Staub & Bar-Tal, 2003). Truth and justice have already become part of conventional thinking as requirements for reconciliation (see *Proceedings of Stockholm International Forum on Truth, Justice and Reconciliation*, 2002). Montville (1993) has suggested that healing from past wounds is important to reconciliation; we see it as an essential aspect of reconciliation.

The Impact of Victimization on Survivors and Perpetrators

The impact of genocide on survivors is enormous. Their perception of themselves and of the world is deeply affected. They feel diminished, vulnerable. The world looks dangerous and people, especially those outside one's group, untrustworthy (Staub, 1998, 2011, 2014). These psychological disruptions may give rise to intense trauma symptoms such as nightmares, flashbacks, and emotional numbing, as well as disruptions in survivors' world view, relationships with self and others, and identity (McCann & Pearlman, 1990a; Pearlman & Saakvitne, 1995). Since identity is rooted, in part, in group membership, even members of the victim group who were not present when the genocide was perpetrated may be greatly traumatized (Staub, 1998). In Rwanda, this means "returnees," mainly children of Tutsi refugees from earlier violence who came back from neighboring countries after the genocide to devastated families and community. This traumatization may be especially likely since these returnees were not accepted and integrated in the countries of their former refuge, which strengthened their identities as Tutsi from Rwanda. Some of them came back as part of the Rwanda Patriotic Front, the mainly Tutsi group that entered from Uganda in 1990 and initiated a civil war. In April 1994 the genocide began. The RPF defeated the government and ended the genocide. Other Tutsis came back after this.

The psychological consequences of victimization include extreme sensitivity to new threat. When new conflict with another group arises, it is more difficult for survivors to take the perspective of the other and consider the other's needs. Without corrective experiences, they may believe they need to defend themselves even when violent self-defense is not necessary. In response to new threat or conflict they may strike out, in the process becoming perpetrators (Staub, 1998, 2011, 2014; see Chapters 3, 10). Healing from psychological wounds, trauma that can result from victimization, is important to prevent such defensive violence and to enhance the capacity of the group for reconciliation.

Often perpetrators had past experiences of victimization or other traumatic experiences. Their unhealed psychological wounds have contributed to their actions. The extent of their victimization may be substantially less than the suffering they have created, especially in a genocide. Nonetheless, unless others acknowledge their injuries, and they address them, they may be unable to shift from a defensive stance of self-justification to a position of accepting responsibility for their actions, paving the way for reconciliation.

Sometimes past trauma is fixed and maintained in collective memory; it becomes a "chosen trauma" that continuously shapes group psychology and behavior (Volkan, 1997). This seems to have been the case with Hutus in Rwanda. The first author had the opportunity to conduct a prison interview with the person who was justice minister during the genocide. As other Hutus have done, she referred to the group's experience under Tutsi rule before 1959 (actually Belgian rule, the Belgians using the Tutsis to rule in their behalf) as "slavery." While this statement may also be self-justification, this period was traumatic for Hutus and remains a trauma in Hutu collective memory.

In addition, people who engage in intense violence against others tend to be psychologically injured by their own actions (MacNair, 2002; Rhodes, Allen, Nowinski, & Cillessen, 2002). To protect themselves from empathic distress, guilt, and shame, perpetrators often distance themselves from victims. This distancing begins to develop in the course of the evolution of increasing discrimination and violence that usually precedes genocide (Staub, 1989). The lessening of empathy and compassion easily extends to other people as well.

When the violence has ended, perpetrators often continue to blame victims and hold on to the ideology that in part motivated and to them justified their violence. This protects them to some extent from the emotional consequences of their actions. Those members of the perpetrator group who did not participate in planning or executing the genocide but were passive bystanders to it are likely to be also affected, but less intensely. Healing from the psychological consequences of their own or their group's actions may help people to see the humanity of the victims, to feel empathy, regret, and sorrow, and to become more able to apologize and reconcile.

To summarize, healing from wounds that result from being harmed (see also Montville, 1993), having harmed others, or being a member of a group that has harmed others (Staub, 2011, 2014; Staub & Pearlman, 2001) seems important for reconciliation. Reconciliation can help to prevent a continuing cycle of violence, especially between groups that continue to live together. As healing begins, reconciliation becomes more possible.

Healing and reconciliation are interdependent, especially when groups that have engaged in violence against each other continue to live together. Healing is essential both to improve the quality of life of wounded people and to make new violence less likely—the overarching goals of our work in Rwanda. At least some limited degree of safety is needed for healing to begin (Herman, 1992; McCann & Pearlman, 1990a; see Staub, 2014). Widespread severe poverty, the gacaca (community justice process), the release of many prisoners in 2003, the development of a constitution, democratic elections, and the continuing violence in the Congo had significant impact on people in Rwanda. Nonetheless, healing processes have been underway in the country, and apparently, many people feel safe enough to engage in such processes. As reconciliation begins, it increases the feeling of security and perhaps of actual security, which makes further healing easier. Progress in one realm fosters progress in the other. However, there have also been societal problems which we will discuss later.

Promoting Healing and Reconciliation in the Community

In this section, we describe an intervention we developed to promote community healing and reconciliation, and an experimental evaluation of its effects. Our goal was to develop an intervention that people without advanced professional training could deliver, that facilitators could use with groups, and that one could readily integrate into other programs for healing, reconciliation, and community-building.

Developing a group, rather than an individual, intervention seemed essential for a number of reasons. First, the genocide affected most of the population of about 8,000,000 in Rwanda, making an individual approach to healing impractical. Second, the genocide was a community disaster, and healing as part of a group, in the community of others, seems more appropriate and potentially more effective. A group approach also seems more appropriate to Rwandan culture, which, like many African cultures, is community rather than individual-oriented (Wessells & Monteiro, 2001). Further, one of the consequences of victimization is disconnection from other people (Saakvitne, Gamble, Pearlman, & Lev, 2000), and group healing can help people reconnect with others. Social support or connection is an important antidote to trauma, at least in the United States (Wortman, Battle, & Lemkau, 1997). Finally, reconciliation between groups requires the engagement of the whole population, and involving more people in interventions is essential.

Our intention has been to offer both information (content) and a way of delivering it (process) that others can use to *augment* their on-going work. This approach acknowledges the expertise of local staff, allows for cultural adaptation of the material, leaves control in the hands of the local facilitators, and allows each user to identify his/her own specific goals (e.g., healing, reconciliation, forgiving, group coexistence, improved adaptations to daily life).

In the following, we use the terms "facilitators" or "facilitator-participants" to refer to people who attended our seminars in 1999 and in the training-of-trainers in 2003-04. These people were professional helpers with various backgrounds and positions. Some were trained trauma counselors, others public educators for the national unity and reconciliation commission, still others frontline staff in local NGOs, a few were staff of religious organizations. They facilitate varied types of groups in the community, and they were participants in our seminars, hence the names facilitators or facilitator-participants. In describing our research, we use the term "integrated groups" to describe the experimental groups in which facilitators integrated our material with their usual approach to healing, reconciliation, and/or community building.

In our first project in 1999, we conducted a two-week seminar/workshop in Kigali with about 35 Rwandese staff of local and international NGOs that engage in healing and community building. About two-thirds of the participants were Tutsi, one-third Hutu. These participants would eventually facilitate groups in the community. Our local collaborators recruited them, mainly from organizations with which we made contact on our first trip in January 1999.

We developed a workshop based on theory, research, and experience with complex trauma (Allen, 2001; Herman, 1992; McCann & Pearlman, 1990a; Pearlman & Saakvitne, 1995; Esterling, L'Abate, Murray, & Pennebaker, 1999; Saakvitne et al., 2000) and with violence (Staub, 1989, 1998, 1999, 2003). The workshop included brief psycho-educational lectures with extensive large- and small-group discussions after each lecture, and experiential components that gave participants opportunities to apply the material to their personal experience. Our objective was to provide participants with information that they could later use in their work with groups in the community, as well as opportunities to reflect on and process some of their own genocide-related experiences.

Staff from local NGOs who attended a one-day meeting with us in January 1999 identified five elements as potentially useful in their fieldwork. These elements became the basis of much of our later work in Rwanda. We describe the five elements next.

Understanding the Effects of Trauma and Victimization and Avenues to Healing

There is some tendency among professionals who provide assistance in the wake of psychosocial disasters to distinguish and contrast approaches focusing on trauma and on community building. From our perspective, the two approaches are not contradictory, but can be integrated and can support each other. Our approach blends an understanding of complex psychological trauma with a community-centered approach to recovery.

Understanding psychological trauma, including both the symptoms of post-traumatic stress disorder (American Psychiatric Association, 1994) and the profound effects of traumatic experiences on the self, perceptions of people and the world, and one's spirituality can contribute to healing (Allen, 2001; Rosenbloom & Williams, 1999; Saakvitne et al., 2000; Staub, 1998, 2011, 2014). Experiencing senseless, violent cruelty toward oneself and one's group diminishes self-worth. Realizing that the way one has changed is the normal consequence of extraordinary, painful experiences can ease people's distress and open the possibility for further healing.

Providing people with a framework for recovery offers hope, a fundamental aspect of healing (Saakvitne et al., 2000). Traumatized people often carry their pain and sense of danger into the present. Engagement with their painful experiences—remembering the events and feeling the emotions related to what happened—under empathic, supportive conditions, can help people move constructively into the future. It can also help them gain new trust in, and reconnect with, people.

Trauma specialists have found that another aspect of healing is creating a story of one's experience that makes sense of it. By symbolizing or representing traumatic experiences through narratives, dramatizations, or art, people can create meaning (Harvey, 1996; Herman, 1992; Lantz, 1996; Newman, Riggs, & Roth, 1997; Pennebaker & Beall, 1986), such as trying to prevent such suffering by others (Higgins, 1994). Indeed, some research has found that traumatic experiences stimulate a search for meaning (Tokayer, 2002).

Encouraging people to talk about their painful experiences, or exposure, can overcome the avoidance that maintains trauma symptoms (Foa, Keane, & Friedman, 2000). While there is some disagreement about the need for survivors to talk about their traumatic experiences (Bonnano, Noll, Putnam, O'Neill, & Trickett, 2003), the preponderance of clinical and empirical evidence suggests that doing so is helpful for many survivors. Survivors of sudden, traumatic loss also need to understand traumatic grief and the need for mourning (Rando, 1993).

We provided a broad understanding of the psychological aftermath of traumatic experiences, "beyond PTSD," helping people understand the behavioral, cognitive, emotional, interpersonal, spiritual, and physiological aftermath of violence. We also conveyed to workshop participants that trauma does not imply psychopathology or dysfunction. Furthermore, communities can use a neighbor-to-neighbor approach to address trauma: we support people in participating actively in their own recovery. This perspective seems to have energized and empowered the people with whom we have worked in Rwanda.

Understanding Genocide

People often see genocide as incomprehensible evil. People also often see their own suffering as unique. Learning about similar ways that others have suffered and examining the psychological and social roots of such violence can help people see their common humanity with others. It can mitigate negative attitudes toward oneself, and even toward perpetrators, helping victims to see perpetrators (as well as passive bystanders) as human beings, in spite of their horrible actions. This experience should make reconciliation with members of a perpetrator group more possible. We hypothesized that exploration of the influences that lead to genocide, based primarily on the conception developed by Staub (1989, 1996, 1999, 2003; it is mentioned in several chapters) and enriched by other conceptions (Chorbajian & Shirinian, 1999; Totten, Parsons, & Charny, 1997) would contribute both to healing and reconciliation.

In our brief lectures about the origins of genocide, we did not describe how the influences that lead to genocide apply to Rwanda (which is described in Staub, 1999 and greater detail in Staub, 2011). Instead, we presented the concepts and their application to other genocides (Staub, 1989), and then asked the participants to apply them to Rwanda. They did so very effectively.

Understanding Basic Psychological Needs

The frustration of basic psychological needs by social conditions is one cause of groups turning against other groups (Burton, 1990; Kelman, 1990; Staub, 1989). We hypothesized that understanding basic psychological needs could contribute to understanding the origins of genocide and its impact on people, and further promote healing. Traumatic experiences frustrate or disrupt basic needs (McCann & Pearlman, 1990a; Pearlman, 2003), and healing promotes the fulfillment of those needs. Basic psychological needs on which we focus include security or safety, trust, esteem, positive identity, feelings of effectiveness and control, positive connections to other people, a comprehension of reality and of one's own place in the world, and transcendence (or spiritual needs) (McCann & Pearlman, 1990a; Pearlman & Saakvitne, 1995; Saakvitne et al., 2000; Staub, 1989, 2003).

Engagement with Experience

We planned to have participants engage with what happened to them during the genocide by first writing (Pennebaker & Beall, 1986), or if they were unable to write, drawing something about their experiences. The next step would be to discuss these experiences in small groups. However, while these facilitator-participants all could write, 50 percent of the population in Rwanda cannot, and many of the people in the community with whom our participants worked have never held a pen or pencil. So instead, we invited the facilitator-participants to reflect privately upon what they experienced during the genocide. Many of them expressed a preference to engage in the exercise in this way.

We discussed the importance of empathic responding to others' experiences, and provided some limited training in it. We demonstrated lack of response, inappropriate responses such as offering advice or immediately beginning to tell one's own story, as well as appropriate empathy. We also invited discussion of culturally appropriate responses. In small groups, participants then told their stories, and often cried with others in this process.

We worked with a mixed group, both Hutus and Tutsis. Given the realities in Rwanda—the genocide by Hutus against Tutsis with the Tutsis now in power—it may not be surprising that the Hutus, who participated actively in the workshop in general, did not tell the "stories" of their experiences during the genocide. Still, we believe that hearing the painful stories of Tutsis—stories that mainly focused on what happened to the victims, hardly mentioning perpetrators—could promote empathy in Hutus and contribute to reconciliation. The empathic participation of Hutus in the small groups may have further helped Tutsis toward healing and reconciliation. Scholars at the Stone Center have written about the central role of empathy in healing and connection (Jordan, Walker, & Hartling, 2004).

Vicarious Traumatization

Vicarious traumatization (VT) is a transformation in the self of the helper that comes about through empathic engagement with trauma survivor clients and a sense of commitment or responsibility to help (McCann & Pearlman, 1990b; Saakvitne et al., 2000; Saakvitne & Pearlman, 1996). While research findings are mixed, the preponderance of evidence suggests that VT may be more common in helpers with a personal trauma history than those without such a history (Arvay, 2001). We introduced the notion to our Rwandese facilitator-participants, most of whom may be considered "wounded healers," who immediately grasped the VT concept. They seemed grateful for this acknowledgment of the challenges of their work and relieved by the normalization of their experience. They collaborated enthusiastically to explore work-related stressors as well as sharing possible coping strategies and ways of addressing and transforming their vicarious trauma.

Informal observations

The information we provided in our workshop about the origins of genocide and mass killing, exemplifying principles by reference to various cases, and the discussions that followed in the course of which participants applied the principles to the genocide in Rwanda, had a visibly powerful impact on participants. Learning that people elsewhere had suffered similarly and coming to understand how certain influences contribute to genocide seemed to help participants feel that they were not outside history and human experience. They seemed moved and rehumanized by the understanding that what had happened in their society is a human, albeit horrific, process. One woman said, "If this has happened to other people, then it doesn't mean that God abandoned the people of Rwanda." Echoing several others, another person said, "If we can understand how this happened, we can act to prevent it in the future." Applying the influences leading to genocide to what happened in Rwanda, participants seemed to gain a deep, *experiential understanding* of the roots of genocide in Rwanda.

Two aspects of the presentation about trauma seemed to provide some relief to participants. The idea that the widely varied adaptations in thoughts, feelings, behavior, relationships, and spiritual experience they experienced and observed in others are normal responses to abnormal events was depathologizing. The additional notion that traumatized people can be effective in their lives seemed to provide hope. It also may have provided permission for people to acknowledge their pain without fearing that others would see them as "crazy."

Our informal observations, along with the results of our formal evaluation (described later in the chapter and in detail in Staub, Pearlman, Gubin, & Hagengimana, 2005), suggested that Tutsis' orientation to Hutus became more positive as they came to understand that perpetrators acted in response to societal, cultural, and psychological forces. Such an understanding may help people to realize that preventing mass violence requires inhibiting the social processes that lead to it, which profoundly shape and form potential perpetrators. Our formal research results suggested that the training also helped the Hutu seminar participants, who presumably did not actively harm others (people known to have been perpetrators were either in jail or had fled the country) to have a way of understanding the horrible events of the genocide.

We intended our facilitator-participants to use the new material with groups in the community, in combination with their traditional methods or approaches, the latter presumably reflecting their understanding of the community, its history and needs (see Wessells & Monteiro, 2001). Part of the seminar focused on integrating our approach with the facilitators' own quite varied approaches. We encouraged them to develop further this *integrated approach* in their work with groups in the community.

Measuring Impact

There has been a great deal of research on the effects of contact between members of different groups in overcoming prejudice or devaluation (Pettigrew & Tropp, 2000). However, the evaluation of interventions to reduce conflict between groups is mostly informal and anecdotal, rather than systematic research (Ross & Rothman, 1999). We conducted an experimental study to assess the impact of our intervention—not on the people in our seminar, but on members of community groups which they subsequently facilitated (Staub et al., 2005).

Following the seminar, some of the facilitator-participants *integrated* our approach with their own in working with community groups comprising the different segments of the community: Tutsis, among them women who were tortured through rape; widows; HIV-affected persons; Hutus; and Twa (about 1 percent of the population). For our research purposes, these were the experimental groups. Other staff from the same organizations who had not participated in the workshop used their usual or *traditional* approach with equally diverse community groups. Both types of groups (integrated and traditional) were newly created for the purpose of the study, meeting three hours, twice a week, for three weeks. Participants were 194 people, with approximately 60 percent self-identified as Tutsi, 16 percent as Hutu or Twa, and 23 percent providing anomalous identifying information, with some changes in self-identification across measurements. There were about 16 people in each of the research groups.

The organizations for which our facilitators worked, with the assistance of our Rwandan research associates, created these groups and assigned participants to treatment and control groups. As far as we know there was no selection bias in assigning them to groups. However, since we had no direct control over the assignment, it cannot be considered a random assignment. We control for possible initial differences by comparing groups from before to after treatment, and using statistical method to address any pretreatment differences.

The activities of the groups were of the kind the facilitators normally worked with. Some focused on healing, others on community-building (talking about their difficulties and providing support to each other in the course of agricultural work), with the seminar material integrated into these activities in the experimental groups. *Control* groups were also created, which were simply evaluated for changes over time. Both the *integrated* and *traditional* groups filled out questionnaires before they began to meet, about a month later (just after facilitators stopped working with them), and two months after that. Members of the *control* groups filled out the same questionnaires at about the same times.

We found that trauma symptoms decreased in the *integrated* groups led by the facilitators who participated in our seminar both over time, from before the trainings to two months after it, and in comparison to changes in the other groups. Symptoms increased somewhat in both the *traditional* groups led by facilitators who did not participate in our seminar and the *control* groups. We also found an increase in positive orientation toward the other group in the groups led by facilitators we trained, both over time and in comparison to the other groups.

The elements of this positive orientation included (1) seeing the genocide as having complex origins (rather than simply resulting from the evil nature of the perpetrators, or bad leaders), (2) expressing willingness to work with the other group for important goals (e.g., a better future), and (3) expressing willingness to forgive the other group if its members acknowledged what they did and apologized for the group's actions (see Staub, 2003; Staub et al., 2005).

In summary, relatively limited participation in groups led by facilitators who participated in our seminars contributed to both healing and to a more positive attitude by groups toward each other. We subsequently further developed elements of this approach, which we used in our work with varied groups.

Working With National Leaders

We conducted two seminar/workshops, both organized in collaboration with the National Unity and Reconciliation Commission (NURC), with high-level national leaders. The 35 participants in a four-day meeting in August 2001 were government ministers, members of the supreme court, heads of national commissions (electoral, constitutional), the heads of the national prison system and of the main Kigali prison, an advisor to the president, leaders of religious organizations, and commissioners of the NURC. In January 2003, the 60 to 70 participants in a one-day seminar were a similar group, with more government ministers, both the president and vice-president of the Supreme Court, heads of political parties, and members of parliament. While both of these seminars were mixed, the current leadership is predominantly Tutsi and there were more Tutsi than Hutu leaders present.

We designed the 2001 seminar to advance leaders' understanding of the impact of genocide both on themselves and on the people of Rwanda, and to consider avenues to healing that leaders might promote. Two important purposes were to provide an understanding of (1) how genocide and mass killing originate and (2) policies and practices in the society that might reduce the likelihood of renewed violence and promote positive relations between groups in Rwanda, in the hope that leaders would advance such policies and practices. The social context was the planned gacaca, or nationwide community justice process, and leaders' expressed concern that one undesirable byproduct of it would be retraumatization. Probably their unexpressed concern, and our strong concern, was also that the testimonies of horrible actions in front of the gacaca would create renewed anger in both groups, and possibly renewed violence. By January 2003, the context included the release of large numbers of prisoners earlier that month, and the experience of some pilot work with gacaca.

As in our previous work in Rwanda, in the leaders' seminars we suggested that both difficult economic and political conditions and group conflict are starting points for the evolution of group violence (Staub, 1989, 1999, 2003; Staub & Bar-Tal, 2003). We discussed the important roles of scapegoating, destructive ideologies, devaluation of members of another group, unhealed wounds from past traumatic experiences, excessive respect for authority, the importance of pluralism, the gradual evolution of increasing violence, and the role of bystanders—both people inside a group and outside groups and nations. We provided leaders with a form to help them evaluate policies and practices. One endpoint on each line on it identified an influence that would make violence between groups more likely, while the other endpoint the opposite influence that would make it less likely (such as devaluing another group—humanizing the other group).

The participants identified and discussed policies and practices from the standpoint of these dimensions. For example, how might new decentralization policies affect people's sense of obedience to authority? What is the impact of providing special help to needy survivors of the genocide, but given highly limited resources, not to needy members of the perpetrator group? They considered whether particular practices would make violence more or less likely and what they could do to shape them so that they would reduce the likelihood of future violence. We also discussed avenues to reconciliation following violence, such as truth, justice, healing from past wounds, significant contact between groups as they work together for shared goals, and the creation of a shared history in place of different and conflicting views of history.

The group in 2001 intensely discussed, and supported by the facilitators (ES and LAP), applied this understanding of the origins of genocide and prevention of violence to Rwanda. The group discussed the challenges of addressing harmful elements of culture, such as a hierarchical society with great respect for authority, which serve them as leaders. These elements, including obedience to orders to kill, appear to have contributed in a variety of ways to the genocide in Rwanda, (des Forges, 1999; Mamdani, 2002; Staub, 1999, 2011).

The Meaning of Group

Guided by government policy of "unity," and the strong commitment of individual leaders to this policy, the use of the terms "Hutu" and "Tutsi" has been strongly discouraged and people rarely used these terms in 2001. In response to our discussion of devaluation of the "other group," seminar participants stated that there were no groups in Rwanda. They stated that the Belgian colonizers artificially created divisions. While there is not enough research and experience to offer much guidance, our understanding of the impact of victimization, group relations, and reconciliation suggests that acknowledging feelings of hostility between groups and working to overcome them is more likely to lead to reconciliation and peace than is asserting unity and not addressing such feelings. In the former Yugoslavia, for example, the government discouraged exploration of the mass killing of Serbs (and Jews) that took place during World War II by the Croat republic allied with Nazi Germany. Thus, the deep wounds, fear, and hostility between groups that were likely to remain were not addressed. With such exploration, perhaps the violence of the 1990s would have been avoided.

In our discussions, participants moved toward acknowledging that, whether or not there is a biological basis for the differentiation between Hutu and Tutsi, there has been differentiation socially (in terms of interpersonal behaviors such as discrimination) and psychologically (in terms of seeing themselves and others as belonging to one or the other group). A high-status participant said at one point, "I wonder what they say about each other in their homes."

Creating a Shared History of Rwanda

After violence, each group tends to see the other as at fault. Each blames the other for its own violent acts, claims and sees these acts as necessary reactions to the other's actions or to the danger the other represents (Bar-Tal, 2002; Staub, 2011). The conflicting views about what happened can rekindle hostility and violence.

Especially when groups live together, creating a history that is acceptable to both sides may be essential for reconciliation (Bar-Tal, 2002; Cairns & Roe, 2002; Penal Reform International, 2004; Staub & Bar-Tal, 2003). A French-German commission of historians did this after World War II, with a focus on showing that the two countries had not always been implacable foes (Willis, 1965). In our first leaders' seminar, some participants expressed the belief that history is objective, that there is only one correct factual account of events. Predominantly, however, the group recognized that there can be different perspectives on historical events and agreed that creating a shared history acceptable to all groups in Rwanda is important. They noted that the government had just convened a commission to create a history to be taught in the schools. The hope was that this history curriculum would lay the groundwork for a more peaceful future.

In small group discussions, a group considering how such a history could be created attracted many participants, who had many ideas about how to achieve it. These included each group taking the role of the other in describing history, as well as the recognition of earlier peaceful coexistence. However, in the end many participants expressed skepticism that it would be possible to create such a history at this time, in light of the feelings generated by the recent genocide. In July 2003, the creation of such a history for the schools was in progress. Unfortunately, in the period that followed, the creation and introduction of such a history into the schools was long delayed.

In our subsequent seminars/workshops in Rwanda, we introduced elements of an approach to the creation of a shared history. Using our approach to understanding the roots of genocide, we attempted to make past historical events comprehensible, identifying the social and psychological forces that led to discrimination and violence. By bringing understanding and empathy to historical events and actions, we hoped to help people acknowledge their own group's blameworthy actions and begin to accept the other group.

For example, in the second leaders' seminar, one of the participants referred to the "genocide" in 1959. At that time, there was a Hutu uprising against Tutsi rule, with many Tutsis killed. In response to this comment, we said that as we understood it, what happened in 1959 was mass killing but not genocide (see Staub, 1989, 2011, and Staub & Bar-Tal, 2003, for a discussion of this distinction). We noted that the Belgian colonizers elevated the Tutsis, who ruled in their behalf. The situation of the Hutus was extremely bad and the societal arrangements unjust. We also noted the difficulty in correcting unequal relations between groups and that lamentably, attempts to correct such injustice commonly include violence (Davis, 1969). We noted that under the Hutu rule that followed, there was discrimination and violence against the Tutsis. Had the Hutus created more just social arrangements, the subsequent evolution toward genocide would have been less likely. In the daily anonymous written evaluations that we collect in all of our seminars, one participant wrote that this was the first time that he or she learned that the violence in 1959 was not genocide, that it was a response to injustice, and thanked us for the information.

Challenges of the Gacaca as a Vehicle for Justice and Reconciliation

At the time of our leaders' seminar in 2001, there was great concern about the potentially harmful impact of the upcoming gacaca, or community justice process. The leaders asked for our help in promoting the potential positive value of this process. We responded by initiating a seminar with community leaders and a public education campaign, which we describe later.

In the gacaca process, the populace elected 250,000 people from the general population in October 2001 who were to serve as judges, in panels of 19, in about 9,000 locations around Rwanda. Their task was to judge the large majority of the approximately 115,000 people who were in jail since 1994, accused of perpetrating the genocide. The gacaca law requires the population to be present and participate. The process moves from identifying the crimes committed—ranging from property theft to rape, murder, and the planning of violence—to establishing what community members know about the crimes committed in that community, to judging alleged perpetrators. In the course of this process, people give and hear testimonies about killing, rape, and atrocities of many kinds. Communities gather in the fields each week to engage in this process.

The gacaca pilot process resulted in several changes. Changes were made in the areas of organization, categorization of crimes, moral damages, and sentences. Penal Reform International has described and commented on those changes and presented a preliminary analysis of gacaca (Penal Reform International, 2004).

Members of our group agreed that, while it could have great potential positive effects, the gacaca process was likely to reactivate trauma for everyone. It might also generate renewed hostility in both groups. They expressed concern that everyone—witnesses, alleged perpetrators, judges, families of victims, people who knew alleged perpetrators as neighbors and now see them as enemies—would need support. The participants requested our help in shaping the gacaca process to promote reconciliation. It is our belief that people need preparation in advance, support during the process, and opportunities to process their experience afterwards in order to minimize retraumatization.

Work with Local Community Leaders

In June 2002, we facilitated a four-day seminar/workshop, with approximately 35 Rwandese community leaders from around the country. They were high- and mid-level leaders and staff primarily from Ibuka (the main survivor organization, of which several constituent associations were represented, such as Avega, a widows' organization, and Profemmes, an umbrella organization for women's associations throughout the country), the Ministry of Health, and the NURC. Participants included regional representatives, directors of central medical facilities, commissioners from the NURC, people in leadership roles in the assistance of widows, and others.

Our purpose was to help participants to lessen the potential negative effects and promote the potential positive effects of the gacaca, which was in its pilot phase. We, as the facilitators, and the NURC, which organized the workshop, agreed that the purposes of the gacaca process—justice, healing, and reconciliation—might be advanced if people had ways of understanding how genocide comes about. In addition, understanding psychological trauma and healing might help to minimize the retraumatization that seemed likely to occur as a result of the gacaca hearings, and enable people to support each other in the process. Before we addressed these goals in the seminar, we asked participants to describe the positive effects of the gacaca they anticipated and hoped for, and the negative effects they feared.

The anticipated positive effects included:

- The truth will be established (how relatives were killed, who should be punished);
- The process will create justice;
- Everyone will be involved in the process;
- The whole population will respect the decisions made because they will have taken part in the process;
- When perpetrators are punished, reconciliation will be possible;
- The problems between the two groups will be resolved;
- As the prisons empty, the economic burden on the country will diminish;
- The country can develop as it resolves problems;
- Over time, the effects of trauma will diminish;
- People will find out where their relatives died and can bury them with dignity, which will enable them to mourn properly;
- As circumstances in the country improve, exiles will return.

In addition, we suggested and the group agreed to the following:

- Innocent people can go home;
- Those sentenced and their relatives will know their fate and can turn to the future;
- The whole society will gain closure.

The potential negative effects resulting from the gacaca that people anticipated or feared included the following:

- Retraumatization may occur as people give or hear testimonies;
- Some people may give biased, untrue testimony;
- Some won't tell the truth because, as Christians, they believe they should love their enemy and God will punish them if they accuse people;
- In some cases there won't be witnesses because so many have been killed and others have moved to a different district and won't be found;
- In many cases victimized people live elsewhere, and it will be difficult for them to reach places where they are to testify;
- Witnesses' security won't be ensured;
- Many perpetrators are poor and it will be difficult for survivors to get compensation;
- Taking property of perpetrators for compensation will create problems for their children;
- Hatred will increase between families that testify and the guilty;
- Families may be killed out of revenge or have to flee the country because they testified;

- Conflict will develop within families with mixed ethnic origin as they accuse each other of perpetration;
- Some of those released may take revenge;
- People find out about women who were raped;
- There can be corruption, protecting people in high positions;
- Some people who have been involved in the genocide may now hide as judges;
- The gacaca judges at the cell administrative level will categorize people, and, as many of them have little education, some people will escape punishment;
- People will spend a great deal of time on the gacaca and they won't have time to work, reducing productivity in the country;
- Some people will get psychologically ill due to the stress and there may not be enough response from the ministries;
- Some perpetrators may testify without any spirit of repentance, just telling of their "heroic" deeds;
- Trauma may occur among people who committed genocide who feel ashamed because of their terrible crimes.

Some potential negative effects that we added, to which the group agreed, were as follows:

- New trauma as people learn about something (e.g., rape) that happened to or that was done by someone close to them;
- Renewed anger and rage by survivors, especially if they see perpetrators not sufficiently punished;
- Hostility from members of the perpetrator group who were not perpetrators, as they feel constantly accused in the course of testimonies about horrible acts by members of their group.

One additional element from this meeting seems important to note. In discussing past history, the group rejected the notion that there was significant dominance by, and conflict between, Tutsis and Hutus in the pre-colonial period, even though historical analyses indicate this (see Mamdani, 2002). Their attitude stands in contrast to our experience in a seminar in 2003 that was part of training trainers in our approach. There, the widely respected Vice President of the NURC, referred to such conflict in opening our seminar. Participants accepted this then, and in later discussions. This may have been due to a different group composition, respect for the person who made this comment and his position, or the group members' participation in a previous seminar with us that prepared them to acknowledge a more complex truth.

But our experience in 2004 with the "listener group" interviews for our public education campaign (see following discussion) revealed continuing rejection by people in the community of the notion that there was conflict between Tutsis and Hutus before colonization. In contrast, a report by Penal Reform International (2004) describes comments by prisoners who were released in early 2003 and then went through a reeducation ("sensitization") camp before they returned to their communities. Some of the prisoners objected to the presentation of history in the camp, according to which the Belgians created differences and difficulties between Hutus and Tutsis, as a significant distortion of the truth. Here we have an example of conflicting views of history which, because of their apparent importance to members of the two groups, need to be addressed as part of the process of preventing future violence.

Our 2001 and 2003 groups to some degree engaged with the question, "what aspects of the truth are important for reconciliation?" It was evident that survivors of genocide need their suffering truthfully represented and acknowledged. This helps them heal and feel more secure; it conveys that the world does not simply accept such events as normal, and that steps can be taken to promote justice (Staub, 2011; Staub & Pearlman, 2001). Getting perpetrators to acknowledge their harm doing is extremely difficult. But the discussions also suggested that passage of time after victimization and appropriate preparation are required before people who suffered genocide are ready to consider and acknowledge that their own group may have also perpetrated harm. Our experience also suggested to us that directly presenting particular views of history, as we did in the seminar with community leaders, is less useful than exploring them in the course of discussion. This exploration is best done in the framework of understanding how certain historical events and conditions developed, which we did in our other seminars.

In his 2004 book, Gibson reported research from South Africa. His findings on the relationship between truth and reconciliation suggest that for some groups (whites, Colored South Africans, and those of Asian origin), truth and reconciliation are positively related. But among black South Africans, truth appeared to contribute little to reconciliation. Thus, the relationship between truth and reconciliation may depend on victim/perpetrator group affiliation. If that were true in Rwanda, it would suggest the need for different approaches to the Hutus and Tutsis. It may be that the apparent success of our approach is enhanced by our emphasis on its integration into facilitators' and others' usual way of doing things. They in turn are likely to have special consideration for the context in which they are working.

Seminars for Journalists

The way media report events can have many significant effects. It can intensify group differences and hostility or help people understand others' actions (Staub, 1989, 1999). It can limit pluralism or enhance the expression of varied views. We conducted two seminars for journalists and included journalist participants in two other weeklong seminars.

The purpose of the first seminar, in August 1999, was to help journalists understand trauma and the roots of violence between groups. The one-day seminar included about 35 journalists. The purpose of the second, two-day seminar, in June 2002, was to help the 40 journalist participants to develop constructive ways to report on the gacaca, and thereby to promote healing and reconciliation. Understanding the origins of the events—robbery, rape, murder, killing of neighbors, and so on—investigated in the gacaca could help journalists report on them in ways that generate comprehension among the Rwandan public. Understanding psychological trauma and healing might help them gather information and report to the public in ways that are less likely to retraumatize people or create new trauma. An understanding of retraumatization could help reporters inform people about the ways they can support each other as individuals and as members of communities as they are exposed to the gacaca proceedings. We thought that our seminar might also lessen the retraumatization and vicarious trauma of journalists themselves that is almost certainly generated as they are exposed to stories of great violence and cruelty in the course of interviewing highly traumatized people (McCann & Pearlman, 1990b; Figley, 1995; Pyevich, 2002; Saakvitne & Pearlman, 1996).

Following a lecture and extensive discussion of the origins of genocide, we asked the participants to generate news stories. As an example, we applied information about the roots of genocide to understanding how a young man might have become a participant in the Interahamwe, the militia composed of mostly young men that did a great deal of the killing. In this example, we noted the difficult economic conditions in Rwanda and lack of prospects for young men; the political parties creating youth arms, which provided connection and community as well as identity for such young men (fulfilling basic psychological needs); the history of devaluation of Tutsis and the strong propaganda against them at the time; the power of the political group they joined over them; as well as other elements. We suggested and they developed other story ideas, such as how a man came to kill his own son, someone who tried to save lives and was killed, children of rape, a perpetrator confessing at gacaca with no sign of remorse, and others. They worked in small groups, each group working with one scenario or story idea.

The next day, following a lecture on psychological trauma, retraumatization, and healing, participants continued in their groups on the story they began the first day, now including this new material. In addition to discussing ways to create stories that promote healing and reconciliation, in the large group, the journalists discussed the issue of reporting details in depth, with the possibility of contributing to renewed hostility and retraumatization, or reporting fewer details but perhaps not fulfilling their role as journalists. They expressed the belief that part of their role was to promote constructive social change, but also expressed concerns about how much freedom they had in reporting. The group discussed limitations by the government on their freedom to report and the government's concerns about what may be considered incitement to violence. One well-respected Rwandese journalist challenged the group's self-imposed limitations on what they might report, leading to a lively discussion.

We are continuing to work with journalists on a project we have initiated to develop extensive educational radio programs for Rwanda on the themes we have described here. They are produced by Radio La Benevolencija (sponsors include the Dutch government, the Belgian government, and USAID). Radio is the primary means for the population in Rwanda to receive information. The radio programs, which began broadcasting in May 2004, include a radio drama with embedded information, direct informational/educational programs, and art such as poetry and stories created by listeners. Grassroots activities will aim to foster community discussions about the informational content and transform it into action. The aims are to inform the population about the origins of genocide, as well as prevention and reconciliation; help them understand the perpetrators who are tried by the gacaca or are released from prison; and inform people about trauma, retraumatization and healing, thereby helping people find ways to assist and support each other and to protect themselves from retraumatization.

This public education campaign includes two research elements. The first research element is based in a series of listener groups. The then-local senior producer of this project, Suzanne Fisher, organized a representative sample of the population who met with Rwandan research assistants and engaged in discussions of their attitudes toward, and understanding of, the information and themes to be broadcast in the radio programs (Fisher, 2004). Fisher has taken care to include people who represent the diverse backgrounds of persons now living in Rwanda in the research: Tutsi who were in Rwanda during the genocide, Tutsi who returned from the Diaspora during and since 1994, prisoners who generally are Hutus, Hutus who did not actively participate in the killing, and Twa. These groups are being queried over time to provide comments to the radio team about how the programs are being received (Fisher, 2004). Radio personnel refer to such a process as "formative research," as it shapes the programs on an on-going basis.

The second research is an outcome study (which radio personnel refer to as "summative research"). A Yale University researcher has designed a systematic, controlled study to assess the impact of these radio programs on the population (Paluck & Green, 2004; See Chapter 19).

Issues and Contemporary Societal/Political Processes Important to Reconciliation

Ultimately, the effectiveness of our work and that of all third parties in post-conflict situations depends on the social and political context within which one conducts it. For example, development efforts to mitigate the extreme poverty in which most of the population lives, the vast public health disaster posed by the approximately 15 percent rate of HIV infection in Rwanda, and the approximately 50 percent literacy rate would undoubtedly help with reconciliation. We discuss here a few additional issues we regard important.

During the genocide, some Hutus spoke out against the killings or publicly attempted to protect Tutsis and were consequently killed (des Forges, 1999). Others successfully saved lives by hiding Tutsis, or even by stopping those who came to take a Tutsi away (Staub & Pearlman, 2001). Acknowledging such heroic rescue could help Hutus feel that others do not blame and devalue them *as a group*. In our 2001 leaders' seminar, we discussed the potential contribution to reconciliation of acknowledging and honoring Hutus who had tried to help Tutsis. Participants thought it might be too early for such an acknowledgment, that it would be too difficult psychologically, given the deep psychological wounds of Tutsis.

We again discussed this issue in the community leaders' seminar in 2002, where participants had similar feelings. In our January 2003 seminar, the head of commemoration in Ibuka who was also present in the 2002 seminar reported that Ibuka was now planning to include such acknowledgments in future genocide commemorations. This did happen in the commemoration of the genocide in April 2003 and 2004. Among other likely influences promoting this was a book published by African Rights in 2002 about heroic helpers, *Tribute to Courage*. The development of an inclusive history, a description of the past that includes multiple perspectives seems important to promote reconciliation. Others have shared this observation (Gibson, 2004).

An even more difficult issue is the acknowledgment by Tutsis of violence against Hutu civilians. Such violence took place in the course of the civil war. It was also an aspect of fighting infiltrators who came into Rwanda to kill Tutsis for several years after the genocide (des Forges, 1999). Also unknown numbers of Hutus were killed among those who escaped from Rwanda into Zaire (now the Congo) after the genocide was ended by RPF victory over government forces. In response to incursions into Rwanda and continued killings by perpetrators who escaped into the Congo, the new Rwandan army invaded the Congo to fight them.

We discussed in our workshops the exploitation of Hutus by Tutsis during the colonial period. While we also introduced the issue of violence against Hutus, there was no significant discussion of this. Later reports indicated that over 200,000 Hutu civilians were killed (Prunier, 2009). Justice that addresses violence against Hutus as well, starting with acknowledgment of it, seems essential to reconciliation. But if the government will not initiate justice processes, acknowledgment and apology, in the context of examination of violence against perpetrators after other historical events, for example, against Germans after WWII, may help to some degree mitigate reactions by Hutus to this violence and prevent future cycles of violence (Staub, 2011).

Contemporary social processes will also contribute to or impede reconciliation. Many of these processes have been positive in Rwanda. These include the repatriation of Hutus who left the country after the genocide was stopped by the RPA and their reintegration into society and even into the army; the gacaca; the release of prisoners in 2003—those old and sick, those who had confessed and others who had already spent as much time in prison as their punishment would have been, given the crimes of which they were accused; decentralization, consisting in part of local elections; educational and other processes in reconciliation; efforts to improve the educational system, including free primary schools starting in 2003 and new universities; the development of a new constitution; and more.

Other processes such as free speech and the national elections in 2003 have been more problematic. The Tutsi minority, about 14 percent of the population, may justifiably have feared the outcome of totally free elections that might have brought Hutu leadership to power only nine years after the genocide. The international community was most likely unwise to pressure Rwanda, which desperately needs the financial support of this community, to hold elections at this time (Uvin, 2003). Continued decentralization, increased free expression and pluralism, and the building of civil society before elections would probably have contributed more to democratization.

Given the existing situation, certain restrictions or limitations on the free expression of ideas (certainly limiting hate speech and ideologies of hate like those that preceded the genocide) may be required to ensure the safety of the minority, and even as a protection of the majority from those who would initiate new violence. The more openly such limitations and the reasons for them are discussed, the less likely that they will create additional conflict between groups.

But open discussion can take place only if the limits created are reasonable. There are sections in the newly adopted constitution that can give the government power to limit free expression, depending on how they are interpreted. Moreover, in 2003, the MDR, one of the major parties, was the object of parliamentary investigation, accused of being "divisionist," and banned by the government. Leaders are often seen as limiting opposition to protect their interests. But the experience of intense victimization, particularly genocide, may lead to such a strong sense of vulnerability that any opposition can be seen as extremely dangerous. Since members of a group who are not present at the time of a genocide are also deeply affected (Staub, 1998), this is likely to be true of the Tutsi leaders who have returned from other countries. We have talked to survivors and returnees who were genuinely afraid of losing the election and of what might happen as a result. Many in the general population were fearful because in the past, the existence of political parties and elections were connected to violence. Even members of opposition parties expressed fear, and some supported the current President, Paul Kagame, because they value the stability and security that his government brought.

While the actions of the leadership are understandable in these terms, they are nevertheless problematic for the future democratic process. In addition to banning the MDR, several individuals, members of the MDR and others, have disappeared, their fate unknown (Human Rights Watch, 2003). In addition to the meaning of this as a human rights violation, intimidating participants in the political process is likely to restrict the movement toward democracy. Most recently, members of an independent human rights organization, Lipradhor, left the country, presumably afraid when the parliament asked that the organization be banned (Penal Reform International, 2004). The absence of pluralism is one of the influences contributing to violence between groups (Staub, 1989, 2003), and thus signals a potential turn away from a healthy society.

The election of Paul Kagame and the Tutsi-dominated RPF could enhance feelings of security and pave the road to democracy. However, government actions so far have not shown this. For this to happen, the involvement of the international community as an active bystander that speaks out about problematic policies and practices, as well as a constructive, supportive force, will be of great importance.

Finally, it is important to understand that reconciliation and the creation of a peaceful society have been challenged by many upheavals that Rwanda has experienced not only before and during the genocide, but also in its aftermath. Fighting infiltrators in the northwest of the country, the war in the Congo, the return of a huge number of refugees, recent hostilities with Uganda, the release of 22,000 prisoners in early 2003, the adjudication of property claims between members of the different groups, the gacaca, the creation of a constitution, and new political parties are a partial list of the many processes that have psychological effects that must be managed if they are not to contribute to a renewed cycle of violence.

As a very brief afterword: Rwanda has experienced great economic progress over the decade since we wrote this chapter, but the restrictions on political processes have continued.

Conclusions

Our work in Rwanda has aimed to contribute to healing from psychological wounds, to foster reconciliation, and to help to prevent violence and build a peaceful society. One major issue is the evaluation of the benefits of such work; another is, if there are benefits, how they can be maximized.

The experimental evaluation of our first project showed positive effects, as summarized previously. Less formal and anecdotal indicators suggested that our later seminars/workshops also had positive effects. In anonymous evaluations that we conducted both every day and at the end of each seminar/workshop, participants overwhelmingly said that their experiences were very useful to them. Frequently, they commented that all Rwandans should receive the information they gained.

We organized our first project in collaboration with a local NGO, le Mouvement Chretien pour l'Evangelisation, le Counselling et la Reconciliation (MOUCECORE). Our later seminars, in collaboration with the NURC, were all formally opened and closed by high-level officials. In introducing a seminar with journalists, the speaker, who had participated in our first leaders' seminar a year earlier, gave a detailed and highly accurate summary of the key points from that seminar. In conversations with participants in our prior seminars, including leaders, we have heard them express ideas and discuss policy matters using concepts and orientations we have presented and developed in our seminars. The continued interest of the NURC, leaders, and journalists to work with us has been another positive indicator. Not long after the January 2003 leaders' seminar, a BBC interviewer asked the head of the NURC, who participated in the seminar, what the curriculum in the reeducation camps for released prisoners would include. She replied that they intended to teach them about the origins of genocide, about the psychological damage to both survivors and perpetrators as a result of the genocide, and the need for everyone to heal.

An important and often difficult issue for those who engage in third-party efforts is to extend the benefits of their work beyond the small numbers of people with whom they work directly (Ross & Rothman, 1999). We have worked with leaders, whose willingness and interest in working with us has been astounding, and with facilitators who work with groups in the community, in order to maximize the reach of our work. In addition, in January and June 2003 and January 2004, we conducted seminars that are part of training of trainers in our approach. The creation of the public education campaign mentioned earlier is another way to extend the beneficial influence of our approach.

The success of limited interventions like ours will depend on the political and social processes in the country. By working with leaders and journalists, by extending the reach of these efforts through radio programs and training trainers, we hope to have some positive influence on these processes. But the challenges to the creation of a viable social, political, and cultural system are great in Rwanda. Some of these include the psychological consequences of past history and the genocide; the destruction of basic infrastructure, social institutions, and culture (like the justice system and communal relations) in the course of the civil war and genocide; social problems like profound poverty and HIV/AIDS; and the social upheavals mentioned earlier. The government limiting democratic institutions and processes over time is another challenge.

The more the government ensures security, allows the expansion of pluralism, and succeeds in ensuring that people can expect just relations between groups (Leatherman, DeMars, Gaffney, & Vayrynen, 1999), the more hope people will have for a better future. Improving economic conditions in the country will also help. The international community, whose passivity in the face of the genocide (Powers, 2002) was so extreme that it might be regarded as evil (Staub, 1999), could help in this realm. The indications are, however, that passivity, sadly the rule in the face of mass killing and even genocide (Staub, 1989), will again characterize the behavior of the international community.

A final issue is the relevance of the approach we have developed to other places and times. Information about the impact of violent victimization and other traumatic experiences and about avenues to healing; coming to understand roots of violence against one's group and oneself as part of the group, as well as one's group's violence against others and the nature of one's own role in it (as perpetrator, passive bystander, and so on); and engagement with painful experiences under supportive conditions are important for promoting healing and reconciliation between groups in many places around the world. Presumably this approach, or elements of it, could be applied to the Israeli-Palestinian conflict, to reconciliation and peace-making between Sunni and Shiite Moslems and Kurds in Iraq as well as to Serbs, Croats, and Muslims in Bosnia. We invite and encourage others to use the material we have developed, to adapt it to other situations, and to assess its effectiveness. Our approach has always been to offer, not to impose; to augment, not to replace; to collaborate, not to dominate. Such a stance seems more likely than its converse to open more doors and ultimately to assist more people.

References

African Rights. (2002). *Tribute to courage*. Kigali, Rwanda: Author.

Allen, J. G. (2001). *Traumatic relationships and serious mental disorders*. West Sussex, UK: Wiley.

American Psychiatric Association. (1994). *Diagnostic and statistical manual of mental disorders* (4th ed.). Washington, DC: Author.

Arvay, M. J. (2001). Secondary traumatic stress among trauma counsellors: What does the research say? *International Journal for the Advancement of Counselling, 23*, 283–293.

Bar-Tal, D. (2002). Collective memory of physical violence: Its contribution to the culture of violence. In E. Cairns & M. D. Roe (Eds.), *Memories in conflict*. London: Macmillan.

Bonnano, G., Noll, J., Putnam, F., O'Neill, M., & Trickett, P. K. (2003). Predicting the willingness to disclose childhood sexual abuse from measures of repressive coping and dissociative tendencies. *Child Maltreatment, 8*(4), 302–318.

Burton, J. W. (1990). *Conflict: Resolution and prevention*. New York: St. Martin's Press.

Cairns, E., & Roe, M. D. (2002). *Memories in conflict*. London: Macmillan.

Chorbajian, L., & Shirinian, G. (1999). *Studies in comparative genocide*. New York: St. Martin's Press.

Davis, J. L. (1969). The curve of rising and declining satisfactions as a cause of some great revolutions and a contained rebellion. In H. D. Graham & T. R. Gurr (Eds.), *Violence in America*. New York: Bantam Books.

De la Rey, C. (2001). Reconciliation in divided societies. In D. J. Christie, R. V. Wagner, & D. D. Winter (Eds.), *Peace, conflict, and violence: Peace psychology for the 21st century* (pp. 251–261). Upper Saddle River, NJ: Prentice Hall.

Des Forges, A. (1999). *Leave none to tell the story: Genocide in Rwanda*. New York: Human Rights Watch.

Esterling, B. A., L'Abate, L., Murray, E. J., & Pennebaker, J. W. (1999). Empirical foundations for writing in prevention and psychotherapy: Mental and physical health outcomes. *Clinical Psychology Review, 19*(1), 79–96.

Figley, C. R. (1995). Compassion fatigue as secondary traumatic stress disorder: An overview. In C. R. Figley (Ed.), *Compassion fatigue: Coping with secondary traumatic stress disorder in those who treat the traumatized* (pp. 1–20). New York: Brunner/Mazel.

Fisher, S. (2004). *Tuning into different wavelengths: Listener clubs for effective Rwanda Reconciliation Radio.* Manuscript in preparation.

Foa, E. B., Keane, T. M., & Friedman, M. J. (Eds.). (2000). *Effective treatments for PTSD: Practice guidelines from the International Society for Traumatic Stress Studies*. New York: Guilford Press.

Gibson, J. L. (2004). *Overcoming apartheid: Can truth reconcile a divided nation?* New York: Russell Sage Foundation.

Harvey, M. (1996). An ecological view of psychological trauma and trauma recovery. *Journal of Traumatic Stress, 9*, 3–23.

Herman, J. (1992). *Trauma and recovery: The aftermath of violence from domestic abuse to political terror*. New York: Basic Books.

Higgins, C. (1994). *Resilient adults overcoming a cruel past*. San Francisco: Jossey-Bass.

Human Rights Watch. (2003, May). *Preparing for elections: Tightening control in the name of unity*. New York: Author.

Jordan, J. V., Walker, M., & Hartling, L. M. (Eds.). (2004). *The complexity of connection: Writings from the Jean Baker Miller training institute*. New York: Guilford Press.

Kelman, H. C. (1990). Applying a human needs perspective to the practice of conflict resolution: The Israeli-Palestinian case. In J. Burton (Ed.), *Conflict: Human needs theory*. New York: St. Martin's Press.

Lantz, J. (1996). Logotherapy as trauma therapy. *Crisis intervention and time-limited treatment, 2*(3), 243–253.

Leatherman, J., DeMars, W., Gaffney, P. D., & Vayrynen, R. (1999). *Breaking cycles of violence: Conflict prevention in intrastate crises*. West Hartford, CT: Kumarian Press.

Lederach, J. (1995). *Building peace: Sustainable reconciliation*. Tokyo: United Nations University.

Lederach, J.P. (1997). *Building peace: Sustainable reconciliation in divided societies*. Washington, D.C.: United States Institute of Peace Press.

MacNair, R. M. (2002). *Perpetration-induced traumatic stress: The psychological consequences of killing*. Westport, CT: Praeger/Greenwood.

Mamdani, M. (2002). *When victims become killers*. Princeton, NJ: Princeton University Press.

McCann, I. L., & Pearlman, L. A. (1990a). *Psychological trauma and the adult survivor: Theory, therapy, and transformation*. New York: Brunner/Mazel.

McCann, I. L., & Pearlman, L. A. (1990b). Vicarious traumatization: A framework for understanding the psychological effects of working with victims. *Journal of Traumatic Stress, 3*(1), 131–149.

Montville, J. V. (1993). The healing function in political conflict resolution. In D. J. D. Sandole & H. Van der Merve (Eds.), *Conflict resolution theory and practice: Integration and application*. Manchester, UK: Manchester University Press.

Newman, E., Riggs, D. S., & Roth, S. (1997). Thematic resolution, PTSD, and complex PTSD: The relationship between meaning and trauma-related diagnoses. *Journal of Traumatic Stress, 10*(2), 197–213.

Paluck, E. L., & Green, D. P. (2004, May/June). *Overview and working plan for the LaBenevolencija impact evaluation study: The impact of Musekeweya: Changes in knowledge, attitudes, and behaviors. A randomized controlled trial*. Unpublished manuscript.

Pearlman, L. A. (2003). *Trauma and Attachment Belief Scale manual*. Los Angeles: Western Psychological Services.

Pearlman, L. A., & Saakvitne, K. W. (1995). *Trauma and the therapist: Countertransference and vicarious traumatization in the treatment of incest survivors*. New York: W. W. Norton.

Pennebaker, J. W., & Beall, S. K. (1986). Confronting a traumatic event: Toward an understanding of inhibition and disease. *Journal of Abnormal Psychology, 95*, 274–281.

Pettigrew, T. F., & Tropp, L. R. (2000). Does intergroup contact reduce prejudice? Recent meta-analytic findings. In S. Oskamp (Ed.), *Reducing prejudice and discrimination.* London: Lawrence Erlbaum Associates.

Penal Reform International. (2004, May). *Research report on the Gacaca VI. From camp to hill, the reintegration of released prisoners.* PRI Rwanda. BP 370. Kigali, Rwanda.

Powers, S. (2002). *A problem from hell: America and the age of genocide.* New York: Basic Books.

Proceedings of Stockholm International Forum on Truth, Justice and Reconciliation (2002). Stockholm, Sweden: Stockholm International Forum.

Prunier, G. (2009). *Africa's world war: Congo, the Rwandan genocide, and the making of a continental catastrophe.* New York: Oxford University Press.

Pyevich, C. M. (2002). *The relationship among cognitive schemata, job-related traumatic exposure, and PTSD in journalists.* Doctoral dissertation, University of Tulsa.

Rando, T. A. (1993). *Treatment of complicated mourning.* Champaign, IL: Research Press.

Rhodes, G., Allen, G. J., Nowinski, J., & Cillessen, A. (2002). The violent socialization scale: Development and initial validation. In J. Ulmer & L. Athens (Eds.), *Violent acts and violentization: Assessing, applying, and developing Lonnie Athens' theories* (Vol. 4, pp. 125–144). London: Elsevier Science.

Rosenbloom, D. J., & Williams, M. B. (1999). *Life after trauma.* New York: Guilford Press.

Ross, M. H., & Rothman, J. (1999). *Theory and practice in ethnic conflict management: Theorizing success and failure.* New York: Macmillian.

Saakvitne, K. W., Gamble, S. G., Pearlman, L. A., & Lev, B. T. (2000). *Risking connection: A training curriculum for working with survivors of childhood abuse.* Lutherville, MD: Sidran Press.

Saakvitne, K. W., Pearlman, L. A., & the Staff of the Traumatic Stress Institute. (1996). *Transforming the pain: A workbook on vicarious traumatization.* New York: W. W. Norton.

Staub, E. (1989). *The roots of evil: The origins of genocide and other group violence.* New York: Cambridge University Press.

Staub, E. (1996). The cultural-societal roots of violence: The examples of genocidal violence and of contemporary youth violence in the United States. *American Psychologist, 51*, 117–132.

Staub, E. (1998). Breaking the cycle of genocidal violence: Healing and reconciliation. In J. Harvey (Ed.), *Perspectives on loss.* Washington, DC: Taylor & Francis.

Staub, E. (1999). The origins and prevention of genocide, mass killing and other collective violence. *Peace and Conflict: Journal of Peace Psychology, 5*, 303–337.

Staub, E. (2003). *The psychology of good and evil: Why children, adults and groups help and harm others.* New York: Cambridge University Press.

Staub, E. (2011). *Overcoming evil: Genocide, violent conflict and terrorism.* New York: Oxford University Press.

Staub, E. (2014). Reconciliation between groups: preventing (new) violence and improving lives. In M. Deutsch & P. Coleman (Eds.), *The handbook of conflict resolution: Theory and practice* (3rd ed.). San Francisco: Jossey-Bass.

Staub, E., & Bar-Tal, D. (2003). Genocide, mass killing and intractable conflict: Roots, evolution, prevention and reconciliation. In D. Sears, L. Huddy, & R. Jarvis (Eds.), *Handbook of political psychology.* New York: Oxford University Press.

Staub, E., & Pearlman, L. A. (2001). Healing, reconciliation, and forgiving after genocide and other collective violence. In S. J. Helmick & R. L. Petersen (Eds.), *Forgiveness and reconciliation: Religion, public policy and conflict transformation* (pp. 195–217). Radnor, PA: Templeton Foundation Press.

Staub, E., Pearlman, L. A., Gubin, A., & Hagengimana, A. (2005). Healing, reconciliation, and the prevention of violence after genocide or mass killing: An intervention and its experimental evaluation in Rwanda. *Journal of Clinical and Social Psychology, 24*(3), 297–334.

Tokayer, N. (2002). Spirituality and the psychological and physical symptoms of trauma. (Doctoral Dissertation, University of Connecticut). *Dissertation Abstracts International, 63*, 1052.

Totten, S., Parsons, W. S., & Charny, I. W. (Eds.). (1997). *Century of genocide.* New York: Garland.

Uvin, P. (2003, June). *Wake up. Some policy proposals for the international community in Rwanda.* Unpublished manuscript.

Volkan, V. (1997). *Blood lines: From ethnic pride to ethnic terrorism.* New York: Farrar, Straus, Giroux.

Wessells, M., & Monteiro, C. (2001). Psychosocial intervention and post-war reconstruction in Angola: Interweaving western and traditional approaches. In D. J. Christie, R. V. Wagner, & D. D. Winter (Eds.), *Peace, conflict and violence: Peace psychology for the 21st century* (pp. 262–275). Upper Saddle River, NJ: Prentice Hall.

Willis, F. R. (1965). *France, Germany, and the New Europe, 1945–1963.* Palo Alto, CA: Stanford University Press.

Wortman, C. B., Battle, E., & Lemkau, J. P. (1997). Coming to terms with the sudden traumatic death of a spouse or child. In A. J. Lurigio, W. G. Skogan, & R. C. Davis (Eds.), *Victims of crime: Problems, policies and programs.* Newbury Park, CA: SAGE.

19

Public Education for Reconciliation and Peace: Changing Hearts and Minds

Musekeweya, an Educational Radio Drama in Rwanda

In societies where there is enough freedom to allow this, public education can help create resistance to violence and promote reconciliation and peace building. An important form of public education is the radio, especially in countries where radio is still the primary source of information and entertainment accessible to the population.

Creating Educational Components

We have created both informational radio programs and an educational radio drama in Rwanda, and later in Burundi and the Democratic Republic of the Congo. Here I describe our first educational radio program in Rwanda, the radio drama *Musekeweya* (meaning "new dawn"). It began to broadcast in 2004 and is still ongoing in 2015. I also describe a "grass roots" project connected to it.

We created the educational content for all our radio programs on the basis of separate theories Laurie Pearlman and I developed about of the origins of genocide, its traumatic impact, healing, prevention, and reconciliation, and the Staub-Pearlman approach we used in seminars/workshops in Rwanda (see Chapter 18 for the approach and references to the theories). On these bases we created 12 "communication messages" (see Table 19.1), as well as ideas for the story of the radio drama, in extensive meetings in Kigali between myself, Laurie Pearlman, George Weiss the Director of Radio LaBenevolencija that was going to produce the programs, and others associated with this nongovernmental organization located in Amsterdam, a Western radio producer, Suzanne Fisher, experienced in working in Africa,

Reprinted with permission and minor changes from Chapter 16, "Changing Hearts and Minds," in Staub, E. (2011), *Overcoming evil, genocide, violent conflict and terrorism.* New York: Oxford University Press.

TABLE 19.1 **"Communication Messages" of the Rwandan Radio Drama**

1. Life problems in a society frustrate basic needs and can lead to scapegoating and destructive ideologies.

2. Genocide evolves as individuals and groups change as a result of their actions.

3. Devaluation increases the likelihood of violence, whereas humanization decreases it.

4. The healing of psychological wounds helps people live more satisfying lives and makes unnecessary defensive violence less likely.

5. Passivity facilitates the evolution of harm doing, whereas actions by people inhibit it.

6. Varied perspectives, open communication, and moderate respect for authority in society make the evolution of violence less likely.

7. Justice is important for healing and reconciliation.

8. Significant connections and deep engagement between people belonging to different groups help people overcome devaluation and hostility and promote positive relations.

9. Trauma can be understood.

10. It is important to tell one's trauma story, and there is a way to tell it that is emotionally safe and constructive.

11. People can help their neighbors heal and help them tell their stories as part of the healing process; everyone can participate in and can contribute to healing.

12. Healing is a slow process.

Source: Reprinted from Staub & Pearlman, 2009. We are grateful to the American Psychological Association for permission. These messages are based on the research and theories of Ervin Staub and Laurie Anne Pearlman and the Staub–Pearlman approach they developed for trainings/workshops in Rwanda (see Chapter 18).

the Rwandan writers who were going to write the episodes of the drama, other Rwandan staff and Rwandan consultants, as well as an educational radio specialist.

The 12 messages guided the writers in including educational content into the radio drama from May 2004 when it began to broadcast, until 2007. I also developed a corresponding "continuum" of how the different influences enter into moving a group toward genocide, or preventing it. In 2007, we expanded the communication messages to 35 to include more on prevention and reconciliation. We have continuously trained writers and producers in the educational material they are to convey in the radio programs.

The weekly episodes were translated into English from Kinyarwanda, the local language, and Laurie Pearlman and I commented on their educational content in the first couple of years. Then "our academic team" in Massachusetts expanded and others also participated in this work, as well as in training staff and other elements of the project.[1]

The Story: Conflict Between Two Villages

The radio drama became extremely popular in its first year, with almost 90% of the population listening to it, and it has remained as popular. It is a story of two villages in conflict. We learn early in the drama that some time in the past the authorities gave a fertile valley lying between the villages to one of them, Bumanzi. There is a drought, and people in the other

---

1. They include Rezarta Bilali, Adin Thayer and Johanna Vollhardt, who are still working on the project, and for a short period Terri Haven.

village, Muhumuro, go hungry. A man instigates hostility and violence. He attracts followers and is elected the leader of Muhumuro. They attack the well-to-do village and steal the harvest.

The radio drama moderates respect for authority, one of our goals, by showing the complexity of the motivation and character of the destructive leader, Rutanagira, and by dramatizing the behavior of bystanders. He responds to the conditions in his village, the drought and scarcity of food. He blames the other village, Bumanzi. But he also acts out of personal grievances and animosities. His father had a second wife in Bumanzi. The father, when he died at the beginning of the story, contrary to tradition, appointed his son in Bumanzi as the head of the family, even though Rutanagira is the oldest son. He cannot accept this. In the dark of a night he attacks and beats up his half brother. His mother, Zaninka, driven by jealousy, instigates him against the other village. In addition, in a storm, his daughter falls off a small bridge, which the two villages built together in a period of cooperation, and drowns in the creek. For this also he blames the other village.

The villagers in Muhumuro are affected by the injustice that the fertile land was given to the other village, which makes them permanently poor, and by the current drought and scarcity. The frustration of their material and psychological needs makes them vulnerable to instigation. The instigator's influence in this authority-oriented culture greatly increases when he is elected village headman.

In the course of the conflict, active bystanders speak out against the leader and the faction that incites and engages in violence. Some older people maintain friendships across village lines. One man courageously goes to and speaks against violence at a meeting of the leader with his followers, and he continues to speak out after his house is burnt down. The most powerful example of a positive bystander is Batamuliza, the sister of the destructive leader. There is a love story between her and a young man, Shema, from the other village. Over the years of the program, the two of them are central in the activities of the young people of the two villages who organize and speak out against the violence.

Batamuliza and Shema undergo many trials. One of them is her kidnapping by one of her brother's followers, a man to whom her brother had promised her as a wife, without her knowledge. She manages to free herself and continues to defy her brother and mother. Many of the characters in this radio drama have become immensely popular and when, after many challenges, Batamuliza and Shema are married in one of the episodes in February 2009, people were sending real presents for the couple.

Other characters in the radio drama provide models of active bystandership as well. A young boy encourages another boy who is about to be sent home from his secondary school, because his family cannot pay the tuition, to ask the principal to allow him to stay. In Rwanda, where decisions by authorities are customarily not questioned, such an action demonstrates and encourages more moderate respect for authority. There is a village "fool," in fact a wise man in the mold of a Shakespearean fool, who, in his foolish way, says things to the leader and his followers that show how wrong their actions are. The drama explores justice processes, including its imperfections. It shows corruption and bias by officials.

In the first three years of the story, there is hostility, attacks, and counterattacks. When Bumanzi, the wealthier village, counterattacks, the inhabitants of Muhumuro become refugees. They leave their village and live under very poor conditions. There is continued hostility, with factions in both villages that persist in advocating against the other village. Some sympathizers from Bumanzi join and live with the refugees. They, and others who speak for reconciliation and peace, are the objects of suspicion and hostility. But slowly, opinions turn, and reconciliation begins. At a later time, when there is the threat of new violence in the region, the two villages join, using their past experience to stop the violence by nonviolent means. There is a transformation in some important characters, such as Rutanagira, the bad leader. He is tried, there is increasing hostility to him by "bystanders," and slowly over time he changes, joining those who work for reconciliation and peace.

Rwandan leaders say they want reconciliation; they promote it, and also limit open discussion and political processes. But this public education program that, among other things, encourages moderate respect for authorities and pluralism, people speaking their minds, has been allowed to continue to broadcast each of its episodes twice a week.

Evaluations and Further Story Content of *Musekeweya*

The effects of the radio drama were studied in experimental research in the first year and after that by research using other methods. The evaluation covered the period of hostility and attacks, with resistance by active bystanders, but not the programs on reconciliation. It included individual interviews with participants, their responses to questions about program effects, focus group discussions, and an "unobtrusive" measure when participants did not know they were evaluated. I will describe the evaluations in the first and second year separately, except when a later finding clarifies an earlier one.

Before the broadcasts began, "listening groups" were set up around the country and were visited each month to assess their reactions first to pilot programs and, during the first 3 years, to actual programs. Their reactions were used to shape program content. Following this model, as part of her doctoral dissertation research, Elizabeth Paluck set up, during the first program year, groups in six communities (identified as treatment or reconciliation groups) that listened together once a month, on audiotapes, to the four weekly programs of *Musekeweya*. In six comparison (or health) groups, people listened together to a radio program about health practices. There were a total of 480 people in the study. These were mixed groups of Tutsis and Hutus, but there was also one group in each condition made up of survivors only, and one group of prisoners. Health group members were promised a small reward and agreed not to listen in the course of the first year to *Musekeweya* broadcasts. If they listened in spite of their agreement, one would expect smaller differences between the groups (Paluck, 2009; see also Staub & Pearlman, 2009).[2]

2. The evaluation research was done by Elizabeth Levy Paluck as part of her dissertation in psychology at Yale. We (Staub, Pearlman, and La Benevolencija) invited applications by individuals and organizations to do the evaluation and selected her from several interested parties. She did an outstanding study, but we (Staub & Pearlman, 2009) disagree with her interpretation of the findings. She sees the changes in listeners as indicating that their beliefs have changed about what are the social norms in their society (Paluck, 2009). This seems highly unlikely to us. We interpret the results as changes in individuals' understanding, personal beliefs, and values, which are then expressed in some behaviors. Changes in norms would follow as many members of the group change. (See Pearlman & Staub, 2009, and later discussion in this chapter.)

The effects of the radio drama were evaluated in the second year by comparing former reconciliation group members, and health group members who after the first year could also listen to the program, as well as assessing differences among all participants as a function of how much they listened to the programs. In addition to self-report, knowledge of drama content, which corresponded well with participants' reports, was used to indicate amount of listening. Former treatment group members listened more to the program. Not surprisingly, people who listened more showed greater changes (Paluck, 2006). Another group was also added to the evaluation—elites in the communities where the first-year participants were located.

The evaluation showed that the program has affected both attitudes and behavior. Among varied effects, listeners to *Musekeweya* were more likely than members of the comparison group to believe in speaking their minds and to actually do so, to express controversial views, and to show independence from authority.

Effects on Behavior

At the end of the first year, at a party to acknowledge their participation, each group received audiotapes of the whole year's *Musekeweya* programs and a tape recorder. In every one of the six health groups, participants decided, after very little discussion, to have the village headman be in charge of them. In each case one person suggested this, and it was agreed to without further discussion. In all six of the reconciliation groups, participants engaged in long discussion of where they should keep the materials they received and who should be in charge of them. They decided that either the group jointly would be in charge, or one of its members would be in charge and make them available to the others. Usually, in the reconciliation groups, one person suggested that they give the material to the village headman to manage, but others disagreed, and a long discussion followed (Paluck, 2009; Staub & Pearlman, 2009). In this unobtrusive measure, at a time when participants thought the project had ended, people who listened to the radio drama showed freedom to express their views and independence of authority.

In individual interviews, listeners to *Musekeweya* disagreed more with the statement, "If I disagree with something that someone is saying or doing, I keep quiet." This was one of the strongest effects of the radio drama. Listeners' behavior was consistent with this in the unobtrusive measure of what to do with tapes of the show. In addition, in individual interviews, participants in both health and reconciliation groups agreed that there was mistrust in their communities. When this was later discussed in focus groups, those who listened to *Musekeweya* were much more likely than participants in the comparison groups to express this view, countering a cultural tendency to hold such opinions privately.

The Effect on Empathy

In individual interviews, people who listened to *Musekeweya* expressed more empathy for varied groups of Rwandans: people in prison because of their role in the genocide, survivors, poor people, and political leaders. This is consistent with what we found in our earlier study, that members of community groups guided by facilitators we trained in our approach, on which the radio drama was based, had a more positive orientation to people in the other ethnic group (Staub et al., 2005).

It is likely that one source of empathy and positive orientation to others was increased understanding of the influence of events on people, their psychological impact, and effects on behavior. Understanding how personal experiences, the conditions in the society, and the influence of other people jointly lead to actions, including extremely harmful ones, is a form of cognitive empathy that can foster at least some openness to harm doers—whether direct perpetrators or leaders—and to passive bystanders. The programs also showed the trauma and psychological wounds resulting from the attacks, which presumably increased empathy with survivors of the genocide. Perpetrators, and many passive members of a perpetrator group, stop thinking about the victims' suffering. They tend to minimize what they (or their group) did and its harmful effects (Baumeister, 1997). The radio drama increased awareness of pain and suffering created by violence, as people in the village that was attacked struggled with anxiety, sexual difficulties, and intimacy.

In creating empathy, understanding the influences leading to and the effects of violent actions presumably joined with identification with positive characters in the story and the values they expressed (Paluck, 2009; Staub & Pearlman, 2009). A Penal Reform International (PRI) report on rescuers in Rwanda concludes that "belief in values that affirm the humanity of the victims, creating a deep empathy with them. . . . as well as the existence within their social environment, particularly within the family, of positive examples of interethnic coexistence" were the primary characteristics of the "righteous" who saved Tutsi lives during the genocide (PRI, 2004, p. 3). Their feelings of empathy, beliefs, and values enabled them to deviate from then dominant norms of conduct.

Other Changes

The changes I just described and those that follow suggest that the radio drama affected beliefs and values, that listeners came to see certain outcomes (such as less dependence on and subservience to authorities) and actions (speaking what one believes) as desirable. This is an especially impressive finding in that during the first year of the radio drama the words and actions of active bystanders did not stop hostility and violence. In some cases there were negative consequences to them.

Research studies have shown that the example of models can lead to imitation, even if their actions are not rewarded. This does not happen, however, if the models' actions lead to negative consequences for them, and it is unlikely to happen if their behavior is evidently ineffective. But in the radio drama the active, positive bystanders were guided by strong values that served positive ends. The rewards to them were intrinsic, as they lived up to these values. They were also "rewarded" by good relationships to each other, even across village lines. And they acted in the context of understanding the importance of resisting influences that move people to violence.

The radio drama also showed trauma. The invaders intruded into people's houses during the night, attacked them, and stole their crops. One character later struggled with giving testimony at a trial, finding it difficult to talk about her experience, as traumatized individuals often do, the difficulty intensified by an initially insensitive judge. Another character began to avoid his wife, avoiding intimacy and sexual relations. She began to suspect that he had another woman in his life. Slowly she learned that his behavior was the result of the attack, which created difficulty in his sexual functioning; this made him ashamed and led him to avoid her.

Educational radio dramas need to entertain to be effective. The writers have infused the story with a great deal of humor, for example, when the wife follows the suggestions of a village healer to regain her husband's affections by stealing one of his pubic hairs—before she understands that he has been traumatized. In this and other cases of trauma, other characters invite traumatized people to talk about their experiences. Those who listened to the program were more likely to believe that one should talk about painful, traumatic experiences and that other people can help make this happen and provide support.

Rwandans experienced great violence in their society, in spite of intermarriages, and neither evaluation group believed that marrying across group lines contributes to peace, although listeners to *Musekeweya* believed slightly more that it does. However, while in a small number of instances participants talked about intermarriages ending in bloodshed, more often they mentioned Tutsis who were saved through their connection to Hutus. The PRI report about rescuers found that a majority of those who saved Tutsis were connected to them through intermarriage (PRI, 2004).

Asked about their personal preferences, reconciliation group members were more likely than health group members to believe that intermarriage should be allowed in their family and that children should not be advised against it. In individual interviews and focus groups, they said that it can be a force for good, creating bonds and reducing division and discord between groups. Both the discrepancy between their belief based on past experience that intermarriage does not contribute to peace and their belief that it should be allowed and can create bonds, and some other findings suggest that the program has generated hope, an expectation and belief that people can take effective action to make the future better. Both values that motivate people and such positive expectations are necessary for people to take action (Staub & Pearlman, 2009).

While the majority of the participants in both groups believed that trust can be rebuilt in their communities, a compelling difference was in the ways people thought about rebuilding trust. For those in the reconciliation group, interaction was one avenue, such as engaging with people, socializing, and sharing resources. Another was mutual forgiveness, asking pardon, and establishing the truth about the past. Those in the health groups emphasized these less, and government policies more, such as government information programs (called sensitization in Rwanda) and laws prohibiting divisionism and political favoritism (Paluck & Green, 2005).

While there were substantial changes in listeners, there were no differences from the control group on some dimensions. One of them was that neither group agreed with the view that violence evolves gradually. One explanation is participants' own experience, the way they perceived the genocide. Although they could see the progressive increase in tension and hostility in the country, they experienced the beginning of the genocide as sudden and surprising. This was also reported by others (Ilibagiza & Erwin, 2006). People get accustomed to gradual small increases in hostility and violence and are surprised when there is a great shift in intensity. There was also no difference, probably again due to the constraining effect of personal experience during the genocide, in reactions to the statement, "If I stand by while others commit evil actions, I am also responsible." Members of both groups agreed somewhat with this statement. But they said that during the genocide it was not possible to intervene. Once the genocide began, intervening meant significantly endangering one's life.

The lack of difference on some items at the end of the first year could also be due to members of the comparison groups actually listening to a limited extent, which brought them some knowledge but not enough to change deeper attitudes and actions. Even more likely was the spread of the effects of the educational radio drama through public discussion. Past research has found that the effects of programs about HIV/AIDS and reproduction spread through discussion between spouses and in the community (Bandura, 2006; Staub et al., 2010). Both participants in the reconciliation groups and others interviewed in the second year reported extensive discussion of the programs. Reconciliation group members talked about them to others, and they were discussed in families and among community members. Children and adolescents, who have been avid listeners, often initiated discussion with their parents (Paluck, 2006).

People in the community in Rwanda often listen to the radio together; their discussion of the programs is likely to enhance their effects. This was probably the case with people listening together in the evaluation study. In the second year, elites in the communities where the study took place reported that members of these groups continued to have strong ties, and that the study had a positive effect on their communities.

Another explanation for the absence of some differences may be that, depending on particular issues, creating change may require more exposure to influential content. This is especially so if change goes contrary to recent powerful experience, such as the perceived sudden beginning of the genocide. In the second-year evaluation, there was again no difference between the two groups on the question about the evolution of violence. But people from either group who listened more to the radio drama, as measured by the number of characters they could name, disagreed more with the view that violence comes about suddenly.

Participants expressed views about a couple of matters contrary to what we expected. Contrary to our intention to communicate that violence is a societal process, and the importance of followers, people who listened to *Musekeweya* agreed more that "evil people cause violence." This was most likely due to actual program content. Given the strong prevailing view in Rwanda that genocide was the result of bad leaders, and given the cultural emphasis on authorities, we did not initially succeed in our attempt to change the perspectives of the writers of the radio drama, through training and editing their work. In the first year the writers continued to emphasize the role of the bad leader in the poor village, and his mother who exerted a strong negative influence on him. But the way they depicted the character of the bad leader, and the role of his personal/family relations in his actions, helped moderate respect for authority, as the behavior of listeners showed.

The joining of cultures, as external and internal parties work together, can be challenging. At a staff meeting a member of our "academic team" realized that the writers resisted the concept of moderating authority because they thought it meant that children need not obey their parents. We clarified that what we meant was that children and adults should learn to judge if their elders, leaders, or society engages in harmful, immoral action, and people should speak out against and attempt to correct such actions.

On another item, those who listened to *Musekeweya* were less likely to believe that trauma recovery is possible. The radio drama was planned to last for a number of years, with evolution in its content. Some of the items in the evaluation assessed the program's intended effects as indicated by communication statements, not its likely effects based on its actual content. The radio drama in the first year showed people traumatized by conflict and attacks, and others encouraging them to talk about their painful experiences. We did not yet show healing and recovery, in part because we were intent to truthfully represent what Rwandans also know from personal experience, the difficulty of and time required for recovering from the trauma of victimization (see message 12 in Table 19.1).

The Effects of the Radio Drama in the Second Year

In the second year, when everyone could listen to the program, some of the differences between reconciliation and health group members disappeared. For example, all groups said that they supported intermarriage, and that they would speak up if they disagreed with something someone did or said. But the amount of listening was important. Regular listeners believed more in speaking what they believed (Paluck, 2006).

The major conclusion suggested by the research findings in the second year is that people who listened more to *Musekeweya* were more ready, willing, and able to express their views. They were more likely to say that there is mistrust in their village, in keeping with what both observers and surveys authorized by the Unity and Reconciliation Commission indicated—that there is mistrust in Rwanda, due to the genocide and reawakened by the *gacaca*. They expressed more concern about the return of prisoners who perpetrated violence and who were released into their communities. Reflecting a widespread cultural fear in Rwanda about poisoning, regular listeners expressed more concern about drinking a beer with a member of a group that has offended them if this person opens the beer out of their sight. These findings indicate that *Musekeweya* contributes to people using their judgment and being more truthful in expressing their views.

Everyone in the second year reported that they participated in reconciliation activities; those who were in the reconciliation group during the first year participated in these activities slightly more, and regular listeners substantially more. Members of the former health groups reported more often that they encouraged others to reconcile: helping neighbors resolve conflicts at home, encouraging forgiveness, or talking to people about the *gacaca*. Regular listeners reported more directly engaging in activities promoting reconciliation. They shared land with people who killed their family, talked to returned prisoners who killed members of their family, returned goods stolen by a son to a survivor, and asked for forgiveness. The evaluator concluded that "The actions of Musekeweya listeners are exceptionally personal" (Paluck, 2006, p. 42).

The Value of Public Education

Public education can take many forms: trainings in seminars and workshops, courses in schools and universities, radio and television programs, and information disseminated in newsprint and on the Internet. Longer exposure matters, especially when the goal is to change deep-seated beliefs, attitudes, norms, and behavior. As these change, slowly the culture changes, including the standards of acceptable conduct. The idea of changing another group's culture may seem arrogant. But Rwandans themselves agree that there is too much respect for authority, not enough pluralism, and a history of devaluation. To moderate orientation to authority requires a focus on the merits of authorities and reevaluation of the relationship between leaders and citizens.

The trainings we conducted with groups in Rwanda, described in Chapter 18, affected understanding of the roots of the genocide, created more positive orientation by members of the two groups toward each other, and conditional forgiveness (Staub et al., 2005). The radio drama seemed to contribute to a "critical consciousness" by listeners, to their use of their own judgment, and greater willingness to engage in discussion and publicly express views. It also affected behavior, some self-reported, some observed. There are public education projects of many kinds and they show that public education can have what seems not only a statistically significant, but also a practically significant impact. In the complex and difficult social world of post-genocide Rwanda, the changes our programs produced provide hope for more active bystandership on behalf of reconciliation and peace.

Audience Feedback

At some point audience members began writing letters with their thoughts and feelings about the programs, and when LaBenevolencija provided a telephone number, they began to call in large numbers. Their reactions were highly positive and also informative about program content. Later, to further involve the audience, there were poetry competitions with themes related to *Musekeweya*, with small awards given to the winners. Starting in 2008, some letters that reinforced program messages were read on the radio. I quote and paraphrase a few letters in one week in early May 2009, some responding to the preceding week's drama episode:

- "Hello you teachers of hearts filled with hatred . . . you have not stopped teaching us in Rwandan society. The importance of *Musekeweya* is inexpressible." Speaking to Zaninka, the mother of the bad leader, the writer admonishes her for her bad behavior in relation to her daughter and wants to exile her. "Good riddance." He also advises Shema to let his wife, Batamuliza, go work in the village that now has problems. "That will bring good results."
- "The seed you have planted has begun to grow. The intelligence and wisdom that you have used to teach us is of great value. *Musekeweya* is a boat, where all of us who are listening are together. Shema, Batamuliza, (Kigingi, Hirwa—other characters in the drama) have the techniques rowing us, and we are sure to arrive at a good port." This writer also speaks directly to the characters and says to Zaninka, "Where has your soul gone?" He also admonishes Shema not to get angry at Batamuliza, if she goes to the other village to

help—"You and others have much to gain, and you can also go to help. . . . I am resolved to be your ambassador among us."

- ". . . the seed you have sown in the heart of the afflicted . . . has given the fruits of human-ism, tolerance, love, and unity. In the fashion of Shema and Batamuliza, we are ready to give testimony of what we have pulled from this tree."
- "I am thanking you for showing the hearts of people directed by hatred, rancour, and wrath . . ."
- "Please read this message to the listeners. . . . For those who have not won a prize in the poetry competition, try to find some reward for them—they have participated. That would make them happy."
- One letter asked that the programs cover rape (which has been done in the radio dramas in Burundi and the Congo but not in Rwanda) and that Batamuliza be a counselor to rape victims.

Some of the content of these letters may be motivated by the hope that they will be read on the radio.

Ongoing Program Development

In developing the radio programs there has been an increasingly deep and equal relation-ship between internal and external parties. There are training workshops on the underlying conception and approach, and design and storyline development workshops. These bring local staff, producers, and some members of the academic team located in Massachusetts and the executive team from Amsterdam together. Stakeholders—representatives of local organizations and leadership groups—are often included for part or all of them.

In January 2009, at one of these workshops, there was discussion of the communica-tion messages that the programs would focus on in the following year. One of these was "establishing the complex truth about past group relations and about conflict and violence and developing a shared view of history are important for reconciliation." In the course of the discussion, participants commented that the notion of "shared history" should reflect not only two versions of what happened in Rwanda, as represented by the two main groups, Hutus and Tutsis, but many versions. In real life there are not only the two primary groups but also divisions by region, status and wealth, and others, each with their own perspective on history. (One of these other divisions is between Tutsi survivors and "returnees," Tutsis whose families were refugees in neighboring countries and returned after the genocide. It was primarily refugees in Uganda who fought the civil war and then ended the genocide.)

The educational content aims to promote knowledge, attitudes, and actions in relation to each communication message. The following guidance to producers and writers (and eval-uators) for the message described earlier was drafted by a member of the "academic team" and then developed further in the January workshop. It specifies the aims of the programs that are to be developed.

KNOW:
- That establishing the complex truth about past group relations is a difficult task, since the two parties in the conflict have different perspectives
- The importance of having a shared history, including both sides' experiences, the two versions of the conflict, rather than having a history presenting the perspectives of one side

DO:
- Have an overall view of the past; always engage to confront one-sided versions of history
- Continue to discuss the past conflict with others, with a mind open to various perspectives and ready to understand that those various visions can complete each other (even when there are disagreements)

HAVE AN ATTITUDE OF:
- Eagerness to understand the past conflict between the two groups
- Willingness to make others question their exclusive version of history

A Grassroots Project and Further Evaluation of *Musekeweya*

Using the radio drama as a base, LaBenevolencija created a companion project to engage citizens in reconciliation. It trained "agents of change" in communities to notice and address problems between people before they become severe, help resolve conflicts, and foster peaceful relations. Thirty-seven communities were identified that were especially strongly impacted by the genocide, and where recovery, in terms of social cohesion, the absence of conflict, and economic activity, was slow. With the help of local officials, LaBenevolencija staff selected for training as agents of change highly diverse groups of people in each community, with varied backgrounds and positions in society. They included genocide survivors, prisoners returned to the communities, poor people, people with some "deviant" behaviors, elected and appointed officials, pastors and teachers, and agricultural and health advisors. The aim was not to duplicate the activities of local officials, but to help people with social cohesion, with problems that affect people's everyday relations.

Those selected received 5 days of training in the Staub-Pearlman approach, by staff that was previously trained in and had been using the approach in creating the radio programs. The training focused on the communication messages, used segments from *Musekeweya*, and included role playing. After the training, local and national coordinators worked with the local agents. The team engaged by LaBenevolencija to evaluate the effects of the program wrote: "The grassroots programme has the objective to amplify the messages through a direct intervention on the ground in localities that encounter serious problems in the domain of conflict resolution, prevention and reconciliation" (Ingelaere, Havugimana, & Ndushabandi, 2009a).

This team first evaluated whether the agents of change understood the communication messages. When shown varied segments from *Musekeweya*, they were substantially better at identifying their meaning—for example, a segment showing passivity by bystanders— than other people from the same communities. They were then asked to describe the type of conflicts they encountered and identify the most important ones. Theft and internal household problems were frequent. Land redistribution was in progress and the government had people stop growing their customary crops and replace them with different crops. Land conflict, and conflict related to the *gacaca*—both in a general sense and specifically in terms of returning property—were both frequent and described as the most important.

The evaluators compared communities with change agents to others in the same area. They concluded that while "gacaca-related conflicts receive the highest ranking overall . . . (they) are not ranked highest in the grassroots sites." They speculated that "this might be due to the grassroots activities since they have the objective of conflict resolution (especially related to issues dealt with in gacaca) and fostering social cohesion and reconciliation issues that are apparently most negatively affected by the introduction of the gacaca in rural life" (Ingelaere, Havugimana, & Ndushabandi, 2009a).

People have become less fearful of cohabitation, living their everyday lives together— sharing a beer, attending a wedding, helping to take a sick person to the hospital. But interpersonal reconciliation, a "matter of the heart," trust and confidence in neighbors, in members of the other ethnic group, is more challenging. The evaluators regard this as the realm of social cohesion. In open questions, when people can say whatever they want, community respondents identified *Musekeweya* (25%), or LaBenevolencija in general (23%) and activities organized by it, and the agents of change in particular (10%) as sources of increasing cohesion over the past 2 years. In this open format, 54% of respondents identified LaBenevolencija-initiated activities as sources of social cohesion. Local community gatherings organized by officials were identified by 25% of the respondents. When asked a direct question, "Did LaBenevolencija play a role in the increase of social cohesion in your community over the past 2 years?" Ninety-six percent said it did. (However, people in Rwanda often say what they believe they are expected to say—especially by people they regard as authorities, which can include researchers.)

In 2008, to create cohesion among the change agents and make their activities more sustained, the coordinators helped them develop associations around agricultural activities, initiated by small grants to the groups. For people who normally would have little contact, coming together in associations, especially after the genocide, seemed to have special value. However, in an in-depth look at two associations, the evaluators found that only one had a highly mixed membership. In that community, agents of change were highly active. Not surprisingly, in that community they received more credit for social cohesion.

Reconciliation activities have often focused on national processes, such as truth commissions, tribunals to bring about justice, or political arrangements. But reconciliation at the local level, between parties who have harmed each other and now have to rebuild their lives living next to each other, such as former prisoners living next to survivors in Rwanda, is crucial. Mozambique has moved from violence to relative peace without a national reconciliation process, but with reconciliation activities at local levels (Broneus, 2008). The aim of

Musekeweya was to reach the population, and the grassroots project, engaging with people directly, seemed to have enhanced its influence.

Musekeweya and the Democratic Forces for the Liberation of Rwanda

We began to hear reports that members of the FDLR in the Congo, the militia led by former genocidaires, have been listening to *Musekeweya*. Some of them left their group and returned to Rwanda, and according to these reports, they were influenced by *Musekeweya*. LaBenevolencija commissioned the same researchers who evaluated the grassroots project, and they conducted interviews in Rwanda with ex-rebels in a demobilization and reintegration camp and on a rural hill. They interviewed 101 ex-rebels in the course of several weeks (Ingelaere, Havugimana, & Ndushabandi, 2009b).

The FDLR members in the Congo have listened a great deal to radio stations such as the BBC, Voice of America, and Radio Rwanda. They listened to Radio Rwanda to keep up with the developments in the country and to understand what might be the situation of family and friends. The most popular programs were *Urunana* and *Musekeweya*, both radio dramas. Most of 101 ex-rebels followed the weekly broadcasts of *Musekeweya*, and according to them most of the Kinyarwanda speakers in the Congo, regardless of ethnicity, listen to the program. For the former members of FDLR, the theme of reconciliation between the villages was especially striking. The change in Rutanagira, the bad leader, made a strong impression on them, as he became active in working for reconciliation and peace.

Coming to learn about the changing nature of Rwanda, mainly from telephone conversations with family in Rwanda and visitors from Rwanda, played a role in their return. So did issues within the FDLR, such as lack of objectives, conflicts and incompetence of leaders, the hard life in the Eastern Congo, and separation from families in Rwanda. While *Musekeweya* is an educational radio drama, a story, the researchers write that "It is evident that radio broadcasts have played a major role in the spread of" a new image of Rwanda. "The theme of reconciliation underlies a great number of the striking episodes mentioned by the ex-rebels." Although there is no evidence that it "played a decisive role in their final decision to return home . . . the radio soap is somehow at work in a dynamic of competing ideologies and mindsets" (Ingelaere, Havugimana, & Ndushabandi, 2009b, pp. 1–2). Interestingly, in addition to getting trustworthy information about Rwanda, a main obstacle to return was a practical one, finding demobilization points in the Democratic Republic of Congo.

Other Radio Programs

Like all forms of prevention and reconciliation, to be effective educational efforts must be informed by the actual conditions of group conflict, history, and culture. The extensions of our project, radio dramas in Burundi and the Congo, were guided by the same conceptual approach as *Musekeweya*, but their content was adjusted according to differences in conditions from Rwanda. The differences are especially great with the Congo, where more groups are involved in the conflict and in addition to tribe and ethnicity, conflicts over local (and national) power and land ownership and material resources have significant roles.

Summary

Public education, especially if it involves extensive exposure, can and has been found to change attitudes, beliefs, and behavior. Public education can include lectures and work-shops, literature, various media, and the Internet. Our educational radio drama in Rwanda, its educational content informed by the Staub-Pearlman approach, had a variety of positive effects on beliefs, values, and behavior. Listening to the radio drama made it more likely that people use their own judgment about the meaning of events and about what to do, and express and/or act on their beliefs.

Both the radio drama and local agents in a "grassroots project" building on the radio drama were believed by local people to have contributed to social cohesion. Other radio programs also had positive effects. Public education has to consider local conditions, and the radio dramas created for Burundi, and especially the Congo, applied the same conceptual approach to the different local conditions.

References

Baumeister, R. F. (1997). *Evil: Inside human violence and cruelty*. New York: Freeman and Co.

Bandura, A. (2006). Going global with social cognitive theory: From prospect to paydirt. In S. I. Donaldson, D. E. Berger, & K. Pezdek (Eds.), *Applied psychology: New frontiers and rewarding careers*. (pp. 53–79). Mahwah, NJ: Lawrence Erlbaum.

Brounéus, K. (2008). Analyzing reconciliation: A structured method for measuring national reconciliation initiatives. *Peace and Conflict: Journal of Peace Psychology, 14*(3): 291–313.

Ilibagiza, I., & Erwin, S. (2006). *Left to tell: Discovering God amidst the Rwanda Holocaust*. Carlsbad, CA: Hay House.

Ingelaere, B., Havugimana, J., & Ndushabandi, S. (2009a). *LaBenevolencija grassroots project evaluation*. Research reports prepared for Radio LaBenevolencija. Unpublished manuscript.

Ingelaere, B., Havugimana, J., & Ndushabandi, S. (2009b). *Musekeweya in the Congo: Radio listening habits of ex-FDLR combatants in Eastern-DRC*. Research reports prepared for Radio LaBenevolencija. Unpublished manuscript.

Paluck, E. L. (2006). The second year of a "new dawn": Year two evidence for the impact of the Rwandan reconciliation radio drama Musekeweya. LaBenvolencija evaluation report. Unpublished manuscript.

Paluck, E. L. (2009). Reducing intergroup prejudice and conflict using the media: A field experiment in Rwanda. *Journal of Personality and Social Psychology, 96*, 574–587.

Paluck, E. L., & Green, D. P. (2005). *LaBenevolencija's reconciliation radio project: Musekeweya's first year evaluation report*. LaBenevolencija evaluation report. Unpublished manuscript.

PRI. (2004, November). Report on monitoring and research on the gacaca. The righteous: Between oblivion and reconciliation? Example of the province of Kibuye. Retrieved from http://www.penalreform.org/resources/rep-2004-gacacaKibuye3-en.pdf

Staub, E. (2011). *Overcoming evil: Genocide, violent conflict and terrorism*. New York: Oxford University Press.

Staub, E., & Pearlman, L. A. (2009). Reducing intergroup prejudice and conflict: A commentary. *Journal of Personality and Social Psychology, 96*, 588–594.

Staub, E., Pearlman, L. A., & Bilali, R. (2010). Understanding the roots and impact of violence and psychological recovery as avenues to reconciliation after mass violence and intractable conflict: Applications to national leaders, journalists, community groups, public education through radio, and children. In G. Salomon & E. Cairns (Eds.), *Handbook of peace education* (pp. 269-287). New York: Psychology Press

Staub, E., Pearlman, L. A., Gubin, A., & Hagengimana, A. (2005). Healing, reconciliation, forgiving and the prevention of violence after genocide or mass killing: An intervention and its experimental evaluation in Rwanda. *Journal of Social and Clinical Psychology, 24*(3), 297–334.

20

Preventing Violence and Terrorism and Promoting Positive Relations Between Dutch and Muslim Communities in Amsterdam

Introduction and Background

One consequence of terrorism and the war on terror has been an increase in previously existing tensions between the original national/ethnic groups and immigrant Muslim minorities in several European countries (Buijs & Rath, 2002). The 9/11/2001 attacks, U.S. responses like the war on terror, subsequent terrorist attacks, especially in Europe, their psychological impact, and political and social reactions in response to these events have led to the intensification and forceful public expressions of negative attitudes and of concerns about future relations between groups (Buijs & Rath, 2002; Cesari, 2002, 2003; Rath et al., 1999).

The primary purpose of this article is to consider ways to help groups with problematic, hostile relations to resolve antagonism, reconcile, and develop peaceful, harmonious relations. I will focus on the Netherlands, where after violence between Muslims and the ethnic Dutch. I was invited to study circumstances and make proposals to improve group relations. However, the principles, analyses, and practices I propose can be applied, with appropriate consideration of the specifics of the situation, to other countries as well.

In the Netherlands, the problems after 9/11 have been accentuated by politicians attacking—rather than constructively engaging with—Islam as a religion and with

Reprinted with permission and minor changes from Staub, E. (2007). Preventing violence and terrorism and promoting positive relations between Dutch and Muslim communities in Amsterdam—with relevance to other European countries. *Peace and Conflict: The Journal of Peace Psychology, 13*(3), 1–28.

Muslim culture and social arrangements. The attacks had already started before 9/11 (Fortuyn, 1997). Subsequent events included the harsh critique by Hirsi Ali, a Somali immigrant of Muslim origins and a member of parliament from 2002 to 2006, about the treatment of women in Muslim families. She and Theo van Gogh created a television film, "Submission," that Muslims perceived as presenting them in an intensely negative light and in a blasphemous manner. Theo van Gogh was murdered by a Muslim man and the life of Hirsi Ali was threatened, followed by the burning of mosques, Muslim schools, and churches (Caldwell, 2005).

Violence, especially terrorism, can be the result of social conditions and culture at a particular place at a particular time, or due to instigation and actions by outside groups. The assumption in this article is that when violence-producing conditions are present in a society, terrorism instigated from the outside is more likely. Violence between groups, and the psychological and social processes that lead to it, usually evolve. In the Netherlands, some underlying conditions for violence appear to exist, at least to a moderate degree, but the evolution is in its early stages.

This article focuses on developing policies and practices in countries with large Muslim minorities—particularly in the Netherlands—with the goal of improving group relations and decreasing the likelihood of terrorism and violence from both inside and outside of the country. The approach in this article to overcoming antagonism and promoting reconciliation is based in part on the study of the roots of mass violence (Staub, 1989, 1996, 2003, 2011), applied to and tested through interventions in field settings, such as Rwanda (Staub, 2006a, 2011; Staub & Pearlman, 2006; Staub et al., 2005: see Chapters 18 and 19). It is also informed by scholarship in genocide studies (Fein, 1979; Melson, 2003; Smith, 1999), and the study of conflict (Bar-Tal, 2000; Coleman, 2000; Kelman & Fisher, 2003; Kriesberg, 1998; Lederach, 1997; Staub, 2011).

The primary Muslim groups in Amsterdam are the Turks and Moroccans, and their populations are continually increasing (*Diversiteits- en Integratiemonitor* 2004). Antilleans and Surinamers, the two other major ethnic communities, come from former Dutch colonies, are primarily Christian, and are better adapted to Dutch society. How can this mixed society be peaceful and grow in positive ways?

There are genuine issues and cultural differences between the ethnic Dutch and the Muslim immigrant groups, and the worldwide focus on terrorism enlarges the perception and meaning of these differences. My use of the term "culture" includes differences in religion, perceptions of and interpretations of events, customs and habits, and values and beliefs that are not solely based on the differences between the Muslim religion and the secular Christianity that characterizes the Netherlands, but also on different national/cultural and educational backgrounds (see also Cesari, 2003).

What are the current conditions and concerns of the ethnic Dutch and of Muslim immigrant groups? One of the concerns of the former is whether Islam is adaptable to their pluralistic, democratic culture.

Issues, Concerns, and Grievances: the Dutch

Since 9/11, terrorism has been a primary concern according to various reports (e.g., Dutch General Intelligence and Security Service Report, 2004), the media, and public statements.

An opinion poll in 2002 for the TV program *Twee Vandaag* by NIPO (Nieuwenhuizen, 2003) found that 6 out of 10 Dutch respondents were afraid of violent acts by Muslim extremists, and almost 50 percent reported more negative views of Muslims than before. After Theo van Gogh's murder, fear and negativity seemed to increase substantially.[1]

The Dutch are also concerned with the high crime rates, especially by Moroccans, who are 15% of the population. Among young people, 61% of those who frequently commit crimes are Dutch, and 31% Moroccan; among adults, 41% Dutch, 22% Moroccan, and 19% Surinamese. Among hard-core young criminals, the percentage of Moroccans has been decreasing over the years, from 31% in 1996 to 22% in 2002 (*Diversiteits- en Integratiemonitor,* 2004, Tables 6.1 and 6.2). The public's perception of the Moroccan crime rate is probably greater than its actual level, due to other actions that disturb people, such as harassment by groups of teenage Moroccans (Germert & Fleisher, 2005) and criminal Moroccan youth gangs (Germert, 2004). These activities of young Moroccan males also create concern about the socialization of boys.

Many Turkish and Moroccan men came to work in the Netherlands in the 1960s and 70s, and planned to return home. Instead, they later brought their families and stayed. However, the jobs they came for disappeared. Without knowledge of the Dutch language and with limited education and skills, immigrants—especially Moroccan men—have been supported by the social welfare system. This is another source of resentment.

Many Dutch are also concerned that Muslim religion with its traditions and authoritarian attitude and practices will undermine democracy and Dutch values, such as individuality and openness, or even that Muslim nationalism will attempt to change the political system. The subservient role of women in Muslim culture, forced marriages, especially of underage girls, and honor killings which have been reported in other European countries, clash with Dutch—and European—values (as well as laws). So does Muslim intolerance of free sexuality and homosexuality (Scroggins, 2005).

The Dutch General Intelligence and Security Service report (2004) describes threats posed by different types of radical Islam to a democratic legal order. Radical political Islam aims at political power. Radical-Islamic Puritanism aims to create adherence to Islamic religious belief and practice and advocates isolation or withdrawal from the West, while Muslim nationalism focuses more on being a Muslim than on religion. Although the report briefly reviews counterstrategies and ways to resist these threats, it does not discuss the extent to which these movements are present, or more importantly, absent in current Dutch society, thereby allowing the threat to loom large.

In summary, Dutch and European concerns include the subversion of the democratic state by incompatible theocratic values, beliefs, political aims, and practices; incompatibility in everyday life due to different values and ways of life; a drain on and threat to public resources and the quality of life by the economic needs and antisocial behavior of Muslim immigrants; and terrorism. Some of the threats and concerns I noted are real and material. Others are at least partly psychological, but the perceptions and attitudes they represent

---

1. Looking at the media suggested this, as did conversations with people. After a talk in Amsterdam by the author on promoting positive relations between groups, one person, a social scientist, asked: Are we sitting on a powder keg?

can powerfully shape actions and thereby material realities (see also Buijs & Rath, 2002). Along with these concerns, many Dutch, including government officials, are concerned that their society is becoming intolerant and inhospitable to Muslims and immigrant groups, and about the creation or existence of a social environment that may radicalize Muslims[2].

Issues, Concerns and Grievances: Muslim Groups

Muslim concerns include lack of acceptance, prejudice, discrimination, and hostility and restrictive immigration policies (de Koenig, 2005; *Diversiteits- en Integratiemonitor*, 2004). They fear violence against them—not surprisingly since in the 22 days following van Gogh's murder more than 800 apparently related incidents were reported by police, the large majority directed against Muslims, such as violence against Islamic schools and mosques, threats, intimidation, and verbal attacks (Tweede Kamer der Staten-General, 2005). Because of the likely consequences to them, Muslims greatly fear terrorist attacks (*Diversiteits- en Integratiemonitor*, 2004).

A significant issue for Muslim minorities is unemployment and problems in material existence—not having the knowledge and skills required to participate in the labor force. An important threat is the disruption of community, worldview, and identity due to dislocation and the changes required by adaptation. Muslims seem concerned that on the one hand they are expected to transform their identity as Muslims to be accepted as Dutch, and on the other hand that regardless of their level of adjustment, they will remain outsiders (Twee Vandaag poll by NIPO, 2003). As part of this adjustment, they face the difficulties of integration into a culture that has elements that are strictly prohibited by Islam, especially related to sexuality. However, there is also concern by some about their own cultural practices, especially related to the treatment of women (Scroggins, 2005).

The Extent of Adaptability of Islam to Western Cultures

Can the people in Western, democratic, liberal countries live harmoniously with Muslim minorities? For a long time, scholars have debated how fundamentalist, universal, and rigid Islam is, and how much it can adapt to specific contexts. Many Western scholars have claimed a core opposition between Islam and the West, a clash of civilizations (Huntington, 1996; Lewis, 2005), a radical incompatibility between democracy, freedom, and individualism, and the theocracy and tradition guiding Islam. Mandaville (2005), for example, notes that radical Islam, such as Wahabism and its relatives, is dominant in Muslim countries and has strong advocates in Western immigrant groups.

However, some scholars have described the vast majority of Muslims as moderates, not extremists (Aslan, 2005). Many have been pointing to movements and ideas within Islam that indicate adaptability and change. There are many moderate views in Islam, which develop when there are contexts that support them. Ramadan (2004), a Swiss-Muslim philosopher, has been calling for a European Islam, with coexistence and civic participation, communities that concern themselves with the welfare of all members, and responsible

2. This statement is based on discussions with many people in March 2005, including city officials in Amsterdam.

relations between Muslims and non-Muslims. At a 2005 meeting in Austria, 160 Imams called for gender equality (Scroggins, 2005). New "solidarity citizenship" organizations are also signs of "transformation of Islam, in the Dutch context of life" (Vernooij, 2004, p. 14). The organizations promote shared goals by involving Muslims in volunteer work.

Wickham (2005) describes "revivalist" political organizations in a number of Sunni Muslim Arab states that advocate democratic elections, some even equating them with *shura*, the Islamic principle of consultation. However, they do reject practices that would allow the free commingling of men and women, including voting and running for elected office. They assume that this would create marital discord and divert women's attention from their responsibilities in the home. Wickham notes that these movements have developed in Muslim societies, which contain and limit them. She sees signs of deepening reformist thinking, with an increasing number of opposition leaders supporting the principle of ijtihad, "the right of Muslims to reinterpret the sacred texts in light of new circumstances" and articulate new positions on "intellectual and political pluralism and the rights of women" (p. 3).

Many other authors point to adaptation by Muslim groups to specific contexts. Mason (2004) writes: "an Arab-Australian can be simultaneously loyal to his/her local soccer team, the Brazilian national soccer team, a specific political party within Australia, the Muslim community, the Palestinian community, and the wider Australian community, without any of these loyalties negating another" (p. 239). A small example of adaptation is that when, in a school in Netherlands, girls were not allowed to wear head scarves, an Imam told their mothers that the girls could remove their scarves when entering school and put them back on when they leave—which is what the girls were already doing (de Koening, 2005). There is, however, the question of mutual adaptation—schools allowing students to wear headscarves.

According to Cesari (2002, 2003), Europeans do not understand the transformation created, especially in the younger generation, by living in Western, pluralistic cultures, as well as the differences due to national and cultural origin. Phalet, van Lotrigen, and Entzinger (2004) conducted a survey of 900 people in Rotterdam and found that while young Muslim adults strongly identify with Islam, their Islam is individualistic and pluralistic, allowing room for internal debate, tolerance, and friendships across group lines. This was especially true for survey participants with more educational background, especially females. Furthermore, Dutch participants estimated more discrimination against Muslims than Muslim participants saw against themselves, and the latter perceived discrimination as more structural and less personal.

Proposals for Preventing Hostility and Violence and Promoting Peaceful Group Relations

Both Western nations and the Islamic world see themselves under attack. In the following I will make proposals, which are in part principles out of which specific policies and practices can be developed to prevent the intensification of hostility and foster positive attitudes and peaceful relations. As background for the proposals I briefly discuss the origins and prevention of violence and reconciliation. Understanding the influences leading to violence and avenues for their prevention can themselves bring about changes in people.

Starting Points for Violence: Instigating Conditions

There are two frequent background conditions that are starting points for hostility and violence (Staub, 1989, 2011). One I call *difficult life conditions* in a society: economic problems, political confusion and disorganization, great societal changes, and the social chaos they create. Another is *conflict between groups*, whether over territory, or power, wealth, and privilege between dominant and subordinate groups, or for other reasons. Both types of instigating conditions profoundly frustrate basic human needs—for security, a positive identity, a feeling of effectiveness and control over important events, positive connections to other people, autonomy, and a comprehension of the world and of one's place in it.

In response, people shift from an individual to a group identity, which fulfills some of these needs. As a group they scapegoat others and turn to destructive ideologies which offer hope for the future, but identify another, usually historically devalued group, as an enemy. Violence does not usually erupt; it evolves with progressive changes in individuals and society. An evolution of increasingly harmful actions can lead to mass killing by a dominant group or to terrorism by a less powerful group (Richardson, 2006; Staub, 1989, 1996, 2003, 2011).

Devaluing Versus Humanizing the "Other"

Human beings have a tendency to divide the world into "us," our group, our people, our nation and "them," those outside the group (Fiske & Taylor, 1991; Staub, 1989). Those on the outside are easily and persistently devalued and dehumanized. The roots of the devaluation may be varied: differences in physical features, knowledge, values, beliefs, or general culture; a lower status that arises from historical group differences; difficult life conditions that lead to scapegoating and the creation of ideological enemies; or justification for violence against a group (Staub, 1996). Once devaluation exists, it is maintained by literature, the media, the way people talk about the other, and by discrimination that is justified by further devaluation.

Proposal 1. Humanizing the "other" is essential to overcome devaluation and the danger of violence.

To humanize Muslims, media projects should present the lives of Muslims in ways that makes them understandable, as young and old individuals, families, a community and a culture, instead of abstractions and stereotypes. Providing images of everyday lives, as well as cultural and psychological understanding—for example, what life is like for people who have left their home countries and have to negotiate differences in customs and religion—is important. Since devaluation is mutual, it is important to present side by side the lives of the Dutch and of Muslims from various national groups, with appropriate commentary. This can develop the capacity to take the other's perspective, to empathize, and can humanize each group in the eyes of the other. Informational programs about the importance of and ways to humanize groups and their members would be useful for members of the media, and for community, religious, and political leaders in all groups.

Devaluation between groups is maintained in the Netherlands by limited contact, especially between Dutch people and the older generation of immigrants, and little knowledge by most Dutch of Islam (see *Diversiteits- en Integratiemonitor*, 2004). The knowledge by many Muslims of the Dutch comes from television and public encounters. The media, leaders, and opinion makers should help communities understand the concept of *devaluation:* that it is possible to have a strongly negative view of a group without that view being based on reality or actual knowledge. Devaluation makes it easier to harm people. The more intense the devaluation, and the more it includes a view of the other as morally bad and as dangerous to "us," the greater the violent potential (Staub, 1989).

Those devalued tend to become angry and hostile. Muslim minorities may turn to a more fundamentalist Islam as a way of strengthening identity, in-group connections, and their understanding of reality and the world and their place in it. There can be mutual radicalization. In the Netherlands, right-wing discussion groups on the internet point to Muslims as the country's problem. The burning of mosques and Islamic schools after van Gogh's murder also indicates radicalization, with the burning of churches a response.

In the view of Rath et al. (1999), the prevailing opinion before 9/11 was that "Muslims have an excessive tendency to cling together and resist becoming part of modern Dutch society . . . [and have] . . . preference for traditional, i.e. non-democratic forms of political leadership. They do not treat women as equals to men, adhere to old fashioned views of bringing up children" and are susceptible to external, arch-conservative influence. (pp. 11–12) Such attitudes have become more negative since this research (*Diversiteits- en Integratiemonitor*, 2004).

Limited research shows that Muslims also devalue the Dutch, but to a lesser extent (*Diversiteits- en Integratiemonitor*, 2004). Muslim websites refer to the Dutch society and lifestyle as licentious and "perverted," while also expressing appreciation for liberal social policies. While the word "perverted" is apparently commonly used in Islam to describe practices such as liberal sexual behavior and homosexuality, such words have significant impact. Fortuyn (1997) was one of the early influential politicians who attacked Islam and Muslim culture after an Imam described homosexuality as a sexual disease. Fostering sensitivity to language may be an aspect of cultural awareness and humanization.

Both Turks and Moroccans say, in responses to scenarios presented to them, that they would prefer to be integrated in society. However, Dutch participants believed that they would prefer separation, which the immigrants prefer least and which the Dutch like least (Van Oudenhoven, Prins, & Buunk, 1998). Another study found that Dutch participants showed less prejudice toward immigrants who assimilate (identify with Dutch culture) than those who integrate (both adapt to Dutch culture and maintain their identification with their original group) (Van Oudenhoven & Eisses, 1998).

Learning about the other's culture is one way to humanize the other. The *Diversiteits- en Integratiemonitor* of 2004 describes an increase in cultural education. Fostering both knowledge of a culture and understanding of how that culture has evolved as a function of circumstances the group had faced and their adaptation to them can promote empathy and acceptance (Staub, 2002, 2003). Groups can also humanize the other by fostering awareness of *shared* needs, in part by understanding the lives of members of the other group. In Macedonia, journalists from different ethnic groups interviewed and wrote articles about families belonging to each group, which were printed in the newspapers of each of the ethnic groups (Manoff, 1996). Further, showing *variations* among people in the other group can help to "individuate" them, disconfirming group stereotypes.

Destructive Ideology Versus a Constructive, Shared Vision of a Hopeful Future

One of the most important influences leading to violence between groups, including terrorism, is a "destructive ideology." In the presence of difficult life conditions or group conflict, people often create or turn to an ideology, a vision of how to live life, of relationships between groups, and individuals within groups. In Nazi Germany, Cambodia under the Khmer Rouge, Argentina during the disappearances (Staub, 1989), or Rwanda in the form of "Hutu power" (des Forges, 1999; Staub 2011), visions of "better" futures have been created. However, these visions or ideologies were destructive, in that some group was defined as an enemy that stands in the way of the ideology's fulfillment.

> *Proposal 2. The Dutch and Muslim leaders and communities should engage in dialogue aimed at creating a constructive, inclusive ideology that embraces mutual understanding, accommodation, and a shared vision of a good society to which all groups can contribute and help create.*
>
> *This should involve exploration of all groups' values, beliefs, and customs, acknowledging and engaging with differences, while considering accommodation, common ground and the aim of developing positive social arrangements that encompass all groups. This might be done in living rooms, public meetings, on the radio and television. The involvement of religious leaders of the Muslim communities in such dialogue is crucial, since they have substantial influence in opening (or closing) minds to new perspectives. Political leaders and the media have somewhat similar power on the Dutch side. Given each group's limited knowledge of the other, providing each group with basic descriptive information about the other would be valuable preparation for dialogue. Active involvement in such a societal process, in small meetings and large events, can empower people, change attitudes toward the other group, and help people envision a good community.*

Muslim groups facing difficult life conditions or group conflict may turn to their already existing ideology, Islam, which is likely to become more extreme or fundamentalist in nature. In the face of adversity, being part of a Muslim community provides security, identity, connection and a familiar world view. Those outside the group are then increasingly seen as enemies of the ideal way of life described by Islam. The Dutch facing adversity—great societal changes and the possibility of terrorism—can also shift from being individuals and become more "Dutch" and more negative toward minority groups. Threat to the group is a powerful predictor of hostility to minority groups (Hewstone, Rubin, & Willis, 2002).

In difficult or confusing times it is important to create an inclusive vision of a better future that all groups can work together to fulfill. The creation of such a vision requires exploration and dialogue among all groups. In the Netherlands, historically there has been social organization in "pillars," different groups having their own identity, culture, religious denomination, and educational system. However, among other problems, it has contributed to separation between groups and has been changed to a "civic integration" policy in the 1990s (Joppke, 2004).

A shared, inclusive ideology can only be created through engagement and empathetic dialogue. In the course of dialogue, differences about core values and identities are certain to emerge. However, the Dutch may learn that Muslim practices are adaptable to historical developments and current circumstances (see previous discussion). Issues of hierarchy and authority versus equality and freedom in the values and practices of both groups can be examined, identifying elements of equality and freedom in both cultures and considering relevant practices, as well as in the treatment of women. Extreme ideological groups from both sides will be threatened by engagement and the easing of ideological differences. But dialogue can help people in the middle from moving toward the extreme, and create a shared vision for society. As part of the dialogue, aspects of Muslim religion that are hostile to outsiders or that terrorists have used to ferment hostility and violence ought to be contrasted with other elements within Islam. Islamic teaching on love and tolerance, the tolerance inherent in democratic ideals, and caring for a shared community can be among the building blocks of a shared ideology.

Past Victimization and Healing of Psychological Wounds

People who have been victimized or in other ways traumatized often carry deep psychological wounds. They tend to feel vulnerable, have a diminished sense of self, distrust people and see people and the world as dangerous. When they experience new threat, they may feel the need to use force to defend themselves, thereby becoming perpetrators (Staub, 1998; Staub & Pearlman, 2006). Members of minority groups who left their own countries, especially victims of political violence, are likely to carry such psychological wounds. Devaluation, discrimination, and disruptions of family or community add to their woundedness.

Proposal 3. Facilitate psychological healing to prevent the negative consequences of painful past experiences.

Offer people who have immigrated to the Netherlands opportunities to tell their stories in an empathic context, including stories of dislocation, discrimination, and experiences of victimization before (or after) they immigrated. This can done be in small groups, community meetings, as well as in the media. Engagement with their own and others' stories can help people heal and connect with each other, and can humanize members of a group in the eyes of other communities. It is important to also provide opportunities for people in the ethnic Dutch community, especially young people, to talk about their painful experiences. In schools, children can read, write, and discuss stories about painful experiences, both fictional and autobiographical. This should not be a special activity, but part of the normal functioning of schools—which requires teacher training.

Healing from past wounds, or psychological recovery, can help people differentiate between past and present, and help them reconnect and trust people more. One way to healing is to engage with, rather than avoid, the memories of painful past experiences, by telling one's story while others respond empathetically or by hearing others share similar painful or difficult experiences (Herman, 1992; Pearlman & Saakvitne, 1995; Staub et al., 2005).

People belonging to majority groups can also be psychologically wounded. Many members of racist right-wing groups in the United States are young people, mostly men, who come from difficult—poor and abusive—backgrounds (Ezekiel, 1995, 2002). They are desperately in need of connection to other people and of a world view that helps them make sense of their life experiences. The right-wing groups they join, with their ideologies of superiority, strengthen their identity, give them meaning and connection, and provide a reassuring comprehension of reality. These groups fulfill basic needs, but in destructive ways, turning people against others. While their membership is limited, extreme right groups do exist in the Netherlands, with busy internet traffic. Helping people with such backgrounds heal and find constructive communities and world views would make it less likely that they turn to right-wing extremism.

Moderating Respect for Authority and Increasing of Pluralism

A culture promoting very strong respect for authority is another contributor to violence (Staub, 1989, 2006a). Being accustomed to guidance by authorities, it is difficult for people to stand on their own in difficult times. They tend to turn to and follow leaders, especially leaders who help them fulfill basic psychological needs. There is much concern in Western societies about the "authority orientation" in Muslim cultures (Nisbett-Larkin, 2005). A related contributor to violence by groups against other groups is the absence of pluralism. Genuine pluralism moderates respect for authority.

Proposal 4. Enhancing pluralism and moderating respect for authority are important in inhibiting the evolution toward hostility and violence.

> *To enhance pluralism, provide outlets for leaders and members of minority groups in the Netherlands to express the needs, concerns, and perspectives of their communities. Provide access to media, encourage community and political participation and dialogue. Look for and develop young community/political leaders in immigrant Muslim groups, through leadership seminars and invitations to participate in political activities. Dialogue may also help moderate authority, as people find their own voice and develop their own views (which may promote respect for authority based not on position, but on merit).*

As the United States' example after 9/11 indicates, people in a secular culture with generally moderate respect for authority can also show strong respect for authority in response to difficulties of life, especially threat to the group. People can turn to strong leaders who promise protection, offer people ways to feel effective and in control, strengthen the group's identity, and provide a clear vision in the midst of confusion. All of this can be destructive, however, if the actions of the group do not address the actual causes of the problem, the clarity does not reflect actual reality, and the solutions offered by leaders generate hostility and violence between groups. It is important, therefore, to make people aware of the potential dangers of very strong respect for authority, in a way that is respectful of a culture that values authority.

Pluralism, which moderates respect for authority, has at least two components: the existence in society and the possibility to express a wide range of beliefs and values, and participation by all segments of society in public discourse. The first component of pluralism is strong in the Netherlands. However, subgroups of society differ substantially in their participation in the public domain. Muslim participation is limited and decreasing in local elections, particularly in Amsterdam, while increasing among Turks in Rotterdam with Turkish candidates for council seats (Tillie & Slijper, 2005). Pluralism can be furthered by promoting Muslim participation in public discussion and political life. This can start with dialogue (Kelman & Fisher, 2003), which gives people a voice and a constructive way to engage with each other's values, ways of life, and culture.

Justice and Acculturation

Conflict between dominant and subordinate groups in a society has been a primary source of violence (Fein, 1993). Another source has been the perception by a group that their identity is being denied, leading to nationalism and a desire to establish their separate identity (Chirot & Seligman, 2001). The two are connected, in that the desire for a separate identity often arises out of the perception of injustice. Acculturation is defined here as the immigrants' absorption of and accommodation to their new society. In contrast to Turkish immigrants, for example, there has been only limited business initiative in the Moroccan community, which has therefore provided less work opportunity for Moroccans. Young people in immigrant minority groups in Amsterdam, especially Moroccans, have had less schooling and much lower rates of high school attendance. This situation has been improving, but there are still substantial group differences (*Diversiteits- en Integratiemonitor*, 2004).

Proposal 5. Societal actions to address unfair social practices are important in promoting positive relations. Facilitating the acculturation of Muslim minorities in both work and personal realms is also essential to reducing group differences and increasing social justice.

Rebuilding internal community, better connections to the larger community, and empowerment through engagement in socially constructive and personally meaningful activities can fulfill basic needs, shape positive and integrated identities, promote social justice, and reduce antisocial behavior. To facilitate acculturation and lessen alienation and antisocial behavior, it is important for schools to promote academic and societal participation—to provide young people with language and job training, opportunities for work and participation in positive group activities. Training young people in entrepreneurship would also be helpful for personal and community empowerment.

Moving to a different country with a different majority religion, leaving friends, extended family and often even the nuclear family behind is difficult and creates structural and emotional upheaval in people's lives. Many Moroccan men, only after being occasional visitors to their wives and children in Morocco for many years, brought their families to the Netherlands. Especially for people from a collectivist culture, the disruption of community adds greatly to their psychological dislocation. Many adults did not learn the language, and often children spoke for the family. Fathers, traditionally the source of unquestioned authority, have been diminished by their inability to influence events that affect their families (de Koenig, 2005; Germert & Fleisher, 2005).

Members of the second generation are to some degree acculturated, creating further separation from their elders, but are not effectively integrated into the larger society. The combination of coming from a collectivist, religious society, disconnection from their own community, and lack of integration makes the individuation process that is part of growing up highly complicated, especially for boys (Erikson, 1963). Some search for identity and connection by exploring the meaning of religion in their present life context (de Konieg, 2005), while others, especially Moroccan boys, turn to informal youth groups for identity and connection.

Some of these groups are aggressive, intimidate people, or engage in crime (Germert, 1999, 2004; Germert & Fleisher, 2005). These young men are considered Moroccans within the Netherlands, but strangers when they go to Morocco (Stern, 2005). They feel alienated, disrespected, and humiliated. Their activities on the streets and in gangs, disapproved at home, further disconnect them from their families. However, rather than trying to disperse gangs, which serve useful psychological functions, efforts should be made to transform them into "prosocial gangs" (Goldstein & Soriano, 1994) that engage in constructive business activities, rather than intimidation and crime.

On the basis of 150 interviews in Kuwait after its liberation from the invasion by Iraq, Volkan (2004) writes about fathers who were humiliated by Iraqi soldiers. They did not talk about it to their children, but distanced themselves in an effort to hide or deny their sense of shame. "Frustrated by the distant and humiliated fathers who would not talk to their sons about the traumas of the invasion, they (the sons) linked themselves together and expressed their frustration in gangs" (p. 83). The experience of Moroccan boys in relation to their fathers may be similar. Groups of other youths provide them with the connection and identity so badly needed during that time of development (Germert, 2004).

Fostering a strong internal community, including strengthening family life, would be constructive. Such communities are less negatively affected by a larger culture that diminishes them (Tajfel, 1982). Moroccans in particular have relatively few internal organizations, especially non-religious ones. While Islamic identity remains strong, there is limited religious participation, in terms of visits to mosques and membership in religious organizations throughout the Netherlands and Europe in general (Cesari, 2003; *Diversiteits-en Integratiemonitor,* 2004). Connections to the outside community, through integration at work, in schools, effective participation in the labor market, and political participation are also important. Minority youth gain effectiveness through knowledge of the larger culture and "bicultural competence," the capacity to engage with both groups (Staub, 1996).

Passive Versus Active Bystanders

Witnesses who are in a position to act have great potential power to either facilitate or prevent the evolution of violence (Staub, 1989, 2002, 2003, 2011). Passivity by witnesses or bystanders has a powerful role in allowing the development of negative attitudes and actions. Both perpetrators and bystanders interpret passivity as acceptance or even approval. However, by their words or actions bystanders can influence each other to act. This has been found both in real life situations (Hallie, 1979; Staub, 2003) and laboratory research (Staub, 1974).

> *Proposal 6. Promoting active, positive bystandership by all segments of the population—leaders, the media, community organizations, individual citizens—makes the evolution of hostility and violence less likely. Every person, or organization, can be active in fostering constructive engagement by others.*
>
> *Active bystanders can have powerful influence. Political and community leaders and the media can promote constructive processes by speaking out in opposition to devaluation and verbal and physical attacks. They can also make citizens aware of the influence they can exert by speaking out to counteract negative attitudes and actions, and promote positive ones. Citizens and community groups can, in turn, call upon leaders to engage in constructive actions. Educational workshops and media projects about why people remain passive, about the power of bystanders, and about constructive methods of active bystandership could increase positive bystandership.*

Both politicians and the media have become very vocal in attacks on Muslims and/or Islam. As negative statements about another group increase, some people join in the attacks because of personal inclinations that shifting norms allow expression, others because of political interest, still others because attention now focuses on what is different and problematic about the "other." If a society increasingly turns against a devalued group, it becomes increasingly less likely that members of the society will have the motivation and moral courage to oppose their own group (Staub, 1989, 2003). Correspondingly, as a minority group increasingly moves toward a radical ideology, its members are less likely to be active bystanders to limit this evolution.

Such evolution of mutual hostility has so far been limited in the Netherlands—and Europe in general (*Diversiteits- en Integratiemonitor,* 2004). Active bystandership is more likely if a society fosters moral values, empathy and sympathy, and caring for the welfare of all people that belong to it. Combined with experiences that give people a voice and confidence in their values and views, this can foster the moral courage to act despite opposition by important others and potential ostracism or danger to oneself (Staub, 2005).

The Absence of Contact and Promoting Deep Contact

The absence of contact between groups makes differentiation between "us" and "them" and the devaluation of the other more likely. Contact between members of different groups has been found by social psychologists to be an important avenue to overcoming devaluation, prejudice, and hostility (Pettigrew & Tropp, 2006).

> *Proposal 7. It is important to foster deep contact (significant engagement) between people across group lines as an avenue to overcoming devaluative stereotypes and hostility and developing positive views of the other.*
>
> *To create deep contact, promote physical integration—in housing, in the workplace, and in the schools. Motivate people in authority to create integrated teams in the workplace, working on shared goals. To enhance the effectiveness of contact, develop mutual cultural knowledge and awareness, through workshops and other educational avenues. Expose school personnel to information and training in cooperative teaching and other learning techniques that create deep engagement between students from different groups. Help parents understand the mutual benefits of cross-cutting relations between children in schools. Work to create equal quality schools, in terms of teaching competence and a positive environment. Parents' motivation to send children to integrated schools may be greatly enhanced if children going to such schools do well educationally. Develop stable structures in which Dutch and Muslim students and adults can engage in joint activities, such as sports teams, cultural events, and educational, community, and business projects.*

With differences in culture, hostility between groups in the larger context of terrorism and the war on terror, the conditions are present for a flare-up of (mutual) hostility in the Netherlands and other European countries. Segregation makes this more likely.

Theory and research have specified a variety of conditions that make *contact* effective as a means of overcoming prejudice. Superficial contact does not help (Stroebe, Lenkert, & Jonas, 1988). Opportunities for interaction are important. The more equal the role of interacting individuals, the more authorities support their interaction, and the more they share goals that are super-ordinate to their separate and conflicting goals, the more likely that contact will have positive effects (Allport, 1954; Cook, 1970; Pettigrew, 1998; Sherif et al., 1961). Cross-group friendships are especially valuable in changing perceptions of and attitudes toward the other group (Pettigrew, 1997, 1998). Anxiety inhibits engagement with members of a devalued group. Experience in interaction can help overcome anxiety about who the other is, what the other might do, and how to interact with the other.

The conditions in Amsterdam that would provide significant contact between the Dutch and Muslim communities are limited. In recent years there has been some increase in segregation in neighborhoods, as more people who are not ethnic Dutch move to the outskirts of the city. Due to housing segregation, there are many relatively segregated schools. Only about 10% of Turk and Moroccan students go to substantially integrated schools (*Diversiteists- en Integratiemonitor*, 2004).

Physical integration creates opportunity for contact. But research with children in schools following desegregation in the United States found that White and Black children interacted little with each other. Black children had low self-esteem and did not perform academically according to their potentials. Cooperative learning procedures were introduced. For example, each child had to learn some material and teach it to the other children. Thus children were working on shared goals, with each child both a learner and a teacher (Aronson et al, 1978). Cooperative learning procedures led to improved academic performance and self-esteem by minority children, less prejudice, and more interaction between White and minority children. They did not reduce the academic performance of White children.

Education about the other's culture can make contact more effective. In U.S. schools, White teachers found it insulting when Mexican-American children did what their culture taught them, to look down when the teacher was speaking to them, especially when they were reprimanded (Staub, 1996). In the Netherlands, reports by Moroccan parents and self-reports by youth indicated less problem behavior by youth than that reported by Dutch or Turkish parents and youth, but teachers reported more problem behaviors by Moroccan youth. Possibly differences in culture and expectations have a role in this (Stevens et al., 2003). Teachers, parents, and children may all be helped by education about differences in culture and expectations.

The great value of stable structures in which people interact across group lines and through which they develop cross-cutting identities has been shown in a study in India of three cities in which significant Hindu-Muslim violence occurred when instigating conditions were present, and three cities that remained calm (Varshney, 2002). In the latter cities there were significant institutions that included both Hindus and Muslims. Their members, respected people in the community, were committed to these institutions. They organized themselves to control and combat rumors as they arose, and to engage with politicians and inhibit them from making speeches that inflame tensions—even threatening to publicly speak out against them.

Truth, the Creation of a Shared History and a Shared Future

Groups that have experienced some combination of hostility, conflict, or violence—whether mutual or one-sided violence—usually have different versions of what has happened and why. They tend to blame each other, which makes renewed hostility and conflict more likely (Staub, 2006a).

Proposal 8. Work toward the creation of a mutually acceptable, shared history of the relations between groups. Conflicting views of history can give rise to actual conflict, while a shared view can promote peaceful relations.

Truth is important in promoting reconciliation in pre- and post-conflict settings (Proceedings of the Stockholm International Forum, 2002). Some important aspects of truth are the specification of what has happened, the acknowledgement by groups of their own harmful actions, and correcting misperceptions. The Dutch might believe that Islam is monolithic, without flexibility and variation (Buijs & Rath, 2002), and that Muslims in the Netherlands want to remain separate from the mainstream society (van Oudenhover, Prins, & Buunk, 1998). Among Muslim misperceptions may be exaggerated beliefs about Dutch people living in ways that Islam regards unacceptable.

Since groups and their members tend to deny responsibility for their own violent actions, the creation of a mutually acceptable history is usually extremely difficult (Staub, 2011; Staub & Pearlman, 2006). In the Netherlands and parts of Europe it should be easier to create a shared narrative of the past, since the groups have not severely harmed each other. Some groups, like the Germans and Czechs, have set up commissions to address their shared history, usually some time after the violence occurred (Staub & Bar-Tal, 2003).

The truth and creation of a shared history would be well served by an empathic description and exploration of the lives of members of the groups involved, possibly including the history of Muslim immigration and the evolution of Muslims' relationship to their new country and its Dutch inhabitants. Such a history might describe how the immigrants were first welcomed as workers, how the economy changed, leading to unemployment and reliance on the welfare system. It might consider the impact of all this on individual immigrants, their families and communities, as well as on Dutch society. A shared history might identify the extent to which there has been devaluation, discrimination, and social exclusion, as well as self-exclusion by immigrants; the extent to which members of minority groups engage in antisocial activities; and any history of violence between the groups.

The ideal approach to such an exploration would be an "understanding roots" perspective (see next section), with an empathic exploration of the influences leading to negative attitudes and actions, and the use of the resulting understanding as an impetus for change. A shared narrative would be a valuable underpinning for, and contribution to, creating an inclusive, constructive vision of the future that was discussed in the section on ideology. While creating a shared narrative is often daunting, even working on its creation and progress towards it is helpful (Staub, 2011).

Understanding the Roots and Evolution of Violence and Peacemaking

Our work in Rwanda has strongly suggested the powerful impact on people of understanding the origins of their genocide (Staub, 2006a, 2011; Staub et al., 2005; Staub & Pearlman, 2006). We found that presenting information about the influences that usually lead to group violence and genocide, with examples from other genocides, and having Rwandans apply their understanding to their own genocide, made Rwandan survivors feel humanized. What happened to them was not the result of incomprehensible evil or God's will, but of understandable, even if tragic, human social and psychological processes. This information helped reduce trauma symptoms and created a more positive orientation toward the other group in both Tutsi survivors and Hutus who were themselves not perpetrators. Many participants also commented that understanding how violence originates can lead to action to prevent it.

Proposal 9. Identifying influences that lead to violence, the extent they are present in the Netherlands and other European countries, and understanding why they lead to violence, can motivate actions to prevent violence and build peaceful relations (Beaman et al., 1978; Staub, 2006a, 2011).

The central influences in the Netherlands include many factors already discussed: mutual devaluation, the woundedness and humiliation of immigrant groups, reactions of the Dutch to antisocial behavior, social dependence, the perceived incompatibility in values, and fear by the Dutch of terrorism and the subversion of democracy. Important aspects of understanding are the principles of psychological and behavioral evolution—of destructiveness and helpfulness. Individuals and groups change as a result of their actions (learning by doing). Actions that create limited harm make it easier to do greater harm and more difficult for bystanders to engage in opposition.

Through workshops, media projects, lectures, and other public events, information should be presented to help politicians, leaders of institutions like churches and schools, the media itself, and the public in general to develop understanding of the psychology of group relations—and the psychological, cultural, and social influences that generate hostility and lead to violence. People also need information about ways to diminish hostility, prevent violence, empower active bystandership, and promote an evolution of positive group relations.

It can make a difference if people understand that perpetrators justify their actions by further devaluing those they harm (Lerner, 1980). Passive bystanders also devalue victims. They distance themselves from and tend to blame those who suffer, so as to avoid feeling empathic distress and guilt (Staub, 1989). Societal norms, standards, and institutions, such as the media, schools, the police, and the government, all change in relation to an increasingly victimized group. Sometimes new institutions are created that serve persecution (Staub, 1989, 2011).

Understanding that negative images about Muslims in the media are likely to contribute to hostility might create more responsible reporting and efforts to humanize, rather than devalue, Muslims. The public acquiring such understanding might lead to holding the media accountable.

Raising Inclusively Caring Children and Altruism Born of Suffering

Children in many places engage in bullying (Olweus, 1993), often directed at children from devalued groups. For children to care about others, including others who do not belong to their community, requires love, affection, guidance, the example of caring by adults, and the involvement of the children in helpful actions (Eisenberg, 1992; Eisenberg & Fabes, 1998; Oliner & Oliner, 1988; Staub, 1979, 2005, 2006b).

Proposal 10. It is crucial to develop inclusive caring in children as an aspect of long-term peacebuilding. This means caring that extends beyond the boundaries of their own group, however that group is defined, and specifically caring about members of other groups in their society, including previously hostile groups. In addition, especially for children who are members of groups that have suffered from victimization and other trauma, it is important to facilitate "altruism born of suffering" (Staub, 2003, 2005; see Chapter 10).

To facilitate the development of caring, provide school personnel training in creating "caring classrooms" that promote both positive interaction with and connections between teachers and students and among students (Staub, 2003, pp. 267–289). Involve students in developing rules for the classroom, which, in addition to increasing adherence, can empower them and contribute to moral courage to be active bystanders when their peers engage in harmful actions (Staub, 2005). Enhance teacher effectiveness in these realms, for example, by helping teachers gain awareness of their attitudes towards children from various groups and toward sharing authority. Involve parents in school life and provide them some training in ways of raising children that is consistent with the principles of "caring schools." The schools provide a natural milieu for engaging parents and helping them acculturate in the realm of child rearing. While minority parents don't always easily engage with schools (at least in the U.S.), parents can be involved through their interest in their children's art, performances, and well-being.

In addition, the school curriculum can include material that humanizes all groups and thereby fosters inclusive caring. It can also engage children with their own painful experiences, provide support for them, and thereby promote altruism born of suffering.

Research on altruism has focused on positive roots, such as love and good guidance. Research with people who have been victimized or endured harsh treatment or other painful experience as children has pointed to its connection with aggressiveness (Dodge, et al, 1990; Gilligan, 1996; Rhodes, 1999; Widom, 1989a, b) or psychological problems (McCann & Pearlman, 1990; Herman, 1992). However, case studies (O'Connell Higgins, 1994) and observations indicate that some people who have suffered become helpful, caring people ("altruism born of suffering"; Staub, 2003, 2005). Participants in a study who have suffered from either victimization in their homes or political violence against their group were more empathic, felt more responsible to help and were more willing to volunteer to collect money for victims of a tsunami.

As this article has suggested, many Muslim immigrants (Gonneke et al., 2003), and some members of the Dutch population, were likely to have had significant experiences of suffering. The same is likely to be true of groups in other European countries. Groups relations can be improved by providing sufferers with opportunities for healing, support, and information that helps them understand their experiences (Staub, 2006a; Staub & Vollhardt, 2008; Chapter 10).

The Role of Leaders

Under difficult life conditions, or in the presence of conflict, leaders often emerge who propagate scapegoating and promote destructive ideologies. Groups turn to such leaders because they offer speedy solutions, if not by resolving real problems, at least by addressing frustrated psychological needs for identity and comprehension of reality. While violence between groups arises out of societal processes, such leaders are in the vanguard of facilitating the evolution of increasing hostility and violence (Staub, 2006b, 2011).

> *Proposal 11. Provide training to political, civic and religious leaders that helps them lead their group to engage constructively with the other group. Develop understanding of the roots of hostility, violence, and peacemaking, including awareness of how past victimization and trauma and current adverse social conditions affect members of both groups, as well as themselves as leaders (Staub, 2011; Staub & Pearlman, 2006).*

On the Dutch side, leaders can help the group deal with anxiety about terrorism and the differences between the Dutch and Muslim communities by talking about these complexities in constructive ways and engaging in public dialogue with Muslim leaders. Muslim leaders, instead of helping people "escape" from the difficulties and challenges of their lives by turning to extreme Islamic fundamentalism, can help them engage with the Dutch and work on creating a shared vision of life together. The leaders of all groups in the society can jointly address specific problems in the situation of Muslims in the country and in the two groups living together.

Implementing Proposals

The proposals in this article, even as they are expanded through some specific ideas for implementation, are statements of principles. They require translation into everyday realities, and a great deal of elaboration in their application through specific projects.

All the communities involved need to participate in deciding about and developing specific programs. The concepts of contact, dialogue, truth, and shared history all point to joint work on the prevention of hostility and violence, healing, reconciliation, and peacemaking. One group creating a project may draw on "truth" that is unacceptable to the other group, or offer an understanding of the other group that is at variance with its self-understanding. Even if programs are created that do not directly touch on history and group relations, joint engagement increases sensitivity to each group's concerns. It also empowers the less powerful group.

Conclusion

A conservative, fundamentalist orientation, which focuses on rigid adherence to rules, is wide-spread in contemporary Islam. But a number of voices describe changes within Islam.

Some describe the original message of Islam as "equalitarian, inclusive, progressive and liberating" (Rodenbeck, 2005, p. 10; see also Aslan, 2005).

Both historically (Armstrong, 2000) and today there are debates about what forms Islam should take. There are reports of intense discussions among Muslims on the Internet on many issues, including how Muslim minorities should engage with and adapt to the societies they live in. A number of authors have argued that the forms religion in general, and Islam in particular take are a product of the historical period and particular societal context. Aslan (2005) argues that there is an internal struggle to define what Islam will be, to define the Islamic Reformation that is already under way in the Muslim world. He believes that the conflicts are internal and the debate must be internal.

Living together in the same societies makes the local ethnic groups in European countries much more than witnesses or bystanders to an internal process in Islam. They are concerned, involved parties. The relations that evolve between Muslim minorities and local ethnic groups will shape both Islam and the nature of these societies. The proposals in this article aim to identify policies and practices that help fulfill the basic psychological needs of people, help develop constructive relationships that make violence, including terrorism, less likely, and help develop societies in which different groups can live harmoniously and be enriched by each other. These are long-term goals that require commitment and persistence.

References

Allport, G. W. (1954). *The nature of prejudice.* Reading, MA: Addison-Wesley.

Armstrong, K. (2000). *The battle for God.* New York: Knopf.

Aronson, E., Stephan, C., Sikes, J., Blaney, N., & Snapp, M. (1978). *The jigsaw classroom.* Beverly Hills, CA: SAGE.

Aslan, R. (2005): *No god but God: The origin, evolution and future of Islam.* New York: Random House.

Bar-Tal, D. (2000). *Shared beliefs in a society: Social psychological analysis.* Thousand Oaks, CA: SAGE.

Beaman, A. L., Barnes, P. J., Klentz, B., &McQuirk, B. (1978). Increasing helping rates through information dissemination: Teaching pays. *Personality and Social Psychology Bulletin, 4,* 406–411.

Buijs, F., & Rath, J. (2002). *Muslims in Europe: The state of research.* Unpublished manuscript. Prepared for the Russell Sage Foundation, New York.

Caldwell, C. (2005, April 3). Daughter of the Enlightenment. *The New York Times Magazine,* pp. 26–31.

Cesari, J. (2002). European Islam. In S. T. Hunter (Ed.), *Islam in Europe and in the United States: A comparative perspective* (pp. 11–15). Washington, DC: Center for Strategic and International Studies.

Cesari, J. (2003). Muslim minorities in Europe: The silent revolution. In J. Esposito & F. Burgat (Eds.), *Modernizing Islam: Religion in the public sphere in the Middle East and in Europe* (pp. 251–69). Rutgers, NJ: Rutgers University Press.

Chirot, D., & Seligman, M. E. P. (Eds.). (2001). *Ethnopolitical warfare: Causes, consequences and possible solutions.* Washington, DC: American Psychological Association.

Coleman, P. (2000). Intractable conflict. In M. Deutsch & P. T. Coleman (Eds.), *The handbook of conflict resolution: Theory and practice* (pp. 428–450). San Francisco: Jossey Bass.

Cook, S. W. (1970). Motives in conceptual analysis of attitude-related behavior. In W. J. Arnold & D. Levine (Eds.), *Nebraska symposium on motivation.* Lincoln: University of Nebraska Press.

de Koening, M. (2005). *Young Muslims: Search for a true Islam.* Unpublished manuscript. ISIM–IMES Lecture.

Des Forges, A. (1999). *Leave none to tell the story: Genocide in Rwanda.* New York: Human Rights Watch.

Diversisteits- en Integratiemonitor. (2004). Amsterdam, The Netherlands.

Dodge, K. A., Bates, J. E., & Pettit, G. S. (1990). Mechanisms in the cycle of violence. *Science, 250,* 1678–1683.

Dutch General Intelligence and Security Service. (2004). *From dawa to jihad: The various threats from radical Islam to the democratic social order.* Amsterdam, The Netherlands: Ministry of the Interior and Kingdom Relations.

Eisenberg, N. (1992). *The caring child.* Cambridge, MA: Harvard University Press.

Eisenberg, N., & Fabes, R. A. (1998). Prosocial development. In W. Damon (Ed.), *Handbook of child psychology: Vol. 3. Social, emotional, and personality development* (5th ed.). New York: Wiley.

Erikson, E. H. (1963). *Childhood and society* (2nd ed.). New York: W. W. Norton.

Ezekiel, R. S. (1995). *The racist mind.* New York: Penguin Books.

Ezekiel, R. S. (2002). The ethnographer looks at Neo-Nazi and Klan groups: The racist mind revisited. *American Behavioral Scientist, 46,* 51–57.

Fein, H. (1979). *Accounting for genocide: Victims and survivors of the Holocaust.* New York: Free Press.

Fein, H. (1993). Accounting for genocide after 1945: Theories and some findings. *International Journal of Group Rights, 1,* 79–106.

Fiske, S. T., & Taylor, S. E. (1991). *Social cognition.* New York: McGraw-Hill.

Fortuyn, P. (1997) *Tegen de Islamisering van Onze Cultuur. Nederlandse Identiteit als Fundament.* (Against the Islamization of our culture: Dutch identity as a foundation). Utrecht: Bruna.

Germert, F. van. (1999). The drug trade by Moroccans in the Netherlands: Weighing the cultural factor. In M. Crul, F. Lindo, & C. Lin Pang (Eds.), *Culture, structure and beyond: Changing identities and social positions of immigrants and their children.* Amsterdam, The Netherlands: Het Spinhuis.

Germert, F. van. (2004, August). *Youth groups and gangs in Amsterdam: An inventory based on the Eurogang Expert Survey.* Paper presented at the Congress of the European Society of Criminology, Amsterdam.

Germert, F. van, & Fleisher, M. (2005). In the grip of the group: Ethnography of a Moroccan street gang in the Netherlands. In F. Weerman & S. H. Decker (Eds.), *European street gangs and troublesome youth groups: Findings from the Eurogang Research Program.* Walnut Creek, CA: Altamira Press.

Gilligan, J. (1996). *Violence: Our deadly epidemic and its causes.* New York: Putnam.

Goldstein, A. P., & Soriano, F. I. (1994). Juvenile gangs. In L. D. Eron, J. H. Gentry, & P. Schlegel. (Eds.), *Reason to hope: A psychological perspective on violence and youth* (pp. 315–333). Washington, DC: American Psychological Association.

Gonneke, W. J., Stevens, G., Pels, T., Bengi-Arslan, L., Verhulst, F., Vollebergh, W., & Crijnen, A. (2003). Parents, teacher, and self-reported problem behavior in the Netherlands—Comparing Moroccan immigrant with Dutch and Turkish immigrant children and adolescents. *Journal of Social Psychiatry and Psychiatric Epidemiology, 38,* 576–585.

Hallie, P. P. (1979). *Lest innocent blood be shed. The story of the village of Le Chambon, and how goodness happened there.* New York: Harper & Row.

Herman, J. (1992). *Trauma and recovery.* New York: Basic Books.

Hewstone, M., Rubin, M., & Willis, H. (2002). Intergroup bias. *Annual Review of Psychology, 53,* 575–604.

Huntington, S. P. (1996). *The clash of civilizations and the remaking of world order.* New York: Simon & Schuster.

Joppke, C. (2004). The retreat of multiculturalism in the liberal state: Theory and policy. *British Journal of Sociology, 55,* 237–57.

Kelman, H. C,. & Fisher, R. J. (2003). Conflict analysis and resolution. In D. Sears, L. Huddy, & R. Jervis, (Eds.), *Political psychology* (pp. 315–357). Oxford: Oxford University Press.

Kriesberg, L. (1998). Intractable conflicts. In E. Weiner (Ed.), *The handbook of interethnic coexistence* (pp. 332–342). New York: Continuum.

Lederach, J. P. (1997). *Building peace: Sustainable reconciliation in divided societies.* Washington, DC: United States Institute of Peace Press.

Lerner, M. (1980). *The belief in a just world: A fundamental delusion.* New York: Plenum Press.

Lewis, B. (2005). *From Babel to Dragomans: Interpreting the Middle East.* New York: Oxford University Press.

Mandaville, P. (2005). Sufis and Salafis: The political discourse of transnational Islam. In R. Hefern (Ed.), *Remaking Muslim politics.* Princeton, NJ: Princeton University Press.

Manoff, R. (1996). *The mass media and social violence: Is there a role for the media in preventing and moderating ethnic, national, and religious conflict?* Unpublished manuscript. Center for War, Peace, and News Media, Department of Journalism and Mass Communication, New York University.

Mason, V. (2004). Strangers within in the "Lucky Country": Arab-Australians after September 11. *Comparative Studies in South Asia, Africa and the Middle East, 24,* 233–243.

McCann, I. L., & Pearlman, L. A. (1990). *Psychological trauma and the adult survivor: Theory, therapy, and transformation.* New York: Brunner/Mazel.

Melson, R. (2003). The Rwandan genocide. In R. Gellately & B. Kiernan (Eds.), *The specter of genocide mass murder in historical perspective* (pp. 325–339). Cambridge, UK: Cambridge University Press.

Nieuwenhuizen, E. (2003). Publieke opinie en de multiculturele samenleving in Nederland – Factsheet (Public opinion and multicultural society in the Netherlands). Rotterdam: Landelijk Bureau ter Bestrijding van Rassendiscriminatie (National Bureau against Racial Discrimination). http://www.lbr. nl/?node=1926

Nisbett-Larkin, P. (2005, July). *The socio-political contexts of identity formation.* Paper presented at the meeting of the International Society for Political Psychology, Toronto.

O'Connell Higgins, G. (1994). *Resilient adults overcoming a cruel past.* San Francisco: Jossey-Bass.

Oliner, S. B., & Oliner, P. (1988). *The altruistic personality: Rescuers of Jews in Nazi Europe.* New York: Free Press.

Olweus, D. (1993). *Bullying at school: What we know and what we can do.* Oxford: Blackwell.

Pearlman, L. A., & Saakvitne, K. W. (1995). *Trauma and the therapist: Countertransference and vicarious traumatization in psychotherapy with incest survivors.* New York: W. W. Norton.

Pettigrew, T. F. (1997). Generalized intergroup contact effects on prejudice. *Personality and Social Psychology Bulletin, 23,* 173–185.

Pettigrew, T. F. (1998). Intergroup contact theory. *Annual Review of Psychology, 49,* 65–85.

Pettigrew, T. F., & Tropp, L. R. (2006) A meta-analytic test of intergroup contact theory. *Journal of Personality and Social Psychology, 90,* 751–783.

Phalet, K., van Lotrigen, C., & Entzinger, H. (2004). Islam in the multicultural society: The views of young people in Rotterdam. Faculty of Social Sciences, Utrecht University.

Proceedings of the Stockholm International Forum. (2002). *A conference on truth, justice and reconciliation,* April 23–24. Stockholm: Regeringskanliet, Sweden.

Ramadan, T. (2004). *Western Muslims and the future of Islam.* Oxford: Oxford University Press.

Rath, J., Penninx, R., Groenendijk, C., & Meyer, A. (1999). The politics of recognizing religious diversity in Europe: Social reactions to the institutionalization of Islam, the Netherlands, Belgium and Great Britain. *Netherlands' Journal of Social Sciences, 35,* 53–68.

Rhodes, R. (1999). *Why they kill.* New York: Knopf.

Richardson, L. (2006). *What terrorists want: Understanding the enemy.* New York: Random House.

Rodenbeck, M. (2005, May 29). The war within Islam. Review of Aslan, R. *No god but God. The New York Times Book Review.*

Scroggins, D. (2005, June 27). The Dutch-Muslim culture war. *The Nation.*

Sherif, M., Harvey, D. J., White, B. J., Hood, W. K., & Sherif, C. W. (1961). *Intergroup conflict and cooperation: The Robber's cave experiment.* Norman: University of Oklahoma Book Exchange.

Smith, R. W. (1999). State power and genocidal intent: On the uses of genocide in the twentieth century. In L. Chorbajian & G. Shirinian (Eds.), *Studies in comparative genocide.* New York: St. Martin's Press.

Staub, E. (1974). Helping a distressed person: Social, personality and stimulus determinants. In L. Berkowitz (Ed.), *Advances in experimental social psychology* (Vol. 7, pp. 203–342). New York: Academic Press.

Staub, E. (1979). *Positive social behavior and morality: Socialization and development* (Vol. 2). New York: Academic Press.

Staub, E. (1989). *The roots of evil: The origins of genocide and other group violence.* New York: Cambridge University Press.

Staub, E. (1996). Cultural-societal roots of violence: The examples of genocidal violence and of contemporary youth violence in the United States. *American Psychologist, 51,* 117–132.

Staub, E. (1998). Breaking the cycle of genocidal violence: Healing and reconciliation. In J. Harvey (Ed.), *Perspectives on loss* (pp. 231–238). Washington, DC: Taylor & Francis.

Staub, E. (2002). From healing past wounds to the development of inclusive caring: Contents and processes of peace education. In G. Solomon & B. Nevo (Eds.), *Peace education: The concepts, principles, and practices around the world* (pp. 73–89). Mahwah, NJ: Lawrence Erlbaum Associates.

Staub, E. (2003). *The psychology of good and evil: Why children, adults and groups help and harm others.* New York: Cambridge University Press.

Staub, E. (2005). The roots of goodness: The fulfillment of basic human needs and the development of caring, helping and nonaggression, inclusive caring, moral courage, active bystandership, and altruism born of suffering. In G. Carlo & C. Edwards (Eds.), *Moral motivation across the life span.* Nebraska Symposium on Motivation. Lincoln: University of Nebraska Press.

Staub, E. (2006a). Reconciliation after genocide, mass killing or intractable conflict: Understanding the roots of violence, psychological recovery and steps toward a general theory. *Political Psychology, 27,* 867–895.

Staub, E. (2006b). The origins, prevention and prediction of collective violence, and the role of leaders. In T. Garling, G. Backenroth-Ohsako, B. Ekehammer, & O. Johnsson (Eds.), *Diplomacy and psychology: Prevention of armed conflicts after the Cold War* (pp. 182–207). Singapore: Marshall Cavendish Academic.

Staub, E. (2011). *Overcoming evil: Genocide, violent conflict and terrorism.* New York: Oxford University Press.

Staub, E., & Bar-Tal, D. (2003). Genocide, mass killing and intractable conflict: Roots, evolution, prevention and reconciliation. In D. Sears, L. Huddy, & R. Jervis (Eds.), *Handbook of political psychology* (pp. 710–754). New York: Oxford University Press.

Staub E., & Pearlman, L. A. (2006) Advancing healing and reconciliation. In R. Sternberg & L. Barbanel (Eds.), *Applications of psychological knowledge to real world problems* (pp. 213–245). New York: Springer Verlag.

Staub, E., Pearlman, L. A., Gubin, A., & Hagengimana, A. (2005). Healing, reconciliation, forgiving and the prevention of violence after genocide or mass killing: An intervention and its experimental evaluation in Rwanda. *Journal of Social and Clinical Psychology, 24,* 297–334.

Staub, E., & Vollhardt, J. (2008). Altruism born of suffering: The roots of caring and helping after experiences of personal and political victimization. *American Journal of Orthopsychiatry, 78,* 267–280.

Stern, J. (2005). Personal communication.

Stevens, G., Pels, T., Vollebergh, W., & Crunen, A. (2003). Patterns of psychological acculturation in adult and adolescent Moroccan immigrants in the Netherlands. *Journal of Cross-Cultural Psychology, 35,* 689–704.

Stroebe, W., Lenkert, A., & Jonas, K. (1988) Familiarity may breed contempt: The impact of student exchange on national stereotypes and attitudes. In W. Stroebe, A. W. Kruglanski, D. Bar-Tal, & M. Hewstone (Eds.), *The social psychology of intergroup conflict: Theory, research and application.* New York: Springer-Verlag.

Tajfel, H. (1982). Social psychology of intergroup relations. *Annual Review of Psychology, 33,* 1–39.

Tillie, J., & Slijper, B. (2005). *Immigrant political integration and ethnic civic communities in Amsterdam.* Unpublished manuscript, Institute for Migration and Ethnic Studies, Department of Political Science, Universiteit van Amsterdam.

Tweede Kamer der Staten General. (2005). *Aanhangsel van her Handelingen, vergaderjaar 2004-2005,* pp. 1505–1506.

van Oudenhoven, J., & Eisses, A. (1998). Integration and assimilation of Moroccan immigrants in Israel and the Netherlands. *International Journal of Intercultural relations, 22,* 293–307.

van Oudenhoven, J., Prins, K., & Buunk, B. (1998). Attitudes of minority and majority members towards adaptation of immigrants. *European Journal of Social Psychology, 28,* 995–1013.

Varshney, A. (2002). *Ethnic conflict and civic life: Hindus and Muslims in India.* New Haven, CT: Yale University Press.

Vernooij, J. (2004). *Religion for migrants: The case of the Netherlands.* Paper presented at the IAMS Assembly, Malaysia.

Volkan, V. D. (2004). *Blind trust.* Charlottesville, VA: Pitchstone.

Vollhardt, J., & Staub, E. (2005). Altruism born of suffering: Altruism in relation to the tsunami as a function of different kinds and degrees of past suffering. Unpublished data, Department of Psychology, University of Massachusetts at Amherst.

Wickham, C. (2005, June). *Debates on democracy, pluralism, and citizenship rights.* Paper presented at the PISAP/NESA annual conference, Political Islam: Critical and Emerging Ideologies and Actors.

Widom, C. S. (1989a). Does violence beget violence? A critical examination of the literature. *Psychological Bulletin, 106,* 3–28.

Widom, C. S. (1989b). The cycle of violence. *Science, 224,* 160–166.

21

The Impact of the Staub Model on Policymaking in Amsterdam Regarding Polarization and Radicalization

Jeroen de Lange

The 2004 assault on Theo van Gogh deeply shocked and wounded the people of Amsterdam and the Netherlands. It confronted politicians with a formidable challenge. The self-image of the Dutch had always been that of a stable, pragmatic, tolerant, and liberal country. Immediately after the assault, violent acts against Muslims took place—257 in total (see the larger number of mutual attacks reported in Chapter 20). Thus the assault on Theo van Gogh, and the escalation that followed, confronted politicians with a new reality, a reality that was unknown to the Dutch.

The academic writing and theories of Ervin Staub have had an impact on politicians and policymaking of authorities in Amsterdam. Three types of influence can be discerned:

1. Staub's model helped politicians and policymakers make sense of and come to grips with the new reality of terrorism, radicalization, and polarization between groups. It helped frame the reality, give it meaning, and make it more understandable and thereby less threatening.
2. The model helped give legitimacy and an academic foundation to the already existing de facto policy of the mayor of Amsterdam, Job Cohen, who had been ridiculed for drinking tea with Muslim leaders during the very polarized public debate in the Netherlands. It gave legitimacy as well to the existing Amsterdam approach to integration issues, which was seen as very soft.

Reprinted with permission from de Lange, J. (2007). The impact of the Staub model on policy making in Amsterdam regarding polarization and radicalization. *Peace and Conflict: Journal of Peace Psychology, 13*(3), 361–364.

3. The model led to concrete projects and programs, as described in the following.

First instance: One day after the assault on Van Gogh the head of staff of the city manager was asked by the mayor and aldermen to come up with an analysis and action plan for the months to come. By coincidence, the head of staff was familiar with the thinking of Ervin Staub as he had worked as a diplomat in Rwanda. The policy paper that was written and the action plan titled "We the People of Amsterdam" were based on many elements of Staub's work (the model with the policy variables) and on general conflict theory. The dimensions of Staub's conflict model were crucial in giving us an alternate language to comprehend the new reality. The policy paper introduced totally new concepts to the politicians and policymakers. This led to a change in discourse. The mayor accepted the terminology that Amsterdam/The Netherlands was locked in a conflict cycle. The model helped politicians to make sense of what was happening and to come to grips with the new reality. Because the policy paper was presented one week after the assault, it created a degree of order and direction among the responsible politicians that, in itself, was important in the whole chaotic and unstable situation.

There was strong opposition at first to the use of Staub's model. From the beginning, some parts of the bureaucracy who had not been involved in the writing of the policy paper felt they had been ignored or overruled. The more leftist policymakers and advisors in particular were against this way of reasoning because they wanted to look at the positive aspects of society and not through the lens of a model that aims at understanding the roots of violence. They were afraid that headlines like "Mayor Sees Conflict Potential in City" would lead to more problems. In fact, the implications of the Staub model were the underpinning of the mayor's de facto policy. While he was heavily attacked in the political debate for being soft on Islam, the Staub model in a sense reassured him and his chief of staff that his approach was the right one, which in turn produced more support for using the model.

Second instance: In March 2005, Ervin Staub gave a lecture to all the politicians and major policymakers of Amsterdam. This occasion gave the audience a chance to become more familiar with Staub's model, which thereby gained greater legitimacy.

Third instance: An extended article written by Ervin Staub on "Understanding the Roots of Violence and Avenues to its Prevention and to Developing Positive Relations Between the Local Ethnic Group and Muslim Minorities in Amsterdam, in the Netherlands—and the Rest of Europe" has had an impact on policymakers and politicians because of its in- depth analysis of the origins of hostility and violence and concrete proposals for action. Since the distribution of the article, the mayor has mentioned the model in several keynote speeches, and relevant policymakers have begun to speak of applying "the Staub model." Taking the step to concrete projects, however, is another matter. The local administration is not very well organized, and policy papers are easier written than concrete projects are implemented. Another problem is the lack of analysis at the level of local administration. Much too easily, projects were lumped together under the heading "Implementation of Staub's policy suggestions." Even though there were many discussions within policy circles, the department on social and cultural policy still felt left out of the debate. The implementation of projects, therefore, had to be directed from city hall.

The following projects and programs have been partly or fully based on Staub's policy suggestions. However, since implementation has been rather slow, concrete results in the city cannot yet be assessed, and several programs are still in the preparatory phase.

- In Amsterdam, a debate, exhibition, and study center on Islam will be founded (Foundation Merhaba). This center should facilitate debate about what it means to be a Muslim in a secular society. It will house exhibitions about Islam and Islamic culture. By doing so, it will help heal wounds of migration because it opens dialogue about the background of migrants and can make them feel proud of their heritage (Staub Proposal 3: Healing; note that all references to "proposals" are taken from the article that is reprinted in Chapter 20). It should also provide information to non-Muslims about Islam (Proposal 1: Humanizing the Other). The physical building itself will serve to symbolize the equal participation of Muslims in the society. In that sense, it will give a voice to Muslims (Proposal 4: Enhance Pluralism).
- During Ramadan, the Ramadan festival took place, funded by city hall. It consisted of many meetings and debates about Islam in the Netherlands. Part of the festival included Muslim families inviting non-Muslims to share dinner with them after sunset. The festival contributed to humanization of the other (Proposal 1) and facilitated dialogue among Muslims and non-Muslims about what kind of city we want to be (Proposal 2: Shared Vision).
- During the year, days of dialogue took place in Amsterdam where citizens could meet to talk about shared concerns (Proposals 1, 2, 7, and 8: Humanizing the Other, Dialogue, Contact, and Shared Vision).
- In some parts of the city, projects were carried out in which children of migrants interviewed their parents about their background and about the migration story. These stories were shared with non-Muslims via Internet and publications (Proposals 1 and 3: Humanizing the Other and Healing).
- A council of young Amsterdam Muslims has been set up in order to facilitate giving voice to their needs and concerns (Proposal 4: Enhance Pluralism; Proposal 5: Promoting Active Bystandership—which includes speaking up for one's own group).
- A "soap" series on local television is being made. In the series, local people will play the roles of White Dutch and Muslim Dutch (Proposal 1: Humanizing the Other).
- An active campaign via billboards throughout the city tells youngsters that whenever they feel discriminated against, they should tell a special organization set up to combat discrimination and racism. Police have received training to be more attentive to discrimination against young Muslims (Proposal 5: Active Bystandership).

- Projects have been carried out to combat the city's segregation, for example, facilitating meetings between Muslim children who attend the so-called "Black schools" and children who attend the "White schools." The project, called "Welcome to my Neighborhood,"will be extended to more neighborhoods (Proposal 7: Contact).
- An organization has been set up to give advice to school personnel who are confronted with polarization and radicalization in their classes (Proposal 10: Develop Inclusive Caring).

22

The Roots of Helping, Heroism, and Resistance to and the Prevention of Mass Violence

Active Bystandership in Extreme Times and in Building Peaceful Societies

Helpful, prosocial behavior, or active bystandership, is of great importance both for individuals in need and to improve society. In this chapter I consider how personal characteristics, the immediate circumstances, and the larger social circumstances in society affect whether people help others and whether they attempt to save lives under extreme conditions such as genocide. What are ways to increase resistance to increasing hostility and violence, promote preventive actions, and build peaceful societies? To change the behavior of groups, cultures, institutions, and political systems normally requires the joint effort of many individuals. But it is striking that even a single person can sometimes make a difference in whole systems and even in the life of a society.

I mentioned Ron Ridenhour as an example of this in Chapter 12. He was a soldier in Vietnam. He received basic training with other soldiers who were later at My Lai, where American soldiers, not finding enemy fighters, killed about 500 unarmed civilians—old men, women, and children. Having been told about this, Ridenhour could not rest. In spite of the advice of his family that this was not his business, he wrote many letters to people in government, politics, and the media. This ultimately led to Congressional hearings,

Reprinted with permission and minor revisions from Staub, E. (in press). The roots of helping, heroic rescue and resistance to and the prevention of mass violence: Active bystandership in extreme times and in building peaceful societies. In D. A. Schroeder & W. G. Graziano (Eds.), *The Oxford handbook of prosocial behavior*. New York: Oxford University Press.

This chapter is an overview. It includes material that has been discussed in other chapters but also has a substantial amount of valuable additional information in it.

newspaper reports, judicial proceedings, and engagement by the whole country, making other My Lais less likely. Another example is Joe Darby. On returning from leave, a fellow soldier at Abu Ghraib showed him the now famous photos of prisoner abuse. After struggling with his conscience, and consulting with others about a supposedly hypothetical matter, he slipped a disk with the photos under the door of a superior. He later came forward as the person who did so (Thalhammer et al., 2007; Staub, 2011). The uproar that followed the publication of the photos made the continued abuse of prisoners not only at Abu Ghraib but also other US-run prisons in Iraq less likely.

On a smaller scale, single bystanders have had positive effects in many systems. A recent example I encountered was Lily Kruglak, a senior at Juniata College in Pennsylvania, who invited me to give a talk there to begin their genocide awareness week. She spent part of her junior year abroad in Rwanda, where she was immersed in the aftermath of the 1994 genocide. She became deeply concerned with the prevention of genocide. On returning to her college she engaged faculty members, the administration, and other students to create a week-long series of events. As part of it over 200 students and faculty recreated the sequence of the events in the Rwandan genocide, acting as Hutu perpetrators, Tutsi victims, bystanders, as well as Hutu victims such as the prime minister who was assassinated on the day the genocide began, because it was believed that she would oppose it (des Forges, 1999). Her college is institutionalizing genocide awareness week. She graduated in 2011 but has gone to Rwanda with faculty members to do groundwork for the establishment of a program of study in Rwanda for students of her college.

I consider a bystander *a witness, someone who is in a position to know what is happening and is in a position to take action* (Staub, 2003). This definition includes "a position to know" because potential witnesses sometimes avoid knowing, either automatically avoiding information or making efforts not to know. I mentioned one of our studies in which when a young man collapsed on the street, some passerby approaching on the other side of the street after a single glance looked away and never looked again (Staub & Baer, 1974).

Because harmful societal processes usually evolve progressively, it can be quite easy for people both in that society and in the rest of the world to avoid knowing. Usually there is no compelling stimulus right in front of them. Within the country, the media can be prohibited or too frightened to cover events, or may give biased information justifying harmful actions. On the outside information is often quite limited, as the media usually covers little news from obscure places, like Rwanda was to most people before the 1994 genocide. The US media barely noticed the violence in the Congo, as millions of people died. While nowadays much can be learned from the Internet, to search for information requires already active motivation.

We have learned a great deal in the past several decades about the influences that lead individuals to help others. Most of this knowledge is about individuals helping other individuals in a situation of direct, immediate need and about people helping others when the danger to themselves is limited (Dovidio, Piliavin, Schroeder, & Penner, 2006). Some of it is about rescuers (Fogelman & Wiener, 1985; Tec, 1986; Staub, 1989, 1997, 2011; Oliner & Oliner, 1998; Africa Rights, 2002). A small amount is about outsiders, groups or "bystander nations" (Staub, 2011; Thalhammer et al., 2007). To promote human welfare in any society, and to create societies that make internal and external violence unlikely requires many active bystanders—educators and other professionals, the media, citizens and leaders. Heroic rescuers act when great violence is already in progress. One of the aims of this chapter is to consider how bystanders can be moved to act early, to prevent the evolution of increasing violence, and to prevent "extreme times."

The aims of this chapter are

- To discuss influences—personal characteristics, circumstances, and their combination—that lead people to help others, and especially how people become rescuers.
- To briefly discuss the influences that lead to violence by groups against other groups and the forces that contribute to passivity by bystanders.
- To consider principles and practices that can move witnesses/bystanders, members of a population, including leaders, who are neither perpetrators nor chosen targets, as well as parties external to a group or society, to act early to (a) inhibit the evolution and prevent violence and (b) build harmonious, peaceful societies.
- To consider socialization and experience that promote inclusive caring, altruism born of suffering, moral courage, and thereby active bystandership.

The Role of Personality and the Situation in Leading to Help/Rescue, Resistance, and Prevention

It is a truism in psychology that behavior is a function of people's personality and the situation they are in. In recent social psychology the focus has been on the situation as a primary influence on action, in particular on moral actions such as evil, goodness, helping, and heroic helping. People administering increasing shocks in Stanley Milgram's (1974) obedience studies, the aggressive behavior of the guards in the Stanford prison study (Zimbardo, 2007), and other bystanders in a position to help making it less likely that any one person acts in the emergency studies of Latane and Darley's (1970) have all been interpreted with a focus on the power of the situation.

Yes, situations can be powerful. But except for the most powerful of situations, they exert their influence through personal characteristics that give rise to the motivation for action. There is reason to believe that the students who responded to an ad to participate in a "study of prison life" (Zimbardo, 2007) had personality characteristics that predisposed them to violence (Staub, 1989). Carnahan and McFarland (2007) found that people who responded to ads for a *psychological study of prison life* were more hostile, Machiavellian, and less empathetic than people who responded to ads for a *psychological study*. Such characteristics can then be activated by the power differentials and roles created in the Stanford "prison," including encouragement of the "guards" by the superintendent to pressure and test the "inmates" (Staub, 2007a). The role of personality was also demonstrated in the behavior of one guard, who was dominant and especially punitive with the "inmates." However, this guard, whom the researchers came to refer to as John Wayne, was part of the situation for the other guards, by his example influencing others (Zimbardo, 2007). In Milgram's studies, participants with high scores on a test of authoritarianism were more likely to continue to administer shocks (Elms & Milgram, 1969), while those with a moral orientation of responsibility were less likely (Kohlberg & Candee, 1984).

Most of the time circumstances exert differential influence on people as they activate relevant personal characteristics. This has to be true in complex life situations when out of many people a very few take action, or when someone acts *in spite of* seemingly powerful forces to inhibit action. This was the case for all the heroes I wrote about (see especially Chapter 12). For motivation to be expressed in action—and to some extent even to arise—people also need to have certain "supporting characteristics" (see later section). Circumstances can also activate powerful social norms, or inclinations probably held by most people, such as responding to the need of a young child drowning in shallow water.

The Personal Origins of the Motivation to Help/Rescue, Resist, Prevent Violence

Moral Values, Caring, and Empathy

There seem to be two primary personal sources of the motivation for unselfish helping: (a) moral values such as justice, the rights of individuals, and the sanctity of life (*moral orientation*) and (b) caring about others' welfare and feelings of empathy or sympathy with people in distress or danger (*caring orientation*). In addition, fear of negative reactions by other people for not helping, adherence to community standards of behavior, the desire for approval and gain, and the intention to generate positive reciprocity can all motivate helpful behavior.

While I discuss separately the influence of the situation, usually personal orientation and context are deeply intertwined in their influence. A family history of volunteering, membership in religious organizations, and civic participation all make volunteering more likely (Penner, Dovidio, Piliavin, & Schroeder, 2005; Dovidio et al., 2006). The groups people enter depend partly on who they are, but they in turn exert substantial influence. People enter terrorist groups often through relatives, friends, or acquaintances who are already members, and in the group members exert powerful influence on each other (Sageman, 2004; Staub, 2011). Context is especially important in affecting passivity or action in complex situations involving societal events.

While there have been discussions of whether acting according to moral values or caring, empathic feelings are genuinely unselfish—true altruism—this is a definitional discussion and not especially important for our purposes. It is true that people can feel distress about not living up to their moral values, and feel good about doing so, or feel empathic distress seeing someone suffer and empathic satisfaction in another's increased well-being. But apart from "personal distress," which looks like empathy but which people can terminate by escaping from exposure to others' distress (Eisenberg, Fabes, & Spinrad, 2006), these enduring personal dispositions *can* motivate people to help without consideration of personal gain, material or emotional. And it is part of our nature to feel good after having helped if we possess such dispositions.

People with moral or caring orientations may consider how bad they will feel if they do not help or how good they will feel if they do help. But since my primary concern here is whether witnesses to others' need will or will not become "active bystanders," this is a problem only if the resulting help is dictated by the needs of the helper, and therefore potentially unhelpful, rather than the needs of those who are to be helped. Since rescue, resistance, and preventive actions in the situations I am focusing on require committed, persistent action, it also matters whether these personal dispositions represent different potentials for these. Laboratory research shows that both types of "unselfish" dispositions are related to helping (see Staub, 1978, 2003, 2005; Hoffman, 2000; Penner et al., 2005; Dovidio et al., 2006; Eisenberg et al., 2006). They are also related to long-term, committed helping in real life, such as by Christian rescuers of Jews in Nazi Europe (Oliner & Oliner, 1988).

Moral values represent commitment to principles. Caring feelings connect human beings to each other. Oliner and Oliner (1988) found that some rescuers were primarily motivated by moral values, such as justice (e.g., seeing what was done to the Jews as unjust), others by empathy (often deciding to help after they saw cruel actions against Jews). However, certainly the same person can have a combination of these two orientations. Such a combined moral/caring orientation appears to be the source of powerful motivation to help.

Personal Dispositions That Influence Helping: Responsibility, Inclusive Caring, Moral Courage

Such a combination seems represented in what I have called a *prosocial value orientation*. Prosocial orientation combines, as indicated by the measures used to assess it, concern about the welfare of other people, which is a likely source of empathy, a positive view of human beings, and possibly its central component, a belief in and feelings of personal responsibility for others' welfare (see Staub, 1974, for a study using a set of previously existing measures, and Staub, 2003, and its appendix, for a measure specifically developed to assess it). Empathy and sympathy are emotions that can change with shifting circumstances. They can also be ends in themselves, felt without giving rise to action. Moral values can be subverted by changes in their position in a hierarchy of values (discussed in earlier chapters and later in this chapter). That a combination of beliefs, attitudes, and values that make up prosocial orientation is an important source of helping is consistent with the view and findings (Penner, Fritzsche, Craiger, & Freifeld, 1995) that a combination of characteristics make up a prosocial personality and is associated with helpful action.

Responsibility has strong action implications. People with a stronger prosocial value orientation have helped more a person in physical distress. On hearing sounds of distress from another room, they were more likely to go into that room. If the distressed person came into the room where they were working on a task, they were likely to help more in both less effortful ways (such as accompanying the person to another room to rest or calling a roommate to come and get a prescription filled) and in a more effortful way, by going to a pharmacy about 10 minutes away fill the prescription (at which point they were told that this was a study of helping; Staub, 1974).

People with such an orientation were also more likely to help a person in psychological distress, a women upset about her fiancé breaking off their relationship and refusing to give an explanation (Feinberg, 1977; Grodman, 1979—see Staub, 1978, 1980). In another study using self-report measures, people with strong prosocial value orientations reported more helping in a variety of ways (Staub, 2003). Oliner and Oliner (1988) found that many rescuers from all around Europe had a stronger prosocial orientation, characterized in similar ways, than people in a control group who under similar circumstances did not rescue.

Prosocial value orientation was also positively related to constructive patriotism, negatively to blind patriotism (Schatz, Staub, & Lavine, 1999) and also negatively related to aggression in boys (Spielman & Staub, 2000). Moral reasoning that focused on one's responsibility was also associated with people stopping to administer shocks in Milgram's obedience studies (Kohlberg & Candee, 1984). Moral values, empathy, and prosocial orientation may make it less likely that people become harmdoers. The motivation of many rescuers included anger at the Nazis (Tec, 1986; Oliner & Oliner, 1988). Resistance and prevention could also be motivated by negative reactions to harmdoers and their actions.

The role of responsibility has also been stressed by Latane and Darley's (1970) interpretation of their findings that diffusion of responsibility is one of the reasons that each person is less likely to help in an emergency when other bystanders are present and my interpretation of varied findings that circumstances that focus responsibility on a person make helping more likely (Staub, 1978). For example, first graders, when they were told that they are in charge in case anything happens while they are working on a task, were more likely to attempt to help in response to sounds of distress from an adjoining room (Staub, 1970a). Either circumstances or personal beliefs and associated feelings can focus responsibility on a person.

Another personal orientations that make active bystandership more likely, especially in resisting and attempting to prevent the evolution of violence toward a subgroup of society, as well as building harmonious societies, is *inclusive caring*. This is caring that expands beyond "us" to "them" (Staub, 2003, 2005, 2011). It is possible, and all too common, for children and adults to learn to care about the welfare of people who are part of their group, however that is defined, but learn to draw a line at the boundaries of the group so that their caring does not extend to other people. This is especially so in relations to members of groups that are devalued, seen in a negative light, the object of prejudice. Adults often teach children in both direct and implicit ways to not to care about such people.

People are likely to vary a great deal in the extent they care about others' welfare, the extent their caring is inclusive, as well as what groups it extends to. Does it extend to all humanity, and are devalued groups included in their categorization of who is human? Morton Deutsch's (1985) notion of the scope of justice is relevant: "The narrower one's conception of one's community, the narrower will be the scope of situations in which one's action will be governed by considerations of justice" (p. 37). I would add: the less will a person's moral consideration and caring expand to other people. The concept of moral exclusion, excluding some people from the realm of humanity in which moral values apply—and moral inclusion—are also relevant (Staub, 1989, 2011; Opotow, 2012).

Another important contributor to helping in the face of adverse conditions is moral courage, the courage to act on moral values and caring emotions in spite of potential negative consequences. Since the negative consequences can be disapproval, ostracism, and at times also physical harm, moral courage at times has to include physical courage.

"Supporting Characteristics" Relevant to Active Bystandership

A number of other individual characteristics are important for motivation to be expressed in action or even for motivation to arise. One of them is *competence*, both feelings of effectiveness and actual competence, such as the ability to swim to save a drowning person or to generate plans of action. The relationship between prosocial orientation and self-reported helping of varied kinds substantially increased when it was combined with people's belief that they have the capacity to influence others' welfare (Staub, 2003; see also Staub, 2005).

Role-taking capacity is another important characteristic related to helping (Staub, 1979; Eisenberg et al., 2006). Without the capacity to consider others' situation, their needs, feelings, and the potential impact of circumstances on them, the motivation to help would only be activated when the need is blatant. Or it may arise in response to inaccurate assessment of others' need, so that the helping action, if any, would not be helpful. The joining of role-taking with motivational dispositions would be especially important when situational cues are subtle and complex, as in the early stages of the evolution of violence in groups. Limited, low-intensity actions against a target group, such as mildly devaluative statements or discrimination that is not blatant, do not call attention to themselves. Noticing them, considering their impact on the targeted people, and the ability to foresee where they might lead, a kind of "societal role taking," would be required for action. The public education we conducted in Rwanda, Burundi, and the Congo to promote understanding the origins of group violence (see Chapters 18, 19), can contribute to such role-taking.

People also greatly vary in their ability to judge and decide about the meaning of events. In an early study, people who were slow in reporting the movement of a light were also much slower and/or less likely to report that when they entered a room a man was taking his hand out of a lady's handbag and speedily left the room (Denner, 1968). Perhaps at times people resist engaging with events because deciding what they mean is difficult and conflictual for them.

It may be another aspect of decision-making that made some people with *marginality in their community* more likely to become rescuers (London, 1970; Tec, 1986). This finding is sometimes questioned, based on the interpretation that it means that rescuers were disconnected from other people, which is not the case (Oliner & Oliner, 1988). Marginality simply refers to people being different in some way: a Catholic in a Protestant community, having one parent from another country, having an unusual personality. One famous rescuer, Oscar Schindler, was marginal in that he was a German who lived in Czechoslovakia, a Protestant who married a Catholic woman from another village. Raoul Wallenberg, the Swede who saved many Jews in Hungary, was marginal in that he was a member of a poor branch of a very rich family (Staub, 1989, 1997).

Being different from others in a group can make people less identified with the group and less embedded in the group's way of thinking. This makes it more possible to use a critical consciousness, to form independent judgments. In many European countries an existing and often deep seated anti-Semitism (Fein, 1979) was freed from its constraints and enlarged by the German persecution of Jews. Marginality, when combined with relevant motivational characteristics, could free people not to adopt, and to be contrary to, such group attitudes. A critical consciousness, independent judgment, is essential for people to become active bystanders in the course of the evolution of increasing hostility and violence against a group.

The Influence of the Environment/Circumstances in Leading to Passivity or Action

The Influence of Immediate Circumstances

Already embedded in the previous discussion was the role of the situation. Latane and Darley's (1970) seminal research and subsequent research on bystander behavior in emergencies identified many influences in the immediate situation. The number of people present reduces the likelihood of help by any one person. Presumably one reason is diffusion of responsibility. Another is pluralistic ignorance—people not showing their feelings in public so that when they look around and see others unconcerned, they decide not to act, or even that there is no reason to act. Pairs of young children, who talk to each other when they hear sounds of distress, help more (Staub, 1970b). These are important inhibitors of action, and even more so in autocratic systems, where it can be dangerous to exchange information about harmful actions against a devalued group.

Facing an emergency alone focuses responsibility on a person to help. Being in a leadership role in a group also focuses responsibility and makes it more likely that the person will help (Myers, 2010). Roles are aspects of situations (but over time can shape personality). Having others nearby with relevant expertise, such as a doctor when someone seems to be ill, makes it less likely that people will help. In group situations many people tend to see leaders and public figures as responsible for taking action, reducing the motivation to act (Staub, 2011).

Other bystanders are an aspect of the situation, and bystanders greatly affect each other's behavior. The passivity of some bystanders makes others' passivity more likely (Latane & Darley, 1970). In Milgram's (1974) studies, others' words and actions substantially affected whether participants continued to administer shocks. Others also affected participants who witnessed an emergency in one of my studies (Staub, 1974). Bystanders can influence others by defining the meaning of a situation, the appropriate action, focusing responsibility on others to act—and by calling attention to a situation such as the persecution of some group.

When the situation exerts extreme power, everyone can be affected. Most of the time, however, people's responses depend on their personal dispositions. For example, the bystander effect is less likely, or does not happen, with people who have a feeling of personal responsibility to help (Schwartz & Clausen, 1970). Their values/beliefs are activated by others' need and presumably focus responsibility on them even when others are present.

The immediacy of the need, the activating power of the situation

There are many different kinds of situations that require helpful actions or active bystandership. On one end of the spectrum are situations that allow time for deliberation and slow, reflective decision-making, such as volunteering (Penner et al., 2005; Dovidio et al., 2006) or taking action to improve conditions in a society. The need might be great, but the response need not be immediate. Even rescuers' decision to hide someone often allowed time for deliberation. At the other extreme are situations that require split-second decisions, such as a person jumping on train tracks to pull someone out of the way of an oncoming train or someone rushing to catch a child falling out of a four-story window—both real events. I have called such actions *spontaneous helping* (Staub, 1978) and proposed that people who help this way have personal characteristics that motivate helping, as well as supporting characteristics required to move from motivation to action. Given their readiness, in response to powerful activation, decision-making is short-circuited, leading to immediate action.

An alternative view holds that there are moral prototypes, such as caring, just, and brave prototypes (Walker, Frimer, & Dunlop, 2010) and that these are associated with different behaviors, such as helping, moral courage, and heroism (Osswald, Greitmeyer, Fisher, & Frey, 2010). Osswald et al. found that activating the just prototype led participants in a study to be more willing to volunteer for a discussion with imprisoned right-wing extremists, in their view an indication of moral courage. It is possible that a child falling out of a window activated for the helper the brave/heroic prototype, leading to brave action. In either case, there is a motivational disposition present, providing a form of readiness.

Many rescuers have reported that they made instantaneous decisions to help. For example, Madame Trocme, the wife of the pastor Andre Trocme in the French Huguenot village LaChambon, reported that when the first refugee appeared at her door, she immediately invited the person to come in. However, Madame Trocme and other villages were to some degree prepared already, as they had engaged in a number of small acts of resistance to the Nazis (Staub, 1989). Subsequently, under the spiritual leadership of her husband, the villagers saved several thousand refugees, the majority of whom were children (Hallie, 1979).

Such reports of instantaneous decisions may be accurate, especially since rescuers were not in danger at the moment they decided to help. But they also may represent changes in people, the result of learning by doing (Whiting & Whiting, 1975; Staub, 1979, 2003; Eisenberg et al., 2006). As people help others they are likely to come to value even more the welfare of people they have helped and over time probably also the welfare of people in general. They come to see themselves as helpful people (Grusec, Kuczynski, Rushton, & Simutis, 1978). This is especially the case when they have helped people for a long time at great cost and while facing great danger, and when afterward they are honored for their actions (although sometimes they are ostracized). When rescuers are interviewed about their actions many years later, they are probably quite different from the already caring people they were many years before.

Many rescuers report such instantaneous decisions. Possibly speedy decisions were made more likely as people were exposed to someone facing great danger, while the threat to themselves, however significant, was at least temporarily in the background. Moreover, inviting a person into the house, and other such initial acts, may have been only the first steps toward making the actual commitment to rescue.

Some heroism requires immediate *physical bravery* but not moral courage. No one is likely to oppose a person catching a child or saving someone drowning in the river. Others, such as rescue, require both, if they involve acting contrary to current community standards. Early opposition to the evolution of violence against a group requires mainly moral courage. At a later time, as leaders and their followers develop increasing commitment to violence, it requires both moral and physical courage.

The Impact of the Larger Social Situation and Its Interaction with Culture: The Origins of Group Violence and Passivity

Even in directly facing someone's need—a person having an accident, a sudden illness—people are affected by the larger social context. The values of the community or society they live in, the level of crime in a society that may make them concerned that someone appearing to need help is a ploy, the seeming ethnicity or race of the person and society's attitude toward that group, and many other aspects of the "larger situation" affect helping. In one of our studies on the street of Cambridge when a healthy-looking young man with normal weight collapsed on the street clutching his heart, helping was less than in other situations or when the scene was enacted by an overweight young man. Showing these actions to students at the University of Massachusetts, many thought that the normal-weight young man collapsed because he was hit by a bullet (Staub & Baer, 1974). This would have been less likely in a society where people are not allowed to possess guns.

In a society moving toward or engaging in violence against a subgroup of society or another group, there are powerful social forces that can inhibit resistance and opposition. The starting points for great violence between groups such as genocide, mass killing, and even terrorism are usually one of two kinds of "instigating conditions." (The brief description of the origins of group violence that follows is based on Staub 1989, 2011). First, it can be difficult life conditions in a society: economic deterioration, great political upheavals and confusion, great and speedy social changes, or their combinations. Second, it can be persistent and seemingly intractable and violent conflict with another group. Both of them frustrate basic psychological needs in large groups of people, for security, a positive identity, feelings of effectiveness and control over important events, positive connection to other human beings, an understanding of the world and of one's place in it.

Feeling vulnerable, the group becomes especially important for people, intensifying their identification with it or, if their group does not address their needs, with some other, usually ideological group. As part of a group they scapegoat another group for life problems or blame the other for the conflict. They help create or adopt ideologies that provide hope, such as nationalism, purity, total social equality, racial superiority and a world ruled by the superior race—themselves. These ideologies are destructive in that they identify enemies who stand in the way of its fulfillment. Scapegoating and the creation of and pursuit of destructive ideologies are group processes that satisfy basic needs—but do so destructively. (For my theory of basic needs see Chapter 4; see also Maslow, 1971). In protracted, violent conflict between groups, each side comes to see itself as right and moral and the other side as responsible for the continuation of the conflict and immoral.

As the group turns against the scapegoat or ideological enemy, an evolution of increasing hostility and violence can begin, "steps along a continuum of destruction." As individuals and the group engage in harmful actions, they "learn by doing" and change in ways that make greater violence easier and more likely. They justify their actions by further devaluing people they harm. They habituate to each level of harmdoing. Moral disengagement can also make harmful actions more possible (Bandura, 1999). This can be followed by the exclusion of a group from the moral realm (Fein, 1979; Staub, 1989; Opotow, 1990, 2012), and then by moral transformation. Learning by doing, that is, the evolution of violence, and the "higher" ideals of an ideology can make for some people killing those in the targeted group the right thing to do (Staub, 1989, 2011, 2013).

The existence of certain cultural characteristics and political conditions in a society makes the evolution of violence more likely. They also create a "cultural tilt" in bystanders, making bystander action less likely. One of them is a history of devaluation that "preselects" a group as the scapegoat or ideological enemy. In difficult times, when people very much need their group, they will be less likely to oppose their group for the sake of people who they have learned to see in a negative light. Another is past victimization of the group or other great group trauma that makes members of the group feel vulnerable and the world seem dangerous. This can lead to unnecessary "defensive violence" in response to a new threat and also makes it less likely that people oppose their group for the sake of an "other." Overly strong respect for authority, often accompanied by the absence of pluralism and an autocratic system, is another characteristic that makes it less likely that people think for themselves and that they resist harmful leadership and oppose harmful group processes.

Witnesses or bystanders need their group in such difficult times for the fulfillment of basic needs. As they remain passive, they distance themselves from victims, thereby reducing their empathic suffering. They also need to justify their passivity; like perpetrators, bystanders tend to do this by increasing devaluation of the victims. All this makes opposition difficult and increasingly unlikely. Perpetrators interpret the passivity of bystanders as affirmation. In the case of protracted, violent conflict, the evolution is furthered by reciprocal violence.

Leaders and elites who become a vanguard propagating scapegoating and destructive ideologies, their followers, and passive bystanders all contribute to the unfolding of the evolution of increasing violence. Prevention requires active bystanders, both to resist influences that lead to violence and to promote positive processes. It requires constructive responses to instigating conditions (e.g., generating a constructive ideology), as well as addressing the cultural characteristics that make violence probable.

The influences and processes I just described make the passivity of "internal bystanders" understandable, even if not acceptable. But "external bystanders," outside groups or nations, have also usually remained passive. Nations have not considered themselves as moral agents. They have tended to focus on their national interests, including commercial interests; this often leads to complicity in continued business relations with an increasingly violent government. Also, international conventions and "laws" of noninterference in other countries' affairs have been supporting, even demanding inaction. These conventions have been changing, but the tendency to blame victims, preoccupation with one's own interests and affairs, and only slowly evolving international conventions without enforcement mechanisms remain powerful hindrances to constructive bystandership by nations. While the United Nations General Assembly passed "Responsibility to Protect," a resolution that proclaims that if nations do not protect their citizens it is the responsibility of the international community to do so, it has no enforcement mechanisms.

Personal Goal Theory: Personality–Situation Interaction Revisited

A society moving toward violence against a group represents a powerful situation. Still, personal goal theory may help us better understand why even people with strong moral/caring orientations remain passive (Staub, 1978, 1980, 2011). According to the theory, every person has values and related goals, which they can arrange in a hierarchy according to their importance. However, this is not a stable hierarchy. Particular circumstances can have strong activating potentials for particular values/goals. Under their influence these values/goals move higher in the hierarchy, thereby lessening the influence of other values and goals. Values of caring and morality can lose their power when circumstances activate, and move to dominance, other values.

In a study relevant to personal goal theory each participant, while working on a task, was exposed to the psychological distress of another person working next to them. The distress was due to a boyfriend/fiancée breaking off the relationship without any willingness to talk about the reason for it. This happened either the day before (high need) or a year earlier (low need). High prosocial subjects helped more than low prosocial ones when the need was great but less when the need was low, and later indicated in that condition that they felt an obligation to help the experimenter by completing the task. Participants with strong prosocial values and weak achievement values responded when the need was strong by stopping to work on the task, paying attention to this other person as she described her distressing experience, and by moderate verbal responses. These participants also liked this person and were interested in continued interaction with her.

People with both strong achievement and weak prosocial values, when the other person's need was high, continued to intensely work on their task, while talking a substantial amount. Talking a great deal to a highly distressed person, who is trying to tell her story, while continuing with one's ongoing activities does not seem especially helpful. Perhaps because it interfered with their work on the task, they liked the distressed person less and believed less that her distress was genuine. People with such a combination of values also talked a substantial amount in the low need condition, when this person's distress was limited. In both conditions their achievement motivation may have led them to both focus on their task and talk a substantial amount—which is also a kind of "achievement" (Feinberg, 1977; see Staub, 1980).

According to the theory, moral and nonmoral values and goals form a single hierarchy. Nonmoral values can be dominant over moral ones in some people's hierarchy. Achievement, or advance in one's career, can be more important to some people than moral values. However, they may be less important but can become dominant under particular activating conditions.

Relevant to how values that lead to immoral actions can become dominant is the concept of *moral equilibration*.

> Facing a conflict between a non-moral motive and a moral value, a person may reduce the conflict by . . . a shift to a different moral value or principle. For example, the moral principles that prohibit killing or harming other human beings are replaced by the principle of "social good" defined (by Nazis) as protection of the German nation from internal subversion or genetic contamination by Jews. Or loyalty and obedience to authority may become the relevant moral principles. . . . Although this can happen consciously, moral equilibration often occurs without awareness. . . . A preconscious or unconscious equilibration circumvents moral conflict. As people progress along a continuum of destruction, moral equilibration becomes more automatic. (Staub, 1989, p. 147)

Research findings by Leidner and Castano (2012) on *morality shifting* support the aforementioned conceptions. They found that when Americans read about atrocities committed by members of their group (US soldiers), they shifted in their "moral foundations." They focused on principles of loyalty and authority, rather than the normally prevalent focus on harm and fairness. This did not happen when they read about atrocities committed by members of another group, such as Australian soldiers. This shift is demonstrated only by people who glorify their group. Leidner and Castano see such a shift as an automatic response to a threat to identity and to one's moral status as a member of one's group. In terms of personal goal theory, members of one's group engaging in immoral acts activates and raises in the hierarchy values of loyalty and authority over genuinely moral values, which in turn can lead to justification of the immoral acts. Such value shifts can make active bystandership to oppose harmful practices or to promote peace and harmony less likely.

These processes are relevant to every potential helping situation but may be especially powerful in complex, multidimensional situations in the real world. Like everyone else, people in leadership positions, such as government officials, are affected both by the immediate situation they face and their overall context. Their context can elevate loyalty to a policy, an ideology, or a leader over moral and caring values, and shape perceptions and actions. A relevant case is described by Powers (2002), as she details the struggles of Peter Galbraith, a government official active in Iraq at the time of the Iraq–Iran war, to reach a judgment about ongoing events.

The United States was supporting Iraq in the war both materially and diplomatically, even as Saddam Hussein's military was using chemical weapons both against Iran and against Kurdish villages within Iraq. In this context it was a great challenge to come to the judgment that contrary to Iraq's claims that the chemical weapons were used by Iran, and Washington's disinclination to acknowledge the truth, it was Iraq doing this.

Environmental activators can be temporary. But lasting environmental conditions can create persistent changes in a hierarchy. Being a member of a gang, a terrorist group, a US government office, or persistent economic problems can all be such conditions. They can elevate nonmoral values and related goals so that they dominate moral ones in a person's "resting" hierarchy. The training of leaders, for example, as in the project in Rwanda (Chapters 18), may help create awareness of and resistance to a context automatically shifting values, perceptions, and actions. Having allies who support one's moral values/goals can also help resist their subversion by environmental conditions.

Promoting Early Action in the Service of Prevention, Reconciliation, and Peace Building

How can active bystandership that begins early be generated so that it prevents the evolution of violence? There are a variety of influences that can move people to preventive actions, including coming to know and understand the influences that lead to violence; humanizing previously devalued groups; generating constructive ideologies that join people to work for shared goals; healing from past group victimization, from the trauma and persistent psychological and cultural wounds that result from violence; and promoting moderate respect for authority, respect that is contingent on the actions of authorities more than on their position. Just like multiple influences give rise to violence, the more positive influences that are present, the more likely they are to move individuals and groups to constructive action.

Understanding the Origins, Impact, and Prevention of Mass Violence

Members of a society, including leaders, do not usually know what leads to genocide/mass killing or why conflict is intractable and cannot be resolved. In Rwanda, after the genocide of 1994 was stopped, the most common explanations of it were "bad leaders" and "ignorance." Learning about the influences that lead to group violence can create awareness of the importance of early events in its evolution and thereby give rise to motivation for action. Understanding can also shift motivation, for example, by realizing that groups become the targets of violence not because they are objectively "bad" but because of long-standing negative views of them that are part of a culture/society.

In our work in Rwanda, my associates and I have conducted many trainings—workshops or seminars—about the origins of violence and its traumatic impact and about avenues to healing, reconciliation, and prevention. We then created educational radio programs with similar content, including a radio drama in which relevant educational material was embedded in the story. Part of our aim was to help people become aware of how relatively small events, such as limited increase in the devaluation of a group or in discrimination, can contribute to an evolution that may lead to great violence and require resistance and opposition.

We evaluated the effects of the training on groups of people led by participants in our training. In comparison to control groups the training reduced trauma symptoms; increased positive attitudes by Tutus and Hutus toward each other; led people to believe that since it is possible to understood how violence comes about they can act to prevent it, and had other benefits (Staub, Pearlman, Gubin, & Hagengimana, 2005; see also Staub, 2011; Staub, Pearlman, & Bilali, 2010; see Chapter 18). Participants were asked to apply the information we presented and discussed with them to Rwanda, which seemed to create beyond knowledge an "experiential understanding."

The radio drama, about conflict between two villages, *Musekeweya* (New Dawn), began to broadcast in Rwanda in 2004 and is still ongoing (see Staub, 2011; Chapter 19). An experimental evaluation (Paluck, 2009; see also Staub & Pearlman, 2009; Staub, 2011) showed that listening to the programs increased empathy with varied groups—survivors of the genocide, bystanders, leaders, even perpetrators. It also increased people saying what they believed and increased independence of authority. Listeners reported more reconciliation behaviors, engaging with members of the other group, in contrast to people in control groups who advocated reconciliation but did not personally engage in relevant actions.

The finding in the first study of more positive attitudes by Hutus and Tutsis toward each other shows that our procedures contributed to the next element I discuss, humanizing devalued others. The lessened trauma in our first study, and greater awareness of trauma reported in the second study also show positive changes relevant to another important matter, healing. (For a detailed description of these projects see Staub, 2011; and Chapters 18 and 19.)

Humanizing the "Other"

A history of devaluation of a subgroup of society makes it probable that the group will be selected as a scapegoat and/or the ideological enemy in difficult times. As harmful actions begin and intensify, they are justified by increased devaluation, moral exclusion, and in the end *moral transformation* that can even make the killing of all members of a group the right thing to do. A similar but mutual process can take place in the course of increasingly violent conflict between two groups (Staub, 2011). Humanizing members of the other group, developing more positive attitudes toward them, ideally before violence begins, can help prevent violence. Seeing others as human beings, with hopes, needs, and aspirations similar to one's own also makes active bystandership in the service of prevention more likely.

We can humanize other people by what we say about them. Words have great power, and most people learn to devalue others through words about them and negative images of them, rather than direct experience. But words and images can also work in a positive direction. In providing a positive image of already devalued others, it seems best to base this on real information about the group and real actions by them, for example, talking about Hutus who endangered themselves to save the lives of Tutsis during the genocide (Africa Rights, 2002). Another example is what journalists from varied ethnic groups did in Macedonia. They jointly interviewed families from different ethnic groups and published articles in the newspapers of the various groups showing similarity in everyday lives, concerns, and strivings (Burg, 1997).

However, the media often dehumanizes members of some groups, thereby contributing to violence. In Rwanda, the media, both newspapers and especially radio, relentlessly advocated against Tutsis (des Forges, 1999). In Amsterdam, relations between the Dutch and Muslim immigrants had started to deteriorate before 9/11. They deteriorated greatly after 9/11 and after terrorist attacks in Europe carried out by Muslims. The killing of a Dutch journalist and film maker by a Muslim man in 2004 because of a film he made about the treatment of women in Muslim societies resulted, in a normally peaceful society, in the burning down of mosques, Muslim schools, and churches (Staub, 2007b; Chapters 20, 21). In 2005, a major newspaper had a full-page picture of a female government minister and an Imam, the minister reaching out to shake the Imam's hand but the Imam holding his hand back. The subscript by the newspaper was about the disrespect he showed, not the minister's disrespect of his religion, which prohibited him from shaking a woman's hand (Staub, 2011). The power of the media and of leaders is great in increasing the devaluation of members of other groups or extending respect to them and humanizing them.

Positive images, such as symbolic actions by leaders, can make a difference. Yassir Arafat and Yitzhak Rabin shaking hands in front of the White House was a powerful image. However, only concentrated action in varied realms can humanize the other. Instead, in both countries but somewhat more among the Palestinians, children have been either taught nothing about the other group or received negative images of it.

As both social psychologists (Pettigrew & Tropp, 2006) and people working in real-life settings (Varshney, 2002; Chirot & McCauley, 2006) have found, contact between people is a potentially highly important avenue to coming to see the humanity of the other. While varied conditions of successful contact have been specified (Allport, 1954; Pettigrew, 1998), probably the two most important ones are deep rather than limited and superficial engagement and that contact be successful in leading to some positive outcome. The positive outcomes can range from personally satisfying interactions to success in achieving the goals of joint efforts. Dialogue between members of hostile groups can be a valuable form of contact (Staub, 2011). Some research even shows that deep engagement in a positive imaginary interaction with a person belonging to a different group, for example, on a train discussing a book, improves attitudes toward that group (Crisp & Turner, 2009). Imaginary encounters may be effective starting points for real interaction.

Societies also humanize subgroups if they create constructive ideologies, visions, and practices that embrace all groups, and if they provide equal rights and equal access to the public domain. This makes it possible for members of all groups to express their beliefs, values, and concerns as part of public discussion and to speak (be active bystanders) in their own behalf.

Creating Constructive Ideologies

Ideologies, visions of social arrangements and human relations, can give people hope in difficult times. They can replace an understanding of reality that people feel were disconfirmed by difficult life conditions or persistent conflict. The visions people adopt often do not address the real problems the group faces but elevate the group, or call forth unrealistic ideals and aspirations, while identifying enemies who stand in the way. Being part of an ideological group or movement can fulfill basic needs for security, identity, effectiveness, and connection, but with certain ideologies they do so destructively as they lead to turning against supposed enemies, to aggression, and often ultimately lead to harm to the group itself (Staub, 1989, 2011).

Constructive ideologies are inclusive, and while they embrace ideals, they also address existing realities. By including all groups in a society in their aims, they humanize each group (Staub, 2011). The work programs in the United States at the time of the Great Depression helped improve the material lives of many people (Alter, 2006). But they also expressed the ideal that everyone belonged to the national community. Israelis and Palestinians could develop a vision of an economic community that would promote peace not only between them but in the region.

Seemingly positive ideologies can be problematic, depending on how they are used. In Rwanda the power is in the hands of the Tutsi minority, led by those who fought against the Hutus and stopped the genocide. The government proclaimed an ideology of unity: there are no Hutus and Tutsis; this division was created by colonial powers; we are all Rwandans (Staub, 2011). It is true that differentiation between Tutsis and Hutus was greatly enhanced by the Belgians as colonial powers (des Forges, 1999). But the differences have been long-standing (Mamdani, 2001) and remain deep-seated after the genocide. The government has passed laws to eliminate discrimination and thereby group divisions. But proclaiming unity and making it difficult for people to talk about issues between the groups, and even passing laws that punish vaguely defined divisionist speech and genocidal ideology, interferes with processes of reconciliation (Staub, 2011). It would be constructive to foster rather than dictate unity and to allow people to identify themselves as Rwandans, but also as Hutus or Tutsis, to hold "dual identities" (Dovidio, Gaertner, & Saguy, 2009).

Generating and promoting positive ideologies requires active bystandership. In turn, they can generate more active bystandership. We human beings are greatly affected by ideas, and especially ideas that express ideals, the possibility of betterment of community and life (Staub, 2011). Individuals can work on generating social movements involving positive ideals by simply talking to other persons; by promoting them in their churches, rotary groups, or other civic organizations; by advocating them in the media or on the Internet. By supporting each other in such efforts, people can maintain commitment and persistence.

Healing from Psychological Woundedness and Altruism Born of Suffering

People who have been victimized, whether as individuals or as members of a group, tend to feel vulnerable and see the world as dangerous. Under conditions of new threat, whether by difficult life conditions or another group, they are more likely to feel the need to forcefully defend themselves, even if this is not necessary. Using unnecessary force, they become perpetrators (see Staub, 1998, 2011; Mamdani, 2001). Healing from past victimization makes this less likely. Healing can also make it less likely that past victimization or trauma becomes a "chosen trauma," a persistent focus for individuals or groups (Volkan, 2001), an important part of their identity and culture, shaping their perception of and responses to events (Staub, 2011).

There has been substantial recent research in psychology on "victim consciousness" (Vollhardt, 2012), the representations of past victimization in beliefs held by members of a group. Survivors of violence and their descendents can have varied types of victim beliefs, which have important correlates. For example, the more Israelis believed that their group has suffered injustice and is vulnerable, the more they endorsed aggressive policies toward Palestinians (Maoz & Eidelson, 2007). Also, "competitive victimhood," the belief that one's group suffered more than one's opponent, was associated with less forgiveness in Chile and Northern Ireland (Noor, Brown, Gonzalez, Manzin, & Lewis, 2008).

Leaders who instigate hostility may simply be intent on gaining followers (Allport, 1954), but they may also be affected by their group's (or their own) past traumas. In addition to victims/survivors, perpetrators, especially people who kill (MacNair, 2002), even if they do so as soldiers (Maguen et al., 2009), are also traumatized. Even passive bystanders can become psychologically wounded. At the very least perpetrators and bystanders will have undergone transformations in personality, such as changes in moral orientations and reduction in empathy.

How can groups of people heal? Since the violence that is the focus of this chapter is perpetrated by groups, and people are victimized in groups, group approaches to healing are likely to be most effective. People can engage with their traumas in small groups, supporting each other (Herman, 1992). Guiding them using a RICH approach (Saakvitne et al., 2000) may be helpful. It consists of *respect*, meaning in part to grant people control over what they talk about and respond with empathy and support; *information,* for example about how the violence comes about and its impact; building *connections* among people and reconnection in the community; and *hope,* strengthening spirituality and hope about the future.

In societies where as a result of extreme violence almost everyone is wounded, like Rwanda, promoting person-to-person empathic engagement can help. In our educational radio dramas we show people recognizing behaviors that are signs of trauma and engaging with each other, telling their stories and empathically responding (see Staub, 2011). Testimonials by people about their experiences, talking about them in supportive groups, and commemorations can be useful approaches to healing. Commemorations will be most beneficial if in addition to helping people engage with loss and grief, which by itself can sustain trauma, a vision of a better future that generates hope is also introduced, a shared future if previously hostile groups continue to live together (Staub, 2011).

As people begin to heal, they are more able to focus on others' experiences and to become active bystanders in relation to the need and distress of others. Healing can contribute to *altruism born of suffering* (Staub, 2003, 2005). This concept refers to the phenomenon that, contrary to the commonly held view that victimized people become aggressive or dysfunctional, many people who have been victimized or suffered for other reasons appear to want to help others and prevent others' suffering. Surprisingly perhaps, in one study people who previously reported that they have been harmed, either as individuals, or because they were members of a particular group, or in natural disasters, were more helpful than people who reported no suffering (Vollhardt & Staub, 2011). They expressed more concern, empathy, and feelings of responsibility to help people who suffered from the tsunami in Asia in 2004 and volunteered more to collect donations for them.

Previous theory (Staub, 2005) and analysis of a substantial body of research that had incidental findings relevant to altruism born of suffering (Staub & Vollhardt, 2008), suggested experiences that help transform victimization or other suffering into altruism. They include having been helped at the time by someone, having been able to help oneself or others at that time, support and care by people after suffering (or before, in the course of socialization and development), healing experiences, and having begun to help others which then leads to learning by doing and further helping (Staub, 2005; Staub & Vollhardt, 2008; see Figure 10.1 in Chapter 10). Helping people at a time of their victimization or other suffering can both protect them and show them that there is caring in the world, thereby contributing to altruism born of suffering.

Groups of people who have suffered can also show altruism born of suffering. This is very important, since active bystandership by groups is usually required to effectively help other groups in need or danger. Constructive or inclusive victim beliefs, in contrast to exclusive victims beliefs that focus on the suffering of one's own group (Vollhardt, 2009), may contribute to altruism born of suffering. Brysk and Wehrenfennig (2010) see linking their group's suffering to others' suffering by leaders and intellectuals as important. They noted that American Jews were highly active both in the civil rights movement and in attempting to stop the violence in Darfur. The Japanese American Citizens' League, which combated discrimination against Japanese people and brought about the recognition of their internment during WWII and compensation for it, challenged after 9/11 the legality of illicit detention of Arab-Americans.

As with individuals, learning by doing can move groups to increasing and persistent positive bystandership. Helping others can increase caring for those one has helped, develop into empathy and feelings of responsibility for others' welfare in general, and become an important aspect of one's self-concept or identity (Staub, 2011).

Promoting Moderate Respect for Authority and Pluralism

One of the contributors to mass violence is overly strong respect for authority in a society. This makes people seek leaders in difficult times and follow them even if they are destructive. Promoting more moderate respect for authority is a way of increasing independence in decision-making and judgment and active bystandership in resisting destructive leadership.

In Rwanda people in six groups who listened for a year to the radio drama *Musekeweya* received a tape recorder and tapes of the first year's programs at a party after their last meeting. They discussed whether the group or a member of it would be in charge of them. People in each of six control groups, who listened to an alternative radio drama, on the suggestion of the first person who spoke decided to hand the material to the head person in the village. In a society where people avoid controversy, those who listened to the educational radio drama also were more truthful about their beliefs, as indicated both in a private interview and in talking to members of a focus group (Paluck, 2009; Staub & Pearlman, 2009; Staub, 2011).

Active bystandership is more likely in a pluralistic society, in which many views can be expressed. In such a society people are more likely to use their critical consciousness to evaluate events, rather than uncritically accept leaders' guidance. In many societies schools and homes are authoritarian. Children are not encouraged to express their views. Giving children a voice can contribute to independent judgment and active bystandership.

Socialization and Experience for Inclusive Caring

An important aspect of active bystandership is caring for and altruistic helping of people beyond family, friends, and the groups one belongs to. But socialization tends to focus on caring about familiar others. The line children and adults draw between "us" and "them" can be natural, the result of our tendency to categorize and have different affective orientations to people we are more or less connected to. But socialization often teaches children to exclude "them," especially members of devalued groups, from the realm of those who should be cared about. This is done both in subtle and at times unintentional ways, by the manner in which adults talk about and respond to members of such groups and through intentional instruction. Groups also imbue children and adults with hostility and aggression toward some others. How can caring be expanded to other groups and ideally to all human beings? A special challenge is to expand caring and active bystandership so that it will be present even under highly challenging life conditions or in the presence of conflict with another group. This would make the unfolding or evolution of increasing hostility and violence less likely.

"Humanizing the other" through words and contact can take place in many settings. I mentioned creating contact through cooperative learning (Aronson, Stephan, Sikes, Blaney, & Snapp, 1978), especially relevant in schools. In the Ivory Coast, farmers received seed money for joint projects between members of different ethnic groups. When violence arose in the region, those involved in these project remained peaceful. Joint projects, with significant interaction and shared goals, help participants experience the humanity of the other.

Fostering Caring and Inclusive Caring

Some core elements of socialization promote caring for and altruistic action in behalf of others (see Staub, 1979, 2003, 2005; Eisenberg et al., 2006). Warmth, affection, and nurturance by important adults generate a positive view of and feelings for other people. Positive guidance, values, and rules derived from them can guide children to caring and helping. Warmth and guidance by reasoning combined with firm but not punitive control, what Baumrind (1975) called authoritative parenting, can lead children to behave according to essential rules that express positive values. Such a combination of practices/influences is associated with prosocial behavior (Hastings, Zahn-Waxler, Robinson, Usher, & Bridges, 2000).

An important form of reasoning is pointing out to children the consequences of their actions on others, what Martin Hoffman (2000) called induction, both the harmful consequences of negative acts, as well as the benefits of helpful acts (Staub, 1979). The example of caring and helpful models is important. Warm, nurturing, empathic parents who provide positive guidance, as well as examples of caring and helping, are most likely to have helpful children (Oliner & Oliner, 1988; Staub, 2003, 2005; Eisenberg et al, 2006).

A further important element is learning by doing, guiding children to engage in positive behavior and the experiential learning that results from this (Whiting & Whiting, 1975; Staub, 1979; Eisenberg et al., 2006). Children who were guided to engage in helpful behavior were later more helpful than children who engaged in an alternative activity. Older children teaching younger children, children making toys for poor hospitalized children, and combining helping with induction have all increased helping by children at a later time (Staub, 1979, 2003). Volunteering was associated with prosocial values, attitudes and identities in adolescents, and later with prosocial behavior as adults (see Penner et al., 2005; Dovidio et al., 2006). Helping increases concern and caring for those we have helped and leads to perception of oneself as a helpful person (Grusec et al., 1978; Staub, 1979, 1989, 2003).

Research on rescuers has found that as they engage in helping, commitment deepens. Rescuers who have initially agreed to help in a limited way became more engaged. They may have initially agreed to hide some people for a few days but ended up hiding them for years, at times taking in additional people. Some of those who succeeded in moving people to a safer place initiated helping more people. Some rescuers who at first agreed to help a Jew who was a former friend or associate, or whom they were asked to help by intermediaries, then decided to help others who were strangers (Oliner & Oliner, 1988; Staub, 1989, 1997).

I already mentioned the Mothers of the Plaza del Mayo in Argentina whose concern expanded from their disappeared children, to other disappeared people, to justice in Argentina and beyond (Burchianti, 2004). In the U.S. many activists against the Vietnam war continued to work against war and for social justice. Some are well known, like Daniel Ellsberg, who provided the Pentagon Papers to the New York Times; others who acquired fame during the war continued as local activists. Francis Crowe in Western Massachusetts, now a small white-haired women in her 90s, continues to move others to action.

Many rescuers were socialized in a way that was consistent with the socialization process described previously as important in developing altruism. They received more love and affection and positive guidance than did others who were in similar situations but did not help. They had parents who, in cultures where physical punishment was common, used explanation instead.

They were exposed to helpful models, such as parents who embodied and expressed in their actions humane values. Many of them had parents who engaged more in interaction with and maintained positive social relations with people outside their own group, including Jews. They also heard their parents make fewer negative statements, if any, about Jews—a group devalued in Germany and in other European countries even before they were occupied by or under the influence of Nazi Germany (Fein, 1979)—than did people in a control group who were in similar position to help but did not do so (Oliner & Oliner, 1988).

Structures that facilitate positive contact are especially important in developing positive attitudes that are essential bases for inclusive caring. School and work provide natural opportunities for deep engagement. Varshney (2002) compared three cities in India in which following instigating conditions there was violence between Hindus and Muslims and three cities without violence. In the cities without violence there were chambers of commerce and other institutions in which Hindus and Muslims closely worked together. In response to the instigating conditions, they joined in exerting influence on the community, as well as on politicians, to stop them from making inflammatory statements, at times threatening to publicly speak out against them if they instigated violence.

In sum, inclusive caring is the extension of caring to "others," ideally to all human beings. It can be developed through words and images that humanize all people, through the example of models who show caring for people regardless of their group membership, through one's own experience of connection to varied people, and through learning by doing. Guiding children (and adults) to engage in helpful action toward people outside their group can be a powerful avenue to inclusive caring.

Common Ingroup Identities and Inclusive Caring

Gaertner and Dovidio (Gaertner & Dovido, 2000; Dovido et al., 2009) advocate "common ingroup identity" as an avenue to expand caring to outgroups. They see contact as one of the practices that can lead people to "recategorize" others, to see their own and the other group as part of a single, superordinate group. This creates more positive attitudes toward that group, increases help for its members, and can contribute to reconciliation after violence (Dovidio et al. 2009). However, when there is strong hostility, creating and maintaining such common identities is difficult (Staub, 2011). Marilyn Brewer's optimal distinctiveness theory suggests, moreover, that people want to both assimilate to and differentiate from others. Emphasizing similarities, such as common university membership of math and humanities students, has intensified negative attitudes, perhaps as a way of reaffirming distinctiveness (Dovidio et al., 2009).

In fostering a common group identity it is important therefore to acknowledge and recognize the nature, characteristics, and differences between the groups involved. Dovidio and colleagues (2009) address this issue by proposing a "dual identity model," emphasizing both a common identity and separate subgroup identities. This makes a great deal of sense. In the United States, people who hold dual identities (e.g., Korean Americans) have more positive attitudes toward members of other racial and ethnic groups. However, dual identities are more challenging to create when people have entrenched identities, such as bankers becoming members of a merged bank, or people becoming members of blended families (Dovidio et al., 2009). It is also challenging when members of dominant groups want minorities to meld into the majority. Muslims in the Netherlands express the desire to have a dual identity, while the Dutch want them to assimilate and have a Dutch identity (Staub, 2007b; Chapter 20). The situation is probably similar in other European countries. In France, in particular, minorities are expected to become French.

Developing what I would call *layered identities* may help: a personal identity, one or more subgroup identities, an identity as part of a nation, and an identity as a human being like all other human beings. An even further extension of identity that fits the spirit of our times and the environmental threats to the earth might be an identity as inhabitant of our planet and part of the larger universe. If each identity is reasonably well developed, such layered identities make it less likely that when a society faces difficult times people shift from their individual identity to an identity as a member of a subgroup of society—and turn against other subgroups. This is often one of the first consequences of instigating conditions for group violence (Staub, 1989, 2011).

Very strong identification with one's group tends to contribute to violence and makes forgiveness and reconciliation less likely (Cairns, Tam, Hewstone, & Niens, 2005). Unfortunately, many groups have what may be called "walled off" identities, such as groups that intensely devalue each other, are in protracted conflict, or carry ideologies of antagonisms (Staub, 2011). Developing common ingroup identities, dual identities, or layered identities would be a substantial challenge for them. While the concepts of inclusive caring and common ingroup identity overlap, the tendency to differentiate ingroup and outgroups is strong. Developing caring for people even if they are seen as members of other groups may be psychologically more possible. We need research to differentiate between inclusive caring and common identities and explore their origins and correlates.

A member of a large group that was walking for peace from North America to various points in South America and all the way to South Africa (taking boats across waters, of course) reports that all along there was conflict between White and Black Americans. They clearly differentiated themselves, continued to spend time with members of their group, and could not resolve their conflicts. They also clearly cared about each other and were united in their vision for peace (Bullock, 2011). Members of different groups, even somewhat in conflict, can unite in working for shared ideals.

Morality, Moral Courage, and Heroism: Determinants and Socialization

I have been using *active bystandership* to refer to positive actions in behalf of individuals or groups. Without moral courage people will not oppose their group, or influential segments of it, as it embarks on an evolution to violence. But before we consider the roots of moral courage, it is important to ask: what is moral, and when is courage moral? Young Nazis in the early days of Hitler's party, National Socialism, believing in its vision and their leader, courageously followed Hitler in spite of opposition and at times ridicule (Merkl, 1980). Hitler already advocated extreme views, and his followers were brutal with opponents. Were the young Nazis morally courageous? They were not, according to my definition of morality as "principles, values, emotional orientations and practices that maintain or promote human welfare" (Staub, 2012, p. 381; see also Staub, 2011).

While until recently there was little research on moral courage and heroic helping in psychology, other than the research on rescuers, these topics, together with morality itself, have recently become of interest (Graham & Haidt, 2012; Mikulincer & Shaver, 2012; Skitka, 2012; Zimbardo, 2007). The meaning of *morality* in some of these current approaches is different from my definition and from earlier approaches. In Kohlberg's (1976) theory of moral reasoning, justice and the sanctity of human life were regarded as the truly moral principles. In my perspective, morality is also based on emotions that connect people to each other, such as empathy, and on responsibility in feelings and beliefs.

In one recent approach to morality, Graham and Haidt (2012) proposed "five innate psychological 'foundations' on which cultures construct widely divergent moral systems: harm/care, fairness/reciprocity, ingroup/loyalty, authority/respect, and purity/sanctity" (p. 15). Applying their conception to the matter of evil, while they agree with others that the "prototypes of evil acts are acts of cruelty and violence and would even agree that these are the most important kinds of evil acts to understand "(p. 17), their theory suggests that perceptions of evil may be based on other concerns as well. They also argue that "evil is something that threatens to hurt, oppress, betray, subvert contaminate, or otherwise profane something that is held sacred" (p. 17) not just by an individual but a group. They note that each foundation can be used to support the sacralization or demonization of varied objects. Sacred values are values that go beyond or are independent of practical utility and that do not accept trade-off, cannot be let go for material gain (see Tetlock, Kristel, Elson, Green, & Lerner, 2000).

Immoral societies and practices can be built on the foundations of authority and loyalty. As I have noted, overly strong respect for authority is a cultural characteristic that contributes to the likelihood of group violence. And values can be sacred but not moral, certainly when looked at from the outside by disinterested parties. For example, blood feuds were deeply set in the culture of many societies. In Serbia spirals of killings could continue through the generations (Grille, 2005), mutual killing apparently a sacred value and regarded as a moral obligation. Graham and Haidt (2012) also note that the sacralization of values can lead to violence.

Even though we psychologists deal with what is—how people think, feel, and behave—not every value that a society holds and considers moral can be accepted as moral. Cultural or individual relativity is acceptable only within bounds derived from universal considerations of morality. In one of my large classes at the very beginning of a semester, students argued that a mother spanking a young child, in essence to protect her life, since she once again ran out into a busy street in front of their house, was wrong. Spanking is always wrong. They also argued that we cannot judge the actions of Nazi Germany, because they had their own culture and value systems.

A recent empirical approach to moral courage focuses on the strength of moral convictions (Skitka, 2012). Stronger moral convictions lead to greater independence of authority, for example, in judging right or wrong or in expressing trust in authority. They also lead to greater willingness to express opinions contrary to a majority, for example, when a person holds a moral conviction that torture is wrong and knows that others believe that torture is acceptable in the interrogation of terrorists. These findings suggest the influence of moral courage, as measured by the strength of moral convictions.

Similarly to Graham and Haidt (2012), Skitka (2012) notes that moral convictions can be for harmful causes. In fact, perpetrators of mass killing and genocide often believe that, following their ideology, they are acting for a higher morality that necessitates killing. My focus is on promoting moral courage where morality is defined by standards of justice/fairness and human welfare, as seen by disinterested observers.

Moral courage can lead to heroism. But not all heroism requires moral courage. Endangering oneself to save another's life is heroic but usually socially valued and does not require moral courage. One study (Walker et al., 2010) looked at personality constellations of caring individuals (people who received the Caring Canadian Award for volunteering and serving the community in varied capacity) and brave individuals (people who received the Canadian Medal of Bravery for risking their lives to save others). The clusters or personality constellations of caring people differed from those in a control group, while the cluster of personal characteristics of brave individuals did not differ from those in the control group. The authors suggest that perhaps such bravery is primarily the result of the situation.

However, the authors measured only one personal orientation directly relevant to helping, moral reasoning. They did not measure empathy, moral values that might be connected to helping, or prosocial orientation/responsibility for others' welfare. Moreover, the highest moral stages may not be most related to courageous helping. Kohlberg and Candee (1984) found that people whose reasoning focused on responsibility (at that time Stage 4) were most likely to refuse to continue to administer shocks in the Milgram obedience studies. However, since such refusal required resisting the demands of the person in charge of the experiment, it required moral courage more than bravery.

Several socialization practices, beyond those that promote inclusive caring, might develop moral courage. One of them is to help children develop and use their "voice," to include them in discussions of values and rules to live by in the home and in school, and in decision-making about rules. Another is that parents, as long as the danger to the children is not substantial, should not discourage but encourage their children to express their values in courageous action, for example, to support a schoolmate who is bullied. Having confidence in one's beliefs and the ability to express them and learning by doing are both likely to contribute to moral courage (Staub, 2005) and even to heroic action. Research is needed both to identify the different personal characteristics associated with and presumably leading to moral courage and heroism, and to explore their roots in socialization and experience.

An additional useful practice (Zimbardo, 2007; Franco, Blau, & Zimbardo, 2011) may be to help enlarge children's heroic imagination, primarily through the example of heroic people. Moral courage in the perspective of Zimbardo and Franco et al. is one form of heroism (but for a discussion of the difference between the two see Chapter 23). The example of moral commitment and courage by parents may be especially important. Rosenhan (1970) found that participants in the civil rights movement, during which participation in sit-ins at lunch counters in the South, demonstrations, and other actions required great courage, tended to have parents who engaged in committed actions, ranging from demonstrations for causes they believed in, to fighting in the Spanish civil war. When relations with parents were good, the civil rights activists had strong commitment, expressed in persistent actions. When relations were ambivalent, their participation was limited.

Moral courage requires going against prevailing norms or values, sometimes of individuals, often of the authorities and the system. Actions that are commonly regarded as heroic usually involve physical danger and are often supported and admired by the community. Moral courage can become heroic, however, when it involves significant physical danger or potential violence against oneself. Temperamental characteristics that contribute to action tendencies may contribute to the potential for heroism and to morally courageous action that is heroic. Experience, however, can shape temperament, its expressions, and action tendencies.

Application to the United States

The material in this chapter is relevant to most countries. Many countries have internal divisions, disharmony, and potentially violence-generating conditions. Even if these do not reach the level that would lead to intense violence between subgroups, at times because there are mitigating conditions, they interfere with the fulfillment of basic needs, and reduce satisfaction in life. I briefly consider here conditions that create disharmony in the United States and could contribute to violence.

In the United States, there has been economic deterioration, especially after the financial crisis starting in 2007, with some decline in wages, unemployment, and substantial government debt. Political processes increasingly limit assistance for people in need. Economic deterioration, more than poverty itself, represents a difficult life condition (Harff, 2003; Staub, 2011). Its severity in the United States has not been as great as it is in societies that move toward mass violence. But there is also political chaos and disorganization, a gridlock in which the political parties and groups are so at odds with each other that they cannot create positive social policies. There have been substantial societal/cultural changes: increasing opposition to government, increase in the role of money in politics, changes in the kind of work available to people—the skills needed for jobs in which people can make a living, a great increase in access to, the use of, and the production of information. There has been a lessening of a sense of community, of people caring about each other.

While there are intense political differences, in contrast to societies in which one group is moving toward violence against another, these political differences are not one dimensional. There is no clearly defined group pitted against another group. There are political liberals, conservatives, groups on the extreme right, some small extreme right militant groups that are arming themselves, people in the middle, libertarians who want very little government, and people who are disenchanted and do not know where to turn.

However, while laws protecting individual rights are well established in the United States, in practice there are significant differences in the ways members of different groups are treated, especially racial groups, for example, by police and in the justice system. The differential treatment is clear, with many Black men incarcerated. There has been hostility and some violence against Muslims in the wake of the 9/11 attacks and wars—on terror, in Iraq, Afghanistan, and against ISIS—but no systematic program of devaluation or harmdoing. While there are no discernable steps along a continuum of destruction, disharmony in the society is at a very high level. The high level violence between individuals in the United States that has existed for a long time may in part express this disharmony.

One of the contributors to mass violence in addition to those mentioned before is a highly elevated group or societal self-concept that is disconfirmed by events (Staub, 1989; see also Baumeister, 1997). People in the United States, both citizens and leaders, clearly hold such a view. It is represented in beliefs of US "exceptionalism," pride in superpower status

(Lifton, 2003), and a very high level of patriotism expressed in public by the oft-repeated statement that the United States is the best country in the world. Difficult life conditions, internal chaos, and lessening of influence, relative power, and respect in the world frustrate such beliefs. Leaders and the people wanting to reaffirm such a view of superiority, in their own and in others' eyes, are a potential danger. In spite of the U.S. losing recent wars, it can be tempting to do this by using force against other countries.

Future Directions in Promoting Harmonious, Peaceful Societies

There is disharmony in many societies. What would lead to the development of harmonious societies that are peaceful internally and in their relations to the rest of the world? Practices such as humanizing all members of society, creating constructive ideologies, and the positive socialization of children contribute both to harmony and peace and to active bystandership for improving society.

Promoting certain values and societal institutions contributes to harmony. A prime value in many industrialized societies, spreading around the world, is material wealth. Connected to this are values of competition and winning. If values representing basic human needs and their constructive fulfillment gain prominence, social life will be more harmonious. This means valuing security gained through positive relations; valuing effectiveness that does not harm others; valuing connection to other people, community, and society; gaining positive self-esteem and growing as individuals by positive means; having autonomy—the capacity for choice and initiative—as society makes meaningful choices possible for everyone; and creating and holding a hopeful vision of the world.

Such values can only be developed and maintained if institutions are shaped or created to function according to them. Differences between groups in power and wealth (inequality) has been a major source of conflict and mass violence (Fein, 1993). Institutions that express these values would limit inequality and provide access to opportunity for everyone.

How can such valued be strengthened? Individuals can advocate them in words and action, engaging with their neighbors, with people in their religious and civic organizations. They can do so in conversations, through dialogue, creating committees in schools, churches, rotary clubs, offices, and factories that promote them, through the media, and as candidates for political office. Like our programs in Africa on reconciliation, public education programs on television, radio, and other venues can present information and create understanding of how peace and harmony can be promoted, and their impact on the lives of individuals. Like harmful societal processes, so positive processes evolve gradually. Over time, essential institutions of a society can be transformed: justice, police, corporations, schools, and political institutions (see Chapter 28).

Another contributor to harmony and peace would be to create "healing societies." In addition to group traumas, there are many sources of individual trauma. Many children are physically or sexually abused. In the United States each year, 3 million children are reported to child protective services for abuse and neglect (van der Kolk, 2009). More are likely to be abused, and many more emotionally neglected, which research indicates can lead to even greater harm in a child's development than physical abuse. We suffer sudden traumatic losses when loved ones die in car and plane crashes or of heart attacks. We suffer "life injuries" of many kinds—when we are children and a beloved friend moves to the other side of the country, when parents divorce, when we suffer significant rejection or betrayal.

Creating a society in which there are natural processes that help people heal from their losses and pain would contribute to altruism born of suffering, a sense of community, and harmony. In our educational radio programs in Rwanda we promote, through the example of drama characters, people recognizing others' trauma and responding to teach other with empathy and support (Staub, 2011). Both responding as active bystanders at the time when people suffer, whether from victimization, loss, or life injury, and providing support afterward contribute to altruism born of suffering (Staub & Vollhardt, 2008; Chapter 10). This can be as simple as neighbors recognizing that the home situation of a child is difficult and showing interest in the child, as was the case with one of my friends. Another value change would be to make the need to heal understandable and healing activities widely acceptable. Groups that promote healing and provide community could be developed in all segments of society.

Training Leaders, Training Active Bystanders

Constructive leaders have certain personal characteristics, such as complex thinking, empathy, and a readiness for reconciliation, as in the cases of Abraham Lincoln and Nelson Mandela (Lieberfeld, 2009). The selection of leaders is important. But to some degree such characteristics, and other important ones, may be facilitated by training. Knowledge, understanding, skills, and even empathy and moral courage are possible to promote.

With national leaders in Rwanda, we worked on developing understanding of the origins of genocide and avenues to prevention and reconciliation, as described in Chapter 18. We also engaged leaders in exercises, such as having them consider in small groups, on the basis of the material in the training, whether national policies they were just introducing were likely to contribute to or inhibit hostility and violence (Staub, 2011; Staub et.al, 2010). They then discussed their "findings" in the larger group. In another approach (Wolpe & McDonald, 2008) Hutu and Tutsi leaders in Burundi spent time together to gain comfort with each other and develop skills in engaging and negotiating with each other.

My associates and I developed a curriculum for Training Active Bystanders in schools to prevent harassment, harmful acts, and bullying by students of each other. In the first use of this curriculum we trained 8th and 10th grade students and adults to work in pairs as trainers. They then trained over 700 8th and 10th grade students. The training included information about the inhibitors of active bystandership and about how bystanders can exert influence on other bystanders by defining the meaning of an event and appropriate actions, thereby recruiting them as allies; had them practice varied types of interventions, such as empathic support for victims, removing victims from the situation, and attempting to stop harmdoers in nonconfrontational ways; helped them explore when knowledge of active bystandership can be used in other settings and when it may be too dangerous to use; and more. The first time we employed the training, even while working out various issues in its use, there was a 20% decrease in harmdoing in two experimental schools from before to after the training, about a half a year interval, with no change in two control schools (Chapter 16). This curriculum/training can be adapted to many realms: commercial organizations, government leadership groups, and other settings. For a table showing the influences that can lead a person to be an active bystander in varied settings, see Chapter 27.

Conclusions

It is imperative to act early to prevent violence between groups. Early actions can promote positive attitudes toward everyone, help people join to work for shared goals, and create constructive ideologies that embrace all groups and motivate their members to work for their fulfillment. As a society adopts and lives by caring values, as individuals respond to each other's woundedness and needs, as institutions and a system help people fulfill their basic material and psychological needs constructively, violence becomes unlikely.

All this requires committed action by many people. In this contemporary world with its cacophony of voices, in countries like the United States and many others where there are so many conflicting views and interests, it is easy to be discouraged and remain passive. But beliefs, values, practices, and institutions can and do change. Committed, persistent, and "courageous" actions (Thalhammer et al., 2007; Staub, 2011) are more likely when there is a network of actors and supporters—individuals, organizations, nations. There can be *successful* Arab Springs of many forms, social movements that transform values and institutions and create harmonious societies.

References

Africa Rights. (2002). *Tribute to courage*. Kigali, Rwanda: Author.

Allport, G. W. (1954). *The nature of prejudice*. Reading, MA: Addison-Wesley.

Alter, J. (2006). *The defining moment: FDR's hundred days and the triumph of hope*. New York: Simon & Schuster.

Aronson, E., Stephan, C., Sikes, J., Blaney, N., & Snapp, M. (1978). *The jigsaw classroom*. Beverly Hills, CA: SAGE.

Bandura, A. (1999). Moral disengagement in the preparation of inhumanities. *Personality and Social Psychology Review, 3*, 193–209.

Baumeister, R. F. (1997). *Evil: Inside human violence and cruelty*. New York: Freeman.

Baumrind, D. (1975). *Early socialization and the discipline controversy*. Morristown, NJ: General Learning Press.

Burchianti, M. E. (2004). Building bridges: The mothers of the Plaza del Mayo and the cultural politics of maternal memories. *History and Anthropology, 15*(2), 133–150.

Burg, S. L. (1997, February 19). Preventing ethnic conflict: Macedonia and the pluralist paradigm. Presentation at the Woodrow Wilson Center. Retrieved from http://www.wilsoncenter.org/index.cfm?fuseaction=topics. print_pub&doc_id=18947&group_id=7427&topic_id=1422&stoplayout=true

Brysk, A., & Wehrenfennig, D. (2010). "My Brother's Keeper"? Inter-ethnic solidarity and human rights. *Studies in Ethnicity and Nationalism, 10*(1), 1–8.

Bullock, H. (2011). Personal communication.

Cairns, E., Tam, T., Hewstone, M., & Niens, U. (2005). Forgiveness in Northern Ireland. In E. L. Worthington (Ed.), *Handbook of forgiveness* (pp. 461–476). New York: Routledge.

Carnahan, T., & McFarland, S. (2007). Revisiting the Stanford Prison Experiment: Could participant self-selection have led to the cruelty? *Personality and Social Psychology Bulletin, 33*, 603–614.

Chirot, D., & McCauley, C. (2006). *Why not kill them all? The logic and prevention of mass political murder*. Princeton, NJ: Princeton University Press.

Crisp, R. J., & Turner, R. N. (2009). Can imagined interactions produce positive perceptions? Reducing prejudice through simulated social contact. *American Psychologist, 64*(4), 231–240.

Denner, B. (1968). Did a crime occur? Should I inform anyone? A study of deception. *Journal of Personality,* *36,* 454–466.

Des Forges, A. (1999). *Leave none to tell the story: Genocide in Rwanda.* New York: Human Rights Watch.

Deutsch, M. (1985). *Distributive justice: A social psychological perspective.* New Haven, CT: Yale University Press.

Dovidio, J. F., Gaertner, S. L., & Saguy, T. (2009). Commonality and the complexity of "we": Social attitudes and social change. *Personality and Social Psychology Review, 13,* 3–20.

Dovidio, J. F., Piliavin, J. A., Schroeder, D. A., & Penner, L. A. (2006). *The social psychology of prosocial behavior.* Mahwah, NJ: Lawrence Erlbaum Associates.

Eisenberg, N., Fabes, R. A., & Spinrad, T. L. (2006). Prosocial development. In W. Damon (Ed.), *Handbook of child psychology: Vol. 3. Social, emotional, and personality development* (5th ed., pp. 646–718). New York: Wiley.

Elms, A. C., & Milgram, S. (1966). Personality characteristics associated with obedience and defiance toward authoritative command. *Journal of Experimental Research in Personality, 2,* 282–289.

Fein, H. (1979). *Accounting for genocide: Victims and survivors of the Holocaust.* New York: Free Press.

Fein, H. (1993). Accounting for genocide after 1945: Theories and some findings. *International Journal of Group Rights, 1,* 79–106.

Feinberg, J. K. (1977). *Anatomy of a helping situation: Some personality and situational determinants of helping in a conflict situation involving another's psychological distress* (Unpublished doctoral dissertation). University of Massachusetts, Amherst.

Fogelman, E., & Wiener, V. L. (1985). The few, the brave, the noble. *Psychology Today, 19,* 60–65.

Franco, Z. F., Blau, K., & Zimbardo, P. G. (2011). Heroism: A conceptual analysis and differentiation between heroic action and altruism. *Review of General Psychology, 15*(2), 99–113.

Gaertner, S. L., & Dovidio, J. F. (2000). *Reducing intergroup bias: The common ingroup identity model.* Orlando, FL: Academic Press.

Graham, J., & Haidt, J. (2012). Sacred values and evil adversaries: A moral foundation approach In M. Mikulincer & P. R. Shaver (Eds.), *The social psychology of morality: Exploring the causes of good and evil* (pp. 11–33). Washington, DC: American Psychological Association.

Grille, R. (2005). *Parenting for a peaceful world.* Alexandria, Australia: Longueville Media.

Grodman, S. M. (1979). *The role of personality and situational variables in responding to and helping an individual in psychological distress* (Unpublished doctoral dissertation). University of Massachusetts, Amherst.

Grusec, J. E., Kuczynski, L., Rushton, J. P., & Simutis, Z. M. (1978). Modeling, direct instruction, and attributions: Effects on altruism. *Developmental Psychology, 14,* 51–57.

Hallie, P. P. (1979). *Lest innocent blood be shed: The story of the village of Le Chambon, and how goodness happened there.* New York: Harper & Row.

Harff, B. (2003). No lessons learned from the Holocaust? Assessing risks of genocide and political mass murder since 1955. *American Political Science Review, 97*(1), 57–73.

Hastings, P. D., Zahn-Waxler, C., Robinson, J., Usher, B., & Bridges, D. (2000). The development of concern for others in children with behavior problems. *Developmental Psychology, 36,* 531–546.

Hoffman, M. L. (2000). *Empathy and moral development.* New York: Cambridge University Press.

Herman, J. (1992). *Trauma and recovery.* New York: Basic Books.

Kohlberg, L. (1976). Moral stages and moralization: The cognitive developmental approach. In T. Lickona (Ed.), *Moral development and behavior* (pp. 31–53). New York: Holt.

Kohlberg, L., & Candee, L. (1984). The relationship of moral judgment to moral action. In W. M. Kurtines & J. L. Gewirtz (Eds.), *Morality, moral behavior, and moral development* (pp. 52–73). New York: Wiley.

Latane, B., & Darley, J. (1970). *The unresponsive bystander: Why doesn't he help?* New York: Appleton-Crofts.

Leidner, B., & Castano, E. (2012). Morality shifting in the context of intergroup violence. *European Journal of Social Psychology, 42*(1), 82–91.

Lieberfeld, D. (2009). Lincoln, Mandela, and qualities of reconciliation-oriented leadership. *Peace and Conflict: Journal of Peace Psychology, 15,* 27–47.

Lifton, R. J. (2003). *Superpower syndrome.* New York: Thunder's Mouth Press/Nation Books.

London, P. (1970). The rescuers: Motivational hypotheses about Christians who saved Jews from the Nazis. In J. Macaulay & L. Berkowitz (Eds.), *Altruism and helping behavior.* New York: Academic Press.

MacNair, R. M. (2002). *Perpetration-induced traumatic stress.* London: Praeger.

Maguen, A., Metzler, A. J., Litz, B. T., Seal, K. H., Knight, S. J., & Marmar, C R. (2009). The impact of killing in war on mental health symptoms and related functioning. *Journal of Traumatic Stress, 22*(5), 435–443.

Mamdani, M. (2001). *When victims become killers: Colonialism, nativism, and the genocide in Rwanda.* Princeton, NJ: Princeton University Press.

Maoz, I., & Eidelson, R. J. (2007). Psychological bases of extreme policy preferences: How the personal beliefs of Israeli-Jews predict their support for population transfer in the Israeli-Palestinian conflict. *American Behavioral Scientist, 50*, 1476–1497.

Maslow, A. H. (1971). *The farther reaches of human nature.* New York: Viking.

Merkl, P. H. (1980). *The making of a stormtrooper.* Princeton, NJ: Princeton University Press.

Mikulincer, M., & Shaver, P. R. (2012). *The social psychology of morality: Exploring the causes of good and evil.* Washington, DC: American Psychological Association.

Milgram, S. (1974). *Obedience to authority: An experimental view.* New York: Harper & Row.

Myers, D. (2010). *Social psychology.* New York: McGraw-Hill.

Noor, M., Brown, R., Gonzalez, R., Manzin, J., & Lewis, C. A. (2008). On positive psychological outcomes: What helps groups with a history of conflict to forgive and reconcile with each other? *Personality and Social Psychology Bulletin, 14*(6), 819–833.

Oliner, S. B., & Oliner, P. (1988). *The altruistic personality: Rescuers of Jews in Nazi Europe.* New York: Free Press.

Opotow, S. (1990). Moral exclusion and injustice: An introduction. *Journal of Social Issues, 46*(1), 1–20.

Opotow, S. (2012). Moral exclusion. In D. Christie (Ed.), *The encyclopedia of peace psychology.* New York: Wiley-Blackwell.

Osswald, S., Greitemeyer, T., Fisher, P., & Frey, D. (2010) Moral prototypes and moral behavior: Specific effects on emotional precursors of moral behavior and on moral behavior by the activation of moral prototypes. *European Journal of Social Psychology, 40*, 1078–1094.

Paluck, E. L. (2009). Reducing intergroup prejudice and conflict using the media: A field experiment in Rwanda. *Journal of Personality and Social Psychology, 96*, 574–587.

Pearlman, L. A., & Saakvitne, K. W. (1995). *Trauma and the therapist: Countertransference and vicarious traumatization in psychotherapy with incest survivors.* New York: W. W. Norton.

Penner, L. A., Dovidio, J. F., Piliavin, J. A., & Schroeder, D. A. (2005). Prosocial behavior: multilevel perspectives. *Annual Review of Psychology, 56*, 14.1–14.28.

Penner, L. A, Fritzsche, B. A, Craiger, J. P., & Freifeld, T. R. (1995). Measuring the prosocial personality. In J. Butcher & C. D. Spielberger (Eds.), *Advances in personality assessment* (Vol. 10, pp. 147–163). Hillsdale, NJ: Lawrence Erlbaum Associates.

Pettigrew, T. F. (1998). Intergroup contact theory. *Annual Review of Psychology, 49*, 65–85.

Pettigrew, T., & Tropp, L. R. (2006). A meta-analytic test of intergroup contact theory. *Journal of Personality and Social Psychology, 90*, 751–783.

Power, S. (2002). *A problem from hell: America and the age of genocide.* New York: Basic Books.

Quabbin Mediation, & Staub, E. (2006). Training active bystanders: A curriculum for school and community. Copyrighted manuscript.

Rosenhan, D. (1970). The natural socialization of altruistic autonomy. In J. Macauley & L. Berkowitz (Eds.), *Altruism and helping behavior.* New York: Academic Press.

Saakvitne, K. W., Gamble, S. G., Pearlman, L. A., & Lev, B. T. (2000). *Risking connection: A training curriculum for working with survivors of childhood abuse.* Lutherville, MD: Sidran Press.

Sageman, M. (2004). *Understanding terror networks.* Philadelphia: University of Pennsylvania Press.

Schatz, R. T., Staub, E., & Lavine, H. (1999). On the varieties of national attachment: Blind versus constructive patriotism. *Political Psychology, 20*, 151–175.

Schwartz, S. H., & Clausen, G. T. (1970). Responsibility norms and helping in an emergency. *Journal of Personality and Social Psychology, 16*, 299–310.

Skitka, L. J. (2012). Moral convictions and moral courage: Common denominators of good and evil. In M. Mikulincer & P. R. Shaver (Eds.), *The social psychology of morality: Exploring the causes of good and evil* (pp. 349–367). Washington, DC: American Psychological Association.

Spielman, D., & Staub, E. (2000). Reducing boys' aggression. Learning to fulfill basic needs constructively. *Journal of Applied Developmental Psychology, 21*(2), 165–181.

Staub, E. (1970a). A child in distress: The effects of focusing responsibility on children on their attempts to help. *Developmental Psychology, 2*, 152–154.

Staub, E. (1970b). A child in distress: The influence of age and number of witnesses on children's attempts to help. *Journal of Personality and Social Psychology, 14*, 130–140.

Staub, E. (1974). Helping a distressed person: Social, personality and stimulus determinants. In L. Berkowitz (Ed.), *Advances in experimental social psychology* (Vol. 7., pp. 203–342). New York: Academic Press.

Staub, E. (1978). *Positive social behavior and morality: Vol. 1. Personal and social influences* New York: Academic Press.

Staub, E. (1979). *Positive social behavior and morality: Vol. 2. Socialization and development.* New York: Academic Press.

Staub, E. (1980). Social and prosocial behavior: Personal and situational influences and their interactions. In. E. Staub (Ed.), *Personality: Basic aspects and current research* (pp. 237–294). Englewood Cliffs, NJ: Prentice Hall.

Staub, E. (1989). *The roots of evil: The origins of genocide and other group violence.* New York: Cambridge University Press.

Staub, E. (1997). The psychology of rescue: Perpetrators, bystanders and heroic helpers. In J. Michalczyk (Ed.), *Resisters, rescuers and refugees: Historical and ethical issues.* Kansas City: Sheed & Ward.

Staub, E. (1998). Breaking the cycle of genocidal violence: Healing and reconciliation. In J. Harvey (Ed.), *Perspectives on loss* (pp. 231–241). Washington, DC: Taylor & Francis.

Staub, E. (2003). *The psychology of good and evil: Why children, adults and groups help and harm others.* New York: Cambridge University Press.

Staub, E. (2005). The roots of goodness: The fulfillment of basic human needs and the development of caring, helping and nonaggression, inclusive caring, moral courage, active bystandership, and altruism born of suffering. In G. Carlo & C. Edwards (Eds.), *Moral motivation through the life span: Theory, research, applications* (pp. 33–73). Nebraska Symposium on Motivation. Lincoln: Nebraska University Press.

Staub, E. (2007a, August). Evil: Understanding bad situations and systems, but also personality and group dynamics. [Review of the book *The Lucifer effect: Zimbardo, P. The Lucifer Effect: Understanding how good people turn evil* by P. Zimbardo]. *PsychCritiques.*

Staub, E. (2007b). Preventing violence and terrorism and promoting positive relations between Dutch and Muslim communities in Amsterdam. *Peace and Conflict: Journal of Peace Psychology, 13*(3), 333–361.

Staub, E. (2011). *Overcoming evil: Genocide, violent conflict and terrorism.* New York: Oxford University Press.

Staub, E. (2012). Psychology and morality in genocide and violent conflict: Perpetrators, passive bystanders and rescuers. In M. Mikulincer & P. R. Shaver (Eds.), *The social psychology of morality: Exploring the causes of good and evil* (pp. 381–399). Washington, DC: American Psychological Association.

Staub, E. (2013). Building a peaceful society: Origins, prevention, and reconciliation after genocide and other group violence. *American Psychologist, 68*(7), 576–589.

Staub, E., & Baer, R. S. Jr. (1974). Stimulus characteristics of a sufferer and difficulty of escape as determinants of helping. *Journal of Personality and Social Psychology, 30*, 279–285.

Staub, E., & Pearlman, L. A. (2009). Reducing intergroup prejudice and conflict: A commentary. *Journal of Personality and Social Psychology, 96*, 588–594.

Staub, E., Pearlman, L. A., & Bilali, R. (2010). Understanding the roots and impact of violence and psychological recovery as avenues to reconciliation after mass violence and intractable conflict: Applications to national leaders, journalists, community groups, public education through radio, and children. In G. Salomon & E. Cairns (Eds.), *Handbook of peace education* (pp. 269–287). New York: Psychology Press.

Staub, E., Pearlman, L. A., Gubin, A., & Hagengimana, A. (2005). Healing, reconciliation, forgiving and the prevention of violence after genocide or mass killing: An intervention and its experimental evaluation in Rwanda. *Journal of Social and Clinical Psychology, 24*(3), 297–334.

Staub, E., & Vollhardt, J. (2008). Altruism born of suffering: The roots of caring and helping after experiences of personal and political victimization. *American Journal of Orthopsychiatry, 78*, 267–280.

Tec, N. (1986). *When light pierced the darkness: Christian rescuers of Jews in Nazi occupied Poland.* New York: Oxford University Press.

Tetlock, P. E., Kristel, O. V., Elson, S. B., Green, M. C., & Lerner, J. S. (2000). The psychology of the unthinkable: Taboo trade-offs, forbidden base rates, and heretical counterfactuals. *Journal of Personality and Social Psychology, 78*, 853–870.

Thalhammer, K. E., O'Loughlin, P. L., Glazer, M. P., Glazer, P. M., McFarland, S., Shepela, S. T., & Stoltzfus, N. (2007). *Courageous resistance: The power of ordinary people*. New York: Palgrave Macmillan.

Van der Kolk, B. A. (2009). Afterword. In C. A. Curtois & J. D. Ford (Eds.), *Treating complex traumatic stress disorders* (pp. 455–466). New York: Guilford.

Varshney, A. (2002). *Ethnic conflict and civic life: Hindus and Muslims in India*. New Haven, CT: Yale University Press.

Volkan, V. D. (2001). Transgenerational transmissions and chosen traumas: An aspect of large group identity. *Group Analysis, 34*, 79–97.

Vollhardt, J. R. (2009). The role of victim beliefs in the Israeli-Palestinian conflict: Risk or potential for peace? *Peace and Conflict: Journal of Peace Psychology, 15*, 135–159.

Vollhardt, J. R. (2012). Collective victimization. In L. Tropp (Ed.), *The Oxford handbook of intergroup conflict* (pp. 135–158). New York: Oxford University Press.

Vollhardt, J. R. & Staub, E. (2011). Inclusive altruism born of suffering: The relationship between adversity and prosocial attitudes and behavior toward disadvantaged outgroups. *American Journal of Orthopsychiatry, 81*(3), 307–315.

Walker, L. J., Frimer, J. A., & Dunlop, W. L. (2010). Varieties of moral personality: Beyond the banality of heroism. *Journal of Personality, 78*(3), 907–942.

Whiting, B. B., & Whiting, J. W. M. (1975). *Children of six cultures: A psycho cultural analysis*. Cambridge, MA: Harvard University Press.

Wolpe, H., & McDonald, S. (2008). Democracy and peace building: Rethinking the conventional wisdom. *The Round Table, 97*(394), 137–145.

Zimbardo, P. (2007). *The Lucifer effect: Understanding how good people turn evil*. New York: Random House.

23

Exploring Moral Courage
and Heroism

Psychologists have studied what leads people to help others in need (or remain passive bystanders) since the 1960s. Researchers have also studied one important form of heroism, heroic rescue, individuals endangering themselves to save the lives of designated victims of genocide (Tec, 1986; Oliner & Oliner, 1988; Staub, 1989, 1997). The term *rescuer* was first used in relation to the Holocaust, but there have been rescuers of Armenians at the time of the genocide in Turkey, of Tutsis during the 1994 genocide in Rwanda (Africa Rights, 2002), in Bosnia, and probably in all genocides and mass killings.

Recently, psychologists have become interested in heroism in general (Becker & Eagly, 2004; Franco, Blau, & Zimbardo, 2011). Heroism to me means a person acting to protect others or enhance the welfare of other individuals or society in significant ways, when this involves substantial danger to the actor. Normally this is physical danger, of injury, death, or imprisonment. Heroism can be a single act: jumping on train tracks to pull a person out of the way of a speedily oncoming train, or a soldier jumping on a grenade, sacrificing his life in order to save his fellow soldiers. The teachers at Sandy Hook Elementary School in Connecticut who stepped in front of bullets, protecting the children with their bodies, are outstanding examples of heroism. Heroism can also be persistent action, such as a rescuer hiding people for a long time, or someone working to oppose a brutal, dictatorial system.

It is also recent that psychologists have become concerned with the study of moral courage (Staub, 2003, 2005, 2011; Osswald, Greitmeyer, Fisher, & Frey, 2010). Moral courage means acting on one's moral values and/or on one's caring about and empathy for individuals, a social group, society, or humanity in the face of potential or actual opposition and negative consequences to oneself. Moral courage is of great importance, for individual welfare and the social good. Much happens that is unjust in society and the larger world; individuals or groups of people are unfairly treated or are the object of violence, whether in school, in the workplace, in the justice system, by the police or governments. People speaking and acting to stop harmful actions or right such wrongs is crucial for a well-functioning and harmonious society and a safe and peaceful world.

Not everything that an individual or group identifies as moral is moral. Individuals and societies can and do hold values *they regard* as moral or, an increasingly used term in psychology, *sacred* (Tetlock, Kristel, Elson, Green, & Lerner, 2000), which outsiders may regard as immoral, or which give rise to harmful and destructive acts. For example, respect for and obedience to authority is often held as a moral value, but authorities often lead individuals and a society to destructive acts. Values that in some societies have been regarded as sacred, such as living up to the requirements of a blood feud (Grille, 2005), have led to much violence and suffering. While sacred values can lead to extremely courageous acts, considering such actions as moral (or caring) requires judgments, by disinterested parties, not only about intentions but consequences (see Chapter 8). Do they genuinely serve human well-being?

Without such considerations what a government or a group (or a person) declares as moral becomes moral, and opposition to injustice, moral courage in resisting or opposing the illegitimate use of power, can be defined as immoral or destructive. People who do harm, whether individuals or groups, almost always believe that what they do is right, moral, even an obligation (Fiske & Rai, 2014; Staub, 1989). Salmon Rushdie felt abandoned by many friends when in a fatwa the Ayatollah Khomeini ordered him killed for supposedly sacrilegious writing about Islam. Were they afraid, or did they accept a view that what he wrote was wrong and immoral?

Rushdie (2013) sees people increasingly suspicious of those who take a stand against abuse of power. Governments try to portray them as immoral troublemakers, and people often accept this. He writes about a man imprisoned because he tweeted about the prophet Muhammad in Saudi Arabia, and the governor of Punjab in Pakistan, who was killed by a bodyguard because he defended a Christian woman who was sentenced to death under the country's blasphemy laws. The killer was regarded as a hero. He suggests that the United States is not immune, with people seeing some intellectuals persistently critical of US policies as extremist.

An act can be morally courageous, or heroic, or both. When it is heroism alone, it is usually celebrated by other people and society. When it is moral courage alone, there is less risk or danger. Jumping on train track to pull a person out of the way of an oncoming train requires physical courage; it is a heroic act that does not require moral courage. The actor is likely to be praised, even celebrated. Some acts require moral courage, like speaking out when someone makes racist or anti-Semitic or homophobic statements, but if the potential consequences to the actor are limited, the act is not heroic.

It is also morally courageous when politicians pursue policies that benefit many people or their country but are opposed by their close colleagues or people who elected them. Such politicians, too rare in the United States nowadays, would only be risking reelection in the United States, but usually not their physical well-being or lives. But morally courageous actions, even if they have no immediate physical consequences, can result in disapproval and potential ostracism by one's community. Therefore, the Supreme Court ruling in 1954 against segregation, or a state judge in Massachusetts ruling in favor of gay marriage before that become more accepted by society were also morally courageous acts.

A student attempting to stop a bully in school may be morally courageous or, depending on the size of the bully and other circumstances, also physically courageous and heroic. The young man in Tiananmen Square in China, standing in front of the tanks in order to stop them, is also an example of both moral courage and heroism. Rescue in genocide often involved not only heroism, potentially leading to imprisonment by the authorities or death, but also moral courage. Rescuers often acted contrary to newly developing community beliefs and standards, based on old prejudices, which supported the violence against the victims. In addition to the danger of imprisonment or execution within Germany, or by German forces or governments allied to them in other countries, their actions could lead to disapproval and ostracism in their communities. This happened even after Germany and its allies were defeated. The German Oscar Shindler, who saved the lives of over 1,000 Jews made into slave laborers during the Holocaust, was badly treated in his community after the war.

At times heroes help others near and dear to them, people they love and have close connections to. Most of the time heroes help strangers. For rescuers in genocide, their caring had to be truly inclusive, expanding beyond their group to people their group intended to exterminate. Moral courage by leaders also often means that their caring expands beyond a limited group, as in the case of the Supreme Court in 1954.

Influences Leading to Morally Courageous and Heroic Actions: General Considerations

To revisit definitions, *helping* is action to benefit a person, group, or humanity. *Heroism* is action to benefit individuals or communities that involves extreme danger to the actor, primarily physical danger. There is, however, an indeterminacy in differentiating helping and heroism. Often helping involves some risk and danger. A man lying on the street may have a contagious disease or may intend to attack the person approaching him (or her). *Moral courage* is expressing in action moral or caring values or feelings (such as empathy) in spite of potential or actual opposition by other people or society and negative consequences to the actor. While heroism is often socially valued and celebrated, when the level of danger is high, morally courageous action can also be heroic, involving not only potential physical harm but also great material or psychological harm to the actor or people close to the actor, for example, due to ostracism or financial loss. Here also there is an indeterminacy in when an action is *merely* morally courageous and when it is also heroic.

Essential to heroism is caring about the welfare of others. Caring can be generated by circumstances, especially of intense need. But circumstances are more likely to generate caring in people who have relevant personal dispositions. In one study, the personal characteristics of the majority of "brave individuals" who received an award in Canada for risking their lives to save other people did not indicate any special qualities (Walker, Frimer, & Dunlop, 2010). However, the only personal characteristics measured that seem specifically relevant to heroism were the traits of nurturance and moral reasoning. While high-level moral reasoning seems relevant and did characterize some brave individuals, it requires a cognitive process that would be more likely to lead to helpful action when there is time for decision-making. Empathy, feelings of responsibility for other people, and such enabling characteristics as belief in one's competence were not measured.

One form of caring is *empathy*, feeling what other people feel, or *sympathy*, feeling with and concern about others' distress. A form of caring that has special force includes a feeling of responsibility for other people's welfare. In our research this has contributed to people helping others in either physical or psychological distress. Such feeling of or belief in one's responsibility is also associated with less aggression among seventh grade boys. It is associated with what I call *constructive patriotism*, loving one's country but a readiness to speak out when it acts contrary to humane values (see Staub, 2003).

Heroic acts often require immediate action and do not allow time for deliberation. The heroism of teachers at Sandy Hook Elementary School in Connecticut required fast judgment and a readiness for action, as some teachers stepped in front of the killer, Adam Lanza, to stop the bullets, while others speedily hid children in classrooms. People vary in their inclination to decide quickly about the meaning of a situation, whether action is needed and what kind. The combination of caring—empathy/feelings of responsibility—a belief in one's competence, the capacity for fast judgment, and readiness for action can lead to fast, seemingly "spontaneous helping." The usual work of decision-making is short-circuited. There can be no deliberation as a person sees a child falling out of a fourth-story window—caught by someone later recognized as a hero by the Carnegie Hero Foundation (Staub, 1978).

Great courage but no special competence is needed to step in front of a man with a gun in order to save children, many people with reasonable strength can catch a falling child, and just about anyone who has a basement can hide a person in it. While often little special competence is needed, a feeling of or belief in one's effectiveness is important. In the 2,000 questionnaires we analyzed that readers returned in my *Psychology Today* study of values and helping, the many kinds of helping they reported they engaged in, including helping in emergencies, was strongly related to their concern about others' welfare and feelings of responsibility to help. The connection between this value orientation and helping was even stronger, and substantially so, in people who also believed that they have the capacity to improve others' welfare (Staub, 2003, ch. 9).

Sometimes a feeling of responsibility and heroism arise out of people's roles. Police officers, fireman, and medical people have responsibilities. Part of the staff's responsibility at a school is to protect children. While their normal and expected function does not include putting themselves in the way of bullets, still, the responsibility carried by that role had to be an element in the heroism at Sandy Hook. Roles that carry responsibility and the potential for heroic actions can over time lead to personal feelings of responsibility.

A mysterious ingredient is *courage*. Many rescuers have reported that they never hesitated when faced with someone who needed rescue ("what else could I do but help?"). While I suspect that some of these retrospective reports are the result of changes in people as a result of having devoted themselves to helping others, often for a long time, the reports are frequent enough that we must give some credence to them. Altruistic, heroically inclined people faced with intense need for help may at times forget about their own safety as they focus on others' needs. At other times and for other people, courage may be the outcome of struggle between what they believe is right and the dangers that will ensue, leading to action even if they greatly fear the consequences. Researchers have found that some people, seemingly a small minority, are fearless. Others may be fearless in the moment, as they are caught up in the need for action. Still others who engage in morally courageous or heroic actions do so in spite of their fear (Rachman, 2010).

Influences Leading to Morally Courageous and Heroic Actions: Research Findings

Research on Courage

There has been substantial research on what leads to courageous actions, how fear diminishes in dangerous situations, and how courage develops. Most of this research is with people engaged in military activities, such as parachute trainees, bomb disposal specialists in Northern Ireland who were members of the British Royal Army Ordnance Corps, and soldiers in the field (for a review, see Rachman, 2010). Some of the actions studied were heroic, saving lives, but it was heroism that was part of one's duty and job assignment as a soldier. Special training experiences and successful execution of missions both greatly reduced fear. Both are also likely to bolster morally courageous and everyday heroic actions.

All members of the Royal Corps had to do bomb disposal, but still self-selection in the characteristics of people who joined this service presumably had a role. They also went through a screening process, but fewer than 10% were eliminated. Overall, the screening found that they described themselves as unusually well adjusted and emotionally stable. Those who received decorations for outstanding performance showed even better psychological health and bodily fitness than the rest of the group. A study of their actual responses in a stressful situation also found that those who were decorated had lower heart rate responses than those who were not, and both had lower heart rate than civilians and young soldiers.

Parachute trainees' initial self-confidence, and success in dangerous jumps from a practice tower during training, both led to the reduction of fear. Specialized training also increased the skill and confidence of bomb disposal operators, and "once the inexperienced operators successfully dealt with a genuine explosive device, their confidence and competence quickly rose to a level close to that of experienced operators" (Rachman, 2010, p. 101). Models are also important. The courageous behavior of parents in war increased the courage of children during air raids. Courage in leaders has great influence on soldiers' courage in combat (Stouffer, 1949).

In the studies with soldiers it was not assessed to what extent they were motivated by moral values and altruism and wanting to protect the public, for example, from bomb explosions. Membership in a close-knit group must have had powerful effects, such as feelings of responsibility to fulfill one's role, responsibility to one's comrades, and the desire to gain approval and avoid disapproval. Such effects of group membership can intensify altruistic activities but also antisocial and violent activities, such as terrorism (McCauley, 2004) and the behavior of German reserve police who were sent to kill Jews behind the Eastern front in World War II (Browning, 1992; see Staub, 2011).

Research on Moral Courage

Osswald and associates (2010) assumed that helping behavior and morally courageous behavior (e.g., "intervening at the risk of high social costs and with no or only little hope for reward," p. 151) have different determinants. As one would expect, people see morally courageous behavior as serving moral ends and having higher costs to the actor than helping behavior. In one study (Fisher, Greitemeyer, Pollozek, & Frey, 2006), each participant saw a presumably live broadcast in which a man and a women talked to each other in an adjoining room. The man was becoming intrusive, started to harass the women sexually. The women tried to escape, a brawl started—and then the picture went black. In a "helping condition" the man was small and skinny; in the moral "courage condition," he was strongly built and "thug-like." In terms of the earlier discussion, in both situations the intervener had to oppose the perpetrator, but the intervention would have been valued and praised by other people and society in general. The difference in the two situations was in the latter calling for some degree of *heroism*, given the greater physical danger.

Perhaps one reason these researchers use moral courage to describe this situation is the influence on their work of the concept of *civic courage*, a concept that has been used in Germany and is regarded there as interchangeable with moral courage. Civic courage seems more inclusive than moral courage; it seems to refer to all situations in which action is needed in the service of the social good. It can include acts based on moral values, as well as acts to protect social norms and societal standards in general.

In the abovementioned study there was a solitary condition, and a bystander condition with a passive bystander. The presence of the bystander inhibited helping in the helping condition but not in the moral courage—or what I think of as heroism—condition. In this condition the potential helpers were more aroused and recognized the situation more quickly as a real emergency. The costs were higher not only to the intervener, but facing a more powerful attacker also to the person who needed help. Perhaps when there is an intense and unambiguous need, the passivity of another so contrasts with what is required that it increases awareness of one's responsibility to act.

In further studies this group of researchers also found that while, consistent with previous research, experimentally induced mood affected helping in "helping situations" (positive and to a lesser extent negative mood increased helping in comparison to neutral mood), it did not affect helping in "moral courage" situations (see Osswald et al., 2010). In this research the influences that normally affect helping did so when intervention seemed less dangerous, but not when the danger to the person in need and to the actor was greater.

Osswald, Greitemeyer, Fisher, and Frey (2010) reviewed two studies in which participants witnessed an experimenter insulting and discriminating against a foreign student (who was a confederate). Before this, half of the participants saw a film with scenes in which people showed morally courageous behavior. Participants who saw the film intervened more often. In a second study the researchers found that participants who saw the film reported greater awareness of the situation, more anger, and more responsibility to act. Those participants who after seeing the film felt more anger and more responsibility helped more. Some of the rescuers in Oliner and Oliner's (1988) large study reported that they witnessed the abuse of Jews, responded with empathy, and/or outrage, and this created a readiness in them to help when the opportunity arose. These findings suggest that in addition to the other influences leading to helping, anger or moral outrage sometimes has a role in motivating morally courageous or heroic actions.

In another study Osswald et al. (2010) used again the situation of an experimenter badly treating a foreign student. Participants with more empathy, and more *openness* on the Big Five personality test, intervened more. As Osswald et al. wrote, "openness to new experiences and a broad mind promote acceptance of different ways of life and of persons from other countries and cultures" (p. 168). Participants who denied their responsibility more (i.e., who felt less responsible) helped less. Being open, nonconventional, and feeling responsible can all be important in helping.

Holding conventional values and beliefs may inhibit helping, and especially morally courageous behavior, which often requires going against convention. In one of my early studies, with sounds of a person in pain coming from an adjoining room, a prosocial orientation in which a feeling of responsibility for others' welfare is central was associated with helping, either by entering the other room or by helping after the distressed person came into the room. However, persons for whom cleanliness was an important—a conventional value—helped less (Staub, 1974). In another study, helping by children in response to sounds of distress from an adjoining room increased from kindergarten to second grade but then greatly decreased from fourth to sixth grade (Staub, 1970). In discussions on their reactions with sixth grade participants, we found that children have learned rules of conventional behavior, such as not interrupting work on their task or going into another room in a strange environment (Staub, 1970, 1971; see Chapter 1). In a subsequent study both a prohibition to enter the adjoining room and no instruction (the same situation as before) led to little helping by seventh graders. But having been told that it is all right to go into the adjoining room for *an irrelevant reason,* over 90% of the children did so when they later heard distress sounds. Strongly emphasizing conventional values and rules in raising children may override empathy, relevant moral values, and feelings of responsibility.

Heroism in Men and Women

Becker and Eagly (2004) show in a review of many studies that there is more male heroism in situations of *immediate* physical danger to the actor, such as rescuing someone from a fire or a drowning person, or intervening in muggings and bank robberies. There may be a variety of reasons for this: the greater physical strength and prowess of men; past training that provides them with skills as boy scouts, firemen, or in the military; and past experience with such roles and relevant situations. Such training, and experiences with sports like football, can also increase self-confidence and feelings of competence, which in research on courage with bomb-disposal specialists and paratroopers was associated with courageous behavior (Rachman, 2010). It also appears that men are more motivated to engage in public prosocial behavior, which provides them with prestige and enhances their social status (Becker & Eagly, 2004).

The relevant male tendencies and capacities may be partly related to socialization. For example, mothers caution boys and intervene with them less in potentially dangerous physical situations (Morrongiello & Dawber, 2000). Observers of playground behavior have reported that when boys having climbed a tall jungle-gym show distress, the caretakers with them encourage them to climb down; girls in the same situation are much more often lifted down. Temperamental characteristics with different actions tendencies and testosterone are also likely to have a role. Zuckerman, Kuhlman, Joireman, Teta, and Kraft (1993) proposed that men are characterized by *impulsive sensation seeking*. While there is certainly great variation in such dispositions, some men appear more oriented to immediate action.

In contrast to circumstances that require physical prowess, need immediacy in action, and involve public behavior, in other domains women are heroic somewhat more often than men. This was the case in rescuing Jews in Europe during the Holocaust, in kidney donations, and in volunteering with Doctors of the World to serve people in faraway places (Becker & Eagly, 2004). All of these activities represent physical danger, to varying degrees. In two of these cases, being a rescuer or as a doctor helping people around the world, the helper acts to benefit others outside his or her group. As I have noted, the motivations of rescuers appeared to be caring for others' welfare both as reported by them and by the people they rescued, such as empathy, commitment to moral principles like justice, feelings of responsibility, and the experience of shared humanity (Oliner & Oliner, 1988; Staub, 1989, 1997; Monroe, 1996).

Further Thoughts on Socialization and Experience Leading to Moral Courage and Heroism

The characteristics I described as contributors to heroism are acquired at least partly by socialization in childhood and experience in life. There may be some contribution to heroism by a general action tendency, genetic in part, an aspect of temperament. But even action-oriented males are not likely to greatly endanger themselves without socialization that promotes relevant characteristics. In a study I referred to earlier, among the young men hearing sounds of distress from an adjoining room those who several weeks before scored high on a test of impulsiveness—measuring a fast action tendency—stopped working on their task earlier. They tended to look up, even get up and pace around. But only those who also had a stronger prosocial value orientation were likely to actually enter the adjoining room (Staub, 1974).

While the research on courage has been done with soldiers who were presumably at least somewhat action oriented (although not necessarily fearless), it clearly showed that training, practice and experience, enhance courage. Among people in general, practice and experience can add to the motivation to help that socialization has developed. I have stressed the feeling of responsibility as important, and noted that pointing out to children the effects of their behavior on other people is one way to develop it (Hoffman, 2000). Giving children responsibilities is another.

One study (McNamee & Wesolik, 2014) compared reports of their parents' child-drearing practices by people who received a medal from the Carnegie Foundation for having saved someone's life while risking their own, with reports of childrearing by parents from a group of randomly selected people. The only difference was Carnegie Heroes reporting more that their parents expected them to help people. Such expectation presumably focuses responsibility on children to help. Parents, teachers, and other people can use practices that develop empathy and a feeling of responsibility. Through their example and by guiding children to help others beyond their own group adults can foster responsibility for everyone.

Like disarming bombs or parachuting, moral courage and everyday heroism are likely to be facilitated by "training" and experience. Having children participate in making rules in the classroom or decisions in the family is a kind of training (Staub, 2005; Chapter 3). Learning that others take them seriously, listen to them, engage with what they say, and that they can have an impact develops confidence by children in their thoughts and actions.

Learning by doing is crucial (see Chapter 5). But some parents discourage children from morally courageous actions, worried about their relationship to peers and adults. Moral courage is likely to be fostered when children (and adults) are allowed and encouraged to act on their values, especially when the risk is not too great. The risk of being picked on by peers for protecting another peer, or of a negative response from a teacher for speaking out on some issue of moral relevance that is significant to the child, is usually tolerable. Children and youth can be helped to develop strategies to involve peers and act jointly, when appropriate (Chapter 16).

Learning to use one's judgment, a critical consciousness, is often a prerequisite for action. Moral courage often requires opposition to people with power or to established systems or standards and rules that are unjust and harmful. Rather than accepting the definition of reality by authorities, people need to use their own judgment, based on moral and caring values and emotions. The capacity to be independent in assessing the meaning of events, and good judgment makes actions that prevent harm possible. This is often easier than stopping harmdoing. Since moral courage may be necessary to protect members of devalued groups, or devalued individuals, having learned to include all people in the realm humanity (McFarland, Webb, & Brown, 2012) will contribute to morally courageous or heroic actions.

In summary, morally courageous people and heroes are not born. Adults can raise children in ways that promote characteristics that give rise to them. And all of us can use opportunities for practice and relevant experience—enter situations and take actions that shape who we are, making such behaviors more likely. We can shape and create ourselves.

References

Africa Rights. (2002). *Tribute to courage.* Kigali, Rwanda.

Batson, C. D. (2011). *Altruism in humans.* New York: Oxford University Press.

Becker, S. W., & Eagly, A. H. (2004). The heroism of women and men. *American Psychologist, 59,* 163–178.

Browning, C. R. (1992). *Ordinary men: Reserve Battalion 101 and the final solution in Poland.* New York: HarperCollins.

Eisenberg, N., Fabes, R. A., & Spinrad, T. L. (2006). Prosocial development. In W. Damon (Ed.), *Handbook of child psychology: Vol. 3. Social, emotional, and personality development* (5th ed., pp. 646–718). New York: Wiley.

Fisher, P., Greitemeyer, T., Pollozek, F., & Frey, D. (2006). The unresponsive bystander: Are bystanders more responsive in dangerous situations? *European Journal of Social Psychology, 36,* 267–278. doi:1002/ejsp.297

Fiske, A. P., & Rai, T. S. (2014). *Virtuous violence: Hurting and killing.* New York: Cambridge University Press.

Franco, Z. F., Blau, K., & Zimbardo, P. G. (2011). Heroism: A conceptual analysis and differentiation between action and altruism. *Review of General Psychology, 15*(2), 99–113.

Grille, R. (2005). *Parenting for a peaceful world.* Alexandria, Australia: Longueville Media.

Hoffman, M. L. (2000). *Empathy and moral development.* New York: Cambridge University Press.

McCauley, C. (2004). Psychological issues in understanding terrorism. In C. E. Stout, (Ed.), *Psychology of terrorism* (pp. 33–67). Westport, CT: Praeger.

McFarland, S., Webb, M., & Brown, D. (2012). All humanity is my ingroup: A measure and studies of identification with all humanity. *Journal of Personality and Social Psychology, 103,* 850–853.

McNamee, S., & Wesolik, F. (2014). Heroic behavior of Carnegie Medal Heroes: Parental influence and expectations. *Peace and Conflict: Journal of Peace Psychology, 20*(2), 171–173.

Monroe, K. (1996). *The heart of altruism: Perceptions of a common humanity.* Princeton, NJ: Princeton University Press.

Morrongiello, B. A., & Dawber, T. (2000). Mothers' responses to sons and daughters engaging in injury-risk behaviors on a playground: Implications for sex differences in injury rates. *Journal of Experimental Child Psychology, 76,* 89–103.

Oliner, S. B., & Oliner, P. (1988). *The altruistic personality: Rescuers of Jews in Nazi Europe.* New York: Free Press.

Osswald, S., Greitemeyer, T., Fischer, P., & Frey, D. (2010). What is moral courage? Definition, explication, and classification of a complex construct. In C. L. Pury & S. J. Lopez (Eds.), *The psychology of courage: Modern research on an ancient virtue* (pp. 149–164). Washington, DC: American Psychological Association.

Rachman, S. J. (2010). Courage: A psychological perspective. In C. L. Pury & S. J. Lopez (Eds.), *The psychology of courage: Modern research on an ancient virtue* (pp. 149–164). Washington, DC: American Psychological Association. doi:10.1037/12168-008

Rushdie, S. (2013, April 28). Whither moral courage? *The New York Times Sunday Review,* p. 6.

Staub, E. (1970). A child in distress: The influence of age and number of witnesses on children's attempts to help. *Journal of Personality and Social Psychology, 14,* 130–140.

Staub, E. (1971). Helping a person in distress: The influence of implicit and explicit "rules" of conduct on children and adults. *Journal of Personality and Social Psychology, 17,* 137–145.

Staub, E. (1974). Helping a distressed person: Social, personality and stimulus determinants. In L. Berkowitz (Ed.), *Advances in experimental social psychology* (Vol. 7., pp. 203–342). New York: Academic Press.

Staub, E. (1978). *Positive social behavior and morality: Vol. 1. Personal and social influences* New York: Academic Press.

Staub, E. (1989). *The roots of evil: The origins of genocide and other group violence.* New York: Cambridge University Press.

Staub, E. (1997). The psychology of rescue: Perpetrators, bystanders and heroic helpers. In J. Michalczyk (Ed.), *Resisters, rescuers and refugees: Historical and ethical issues* (pp. 137–147). Kansas City, MO: Sheed & Ward.

Staub, E. (2003). *The psychology of good and evil: Why children, adults and groups help and harm others.* New York: Cambridge University Press.

Staub, E. (2005). The roots of goodness: The fulfillment of basic human needs and the development of caring, helping and nonaggression, inclusive caring, moral courage, active bystandership, and altruism born of suffering. In G. Carlo & C. Edwards (Eds.), *Moral motivation through the life span: Theory, research, applications* (pp. 33–73). Nebraska Symposium on Motivation. Lincoln: Nebraska University Press.

Staub, E. (2011). *Overcoming Evil: Genocide, Violent Conflict and Terrorism.* New York: Oxford University Press.

Stouffer, S. (1949). *The American soldier: Combat and its aftermath.* Princeton, NJ: Princeton University Press.

Tec, N. (1986). *When light pierced the darkness: Christian rescuers of Jews in Nazi occupied Poland.* New York: Oxford University Press.

Tetlock, P. E., Kristel, O. V., Elson, S. B., Green, M. C., & Lerner, J. S. (2000). The psychology of the unthinkable: Taboo trade-offs, forbidden base rates, and heretical counterfactuals. *Journal of Personality and Social Psychology, 78,* 853–870.

Walker, L. J., Frimer, J. A., & Dunlop, W. L. (2010). Varieties of moral personality: Beyond the banality of heroism. *Journal of Personality. 78*(3), 907–942.

Zuckerman, M., Kuhlman, D. M., Joireman, J., Teta, P., & Kraft, M. (1993). A comparison of three structural models for personality: The Big Three, the Big Five, and the Alternative Five. *Journal of Personality and Social Psychology, 65*(4), 757–768. doi:10.1037/0022-3514.65.4.757

24

Nonviolence as a Way to Address Injustice and Group Conflict

It is almost inevitable in human societies that some groups come to have greater power, wealth, and influence. Not infrequently groups limit the rights and opportunities, and harm members of other groups. The more powerful tend to ignore requests by the less powerful for security, rights, and opportunity. This often leads to violence by the less powerful, whether terrorism, guerilla warfare, or revolution—as it did in Argentina in the 1970s, in Syria, and in the complex relations of Israel and the Palestinians. The more powerful usually respond with violence, and a cycle of increasingly intense violence can follow.

It is not simply that the powerful resist giving up privilege. It is also that they develop a worldview or ideology according to which they deserve it—because they are more hard-working, or more intelligent, have better values, or are inherently better as a race or ethnic or religious group. If the less powerful gain power in a violent revolution, since violence tends to expand, often a repressive and violent reign follows.

When people join together, they can accomplish a great deal through nonviolent action. To do so, nonviolence usually needs to be assertive, requiring courage. It can require people putting their lives on the line. Well-known examples of effective nonviolent actions include the people's movement that Gandhi created, which led to India becoming free of British colonial rule, and the primarily nonviolent civil rights movement in the United States led by Martin Luther King. The evolution of civil right in the United States would have been very different if instead of peaceful demonstrators, willing to endanger themselves for their ideals, the authorities and people opposed to expanding civil rights had faced guns and bullets (Chapter 28).

Among other examples of nonviolence, Milošević, who was to a large extent responsible for Serb violence in Bosnia, was overthrown by students and workers. They joined in huge, peaceful demonstrations. They used cars, buses, and tractors to block traffic in Belgrade, the Serb capital. In Chile, when during the rule of Pinochet miners who planned to strike

This chapter is revised and expanded from a *Psychology Today* blog, posted on February 24, 2012.

were surrounded by the military, they asked that sympathizers walk slowly at designated times and flash the lights on their cars. As many people did so, everyone became aware of the degree of opposition to the military dictatorship. Resistance increased, and the days of the system were numbered. The Arab Spring, Egypt and Tunisia, and Occupy Wall Street are important recent examples, even though these nonviolent mass movements led only in Tunisia to lasting benefits. They also showed the Internet as a way to get people informed and engaged. The Internet, unfortunately, as simply a means of reaching people, is also used to promote hostility and violence, including terrorism.

Only recently have social scientists began seriously to study how people move toward group protest. Sociologists, psychologists, and other social scientists have addressed the question of how people come together to form a group. How do they develop a shared perspective on problems and grievances and the willingness for joint action? Discussion and dialogue among individuals can identify problems, help develop a shared sense of grievance, and promote willingness to engage in protest. In the course of such discussion, and especially as people engage in joint action, there is a transformation of beliefs, the evolution of an ideology, and a shift from individual to a collective identity. Leaders can exert influence through ideas and by solidifying the group. This process is not very different for socially constructive protests and for destructive groups that engage in violence.

How effective can nonviolence be? We may think that it would not have been effective in the face of the Nazis' readiness for brutality. But when the German people became aware of the so-called euthanasia program, the killing of mentally and physically handicapped Germans, and relatives, lawyers' groups, and leaders of the Catholic Church protested, the program was halted. There was essentially no protest against the increasing persecution of Jews. But when the genocide was in progress and Jews were deported to extermination camps, the German wives of Jewish men protested in front of government buildings the deportation of their husbands. The deportations stopped, and some of the men already deported were brought back from concentration/extermination camps. Some scholars have suggested that the women succeeded only because in the midst of war the Nazis did not want to alienate the population by turning against German women. But we do not know this, and whether earlier large-scale protests would have been effective.

Events in Syria, where the protests were initially nonviolent but led to violent government response, show the limits of nonviolent action. It is possible, though, that if in spite of the violence inflicted on them the protesters had remained nonviolent, the reactions of the world would have been so overwhelming that the government could not have survived. No outsider can ask, however, that when people are shot at and killed, they should not take up arms themselves. This is a decision only the people involved can make. The fate of the nonviolent movement in Egypt and of Occupy Wall Street show that long-term success also depends on the extent groups can convert the participation of people, and initial success, into political and institutional change.

Diplomatic engagement and bringing parties together for dialogue are a different type of nonviolent action. Success in creating such engagements, and then for them to be fruitful, usually requires overcoming mistrust. It was presumably mistrust of the outside world, and perhaps his own population as well, that led Saddam Hussein to hide the fact that Iraq had no weapons of mass destruction. Perhaps pride also made him less forthcoming, the pride of a dictator. The determination of the US government to create "regime change," and a long-term boycott did not help.

While sanctions and boycotts are not explicitly violent, those who are its targets can consider them a form of war, especially when, as in Iraq, they greatly harm a population and lead to many deaths. The harm done and ineffectiveness led to a shift, sanctions and boycotts focusing on leaders and elites, their money and travel. This has been the focus in boycotting Russia, after its aggressive involvement in Ukraine.

Depending on circumstances and their exact forms, sanctions and boycotts can constitute constructive, nonviolent action. Huge demonstrations by people at many places led corporations to stop doing business in South Africa, contributing to the collapse of the apartheid system, in part because it activated internal actors. This boycott was the outcome of an evolution: lesser actions against the apartheid regime, such as excluding South African athletes from international competition, and seeing nonviolent protests by Black South Africans on television and violent government responses to them.

We have much to learn about what forms of nonviolent actions and what types of engagements work best in what cultures, with what governmental system and what kind of leaders and elites. I mentioned in Chapter 2 that powerful people are not naturally inclined to empathize with the poor and powerless. Research in psychology indicates that while in dialogue less powerful groups want to talk about their grievances, members of the dominant group want to talk about common interests and goals. Still, those with privilege are more inclined to give up some privilege if instead of demands by the less privileged, their difficulties in life and their own relative privilege is highlighted.

Nonviolent action, an important form of active bystandership, needs to become a strong value, skill and technique. People need to exert influence on their leaders to do their utmost to address injustice and resolve conflict without violence. To avoid the human suffering and material costs of violence, we must learn to address legitimate goals in nonviolent ways whenever possible.

25

An Unassuming Hero

Maria Gogan, a Christian woman, came to work for my middle class Jewish family in Budapest five years before I was born. She lived with us. She was my second mother. Her heroic actions in 1944 and her loving presence shaped who I am and my lifelong work on goodness and evil.

Nineteen forty-four, when I was six years old, was the worst of times for Hungarian Jews. About 500,000 people were taken to Auschwitz in the summer of that year, most of them killed immediately in gas chambers. The large majority were taken from the countryside, among them my aunt and two cousins. Those of us who lived in Budapest waited in constant fear.

In October of that year, the Hungarian Nazi party, the Arrow Cross, took over the government. While hardly possible, life got even worse for us. With the yellow star on our chests, we were harassed when we walked down the street or tried to buy bread at a bakery. During the middle of the night, the drunken coal merchant from across the street came into the courtyard of our apartment house and shouted threats at us. Jews were caught on the street and taken to the river Danube. Several of them were tied together, one or two were shot, and then all pushed into the river.

The apartment house we lived in had a number of Jewish families, so we had to put a big yellow star on the gate. Around this time Maria took me and my sister into hiding with a Christian family. I remember walking on the street holding her hand, then into a house and up some stairs—there was an inside balcony surrounding the courtyard with apartments opening from it—entering an apartment, a women sitting on a stool peeling potatoes. I remember nothing else. The neighbors were told that we were relatives from the countryside. Because some seemed suspicious, after a couple of weeks Maria moved us to another family.

Then my mother and aunt managed to get so-called letters of protection, the creative idea of Raoul Wallenberg, the Swedish businessman who was appointed a diplomat and asked to go to Hungary to save Jewish lives. These letters said that their bearers would become Swedish citizens after the war and were now under the protection of Sweden. Wallenberg persuaded the Hungarian government to allow him to protect a few thousand Jews this way, but he handed out many more of these documents. I heard from my mother and aunt the story of their standing in a mob of people outside the Swedish embassy, miraculously getting into the embassy and receiving these life-saving documents. The tragic competition for survival. Wallenberg bought and set up apartment houses in Budapest to which people with this document could move.

Maria brought my sister and me home just before our family, my mother, my aunt, my three cousins and my sister and I moved to one of these "protected houses." The fathers were in forced labor camps. We went there late one night, on dark streets barely able to see our way, with a few possessions on a cart we pushed, scared that someone would stop us, and given our situation, could do to us whatever they wished. Maria, a Christian woman, could have been safe, but she came with us.

The house had a huge number of people in it. We had little food. Maria prepared dough and took it in a baby carriage to a bakery, then brought the bread back the same way. Once she was stopped by Hungarian Nazis. She was made to stand for hours facing a wall, with her arms up, told that she would be killed for helping Jews. Then a Nazi who knew her from the neighborhood walked in and told the others to let her go. She continued with her activities. The bread she baked, and food she scavenged, staved off serious hunger for a good number of people in the house.

Maria also went to my father's forced labor camp. Standing outside a barbed wire fence, she called out to an inmate inside, asking him to send my father there. She handed him a copy of the letter of protection. He later escaped when his group was taken to Germany, during a stopover in Budapest. He simply walked out, and when the guard asked him where he was going, he said he was separated from his group and was rejoining them, giving a location. He was the only survivor of that group. The letter of protection would have been of no use to him, given that he was an escaped slave laborer. But after his death in 1974, when my mother and I talked about his escape, we thought that this letter gave him, a good but not a forceful man, the courage to escape.

When I was 18, after the uprising in 1956 was put down by Soviet troops, I escaped with two friends from Hungary. Maria came with us as we circuitously made our way to the border, ostensibly to report back to my worried parents, but probably also to support me. We said a tearful goodbye one night sitting in a haystack, before a man we found in this border village took us to a strip of bare land and said, "That is the border; run."

Maria's actions, and her loving presence, were a lifelong inspiration for me. I learned from her that life does not have to be what the Nazis made it, that there is love in the world, caring, and the willingness for self-sacrifice. A few years ago a friend, also a "child survivor" of the Holocaust from Hungary, asked how I would summarize in one sentence the lesson I took from my experience in the Holocaust. My summary was, "Even in the worst of times, there are some people who care." He then gave his summary, saying, "People are cruel and one must do all one can to protect oneself." What Maria did and who she was shaped me, my path in life, and my work—studying altruism and the way to raise caring children, the roots of violence between groups, engaging with efforts to help groups reconcile after violence, and promoting "active bystandership" in as many ways as possible.

For many years I continued to go back to Hungary, even after all my blood relatives died, to see Maria. When she was in her late 80s, she and I and a few close friends had lunch in a restaurant. Her hair was all white, her head slightly trembling. I told her that she was the inspiration for the work I have been doing all my life. This modest woman, whom I never knew to put herself forward or take credit for anything, smiled and said, "I know."

26

Bystandership—One Can Make a Difference: Interview with Ervin Staub

NANCY R. GOODMAN AND MARILYN B. MEYERS

I rail against the notion of incomprehensible evil.
ERVIN STAUB (INTERVIEW, *2011*)

Ervin Staub is an exemplary witness of the Holocaust, mass killing, atrocity, and individual acts of dehumanizing behavior. He is not only willing to face all of these terrible events but also fully brings his mind to them. In his scholarly work, he brilliantly creates concepts depicting what factors lead to the horrors of genocide and what can be learned to prevent genocide. Ervin was a hidden child of the Holocaust who was protected by active bystanders who risked their own lives to save him and his family. Ever since, he has been motivated to bring active witnessing and intervention to others. The titles of his recent books speak directly to the aims of his extensive research and direct work on interventions: *The Roots of Evil: The Origins of Genocide and Other Group Violence* (1989); *The Psychology of Good and Evil: Why Children, Adults and Groups Help and Harm Others* (2003); *Overcoming Evil: Genocide, Violent Conflict, and Terrorism* (2011); and *The Roots of Goodness: Inclusive Caring, Moral Courage, Altruism Born of Suffering, and Active Bystandership* (the initially planned title —E.S.). We were determined to end this book by demonstrating the importance of bringing the power of witnessing to all inhumanities and traumas. As we read the work of Ervin Staub, we knew we needed him. We are so grateful to him for helping make his ideas available to the readers of this volume.

Reprinted with permission from Goodman, N. R., & Meyers, M. B. (Eds.), *The power of witnessing: Reflections, reverberations, and traces of the Holocaust*. New York: Routledge.

While I am uncomfortable with reprinting this interview because of its highly complimentary tone, I do so because it gives a worthwhile and accessible overview of my work and its connection to my life experience.

On May 28, 2011, we flew to Bradley International Airport (Windsor Locks, CT) and, with Ervin's directions, found our way to him. His home offered a warm space for settling down to conversation at the dining room table. From the window open to the backyard gardens, we could see a beautiful copper beech tree spreading its branches high and wide, creating shade underneath as the leaves shone in the light of the sun. It seemed to us that this magnificent tree symbolized the largeness of Ervin's witnessing and scholarship to understand and prevent genocide and evil.

Ervin is a leading scholar in understanding the bystander phenomenon. As evidenced in the interview, his personal experience as a child in Hungary under the Nazi threat affected him deeply and influenced his life's work. His family was provided "protective passes" and presumed safe housing by the Swedish humanitarian Racul Wallenberg. Wallenberg was a hero who saved many lives. But it was his beloved housekeeper (Maria, affectionately called Macs), who was the active bystander who influenced Ervin most. She took Ervin and his younger sister into hiding and then repeatedly endangered her life to feed Ervin and his family and other people in their "protected house." In the interview, he also told us about other breathtaking situations when a family member was able to do something to ensure, for that moment and that day, that they would remain alive. He told us that he understands how fortunate he is. There were so many Jewish people who had received no active interventions from anyone around them and had no chance to take effective action on their own behalf.

The situations of active bystandership in Ervin's life left their imprint in enduring ways that he brings continuously to his worldwide efforts to change what happens for individuals and societies when faced with individual and mass cruelty. His long-standing and consistent dedication to the exploration of the motivation for active bystandership brings him not only to genocide and mass murder but also to bullying and other misuses of authority and power and aggression. He has made 17 trips to Rwanda, working to prevent reoccurrence of mass murder through reconciliation. His determination to intervene led to work with the Los Angeles Police Department after the Rodney King incident and with the city of New Orleans after Hurricane Katrina. He also goes into classrooms to raise awareness in children about treating others kindly and to work with teachers to create caring classrooms that help develop positive behavior by children.

In the interview excerpted here, Ervin emphasizes the interconnectedness of genocide, atrocity, altruism, passive and active bystandership, and perpetration. Throughout, he generously lets us be his witnesses as he interweaves and reflects on stories of his personal and professional life. This interview took place between Ervin Staub (ES), Nancy Goodman (NG), and Marilyn Meyers (MM). We chose segments of the interview that highlight Ervin's work and his personal history as a child of the Holocaust. In the interview, we move between past, present, and future. We return often to felt memories of his childhood witnessing and to his development of ideas defining the evolution of genocide and the evolution of caring, active bystandership, and prevention. A better future becomes possible by following how Ervin has brought the power of witnessing to his work and has used it to think fully about atrocity and to prevent further atrocities and genocide.

Evil Is Important

ES: Evil is important to think about, important to comprehend, and important to penetrate. It's not like you are trying to find some mysterious alien substance. It is that you are trying to understand all the layers that are involved. By layers I mean societal conditions, characteristics of the culture, and the psychological impact of the combination of social conditions and culture. I mean the social processes that evolve out of this mix, and then to understand the evolution of hostility and violence and the transformations of individuals, groups, and society. We can transform so that we become better, but unfortunately transformation can take place for evil, and that's what happens to perpetrators. There was this medical thinking among the Nazis, that the Jews were bacilli, the Jews were a virus. What has been written about the Wannsee Conference indicates the consequences of this. Those people, high-level Nazis at the Wannsee Conference, sit around and talk about how to do this, how to exterminate the Jews, and they are not doing it to human beings. They are not thinking about that person as a human being anymore. You are now thinking of how to deal with a problem that must be dealt with, and so this is the tragedy of perpetration, that the experience of the other as a human being with feelings and thoughts and needs is lost and gone and negated. To be able to do great violence to people, you have to devalue them greatly, and this happens in every genocide.

"I Saw All of This": Becoming an Active Bystander

Ervin talked about what he experienced as a child in having Macs standing by his family and the witnessing and many actions by family members that gave them a chance to hide and survive.

ES: I attribute my interest in the active bystander to a number of things. I was recently thinking about this because, as I mentioned, I wrote a little piece to honor Macs, this woman who was our maid in Hungary. In Hungary, middle-class families had maids, and she helped us as best as she could. She lived with us from the time before I was born. I escaped from Hungary when I was 18. She continued to live with my family, and she was the last survivor of that generation. I think that her actions, her taking action on our behalf, her endangering herself by going out and baking bread and bringing it back to the protected house that we were in at that point, and doing other things to help us, and her loving presence, had a large role in inspiring my work on helping behavior, and altruism, and questions about what leads people to help others, and why people remain passive in the face of other people's need, and how we can create more caring—and what I like to think of as inclusive caring. It is perfectly possible for children to be raised in a way that they care about people connected to them, people in their family and people in their group. But then they can draw a line between their group and the rest of the world, and especially draw a line between their group and some devalued group. They can then not care about the welfare of the people in that devalued group. So that has been for a long time my intense concern.

I think there is also another source of what I do, and I am just realizing some of these things now. It's interesting that I'm thinking about this now; it's a nice coming together. In the huge majority of cases, Jews had very little potential to affect their fate. But my experience was that my family did all kinds of things that affected our fate for the better. We were lucky to be in such a context. What do I mean by that?

My aunt and my mother went to stand in this crowd in front of the Swedish embassy in Budapest, and everybody was trying to get in because that seemed to be the one means of survival, and they somehow managed to get in. Now, in truth, I must say that later on I felt guilty about this, that they got in but other people didn't get in. The tragedy of the Holocaust was that in the limited instances when people had an opportunity to do certain things, often there was competition for survival, and people under those circumstances even if they are really good people, what do you do when there is that kind of competition for survival. The point is that they took action. They got these letters of protection. Macs, this woman, took action and took me and my sister into hiding and then brought us back when we were to move to this protected house. She went out to get bread for us and continued to do that.

Macs took a copy of the letter of protection to my father who was in a forced labor camp. She asked somebody to ask my father to come to the fence and gave my father a copy of this letter of protection. That piece of paper was totally useless to him.

Actually in the protected house where we stayed there were constant raids on the house, so it wasn't like we were there and we were safe. In ongoing raids on the house people were taken away, and people were taken away because they were not the right age or they were not something. So while this was of no use to him in a practical sense, my mother and I later believed, we talked about this, strangely, only after he died many years later, that this was probably what gave him the courage to escape. And when his group from his labor camp was being taken to Germany, they had a stopover in Budapest, and during that stopover he escaped.

He came to the protected house where we were, and the superintendent allowed him in. He knew where we were because Macs told him. So he came there and he was in hiding in the building, and once I saw a group of black-uniformed men marching down the street, and I called out, "They are coming!" I don't know whether my mother had this in mind before or just came up with this plan, but she had my father sit down in the corner of the room, pushed an armchair over him, and threw a blanket over the armchair. And these men came into the house, and they looked at everything, pulled out every drawer, and they didn't find him. The point that I'm making is that her actions saved my father. I saw all of this.

One Can Make a Difference and
One Can Change the World

ES: I must have had the feeling at some level that one can take action, one can make a difference, and one can change the world and people can be protected, and violence can be stopped. And all of these experiences probably contributed to my orientation to do work about prevention and active bystandership. From the very beginning, I was doing work to see how things can be changed. As I started to work at Harvard University, for the first few years I was doing—surprise—research on fear and how people can deal with fear and anxiety and how opportunity for control, for exercising control over events, and information about events and so on can diminish fear. So from the very beginning, and all along, I was interested in change processes.

MM: At what point was there for you a conscious connection between your experience as a child in Hungary and the work that you've been doing?

ES: At the very beginning I was working on disconnecting myself actually, disconnecting the work that I was doing from my experience in the Holocaust. I was trained at Stanford, in graduate school, to be a serious experimental researcher. So I saw myself as studying valuable, serious problems, and separating them from my experience. Then some years after I had been doing research on helping behavior, I was reading a book by Leon Uris, maybe it was *Exodus,* maybe it was something else, and I remember feeling teary and I'm thinking I want to do in my work whatever I can so that these things don't happen ever again, and the world will be a different kind of place. And then, as time went on it became very clear that everything that I do has to do with my earlier experience, that all my work and everything grew out of that.

From Passivity and Avoidance to Action and Responsibility

NG: When did studying bystander phenomena occur to you?

ES: It's so integral now to the way I think, that I'm not sure when it started. I began to think about doing research on helping when I talked at Stanford to Perry London, who was a visiting professor there and became my friend. He was the first person to do research on rescuers. So when I got to Harvard, early on I began to do some research on prosocial behavior. I was then influenced by the work by Latane and Darley on emergency helping. Before I was doing work on the Holocaust and genocide, as I was doing this research on helping behavior, it was very clear that sometimes people take action and sometimes they remain passive. In the course of that work I began to see the importance of the passive bystander in encouraging harmdoers. When I started to read about the Holocaust I thought I understood on the basis of my earlier work that somebody who is a witness and remains passive can distance themselves from that situation, even avoid taking in information. When I was at Harvard I had these young Harvard students collapse on the street in Cambridge in one of my studies, as passersby were approaching. An incidental observation was to me the most powerful information from that study. Some people walking on the other side of the street after a single look immediately rushed over. But some others turned their head away and never looked back, and sometimes at the next corner, rather than continue down the street, turned away.

I interpreted this as meaning that they didn't want to be anywhere near, that they wanted to avoid taking in information so that they have no responsibility.

Such avoidance of responsibility and distancing from events I thought early on was probably an important contributor to the Holocaust and to other genocides. And that seems to be the case. Almost always hostility and violence evolve gradually. Perpetrators change as a result of their own action—but so do bystanders. In the course of the evolution of violence there is often general passivity. That is, witnesses become passive bystanders, they don't take action, and as a result they change bit by bit.

MM: Right.

ES: So you are the witness and you can look at it and say, oh well, it's just a small change, and you already distance yourself a little bit from it, from the people who are harmed, and you already begin to justify, because otherwise how do you just stand by? So then, it moves a little further, and having not acted before, you know, when do you decide to act? Then another small thing happens. So it's only when the killing really begins that some people, as we know an extremely small percentage of the population, cannot accept it and they cannot just look on any more.

MM: Yes.

ES: And they take action and become rescuers.

NG: There is action in being a passive bystander.

ES: Internal action, yes. Yes, that's a good point.

NG: And it has implications that are defining of what can happen to people. I mean you could think that you're being passive, but you are doing something.

MM: Making a choice by inaction.

ES: Yes, and exerting influence. The perpetrators interpret this passivity as acceptance, or even approval of what they are doing, so that passivity of bystanders opens the way for more violence by perpetrators.

Understanding That Evil and Goodness Evolve

Ervin told us about his insights about how evil evolves and what the defining features of this evolution are. He developed these ideas through witnessing of atrocity throughout the world. For example, in his book, *The Roots of Evil: The Origins of Genocide and Other Group Violence* (1989), he presented case examples of the Holocaust, the Armenian genocide, Cambodia's autogenocide, and Argentina's mass killings and torture. He also brought his understanding to how rescue behavior comes about. His next inspiration was that since evil human behavior evolves, goodness also evolves, and there are ways to help it evolve, and these ways can be identified and put into action.

ES: Now, as I was doing this work, I came to profoundly believe that at the core to understanding was that evil and goodness evolve. I mean psychological evolution and social evolution. When people begin to do harmful things and there are no constraining forces, they are going to move further in that direction, because they learn by doing. They do bad things, then they justify those actions. They also develop communities around those actions that support them in those actions, so they are likely to move in that direction. But the same thing tends to be true of people doing good things.

If you do worthwhile things and if there are no constraining sources, and especially if there are supportive sources, then you are going to move in that direction. Often the rescuers were in connection to other rescuers. I mean at the beginning they might have started off on their own, agreeing to hide somebody for a period of time, sometimes as a result of a request by an intermediary, and often continued to hide them for much longer times. Some of those who then managed to move the people they hid to safe places, and then decided to continue, connected up with others and did it in connection and support. So this relates to what you talk about in terms of witnessing, in terms of whether there is a receptive other and so on. I think that is important. There are single, heroic actors, and many rescuers were such actors. But difficult, challenging things become more possible and are often done in connection and through the support of the shared vision of people.

Altruism Born of Suffering

MM: I was wondering how you saw Macs's psychology—how you saw her then and how you understand her motivation to be active on your behalf?

ES: In trying to understand Macs's motivation, I do not think it was an intellectual thing. I don't think it was a moral thing to work out, the moral principle in her head and to say, you know, this is what I must do. It was an emotional thing. It was just at the core level, this was the right thing for her to do. I don't think it ever came up in her mind to abandon us. I think we were her family.

One of the things in recent years that I have started to think about and write about is what I call altruism born of suffering. As we know from research, people who are victimized often become aggressive or they become dysfunctional in some ways or they remove themselves from other people, but for some people, when they have certain mitigating experiences, their own suffering becomes a source of caring and altruism. So for Macs, in addition to caring about us, the other thing was, I think, the lesson she took from her own suffering. When her mother died, she had a stepmother who was very cruel to her. She would do some little thing, she was a child, and her stepmother would make her kneel for hours on dried corn, which was very painful, and then from an early age on she was sent out to work as a maid. Fortunately for her, perhaps, part of it was taking care of children whom she loved, and then she came to work for my family and lived with us, starting five years before I was born. She was taking care of my three cousins. So by the time I was six, when these really terrible things were happening, she lived with us for 11 years. So, you know, we were her family, I think she herself suffered, she knew what suffering was like, both of those things were likely to contribute. And basically, also, she was a good person. Not a good person who was holding intellectual values that she was going to live by but in a very basic and core sense a good, empathic, loving person.

When we are caring, helpful bystanders, apart from helping someone who is harmed, who is suffering, I believe we make another contribution. Being helped at the time of one's suffering is, I think, one of those mitigating experiences that transforms victimization into altruism born of suffering.

Remembering Fear

ES: My first very clearly held memory is waking up very early in the morning and hearing sounds from the adjoining room and going into the adjoining room and members of my family were sobbing and my uncle had this pink sheet of paper and he had to go and report at a forced labor camp. And so there was this air of anxiety surrounding us. Anxiety suffused our existence. In the summer of 1944 all Jews from the countryside were taken to Auschwitz. We knew about this; we had relatives in the countryside. My father's sister and her family lived there, and they were taken to Auschwitz. But even a little before that, when Macs and I were walking on Circle Avenue in Budapest, pushing my little sister's baby carriage, and we saw German tanks and troops coming into the city, even though I was not yet quite six years old I knew that something very bad was happening. And we knew about the deportation of the Jews, and so, as I am saying, our life was suffused with anxiety. One story I remember was when we were still in our old apartment, all young men living in the house, boys, teenagers, were supposed to go into the courtyard and line up, and I think we were told that they were going to be taken to do some work somewhere. But, my aunt, not trusting this, told my cousin who was nine years older than I was, so he was 15 at the time, not to go, and he thought that he should go because he was told to go and the best thing was to go, and my aunt, who never did this, slapped him and said you are not going, and so he didn't go. I don't know for sure what happened, but I think those kids didn't come back.

NG: People did things. They interrupted the March to Death, which is what you keep focusing on.

ES: Yes, that's right. Now this is an interruption under extreme and tragic circumstances, and the point is, my focus is really to interrupt it early, because we can point to the signs that indicate that some form of violence is likely.

Interrupting Violence and the Example of Working in Rwanda

ES: Violence evolves, once it begins, and we don't know where it will end, and the later you act, the more difficult it is to interrupt it, because commitment develops. Ideologies, ways of thinking that support the violence against a group, become more and more influential. Those who are victimized are devalued more and more along the way. Systems are created that maintain and increase harmdoing, so it is extremely important to do these things early to increase the chances that one can actually interrupt. And if you interrupt effectively, that also means that you are transforming circumstances in such a way that the society improves. People sometimes say, well, you don't know if actually extreme violence is going to evolve; yes, there may be the likelihood because there are these indicators, but they are not certain so they don't take any action. They don't bother at all. But the thing is that even if it turned out that there would not be serious violence, the kind of actions that we need to take and could take would improve society and the lives of people a great deal. So nothing is lost and everything would be to gain.

NG: Everything is gained. Have you been able to do this? You and your team of people? Have you convinced a government to take steps?

ES: Well, you know, it's complicated. We have been working in Rwanda, and we started out doing workshops and trainings for all kinds of groups. We started first working with people who worked with local community groups that worked with groups in the community. And we trained these people and helped them to interweave their traditional approach with our approach. Then we actually did a very elaborate study to evaluate the effects of this training, not on the trainers, on the people we trained, but on the people *they* trained in turn, to see if our training translates into a larger effect when they work with groups. And we found all kinds of positive effects. In comparison to control groups the attitudes of Tutsis and Hutus in those groups toward each other improved. People showed a more complex understanding of the roots of violence. Their trauma symptoms lessened. Then we did these trainings with media; we did these trainings with high-level national leaders. We talked about the roots of or influences leading to violence; we engaged them in talking about how you prevent violence; we talked about the impact of violence on people, the traumatic impact. You know, my wife and my partner in this work is Laurie Anne Pearlman. She's a clinical psychologist and specialist on trauma. The term *vicarious trauma* was originated with her and one of her coauthors. She is the prime expert on vicarious trauma. So anyway, we did this and we had these leaders work in small groups.

So we did short lectures and then we engaged people in extensive discussion. When I talk in Rwanda about the influences leading to genocide, I never tell the Rwandese this is how it happened here, what happened to you. I tell them in general how these things come about; I give them examples from other places, which in itself is very important to them because it makes them feel that they are not alone; it has happened in other places also. But then they apply it to their own experience. I think the result is experiential understanding, when people take information and knowledge and apply it to their own experience, and then I think that has a different kind of power than just information.

NG: And, people who have been so traumatized.

ES: You begin to ask: How can genocide happen when there is this influence and that influence, how did it happen here, to us? And then you look at the whole society and what happened there, and you see that those elements were present, and somehow I think it becomes more part of you, that knowledge. So, one of the things that we did with leaders was to have them work in small groups, to look at policies that they have been introducing and to consider whether these policies are likely to make violence more likely or make it less likely.

Then we did something that it seems was a good thing. Everybody wanted us to expand the range of our work so that it could reach more people. Leaders also wanted us to do this; so we decided to go to educational media, and we got somebody involved, George Weiss, a producer who lives in the Netherlands, who not long before got in touch with me. He had this vision of creating 10 TV programs, *Hate in Ten Lessons*. He was interested in the roots of hate and the prevention of hate, very much along the lines of what I had been doing In fact, he got the inspiration from reading *The Roots of Evil*. So we invited him, and instead of doing that television series he came to work with us in Rwanda and we set up educational radio programs. Our radio drama immediately became very popular. It is called *Musekeweya*, "New Dawn." Just about everybody in the country, well, about 90% of the people, listen to. It has been going on since May 2004 continuously. It is the story of two villages in conflict, with hostility, violence, active bystanders, slowly over the years moving on to reconciliation and all kinds of positive processes. There is evidence, again from a careful evaluation study, that it had a variety of positive effects even at the end of the first year, from increasing empathy to leading people to speak their minds, to be more independent of authority, since overly strong respect for and obedience to authority contributes to group violence. And the whole community is very involved with it. Children talk to their parents about it.

In addition to the radio drama, we also have straightforward educational programs. Since 2006, we have been doing all these things in Burundi and the Congo as well. All these programs are ongoing.

"Facing History": Teaching Children About the Holocaust and Other Inhumanities

We talked with Ervin about the specific ways in which he has reached out to children to teach them about bystandership and how to be caring people. He told us about Facing History, an organization that he has worked with at times, and how it engages children about lessons in the prevention of cruelty.

ES: Facing History is a wonderful organization that was started many years ago by Margot Strom, a woman who at that time was a teacher in a school in Brookline, Massachusetts, to teach about the Holocaust. It evolved into a very substantial organization that develops materials, trains teachers to teach courses all around the country and also some internationally on the Holocaust. It also evolved from a focus on the Holocaust to using the Holocaust as an avenue to have students understand the role of the individual in the face of these events and concern with human cruelty and violence in general. So they are concerned with other kinds of genocides; they are concerned with racism and so on. It's the individual facing historical events, and the issue for them, like for me, is not to be passive bystanders. By helping students understand what happened in the Holocaust and how this evolved, it is more likely, they hope and believe, that a person will relate to events in a different way.

NG: How do you engage children and teach them to be active bystanders?

ES: Well, one thing that you can do is, you can talk very directly about "us" and "them." That we create divisions between "us" and "them," and we tend to look at some others in a negative light, whether we have a reason to or whether it is because other people tell us things. They recognize that this happens. I give many talks about these things. Sometimes also in the area where I live as a kind of volunteer activity. Just a few days ago I gave a talk to people in Greenfield, about harassment, intimidation, and bullying.

I actually developed a training program with some people here, an organization in the area. They read *The Psychology of Good and Evil* where I have written about bullying, harassment and intimidation, and raising caring children. So they approached me to work with them to develop a training program to train active bystanders, kids as active bystanders. So, one of the things that you can point out to kids, because they don't really think about this, is how when you do certain things it affects and harms others. What's the impact of this on other people? What happens? As part of this training program, we trained kids to be trainers of others. So one of the trainers said afterwards, "I used to do these things. I never thought about the effect of it, of what I am doing."

MM: Right, exactly.

ES: So, you know.

MM: To plant the seed to think about it.

ES: To have them understand how devastating it is. Actually, one of the important contributions to raising caring children is to point out the consequences of their behavior on other people. Not to tell them to be good, but to tell them when you do things, what is the effect on another person; also, to engage children in a conversation about these things. Does it ever happen that something is going on or something is happening to you and nobody is doing anything to help you? And so then they are right there.

MM: They get it.

ES: They understand these things, because it's happening to them—when they need help and somebody else doesn't do anything. Then as they think about it, this can contribute to changing their orientation to such situations.

As part of our training active bystanders we also help young people understand what can inhibit their action. For example, others looking unconcerned and remaining passive often stops us from acting. We also help them realize how much power they have to influence others. I found in one of my studies that just by saying something like, "This seems bad; maybe we should do something" can strongly influence another person's actions. We also train them to turn to other bystanders, to attract allies for joint action.

To raise caring children, it is important to work with adults. Warmth and affection by adults, combined with guiding children to understand caring values and to act according to them, are very important. I also emphasize engaging children in positive action, so that they will learn by doing. I have done research which shows that this increases children's later helping. And to act in caring ways not only to people close to them but toward everyone.

Connecting With the Past: The First Hidden Children's Conference

ES: Around 1990, maybe a little earlier, there was this first hidden children's conference in New York, a big event, something like 2,000 people showed up. I had no intention of going. A couple years before, I met Paul Valent in San Francisco at the ISTSS, the International Society for Traumatic Stress Studies meeting. He's an Australian psychiatrist, also a child survivor from Hungary, and he was leading a child survivor group in Australia. He immediately acted as if we were friends, and I responded and we became close. He and my wife persuaded me to go with him to New York. I said okay I will go for one day, then I stayed, it was two days, maybe three days. I stayed for the whole thing. I had the sense that, I think somebody described this in one of your papers, that I was with others who understood each other. We understood each other's experience. You didn't have to explain. These were people who knew. Then, when I went home I started to talk to my children about this. I talked to them earlier as well, but I did not think I talked that much about my experience. But I'm often surprised, I am not aware that I talked about some aspect of my life, and they seem to know. So I talk more than I think sometimes.

Remembering the End of the War

ES: Yes. The end of the war I remember quite vividly. I remember my father was hiding with us in that house, so at some point we saw some men running down the street and there was street fighting, and my father said, "Those are Russian soldiers," and a couple days later a Soviet tank pulled up in front of the building and we were liberated. I was sick with something and I remember I was bundled up and somebody carried me upstairs, and I remember seeing a couple Russian soldiers standing there and some people talking with them, including my father who was a prisoner of war in Russia in WWI. Pretty soon we heard that people were looting stores, and I remember that my oldest cousin, I don't know if it was any of my other cousins as well, my oldest cousin went off and saw what was going on to see if we could get some stuff. He came back without anything but vividly described people taking things. Of course, nobody had a thing at that time. I wanted to go with him just to see what was happening, but I was too young and they wouldn't let me.

Then I remember moving back into our apartment. We were told it was used first by the Germans and then it was used by Russians, and apparently the Soviets took up horses, it was on the mezzanine, so the horses had to go up some steps. They took horses into the apartment. There were these hoof marks in the floor.

NG: Now that fascinates a child!

ES: I don't know how many days passed, but I remember going out. We had this little store near the apartment where we lived before the war. My parents were selling trousseaus. There was a big pile of bricks in front of the building where the store was, and I remember I was moving bricks away, and I remember walking down the street and there was no bread. There were some people selling cornbread on the street.

NG: It's really in your mind; it was an important thing.

ES: Well, I mean, it was huge! We were going to die, I mean, that was the sense that, you know, there was a clear sense for a long time that our life was in great danger. These little pieces of letters of protection, I mean there were raids on the house and people were being taken away, and it seemed very shaky. So, and then we were liberated! You know, we didn't have to fear for our lives. It was a very big deal.

MM: You go from living in a state of fear and terror to a state of freedom.

ES: I don't remember that actively, the terror, but now as I'm talking about it I remember this kind of vague sense of anxiety that we had all the time. It was a miracle that they didn't find my father and take him away. Apart from that, we never felt secure at all. So, yeah, I mean that was a very big event, the Soviets arriving.

We Have to Ask Again: How Does Genocide Happen?

ES: Well, there are a number of charts and a number of descriptions in different ways in my books. Certain social conditions, what I call difficult life conditions, whether it's severe economic deterioration, political disorganization, or great social change, are starting points. They usually go together, not always, but often go together. While nobody is invulnerable, usually we have some feeling of invulnerability. When events frustrate that, groups can respond in destructive ways. It contributes when there is a history of devaluation of another group who is defined as different from the major cultural group. As I mentioned, some group, usually an already devalued group, is scapegoated for life problems. In addition, people create a vision of a better future, an ideology that is destructive because it identifies another group as an enemy, usually this already devalued and scapegoated group. Sometimes the starting point is conflict between two groups. The conflict can be over land, or water rights, or over power and privilege in society. But if it persists, and if it turns violent, usually each group sees the other group as responsible, as immoral. So the other group is an enemy, and seen in a very negative light.

Whether the starting point is difficult life conditions or group conflict, or often their combination, as you begin to harm the other, that changes you. And you move on and take more harmful actions. Devaluation turns to discrimination, and discrimination turns to small acts of violence, and then to greater violence. All this is supported by the ideology, and the people who become part of the ideological movement. Ideologies, visions of a better future, also develop in group conflict. The passivity of people who don't even say this is wrong encourages perpetrators. So there is this unfolding of increasing violence, and everybody changes along the way. The perpetrators are transformed. They come to see killing these people as the right thing to do. Albert Bandura, an important psychologist, has this concept of moral disengagement, but I think that he is only partly right. At the beginning there may be moral disengagement, but mostly it is moral transformation. Others are excluded from the moral realm, and in the end killing them becomes the right thing, at least for some people.

NG: Your work takes our understanding of trauma and witnessing to an additional level. It is very painful, it's very difficult, scary, and there are wonderful things you can do. You really can do things. You can go into a classroom and help children know how to behave as active bystanders; you can be alert and have your government and groups alert to watching this continuum begin and know that it can be effectively interrupted. I mean, this will give me a way to talk to my grandchildren about why, why bother to know about the Holocaust and other terrible things going on in the world.

Ending our Conversation: Saying Good-Bye

At this point, we were all aware that it was time to stop, to say good-bye. We had to reverse our direction and go back to the airport on the return trip. Being together, telling and receiving stories makes for an intimate and enriching experience. The power of witnessing brings emotion. We were all feeling close, sad, and vital. We together were facing genocide and creating the living surround where our minds and hearts could feel alive. We were grateful. We did not want to let go of Ervin and his plenitude of scholarship and personal presence as witness and intervener. We also knew that this was our last chapter; we were ready to finish our journey into the world of the power of witnessing.

MM: I think it is reflected right now that we are confronting the reality that there is so much more that we could talk about and the recognition that it's never done. In the book we are so aware of that—there are so many other places we could go.

ES: Well you know there is a famous writer who, in either a short story or part of a novel, writes about a painter who wants to paint the perfect picture. He is painting it and repainting it, and this is all done, all it needs is one little touch, and then he does one little touch, and now it's all wrong. . . . So the fact is at some point you have to say, this is the project, life continues, and there are going to be other projects.

We were able to say good-bye.

References

Staub, E. (1989). *The roots of evil: The origins of genocide and other group violence.* New York: Cambridge University Press.

Staub, E. (2003). *The psychology of good and evil: Why children, adults and group help and harm others.* New York: Cambridge University Press.

Staub, E. (2011). *Overcoming evil: Genocide, violent conflict and terrorism.* New York: Oxford University Press.

27

Summary Table of the Roots of Caring, Helping, Active Bystandership, Resistance to Violence, and Creating Caring Societies

Socialization Practices and Related Experiences to Generate Caring and Helping

- Warmth and nurturance. Helps to see people in a positive light, fulfills basic psychological needs
- Positive guidance—focusing on important values. The use of reasoning—for example, pointing out to children the consequences of their harmful and helpful behaviors on other people.
- Firm (but not) harsh guidance/discipline in moving children to act on important values and rules derived from them.
- Warmth, nurturance, and positive guidance enable people to fulfill basic psychological needs constructively rather than destructively.
- Modeling, the positive example of adults and peers.
  - Hypocrisy, saying the "right" thing but acting differently will, at best, lead children also to say the right things but act differently.
- Learning by doing—creating a positive evolution. Individuals (and groups) change as a result of what they do. Guiding children to positive action that benefits others increases caring and helping by them. Also learning by doing in adults—for example, the evolution of rescuers
  - Parents and schools giving children responsibilities to help in the home and school in ways that bring genuine benefit to others.
  - Guiding children to help in the community.
  - Discouraging aggression and violence, which also evolve through learning by doing.

Us and Them

- Devaluation of "others" makes helping less likely and leads to harmful actions.
- The sources of devaluation include a natural tendency to categorize; teaching/modeling by others, with words, images, actions; justification of discrimination and of other bad treatment.

Overcoming Devaluation/Developing Positive Orientation to "Others"

- Through significant positive contact. Joint projects, working for shared goals (e.g., cooperative learning).
- Structures—environments that provide opportunities for deep contact.
- The example of positive models, at home, in school, in the media and literature.
- Moving children to act in behalf of people seen as "others."

Personal Characteristics/Dispositions That Result from Socialization and Experience and Lead to Goodness—to Helping and Resisting Violence

- Dispositions for caring and empathy/sympathy/compassion, responsibility for others' welfare, moral values, and moral courage.
- Seeing the humanity of the "others" and inclusive caring.
- The capacity to take other's role, see other's need or pain; competence; and decision-making ability (about the meaning of events and appropriate actions).

The Impact of Being Harmed, of Having Suffered—on Individuals (at Home, in School), on Groups and Their Members

- Vulnerability—seeing the world as dangerous, other people as hostile. A potential for aggressive "self-defense" even when it is not needed; also for hostile aggression.

Altruism Born of Suffering, by Individuals and Groups

- Some people (and groups) feel empathy and responsibility because they themselves have suffered. They want to prevent other's suffering and/or help others who have suffered.
- Experiences that promote it and can create resilience:
  - Receiving help while suffering
  - Being able to act in behalf of oneself and/or others at the time

- Healing experiences and receiving care and support afterward
- Beginning to help others
- Prior love and affection

Developing Moral Courage

- Participation in decision-making at home, in school—gaining confidence in one's judgment, "voice." In societies/schools/homes in which children are raised in an authoritarian manner, this requires culture change.
- Encouraging children from a young age to act on their values and empathic feelings, to be morally courageous—even when there might be opposition or negative consequences or when the potential harm is not prohibitive. Research on physical courage in the military shows that training and practice/engagement contribute to courage.
- Developing the capacity for "critical consciousness"—independent judgment, to be able to decide when action is needed.

Personal Goal Theory: Resisting the Subversion of Moral Values and Caring

- Personal values/goals develop, in part, out of the ways children and adults habitually satisfy basic psychological needs.
- Every person can arrange his or her values and associated desirable goals or outcomes in a hierarchy.
- These are activated by the environment. Even if a person has strong caring or moral values/goals, circumstances can powerfully activate nonmoral ones so that they become dominant at that time. Persistent activation of these can change the hierarchy.
- Awareness of how circumstances do this can enable us to resist it, as can finding allies to support caring and moral values.

Developing the Understanding and Capacity to Become Active Bystanders in Resisting Violence

- Understanding the roots of violence and avenues to prevention, healing, and reconciliation. Applying information to one's own experience can transform knowledge into "experiential understanding."
- Education about influences that lead to violence by groups, with real-life examples, as well as ways to join with others in action, can lead people to respond to rather than ignore early events and engage in actions that may inhibit the evolution of violence.

Training to Be Active Bystanders (Bullying in School; in Other Settings)

- Learning about inhibitors of action—diffusion of responsibility, pluralistic ignorance, self- consciousness/not wanting to stand out, fear, concern about emotional and material costs.
- Developing skills (which can increase both feelings of and actual competence) for effective bystandership.
- Developing skills and inclinations to invite others as allies, joining in action.
- Creating institutions that facilitate alliances in working for a caring society.
- Helping people to become aware of their potential power as bystanders who can help others and affect social conditions.

Creating Caring Societies

- Propagating values of social responsibility, self-transcendence, and cooperation.
- Learning about and generating nonviolent practices that can change institutions.
- Creating conditions and empowering individuals to satisfy their material needs and to constructively satisfy basic psychological needs.

General Matters

- Members of the population developing community standards of positive behavior and activism and the motivation and skills to generate positive leadership.
- An independent perspective/judgment, a critical consciousness in evaluating events, including the words and actions of leaders and other authorities.

28

Creating Caring Societies
Values, Culture, Institutions

The Nature of Good and Bad, Caring and Not-Caring Societies

What are the characteristics of societies that make violence unlikely and generate goodness in children and adults? Of societies in which people help others, and engage in active bystandership on behalf of other people, the group, and also people outside the group? Of societies in which people of many kinds work on creating policies, practices, and institutions that serve the well-being of all members of society and of people in the outside world?

The concept of "caring societies" can mean different things. Evelyn Glenn (1999) in a symposium article titled "Creating a Caring Society" focuses on "the need to care for children, the elderly and disabled" (p. 84). While the caring I am concerned with includes this, it is much broader. Many people have imagined a good society, sometimes with utopian visions of a perfect society and at other times more realistically considering the complexities of human existence and therefore of good societies. In writing about a good society, authors often write in detail about the bad societies that need to be changed.

A good or caring society cannot be simple or one dimensional. A society organized around any one principle would repress legitimate human impulses, human voices, and the satisfaction of legitimate needs. A good society must allow and help individuals and members of groups to live complex lives, express their divergent views and conflicts, but do so peaceably and find peaceful ways to resolve them. A central characteristic of the good society I am concerned with is caring about everyone's welfare. A caring society provides the conditions and empowers people to at least minimally satisfy material needs and constructively satisfy core psychological needs. It thereby lessens both the frequency and intensity of conflicts.

Amitai Etzioni (2000) notes the contradictory aspects of a good society, such as liberty and social order, and community and individuality (p. 188). A good society, which may be thought of as one large community comprised of many smaller ones, does require reasonable order, which makes life predictable and gives people a feeling of security. So laws, social norms, and appropriate respect for authority must be part of the good society. But the social order ought to be created on the basis of democratic principles and positive values and not be repressive. Etzioni stresses the importance of community, people tied together by shared values and bonds of affection. But he also notes that community can be highly restrictive, preventing spontaneity, creativity, and individualism. A caring community provides people with opportunities to grow.

Good communities and a caring society must allow people to think for themselves, to develop and use their critical consciousness, their ability to judge the meaning of events. It must allow and encourage people to make life choices and moral/ethical decisions and act on them, as well as participate in social decision-making. A caring society would also balance its concern for order with concern for social justice (Janoff-Bulman & Carnes 2013), with creating institutions and policies serving the well-being of all of its members.

Bellah, Madsen, Sullivan, Swidler, and Tipton (1991) describe in their book about the good society the highly problematic conditions in American life—unemployment, homelessness, the potential for ecological disaster, and more—conditions that have grown even more problematic since then. We can now add the huge numbers of people in prison, the shenanigans of our financial institutions, and the legislative and political deadlock. In their view, the problems are the result of the way our institutions function. And the reason for citizen passivity in the face of all this is our deeply held ideal of individualism. At least one added source of inaction is the feeling of powerlessness in the face of the huge forces that govern American political and economic life.

I have stressed in this book and elsewhere (Staub, 1989, 2011) the importance of ideology. In Bellah and colleagues' view, the intense individualism and the problems it has created is the result of the great influence of the powerful ideology of John Locke, with its teaching of the unlimited freedom of the individual and unlimited opportunity to create material well-being for oneself and the need to limit the power of government. In the views of the founders of the United States, individualism would be tempered by a public spirit and common purpose. Bellah and his coauthors argue that this used to be the case, but the military industrial complex and international corporations have greatly lessened concern about the public good, and people in the United States have lost democratic control over their lives. To improve matters, they suggest that we must reform institutions. Their analysis seems even truer in the years leading up to 2015. To change matters, in the United States and elsewhere, citizens must become active bystanders.

This requires that we pay attention to how institutions shape our lives and realize our responsibility in shaping them, and that we exert influence to practice democracy in our families, schools, workplaces, and communities, participating in our institutions both locally and nationally. As we do that, our horizons broaden and we come to see ourselves as part of a larger whole. Positive change can begin with active discussion, debate about policies and practices, societal dialogue, and what Etzioni (2000) calls moral dialogue about the kinds of values that society is to live by and institutions are to represent.

I see engagement in such discussion—by neighbors, friends, members of churches and other institutions—as essential for the beginning of collective actions, and of social movements for change. It is important to generate along the way and propagate a constructive vision or ideology—of positive values, community, common interests, and shared goals that include everyone. Public education is also important (see later discussion).

Bellah and associates (1991) also stress the importance of international collaboration to address significant international problems. A few important ones, from my perspective, are poverty, great inequalities, cruelty by authorities and the mistreatment of groups of people that give rise to violence and huge numbers of refugees, the limited concern by international corporations for the well-being of their workers and even customers, terrorism and the conditions that give rise to it, ecological issues and global warming, and nuclear weapons and arms sales. A caring society will cooperate with others to address these, through international institutions, educational campaigns, and the example of its own actions, and direct help materially and in expertise in promoting economic and social development, fostering conflict resolution and reconciliation.

Principles to Guide the Creation of Caring Societies

The following is a summary of principles I consider central to creating a caring society. These principles describe the "what" that is needed. But also essential are the "how" these are to be brought about and the "who," the individuals and entities that are in best position to bring them about.

Respect for the "other." One aspect of this is opportunity for all groups to participate in societal (and international) processes. This requires coming to value and develop a positive orientation toward people outside one's group, within one's country and outside one's nation.

Promoting positive values to live by as individuals, a society, and the global community— the relationships between societies. An important value is cooperation rather than competition—doing better than others—as the primary value and frame for social relations, for individual achievement and success and the relations of groups. Another important value is justice.

Transforming and creating local, national (and international) institutions so that they express positive values in their practices. Especially important are just institutions, which ensure respect for the rights of all people and freedom from repression and violence. Just institutions that serve just societal arrangements will promote a reasonable degree of equality, not only in opportunity but also in outcomes, while also allowing a reasonable degree of variation in outcomes, since human beings will always vary not only in their capacity but also in their motivation for achievement and success.

Values and practices of empowerment, which include a good education for everyone, that prepares all children, including those from challenging and emotionally and cognitively limiting backgrounds, to develop their potentials. Internationally this means economic and political relationships and cooperation that allow and further social and economic development in every country.

Societal conditions and arrangements that help people fulfill their basic material and psychological needs. That it makes a great difference in people's life to be able to fulfill core material needs is obvious. But so is the ability to fulfill the universal psychological needs I have emphasized—for security, the ability to be effective, to develop positive identities and connections, and a reasonably positive understanding of reality.

The last entry also means that society takes care of its members who, due to age, illness, or other reasons cannot care for themselves. It also means creating ways for people affected by individual and group traumas to heal, whether the abuse of children, or oppression and group violence. Such healing may sometimes require psychological interventions, but especially group healing can to some degree be facilitated by constructive societal processes.

Values to Promote Caring Societies and a Caring Global Community

Values are beliefs about what is good and desirable and accompanying emotions or feelings that give them power. They point to desired outcomes, or goals, as I have proposed in "personal goal theory," and tend to shape attitudes and actions. Values are promoted in the home and are embedded in the institutions and practices of society, its literary and artistic products, in television and other media. Societal values that have shaped parents (and other adults) are transmitted to children in words, the way they guide children, how they themselves behave in the family and in the outside world, through literature, the media, and the arts.

The following are a few positive values that have associations with positive behavior and, broadly held, would contribute to a caring society. It is people with such values, combined with moral courage (see previous chapters) and relevant skills, who are potential agents in shaping values and institutions. I have discussed prosocial value orientation, with its positive view of human beings, and its central element, a feeling of or belief in one's personal responsibility for others' welfare, and the various positive behaviors and orientations it is associated with. Its association with constructive patriotism suggests that prosocial value orientation does not have to do only with the welfare of other individuals but also has a role in the welfare of society.

Another personal disposition, *self-transcendence* orientation, with its values of universalism and benevolence, is associated with more cooperative, altruistic behavior, more openness to helping people in need (Schwartz, 2007), and less harmful behavior. The attitudes and actions of people who have a primarily *self-enhancement* orientation, with values of power and achievement, tend to be the opposite of these. Such values can also characterize societies, expressed in their institutions and practices. Sweden has been described as an example of self-transcendence orientation—caring, protecting the poor and aiding poor countries, and protecting the environment. In Fry and Miklikowska's view (2012) the United States is an example of self-enhancement orientation.

Particular values can be held by a few individuals, or they can be widespread and legitimately considered societal values. Societies consist of many subcommunities, with at times greatly varying values. Overarching values can weave together segments of a society. But particular values are truly societal only if they are embedded in institutions and practices. This is the case, for example, for valuing equality. "Social justice is a property of social systems" (Jost & Kay, 2010, p. 1122). Great income inequality is associated with many negative aspects of social life, including less community participation and more violent crime, and usually also with political inequality. A reasonably degree of equality is important not only for those who are less equal but for all of society. It is associated with greater happiness and health. Among wealthy societies the quality of life of *all* citizens is best among those who have the least difference between rich and poor people (see Janoff-Bulman & Carnes, 2013).

Societies with severe inequality and great poverty of segments of the population disempower many children. A young boy or girl, who has to work from an early age, whether to weave rugs or work in a kitchen or as a brickmaker, does not have the educational opportunities that are the best instruments to improve one's life. Good schools are an important avenue for enablement. In the United States, where each community supports its schools, children in poor communities are disadvantaged. Some states make up for this to some extent by providing extra funding. But most other democracies have policies that aim to equalize educational opportunities (Zakaria, 2013).

A good education, and caring by a community that provides it, have beneficial effects beyond the economic. There is increasing awareness and research showing that well-being is strongly associated with material status at low income levels, but only to a very small extent once basic material needs are satisfied. Social relationships, trust in other people and one's community (Tov & Diener, 2008), and, as I have been suggesting, the fulfillment of psychological needs are important influences on well-being and happiness. A caring society fosters trust and positive relationships.

Beyond Us and Them: Interdependence and Cooperation: What and "How"

As I have discussed in earlier chapters, deep engagement across group lines, joint projects, and cooperation in working for shared goals contribute to positive attitudes toward others. Socialization into inclusive caring does the same.

The structures and practices of institutions, for example schools, can maintain or help overcome divisions. In the American South, even after the integration of schools, in some schools Black children were made to sit in the back of the room. In Rwanda, with discrimination against Tutsis between 1959 until the end of the genocide in 1994, in some schools when children began school they had to identify themselves in front of their classmates as Hutu or Tutsi.

Schools (and workplaces) can be truly integrated or segregated because of housing patterns, related to differences in wealth and group membership. This is the case in Amsterdam, where most Muslim children go to schools with very few Dutch children (Staub, 2007b; see Chapter 20), and in many places in the United States. Or children may separate themselves within schools into groups on racial, ethnic, or religious bases. Schools can do a great deal to create interaction, if they choose, for example, using cooperative learning techniques (Aronson, Stephan, Sikes, Blaney, & Snapp, 1978). Not all separateness is a problem. Only

Baptists would want to be members of a Baptist church. But Baptist churches may be further segregated by race or class, or other criteria, due to prejudice, tradition, housing patterns, and wealth.

Cooperation requires motivation, supporting structures, and the freedom and opportunity to interact. A child may live in a society and family that stresses competition, doing better than others and individual success. This reduces helping, which often requires giving the welfare of others precedence over the goals a potential helper is pursuing at the moment. A society may discourage cooperation, as a value, a practice, and an avenue to achievement. But the successful pursuit of goals almost always requires cooperation. Leaders of corporations will only be successful if they work well with their staff and workers (Aiken & Keller, 2009). Students do well if teachers and students effectively "collaborate" in the learning process. Conflict between groups is reduced through successful collaboration.

Research on cooperation shows wide-ranging benefits (Johnson, Johnson, & Tjosvold, 2012). Individuals in cooperative work/task situations work harder than those in competitive or individualistic activities (spend more time on the task and feel more satisfied working on it) and accomplish more. Cooperative experiences lead to better relationships and promote higher self-esteem, including "joint self-esteem," the perception of competence and value of all participants. They enhance taking the perspective of others and contribute to "moral identity." When it involves working with people in other groups, consistent with material in earlier chapters, it leads to including the others more in the moral universe.

Cooperation fulfills psychological needs: connection, effectiveness, even security. It affirms each person, gives people a positive understanding of the world, and develops trust. In a society that values and promotes cooperation, our human tendency to engage in comparison is likely to be lessened. Success will be judged more by one's own progress, and less by whether one does better than others. It then becomes easier to create a balance between achievement and moral and caring values.

Cooperation means interdependence in achieving goals. Recognizing interdependence (the whole world needs to act together, for example, to address global warming), and creating interdependence, the conditions for working together to accomplish shared goals, and acting collaboratively, expand identity and promote peace. For example, Fry and Miklikowska (2012) write about the successful peace system that the 10 tribes of the Upper Xingu live in. The tribes specialize in different products, "such as hardwood bows, salt, or pottery," and this economic interdependence contributes to a social identity that extends beyond each tribe (p. 232).

In other places as well interdependence leading to collaboration has contributed to peace (Fry & Miklikowska, 2012). Sometimes there is natural interdependence; at other times it needs to be fostered. After World War II a number of leaders called for the reshaping of Europe. Establishing a European Coal and Steel Community in 1952 was a stepping stone toward the establishment of the European Union. I have proposed that a vision and creation of an economic community may contribute to the resolution of the Israeli–Palestinian conflict. There is now collaboration between Israelis and Palestinian on various economic projects, some involving high-tech design and production. Expanding these and creating greater interdependence could lead to adopting a constructive vision for the two societies, replacing the destructive visions of a world without Israel and of a Greater Israel that incorporates Palestinian territories (Staub, 2011).

Communal or collectivist societies put more emphasis on the family, the group, and group goals than individualist societies. Less technologically developed societies tend to be communal, and some live in the peace systems to which I referred. But often in collectivist societies there is a sharper line drawn between ingroup and outgroup (Triandis, 1994; Staub, 2011). People are also less likely to speak out, resist, or oppose when such a society begins to harm some category of people within the group, or even when presumed individual wrongdoers are harmed.

Our experience in Xian, a large city in China, was perhaps an example of this. A woman and a man were following and poking at a man on a side street at a substantial distance from us, as my wife Laurie and I passed by. We had only a limited view and no understanding of what was happening. When we later walked back along the same route, the target of the attack and the attackers were on the main street. The man who was attacked was injured, his attackers still poking at him with a piece of metal. A substantial crowd gathered and was watching. We were trying to get people to intervene. Since we do not speak Chinese and no one seemed to speak English, I was gesticulating, miming some action. No one did anything. Without the ability to communicate, I could have only intervened physically.

Laurie was moving around the crowd looking for an English speaker. She found two young men. Calm and unconcerned, they said that the man who was pursued stole something (which they obviously did not see) and this was a normal consequence of that. We persuaded them to call the police, which they either did or pretended to do. The attack on the man stopped only when he was lying on the ground, moaning. We waited, but the police did not come. While groups of bystanders are often passive at other places as well, someone calling attention to the need for action is often able to activate them.

Conventions and Caring

Caring values may be subverted as societies and families stress conventional values and "appropriate," conventional behavior without the proper balance between these and caring values. Rules and plans or scripts of appropriate behavior are important. However, children and adults may overlearn these and are then less likely to engage in moral and helpful behavior, especially when these require some deviation from convention.

In one of my studies, male students from various colleges in the Boston area, who weeks before when rating their values/goals rated cleanliness as an important value for them, were less likely to go into an adjoining room when, while working on a task, they heard moaning from that room. They also helped less when the distressed person (who said he had a stomach problem) came into their room (Staub, 1974). Since our values form a hierarchy, the importance of cleanliness, a conventional value, suggests a lesser importance of other values.

In two studies with children I described at the beginning of Chapter 1 and referred to again in Chapter 19, adherence to rules of conventional behavior—that one does not stop working on a task one has been given and does not go into a strange room—seemed the reason that older children helped less than younger ones (Staub, 1970). In another study, only when they were told that they were allowed to go into the other room for an irrelevant reason did many children help (Staub, 1971). I have proposed that the behavior of "teachers" in Stanley Milgram's studies, administering what they believed were increasingly intense shocks to a "learner," may have been affected by the desire to behave appropriately (Staub, 2014). Having agreed to participate and placed into the role of teachers, there was an implicit contract to fulfill the tasks of a teacher in that setting. Especially people guided by conventional values would find it difficult to stop cooperating once they entered such an arrangement.

Children and adults learning a balance between convention, appropriate and polite behavior on the one hand, and morality and caring on the other is crucial for both helping and resisting influences that lead to harming others. Parents, teachers, the culture, and its products in literature and media ought to teach children that under certain circumstances other people's need supersedes rules of conventional behavior.

Living in and Creating Institutions

To bring positive values and goals to life, in a society and internationally—as part of a global community (Deutsch, Marcus, & Brazaitus, 2012)—requires building good institutions. Lasting change requires the "creation and reform of institutions . . . and institutional . . . and large social change" (Soltan & Elkin, 1996, p. 2). For this to happen there must be people who already hold positive values and at least the beginning of a positive vision, with the motivation and moral courage to act. Ideas have great power (Staub, 2011). But most ideas, good and bad, that have exerted lasting influence have done so through institutions created around them. The Nazis created a party, and paramilitary groups such as the SA and SS, and after they took over Germany educational and other institutions to propagate Nazi ideals. Americans were inspired by the Declaration of Independence, but also created a Constitution and the institutions to bring about the way life it was to serve. A handful of people created Human Rights Watch and another handful Amnesty International. Beyond ideas and values, a vision and motivation, change agents need to be effective people who create lasting institutions.

Our lives are shaped by institutions: schools, factories, businesses, corporations. Our families may also be regarded as institutions. All of them communicate values to us and affect us by the values expressed in how they operate, the rules they promote, the freedom or inhibition created by their structures. Institutions can be democratic, or they can be autocratic, uninterested in our personal views and desires. Members of a family or the staff of a school may show interest in and respect for a child's thoughts and feelings, or not. Members of an institution may be equally treated, or some may have privileges that others do not. The core values and orientation toward people may be cooperation or competition, trust or suspicion and hostility.

Corporations can show respect for employees by creating safe and clean work places, by inviting and using their ideas, by facilitating caring for their children. They can also be more or less moral in the products they make, advertise, and sell. At one point Coca-Cola used one—liter glass bottles, which occasionally exploded, injuring people. When the use of these bottles was prohibited in the United States, the company continued their use in third-world countries. Baby formulas have been intensely promoted in third world countries at the expense of breastfeeding, which is better for children.

We are greatly affected not only by social/community institutions that we "live in," such as families, schools, and workplaces, but also by many others: our religious community, ethnic community and its organizations, political party organizations, chambers of commerce, rotary clubs, soup kitchens, medical centers and hospitals, television and the media, the justice systems (the police and the courts), banks and other financial institutions. They all express, propagate, and may impose values and orientations on those engaged with them.

A safe society is crucial for the development of positive values, their expression in action, and economic development. The police may protect members of society, ensuring to their best ability the safety of all. But authorities may also routinely engage in criminal activity or intimidate and harm members of the population or of particular groups. An example is the Democratic Republic of Congo, a very poorly functioning state. There have been wars, and violent militias have been operating there since 1996. Due to these conditions, and because they often do not get paid, military units rob the population, kill people, and rape women. In authoritarian/totalitarian political systems, the military and police are usually tools of repression.

But even in democracies, police behavior varies. In the United States, police in some cities has been abusive toward civilians. In many places they act more harshly toward Black and Hispanic Americans. Black and Hispanic Americans are stopped more often and searched more often than Whites, whether on foot or traveling by car. This is so even though the police find drugs or weapons more often from searches of White vehicles (Greenwald & Pettigrew, 2014).

The justice system in the United States brings unequal justice, with harsher punishment of minorities than Whites for the same crimes. A quite widespread practice across the United States is the police confiscating property such as money, jewelry, cars, and houses because of some relationship, presumed or real, to drugs or criminal activities. The laws that enable this practice were aimed at high-level drug dealers and criminal groups. Now the practice has expanded to persons never convicted of a crime, or never even indicted. In some locations people have been stopped as they drive through, their money or other property taken, and they are not allowed to continue until they sign a release, absolving the police of responsibility. A substantial portion of the monetary gain goes to the police, to support police work—and sometimes members of the police. Minorities are much more frequent victims of this practice (Stillman, 2013). A caring society would not tolerate such abuse.

A justice system can serve repression, as it did in Nazi Germany and does so in many countries. It can discriminate against and in favor of individuals and groups. In some countries, including the Congo, judgeships can be bought. In the United States, huge financial contributions to the campaign of a candidate for a judgeship can succeed at buying the seat. Institutions have a life of their own. There is a tendency for people, both who work in them and who interact with them to follow their standards, values, modes of operation. But institutions can also be changed—by people.

The Individual in Harmdoing and in Creating Positive Change

It is individuals who have to act in order to generate changes in values, culture, and institutions.

However, in recent times social psychologists have stressed circumstances or situations determining action. The research of Stanley Milgram on people's willingness to do what they are told as "teachers" and administer intense shocks to "learners" has focused on the role of the situation. The demonstration by Philip Zimbardo of college students assigned to be guards in a study of prison life, with the guards becoming increasingly harsh and punitive, was also interpreted this way. Put people into a particular setting, with a certain structure, a situation powerful enough, and they will become punitive or violent. Robert Jay Lifton coined the term the "atrocity producing situation."

My own conception of the roots of group violence is a system view, which also stresses circumstances—the larger situation, societal conditions such as economic deterioration, political chaos, great and rapid social change, and their impact on people—as a starting point. Violence is more likely when these environmental conditions combine with cultural characteristics such as a history of devaluation of some group, authority orientation, and past group trauma. These cultural characteristics are both situational influences—since other people and institutions shaped by culture surround and affect people—and to the extent they have become internalized by people, taken in as their own, also personal dispositions. Immediate circumstances also have a role. Both people who move a society toward genocide and people who become terrorists can be affected by membership in a smaller group, as well as by relationships with people already involved in the processes leading to violence (Sageman, 2004). So can be people committed to some aspect of goodness.

Among the characteristics of a good or caring society would be the opposites of those leading to group violence, such a positive attitudes by members of a subgroup of society to each other; appropriate, moderate respect for authority that allows people to think and make choices; and healing from group trauma (Staub, 2011; Chapter 22). But if particular societies are characterized by destructive or less constructive values and institutions, and if it is situations that determine behavior, how can change come about?

The long tradition in psychology of understanding behavior as a function of the combination of personality and situation remains correct. As I discussed in Chapter 22 both in the "obedience" studies of Stanley Milgram and the Stanford prison study of Philip Zimbardo, the behavior of participants was not only a function of the situation. Personal characteristics had an important role (Staub, 2007a). Individuals do matter and can generate change. While social conditions affect large groups of people, it is people with certain characteristics who create destructive ideologies and movements. Others who join are likely to do so because of existing personal dispositions—attitudes toward an "ideological enemy," or toward some outsiders, or vulnerabilities that lead to an especially strong effect on them of difficult life conditions. They may also do so because of preexisting relationships to people already involved. A subset of them turns into the executors of the ideological vision and direct perpetrators of violence.

One study of SS members, after Germany was defeated, found that they grew up with authoritarian childrearing and were characterized by authoritarian personal tendencies, as well as by a focus on their careers in the SS (Steiner, 1980). People with authoritarian personalities may feel lost when life is chaotic. Such people fitted the SS perfectly, with their obedience to the authority of those above them and the desire to exert authority over people below them. Some people, such as conductors of trains leading to extermination camps or people in offices dealing with victims' property, may have been involved because of their already existing roles in institutions.

As in experimental situations, so in studying group violence, there has been insufficient attention to and study of the characteristics of the individuals involved, especially of those in leadership roles (Mendel, 2002; Staub, 2011). We also know little about people who remained uninvolved, distanced themselves from participation in genocidal process, or the very few—other than rescuers who acted once a genocide began—who attempted to resist the societal evolution toward genocide. We also do not know about people, if any, who left their jobs, perhaps on the railroad in Germany, because it came to have a role in the perpetration of a genocide.

It is obvious that people with positive inclination and visions are important in moving societies toward peace. Without Nelson Mandela, South Africa would have most likely experienced much violence between White and Black people. Lincoln engaged in gestures of reconciliation immediately, when the Southern armies put down their arms (Lieberfeld, 2009).

I briefly discussed earlier in this chapter personal characteristics that might incline people to work to create caring societies, such as self-transcendence and prosocial orientation. An additional characteristic is political orientation. Janoff-Bulman and Carnes (2013) see the morality of conservatives as more avoidance oriented, more proscriptive, focusing on the prohibition of certain conduct. The morality of liberals is more approach oriented, more prescriptive. Political conservatives tend to focus on social order and respond negatively to deviation in behavior from what is customary in their society. They are more fearful of disorder and more negative about those who are different. Liberals are more concerned with equality.

We do need social order, but we also need change. Janoff-Bulman and Carne' analysis is consistent with observation of political life, which shows that liberals are more motivated to create a society of cooperation and equality. However, it is always a combination of characteristics that shape behavior. The beliefs in justice and responsibility are not just liberal values. Some conservatives work to address poverty. People with different combination of values may be motivated to create different aspects of a caring society.

Political orientations are affected by early childhood experience. Approach and avoidance tendencies can be seen in early childhood, an aspect of temperament, which is partly genetic. But parents' authoritarian attitudes when a child is one month old and their restrictive parenting predicted later political conservatism, while parents' equalitarian attitude predicted liberal political attitudes (see Janoff-Bulman & Carnes, 2013).

Inherent to working on positive social change is opposition to what is in existence. Both relevant values and an independent perspective are required for people to notice and emotionally respond to inadequacies in their society. Working for change involves costs and often requires moral courage. Much of the research on collective action focuses on responses to injustice and the participation of members of underprivileged groups. But some of the privileged also participate (Van Zomeren & Iyer, 2009).

Beyond positive values, the way a person's identity has developed, the way it is constituted, also matters. I have proposed that people can develop disconnected, autonomous, embedded, and connected selves (Staub, 1993). *Embedded selves* are characterized by deep connections to other people and/or a group but also by difficulty in separating from others' expectations. People with *connected selves* are also connected to other people but are capable of standing on their own. They are therefore more able to advocate for and initiate positive change. People also have group self-concepts, conceptions of their group "which tend to be shared by the group and . . . strongly shaped by culture" (Staub, 1993, p. 346). People who strongly hold such group self-concepts, and strongly identify with the group as it is, would be less likely to try to change it.

Different forms of patriotism also affect the likelihood that a person would work for change. Blind patriots in essence believe "my country, right or wrong." They tend to see what their country does as right and moral. They are also proprietary. Young Americans who on a test showed themselves to be blind patriots disliked the Japanese playing baseball because it is an American game. Constructive patriots believe that because they love their country, they must speak out when their country deviates from humane values or its own core values. Constructive patriotism is positively associated while blind patriotism is negatively associated with prosocial value orientation (Staub, 1997; Schatz, Staub, & Lavine, 1999). Constructive patriots would be more likely to oppose immoral, harmful practices by their society and work to promote moral and caring values and institutions.

One of the human tendencies that makes positive social change less likely is self-censorship, people not speaking or writing about important information available to them, usually because it is contrary to currently predominant views in the society or of the authorities. Self-censorship can be the result of culture and social practices or proximal influences such as the editorial policy or climate of a newspaper or TV station. These influences can lead people to pay little attention, even hardly notice certain events, or avoid learning more about them so that they will not feel obligated to respond to them (Staub, 1989). Such avoidance can be automatic or only semiconscious. However, self-censorship can also be conscious and deliberate. Daniel Bar-Tal described many harmful examples of self-censorship in Israel (Eldar, 2013). It is certainly practiced in all societies, presumably more in those that are in the midst of conflict or are intensely politically polarized.

Changing Values, Norms, Institutions, and Culture

To create a caring society requires the joining together or intertwining of many influences. In writing about societies in conflict and based on his work with reconciliation, Lederach (1997) noted that change can start top-down, by leaders, or bottom-up, by people in the community. Or influence for change can come from the middle, such as the media or church leaders, who can exert both upward and downward influence.

Changes in some domains affect changes in others. Teachers may be influenced by their superiors, by parents, by changing values and standards in their society, by their students, and by training they receive. Changes in teachers affect children, which in turn can affect parents. Change is usually a result of an intermixing of influences. It has been a truism among teachers that in the past few decades problematic changes in life in the United States have resulted in many students less prepared to learn, to follow rules and behave in an orderly way. This has affected teachers' capacity to teach.

Many people in a position to and motivated to create positive change may have characteristics that limit their ability to do so. Parents and teachers who are insecure may easily feel challenged by children and react punitively. Or they may not know how to guide children effectively. Parents, teachers, leaders of organizations may be authoritarian rather than democratic. Potential change agents may not know how to influence their colleagues and leaders and may have difficulty creating a sense of community. Self-awareness, awareness of and the impact of one's behavior on people, and developing relevant skills are essential.

A central principle of effective change is attracting allies—or becoming an ally by joining already ongoing efforts. How we can attract allies depends on the situation. Seeing a person harm another, we can say to other people how we see the situation, "defining its meaning," and what we think is necessary to do. But attracting allies for large social causes requires exploring ideas together, drawing on relevant knowledge, and generating visions of the future and common goals.

Public education can be an important tool. In Rwanda our workshops providing information about the origins and traumatic impact of genocide and avenues to reconciliation, and our long running educational radio drama have created changes in people (see Chapters 18, 19). Evaluation showed that the radio drama led people to speak their mind, to participate in reconciliation activities (Paluck, 2009; Staub & Pearlman, 2009; Staub, 2011). Because most Rwandans have been listening to it for 11 years by now, it may have led to culture change.

Long-term, effective education can have powerful effects. So can direct engagement between people. Atul Gawande (2013) describes the often slow process through which new, effective medical practices become actually used. His primary example is a solution of sugar, salt, and water that "you could make in your kitchen" (p. 42). Combined in the right proportions, it can save the lives of people with cholera and severe diarrhea. But people all around the world, in their villages and towns, did not adopt this simple "oral rehydration therapy," resulting in huge numbers of unnecessary deaths, especially of children. In 1980 a Bangladeshi nonprofit organization decided on an approach usually regarded as "impractical and inefficient." It sent a group of 14 young women, a cook, and a male supervisor to go to villages, door to door, using seven easy-to-remember messages to train mothers to use the solution. The program became more effective when young woman, instead of going to 20 households a day, went to 10; when they had mothers themselves mix the solution; and when workers received pay according to how many of the messages the mothers retained when a monitor later followed up. As the program looked effective, the Bangladeshi government hired thousands of workers, who went to more than 75,000 villages. "The program was stunningly successful . . . the knowledge became self-propagating, . . . changed the norms" (Gawande, 2013, p. 43). Gawande stresses the necessity of such person-to-person approaches to change the behavior of both doctors and patients. Going door to door has, of course, been extensively used in political campaigns.

Naturally the media, person-to-person engagement, and change processes in general can serve harmful goals as well. Exposure to violent films (and playing violent video games) reduces later helping (Bushman & Anderson, 2009). Many US lobbyists, who often shape public policy in problematic ways, are presumably successful not only because they have money to spread around, but also because of their personal engagement with government officials. Many members of Al Qaeda have been attracted through friends and relatives (Sageman, 2004). Social media can move people to join terrorist groups.

It requires sensitivity and skill for people with extremely divergent beliefs about the good society to have even somewhat constructive discussion. Even though people tend to attend to media consistent with their beliefs, relevant public education embedded in themes of general interest may help create a more fertile ground for person-to-person as well as public dialogue. This is especially true for people with less extreme views. Actual research findings, for example, that people in all realms of society tend to be less satisfied when inequality gets very high (Wilkinson & Pickett, 2009) can facilitate discussion. If people develop shared opinions about desirable change, shared identities and joining in collective action may follow (McGarty, Bliuc, Thomas, & Bongiorno, 2009).

What Is Required for Popular, Nonviolent Uprisings To Be Effective

Initial mobilization of people for positive action is clearly not enough. A very large group of demonstrators sometimes do and other times do not have success in creating change. Demonstrations against the war in Iraq in 2003 did not stop the Bush administration from going to war. In Israel they did not change internal economic policies. Smaller but still substantial number of committed people in Occupy Wall Street did not bring lasting change. However, demonstrations in the Philippines against the rule of President Marcos led to his ouster. So did demonstrations against Milosovic in Serbia. I mentioned the success of German women during WWII in stopping the deportation of their Jewish husbands to exterminations camps.

Whether such popular nonviolent uprisings create change depends on a number of factors, singly or more likely in combination. One is persistence. Another is whether the dissatisfaction that motivates protesters is shared to some degree by a substantial percentage of the population so that there is at least latent support in the society. Potential support or opposition by powerful institutions matters. Further, are the demonstrators able to affect societal institutions and the political system? Is there a leadership that can attract popular support?

In the Philippines there was general dissatisfaction with the Marcos rule, and the army refused to go against the demonstrators. In the United States the movement against the

Vietnam War, with the large number of people involved and its persistence, affected the general population and institutions like the media and politics. It probably contributed to the United States signing a peace agreement and removing American troops in early 1973, although the war between South and North Vietnam ended only in April 1975 with the victory of North. The photos of suffering and brutality, US atrocities, and many American soldiers dying presumably both helped maintain the antiwar movement and affected the US government.

In Egypt huge demonstrations overthrew President Mubarak and his rule. But the remaining established institutions of potential or actual power were the Muslim Brotherhood and the military. The demonstrations were a people's movement, and no new popular political leadership arose. New leadership also could not develop because of the speedy elections. The problematic new constitution, too rapidly created, and the way the Muslim Brotherhood ruled were unacceptable to the most powerful institution in the country, the military.

Perhaps good scholarship can help predict the probability that a positive, nonviolent social movement, made up of many active bystanders, will be successful. Their success may be less likely in societies with a long authoritarian history and entrenched conservative institutions (like the Egyptian Army), and deep societal divisions (in Egypt between secular and religious groups). However, when there is great dissatisfaction and passion for change, foreseeing difficulties would not stop people from action. But it may help them to work on creating conditions that make success more likely.

Some Principles and Practices of Change

Practitioners working on and writing about changing business organizations suggest varied requirements. Consistent with my focus on a constructive vision, one of these is a "compelling story" (Aiken & Keller, 2009) about what the change would be and why it is necessary and valuable. Michael Shandler, an organizational development consultant, based on his experience with corporations noted that without the leader wanting change, it is very difficult to create it (personal communication, 2013). To create change, leaders have to be able to engage followers. A compelling vision that has relevance to people can help do that. While change is easier if leaders want it, the initiative from it can also come from below—in organizations and society in general. Every person can exert influence through discussion with coworkers, friends and neighbors, and by attempting to mobilize for action in his or her communities, or joining organizations that work for positive change.

Another requirement for change is "role modeling," by visible, important people. A further one is *"reinforcing mechanisms,* because systems, processes, and incentives must be in line with the new behavior" (Aiken & Keller, 2009). Capability building is also important, developing the knowledge and skills needed. All of these seem relevant to changes in values and practices in other institutions as well and in society in general.

Aiken and Keller (2009) see barriers to effectively applying these four conditions, which must be overcome for successful change. People do not automatically accept the story about why change is desirable and what the change should be. Information, or education, and personal engagement with people are useful, as is people having a voice, contributing to the vision and practices associated with them. As both their experience and my own suggests, it is easy to believe—both for bosses and "experts"—that one knows already what is desirable and how to accomplish it. If so, why not simply tell people? But people participating in creating the vision and plans for action results in much more change in behavior (Aiken & Keller, 2009).

Top down pressure and change in regulations and laws can change behavior, followed by changes in attitudes. But change in behavior and systems usually start with change in consciousness and beliefs—in ways of understanding the world. Education can foster such change. In our work in Rwanda information about the origins (and impact and prevention) of genocide led Tutsis, the victims of the genocide there, to change from seeing Hutus as simply evil to human beings who under the influence of many forces have done terrible things, and Hutus to see their former victims in a more positive light (Staub & Pearlman, 2006). Such change can open people to the vision of a society that cares about everyone. The routes to change can include contemplative practices such as meditation, in the course of which people observe and become aware of their ways of thinking. It can include dialogue. Change in thinking will solidify if it leads to change in behavior.

New behavior, to be successful, demands new skills, which require practice. A new consciousness, practice, and skills can enable teachers and parents to engage with children in new and constructive ways, police officers to engage with citizens. They can help members of governments to create good laws. Government official can inform themselves—through imagination, role-play, educational experiences, and observation—about how particular laws will affect citizens' lives. Rather than acting on abstract ideas, as best as possible leaders ought to engage with the potential material, social, and psychological impact of their actions. In Rwanda, working with national leaders, after providing information to them about influences that usually lead to or can prevent violence between groups, they eagerly applied this information to consider whether policies they were about to introduce would increase or help prevent future conflict and violence (Staub & Pearlman, 2006; Staub, 2011). Extensive engagement in such practices can have transformational effects.

An Example of Societal Change: Race in America

Exploring the very great changes in racial relations in the United States can show the intermixture of different sources of change, and raise the question of why further changes have stalled. There were many influences that led to changes in laws and practices related to race. The Supreme Court ruled in 1954 that state laws ordering separate schools for Whites and Blacks were unconstitutional. But this could only happen after some change in public attitude and mood. Black Americans fought in WWII, and after the war President Truman integrated the armed forces. This led not only to contact and familiarity between White and Black soldiers but also relationships between Black and White people around military bases (Reid, 2001; Staub, 2011). Among other influences on the Supreme Court, psychological research indicated that Black children identify with Whites rather than their own group.

Their experiences in the army also led to unwillingness by young Black men to accept again the humiliation of segregation in civilian life. And the Supreme Court decision empowered African Americans. They started an ideologically strong and disciplined non-violent movement (Reid, 2001). Their actions included the Montgomery bus boycott in 1955, marches, and sit-ins by young Black people in segregated restaurants. As they were attacked, as Americans could see waters hoses aimed at peaceful marchers, dogs attacking them, a bomb killing young children in a church, and more, and they remained nonviolent, the movement gained sympathy and support. Young White Americans joined sit-ins; young and old people and spiritual leaders joined marches.

Black churches were heavily involved. The words and images participants used, referring to the Bible, and their gospel songs, also helped generate support. Charismatic leaders were able to energize and maintain the courage of participants. In addition, what may be called internal bystanders in the South, the business community, as in South Africa at the time of the international boycott there, wanted to stop paying the economic price that was already evident (Reid, 2001). Further actions by Southern officials, for example, Governor Orval Faubus of Arkansas calling out his National Guard in 1957 to stop Black students from entering Little Rock High School, and Governor George Wallace of Alabama blocking the entrance to an auditorium at the University of Alabama in 1963 to prevent the enrollment of two Black students, led, respectively, President Eisenhower and President Kennedy to use the National Guards (state or federal) to enforce the entry of Black students (http://en.wikipedia.org/wiki/Brown_v._Board_of_Education#Unanimous_opinion_and_consensus_building). Busing children to schools and other practices were created to promote integration.

Why Has Progress in Race Relations Stalled or Even Reversed?

The civil rights movement was extremely successful in changing attitudes about segregation (Reid, 2001), reducing explicit prejudice, and over time greatly increasing the inclusion of African Americans in public life. However, race relations have not continued to improve. As we saw earlier in the chapter, the police and the justice system continue to act with prejudice. The schools at many places in the country are largely segregated due to housing patterns, with lower quality of predominantly Black schools. Subtle prejudice, for example, people more easily associating good things with White and bad things with Black people when this is measured unobtrusively, has remained widespread (Dovidio & Gaertner, 2004).

When the rules are unclear and judgments need to be made, people discriminate. Whites who judge equally qualified White and Black candidates for a job favor other Whites. According to Greenwald and Pettigrew (2014), favoring the "ingroup," people with shared characteristics, is a stronger force for discrimination in the United States than hostility to the outgroup. This may be so, but the preceding description of police behavior and the justice system suggest that there is also substantial hostility to minorities.

Society does not empower Black youths. Poverty at home and in their communities, the absence of the support children require, and unequal justice including severe sentences for minor drug offenses are among the conditions that have contributed to many young Black men ending up in jail. Understanding why race relations have not continued to improve may help restart a change process.

One likely reason is the still-existing, widespread prejudice. The good news in the election of Barack Obama as president was that it could happen. The bad news was the immediate, vicious attacks on him. This was an extreme example of one of the reasons that progress in race relations halted, the use by politicians of race and usually subtle or at least covert appeals to racism to win votes. As it is widely believed, the subscript in George H. Bush's attack on governor Dukakis of Massachusetts during their presidential campaign using Willie Horton, a man released from jail in Massachusetts who then killed someone, was race.

Another reason may have been the fracturing of the African American community. As some Black Americans moved into the middle class they left their old neighborhoods. Whites, if they lived in those neighborhoods, moved away. Left were the poor, those less able to make it in American society. A group that experiences adversity in a larger society does better when there is strong internal community and support (Tajfel, 1982).

Another reason is society's unwillingness to do what is necessary to make up for the impact of slavery and persecution. Slaves were prohibited from learning to read and write. Afterward, success in a business by a Black man could lead to a White business competitor accusing him of a crime, such as sexually approaching a White women, which led to lynching him (Staub, 1996). Such experiences, together with poverty, discrimination and disintegration of community limit enablement and possibly the motivation for achievement. Affirmative action helped. Head Start and other early education programs have provided cognitive skills, motivation, and the feeling of confidence needed for success in school. However, early education has not been widely enough available.

The American ideal of individualism and the self-made person is another likely contributor. It underemphasizes or even ignores the role of a person's immediate environment and overall societal conditions in promoting—or inhibiting—success. Instead, the assumption is that the individual is responsible, regardless of conditions and experiences in childhood and later life. In addition, research on contemporary prejudice shows that it manifests itself most in situations of ambiguity, when the rules of behavior are unclear. Individualism combined with prejudice makes it easy to ignore people who are disadvantaged because of the history and conditions of their group, and resulting personal history. Related to this is the absence of a vision and practices of a caring society. Such a society would identify what is required to enable children from various backgrounds to be successful as individuals, group members, and citizens and create the institutions and practices required for such success.

The murder of Martin Luther King and the loss of him as a leader, the Black Panther movement that abandoned the ideology of nonviolence, and the Vietnam War absorbing people's attention are also all likely contributors to lack of further progress. Later terrorism and the wars in Iraq and Afghanistan overwhelmed societal issues at home. And American society became increasingly conservative, and increasingly politically polarized, with less caring about disadvantage and race. Moreover, while successful helping and active bystandership tend to evolve into greater helping, as it did during the active phase of the civil rights movement, many people may have felt that enough was done already. This is especially so since the problems I described emerged progressively; initially it was the success that was visible.

Conclusions: A Brief Summary

The civil rights movement demonstrated in practice many of the elements required for creating positive societal change and ultimately a caring society.

- There were *important midlevel institutions* involved, such as the Black churches, preachers, and the media.
- It had strong, *charismatic leaders.*
- The *ideals* and the evolving movement mobilized many people, Black as well as White. They had to have the initial values and motivation to support it. They engaged, identified with the movement, and were willing to expand effort and face the dangers involved in working for its goals.
- Its *ideology* (of integration, equal rights, the dignity of all humans) could be connected to core American principles, enunciated in the Declaration of Independence and the Constitution, and to the Bible. Positive ideologies can usually be connected to important human ideas and universal human values.
- There were strong *cross-group alliances,* with White people participating in the collective movement.
- It brought about not only changes in attitudes but *institutional change* as schools, universities, work and public spaces became integrated, as Black people became increasing participants in the media, sports, and public life.
- In contrast to past history, where Black people were unprotected from White persecution and violence, Presidents Truman, Eisenhower, and Kennedy when necessary using the National Guard, the Supreme Court, and thus the *power of the state,* supported the rights of Black people.
- At its height the civil rights movement involved people and institutions at the *top, the bottom,* and *in the middle.*

Creating a caring society requires change agents at varied levels and changes on many dimensions and in many institutions. A change process often begins at one level, whether with enlightened leaders, or a motivated group in the population, or writers who call attention to injustices, or others. When it is effective, it moves people and institutions at other levels to action. It may be lack of change in important aspects of society—the police, the justice system, schools and the enablement of children—and continued poverty that came to limit improvement in the conditions and life of African Americans in the United States. Still, the example of the great changes in race relations show what can be accomplished when people speak, engage, and act. George Mitchell, the former leader of the US Senate and mediator in a variety of conflicts, said about conflicts: "They are created, sustained, and conducted by human beings ... [and] they can be resolved by human beings." This is also true of the values, institutions, and practices within societies and in the international system. They are created and maintained by human beings, and they can be changed by their coordinated efforts.

References

Aiken, C., & Keller, S. (2009, April). The irrational side of change management. *McKinsey Quarterly*.

Aronson, E., Stephan, C., Sikes, J., Blaney, N., & Snapp, M. (1978). *The jigsaw classroom*. Beverly Hills, CA: SAGE.

Bellah, R. N., Madsen, R., Sullivan, W. M., Swidler. A., & Tipton, S. M. (1991). *The God society*. New York: Alfred A. Knopf.

Bushman, B., & Anderson, C. (2009). Comfortably numb: Desensitizing effects of violent media on helping others. *Psychological Science, 20*(3), 273–277.

Deutsch, M., Marcus, E. C., & Brazaitus, S. (2012). A framework for thinking about developing a global community. In P. Coleman & M. Deutsch. (Eds.), *The psychological components of a sustainable peace* (pp. 227–245). New York: Springer Science and Business Media.

Dovidio, J. F., & Gaertner, S. L. (2004). Aversive racism. In M. P. Zanna (Ed.), *Advances in experimental social psychology* (Vol. 36, pp. 1–51). San Diego, CA: Academic Press.

Eldar, A. (2013, July 17). Israel's plague of self-censorship. *Al-Monitor*. Retrieved from http://www.al-monitor.com/pulse/contents/authors/akiva-eldar.html

Etzioni. A. (2000). Utopian visions: Engaged sociologies for the 21st century. *Contemporary Sociology, 29*(1), 188–195.

Gawande, A. (2013, July 29). Slow ideas: Some innovations spread fast. How do you speed the ones that don't? *The New Yorker*.

Glenn, E. N. (1999). Creating a caring society. *Footnotes: Newsletter of the American Sociological Association, 27*(8), 84–94. Retrieved from http://www.asanet.org/images/members/docs/pdf/special/cs/CS_29_1_Symposium_8_Glenn.pdf

Greenwald, A. G., & Pettigrew, T. F. (2014). With malice toward none and charity for some: Ingroup favoritism enables discrimination. *American Psychologist, 69*, 669–685

Fry, D. P., & Miklikowska, M. (2012). Culture of peace. In P. Coleman & M. Deutsch (Eds.), *The psychological components of a sustainable peace* (pp. 227–245). New York: Springer Science and Business Media.

Janoff-Bulman, R., & Carnes, N. C. (2013). Surveying the moral landscape: Moral motives and group-based moralities. *Personality and Social Psychology Review, 17*(3), 219–237.

Johnson, D. W., Johnson, R. T., & Tjosvold, D. (2012). Effective cooperation, the foundation of sustainable peace. In P. Coleman & M. Deutsch (Eds.), *The psychological components of a sustainable peace* (pp. 15–55). New York: Springer Science and Business Media.

Jost, J. T., & Kay, A. C. (2010). Social justice: History, theory, and research. In S. T. Fiske, D. Gilbert, & G. Lindzey (Eds.), *Handbook of social psychology* (5th ed., pp. 1122–1165). Hoboken, NJ: Wiley.

Lederach, J. P. (1997). *Building peace: Sustainable reconciliation in divided societies*. Washington, DC: United States Institute of Peace Press.

Lieberfeld, D. (2009). Lincoln, Mandela, and qualities of reconciliation-oriented leadership. *Peace and Conflict: Journal of Peace Psychology, 15*, 27–47.

Mandel, D. R. (2002). Instigators of genocide. Examining Hitler from a social-psychological perspective. In L. S. Newman & R. Erber (Eds.), *Understanding genocide: The social psychology of the Holocaust* (pp. 259–285). New York: Oxford University Press.

McGarty, C., Bliuc, A., Thomas, E. F., & Bongiorno, R. (2009). Collective action as the material expression of opinion-based group membership. *Journal of Social Issues, 65*(4), 839–859.

Oliner, S. B., & Oliner, P. (1988). *The altruistic personality: Rescuers of Jews in Nazi Europe*. New York: Free Press.

Paluck, E. L. (2009). Reducing intergroup prejudice and conflict using the media: A field experiment in Rwanda. *Journal of Personality and Social Psychology, 96*, 574–587.

Reid, J. S. (2001). Why there has been no race war in the American South. In D. Chirot & M. E. P. Seligman (Eds.), *Ethnopolitical warfare: Causes, consequences and possible solutions* (pp. 275–287). Washington, DC: American Psychological Association.

Sageman, M. (2004). *Understanding terror networks*. Philadelphia: University of Pennsylvania Press.

Schatz, R. T., Staub, E., & Lavine, H. (1999). On the varieties of national attachment: Blind versus constructive patriotism. *Political Psychology, 20*, 151–175.

Schwartz, S. H. (2007). Universalism values and the inclusiveness of our moral universe. *Journal of Cross-Cultural Psychology, 38*(6), 711–728.

Soltan, K. E., & Elkin, S.L. (Eds.). (1996). *The constitution of good societies.* University Park, PA: Penn State University Press.

Stillman, S. (2013, August 12). A reporter at large: Taken, the shocking injustice of civil forfeiture. *The New Yorker*, pp. 48–62.

Staub, E. (1970). A child in distress: The influence of age and number of witnesses on children's attempts to help. *Journal of Personality and Social Psychology*, *14*, 130–140.

Staub, E. (1971). Helping a person in distress: The influence of implicit and explicit "rules" of conduct on children and adults. *Journal of Personality and Social Psychology*, *17*, 137–145.

Staub, E. (1974). Helping a distressed person: Social, personality and stimulus determinants. In L. Berkowitz (Ed.), *Advances in experimental social psychology* (Vol. 7., pp. 203–342). New York: Academic Press.

Staub, E. (1989). *The roots of evil: The origins of genocide and other group violence.* New York: Cambridge University Press.

Staub, E. (1993). Individual and group selves, motivation and morality. In G. G. Noam & T. E. Wren (Eds.), *The moral self* (pp. 337–359). Cambridge, MA: MIT Press.

Staub, E. (1996). The cultural-societal roots of violence: The examples of genocidal violence and of contemporary youth violence in the United States. *American Psychologist*, *51*, 117–132.

Staub, E. (1997). Blind versus constructive patriotism: Moving from embeddedness in the group to critical loyalty and action. In D. Bar-Tal & E. Staub (Eds.), *Patriotism in the lives of individuals and groups.* Chicago: Nelson-Hall.

Staub, E. (2001). Ethnopolitical and other group violence: Origins and prevention. In D. Chirot & M. E. P. Seligman (Eds.), *Ethnopolitical warfare: Causes, consequences and possible solutions* (pp. 289–304). Washington, DC: American Psychological Association.

Staub, E. (2007a, August). Evil: Understanding bad situations and systems, but also personality and group dynamics. [Review of the book *The Lucifer effect: Zimbardo, P. The Lucifer effect: Understanding how good people turn evil* by P. Zimbardo]. *PsychCritiques.*

Staub, E. (2007b). Preventing violence and terrorism and promoting positive relations between Dutch and Muslim communities in Amsterdam. *Peace and Conflict: Journal of Peace Psychology*, *13*(3), 333–361.

Staub, E. (2011). *Overcoming evil: genocide, violent conflict and terrorism.* New York: Oxford University Press.

Staub, E. (2014). Obedience, joining, following and resistance in the Milgram situation and in genocide and other group violence: Situation, personality, bystanders. *Journal of Social Issues*, *70*(3), 501–514.

Staub, E., & Pearlman, L. A. (2006). Advancing healing and reconciliation. In L. Barbanel & R. Sternberg (Eds.), *Psychological interventions in times of crisis* (pp. 213–245). New York: Springer-Verlag.

Staub, E., & Pearlman, L. A. (2009). Reducing intergroup prejudice and conflict: A commentary. *Journal of Personality and Social Psychology*, *96*, 588–594.

Steiner, J. M. (1980). The SS yesterday and today: A socio-psychological view. In J. Dimsdale (Ed.), *Survivors, victims and perpetrators: Essays on the Nazi Holocaust* (pp. 405–457). New York: Hemisphere.

Tajfel, H. (1982). Social psychology of intergroup relations. *Annual Review of Psychology*, *33*, 1–39.

Tov, W., & Diener, E. (2008). The well-being of nations: Linking together trust, cooperation and democracy. In B. A. Sullivan, M. Snyder, & J. J. Sullivan (Eds.), *Cooperation: The political psychology of effective human interaction.* Malden, MA: Blackwell.

Triandis, H. C. (1994). *Culture and social behavior.* New York: McGraw-Hill.

Van Zomeren, M., & Iyer, A. (2009). Introduction to social and psychological dynamics of collective action. *Journal of Social Issues*, *65*(4), 645–661.

Wilkinson, R. G., & Pickett, K. (2009). *The spirit level: Why more equal societies almost always do better.* New York: Allen Lane.

Zakaria. (2013, August 18). *Global Public Square.* CNN.

Zimbardo, P. (2007). *The Lucifer effect: Understanding how good people turn evil.* New York: Random House.

Author Index

Subject Index